REGISTER OF OXYRHYNCHITES
30 B.C.–A.D. 96

AMERICAN STUDIES IN PAPYROLOGY
VOLUME 25

Editors
Deborah Hobson, Ludwig Koenen,
and Susan A. Stephens

REGISTER OF OXYRHYNCHITES
30 B.C.–A.D. 96

B. W. Jones and J. E. G. Whitehorne

REGISTER OF OXYRHYNCHITES
30 B.C.–A.D. 96

B. W. Jones and J. E. G. Whitehorne

Scholars Press
Chico, California

REGISTER OF OXYRHYNCHITES
30 B.C.–A.D. 96

B. W. Jones and J. E. G. Whitehorne

Library of Congress Cataloging in Publication Data

Jones, B. W. (Brian William)
Register of Oxyrhynchites, 30 B.C.–A.D. 96.

(American studies in papyrology, ISSN 0569-8642 ; v. 25)
1. Oxyrhynchus (Egypt) 2. Romans—Egypt.
I. Whitehorne, J. E. G. (John Edwin George) II. Title.
III. Series.
DT73.0'8J66 1982 932 81-18494
ISBN 0-89130-529-7 AACR2

Printed in the United States of America

FOREWORD

We are indebted to the Australian Research Grants Committee for their generous financial support of this project, and to our own University for assistance with typing costs. Our thanks too to M.A. Hardcastle and R.G. Forzin, who served as our research assistants, and to Susan A. Stephens for her many useful editorial suggestions.

J.E.G. Whitehorne and B.W. Jones
University of Queensland

INTRODUCTION

Our purpose in this Register is to list all persons living in the Oxyrhynchite nome between 30 BC and 96, that is roughly the first century of Roman rule in Egypt. We hope that this will assist in the study of such matters as Roman exploitation of Egypt at a local level, social mobility and class composition, and the identification of further archives among hitherto scattered documents.

The data base comprises all texts dated between 70 BC and 140, known or likely to have come from the Oxyrhynchite or to refer to persons from there. This ensures coverage of those who may still have been alive as grandparents in 30 BC, or who were alive as children in 96. Also included are some texts from a later date where these refer to persons alive within the period covered by the Register. An index of Texts cited by Date is given after the index of Texts Cited.

We have only been able to take limited account of papyri published after 1977.[1] We have however included relevant material from *P. Genov.* II, *P. Köln* II, and *P. Oxy.* XLVI as well as some documents published singly and not yet collected in *SB*.

For the sake of completeness, we have included the demotic ostraca from Oxyrhynchus,[2] although at the time of writing there does not seem to be any overlap between the persons who appear in the demotic ostraca and those in the Greek papyri. We adopt the commonest Hellenised equivalent of the demotic name where one exists and include the name in the main Register. Names with no apparent equivalent in Greek are listed separately after the main Register.

The primary criterion for inclusion in the Register is a connection with the Oxyrhynchite. Accordingly we list local officials including strategi and royal scribes, but exclude officials usually resident in Alexandria or elsewhere. Similarly, Oxyrhynchites temporarily absent in other cities or nomes are included, but not those from elsewhere staying in the Oxyrhynchite, unless they are outsiders who have married into Oxyrhynchite families and so may be regarded as permanently resident there. As is often the case with works of this type, a small residue of examples has defied categorisation and we apologise for any apparent inconsistencies.

......

1 The following editions published from 1978 onwards, which were available to us, contain no material relevant to the Register: *P.Cair.Mich.*359; *P.Coll.Hombert*; *P.Landlisten*; *P.Lett.Carlini*; *P.Laur.*III; *P.Amst.*I; *P.Lugd.Bat.*XX.

2. For publication details see index of Texts Cited. The latest series of *OD Pisa* to be published by E. Bresciani et al., *SCO* 27 (1977) 13-78, reached us too late for inclusion in the Register.

KEY

After the Index Number and Name we record as many of the following items as are known:

(1) Family members:

bro.	=	brother
ch.	=	child, children
d.	=	daughter
gch.	=	grand child, grand children
gd.	=	grand daughter
gs.	=	grand son
m.	=	mother
mat.	=	maternal
s.	=	son
sibs.	=	siblings
sp.	=	spouse

(2) Document date (or date of relevant section); within each name entries run according to date:- 70 BC - 1 BC; i BC; 1-99; early i; late i; i; i-ii; 100-140; early ii; ii; n.d. All dates are AD unless specified otherwise.

(3) Title(s):

gym.	=	gymnasiarch
hypom.	=	hypomnematographus

(4) Occupation(s).

(5) Status, citizenship.

(6) Address:

addr.	=	address
E. Top.	=	Eastern Toparchy
L. Top.	=	Lower Toparchy
M. Top.	=	Middle Toparchy
Thmois. Top.	=	Thmoisepho Toparchy
U. Top.	=	Upper Toparchy
W. Top.	=	Western Toparchy
qtr	=	quarter

(7) Document provenance (doc.pr.) where provenance is not the Oxyrhynchite.

(8) Other information, e.g. age, signalement, names of other relatives, source of address, etc:

a/c	=	account
assoc. w.	=	associated with
dec.	=	deceased
div.	=	divorced
nr	=	near
ref.	=	reference
reg.	=	registered
rep.	=	representative
res.	=	resident

(9) Document reference to ed.pr., as corrected in *BL*. For republications in *Chrest. Mitt.*, *Chrest. Wilck.*, and *Sel. Pap.* and publication details of documents listed by inventory number, see index of Texts Cited. Abbreviations of editions follow the conventions of *BASP* 11.1 (1974), except that all references to texts in *P. Oxy.* are shown by underlining the document number, e.g. I <u>100</u>.3.

REGISTER OF OXYRHYNCHITES

1 A( ); ch. Apynchius(?); 60/61; former landowner in Kleros of Nicanor and Drimax; Oxy.; addr. for s.; II 250.25.

2 A or HA; ch. Harpaesis; 77; priest?; Oxy.; addr. for gs. Apis; II 242.3.

3 A.[.]..[...].; Oct 111; slave; formerly of Diogenes, s. of Theon, now of Ti. Julius Theon, ex-strategus; XLIV 3197.6.

4 A[...]N[; 63/64; city secretary(?) w. Apollophanes; *P. Gen. inv.* 222.1

5 A..OLEAS (or A..OMAS); Oct 111; slave; formerly of Ti. Julius Theon, now of Theon, ex-strategus; snub-nosed; XLIV 3197.7.

6 ABABICI(S); 81-96; VI 984 R.

7 ABARUS; s. of Didymus; Sept 36; weaver; Oxyrhynchite; Oxy.; II 322.4.

8 ABASCANTION; Oct 111; slave; formerly of Ti. Julius Theon, now of Ti. Julius Theon, games victor; Ethiopian (i.e. negroid); XLIV 3197.13.

9 ABASCANTUS; Oct 111; slave; formerly of Ti. Julius Theon, now of Ti. Julius Theon, ex-strategus; XLIV 3197.9.

10 ---; Oct 111; slave; formerly of Ti. Julius Theon, now of Ti. Julius Theon, games victor; Kerkethyris, W. Top.; XLIV 3197.14.

11 ---; ch. Aunchis; 126; III 634 (descr.).

12 ---; ii; III 531.23.

13 ---; ch. Sarapion; ii; "brother" of addressee Sarapion; XII 1582.15 V.

14 ABAU; s. of Apollonius; ch. Papontos; Aug 133; stemma in ed. pr.; *P. Köln* II 100.29.

15 ABI; Sept 6; *OD Pisa* 814 Convesso 4.

16 ABILLA(S?); 50/51 or 64/65; *P. Mil.* II 53.2.

17 ABOK; ch. Petamunis; i BC - i; *OD Pisa* 510 + 568 Convesso ii 2.

18 AC ...; ii; XII 1584 (l.h. margin)31.

19 ACHIL(LAS) or ACHIL(LEUS); ch. Sinth( ); early Roman period; *P. Mert.* III 104.7.

20 ACHILL( ); 98/99; assistant to basilicogrammateus Achilleus; *P. Köln* II 86.25.

21 ACHILLAS; s. of Didymus; March 108; catoecic landholder in Kleros of Zenodorus, E. Top.; III 483.30, 33.

22 ---; early ii; has sons; III 525.6.

23 ACHILLEUS; s. of Proetus; 21; grammateus of Sinary and other villages; Sinary, L. Top.; X 1281.14.

24 ---; ch. Apollonius; 25-37; *PSI* X 1118.1.

25 ---; s. of Pastous; sp. Plutarche; ch. Thermuthion; (1) April 60; (2) March 61; property owner; Oxyrhynchite; Hippodrome qtr; dec. (1); (1) *P. Mich.* III 192.5; (2) 194.4.

26 ---; ch. Achilleus; (1) Mar/Apr 66; (2) 91/92; Oxyrhynchite; Oxy.; addr. for gd. Thermuthion; (1) *PSI* VIII 871.30; (2) XXXVIII 2856.12.

27 ---; s. of Achilleus; sp. Thaisous; ch. Sarapion, Thermuthion; (1) Mar/Apr 66; (2) 91/92; Oxyrhynchite; Oxy.; addr. for d.; (1) *PSI* VIII 871.29; (2) XXXVIII 2856.11.

28 ---; 81-96; agent for Pyrrhus, land superintendent; I 47.2.

29 ---; gs. of Ammonius; m. Sarapous; 91 or 107; slave owner (of 1/3 slave); Oxyrhynchite; Oxy.; age c. 20; signalement; bro. of Sarapas; IV 722.[6], 27, 35.

30 ---; ch. Sinthoonis; 94/95; Oxyrhynchite; Heracles Place qtr; addr. for d.; II 257.18.

31 ---; (1) 98/99; (2) Jan 100; basilicogrammateus; (1) *P. Köln* II 86.3, 25; (2) XLI 2960.1.

32 ---; i; XXXVI 2786.5.

33 ---; ch. Theon; 122/123; Sinkepha distr.; *P. Lips.* 116.10.

34 ---; Jan/Feb 128; Gynaecopolite; doc. pr. Oxy.; accused of harbouring slave; XII 1422.6.

35 ---; sp. Demetria; early ii; Alex., Propapposebasteius, Althaieus; Oxy.; gs. Theon; III 497.20.

36 ---; ch. Dem[etrius] alias Dorion; ii; *P. Sel.* 22.5.

37 ACHORINIS; c. 1; livestock owner; IV 807 ii 3.

38 ACORIS; s. of Aristion, s. of Promachus; m. Hagnes, d. of Ptolemaeus; Aug 72?; property owner; Oxyrhynchite; Nemerae, M. Top.; bro. of Aparous; XLIV 2972.25.

39 ---; s. of Satyris; m. Harseis; ii; landholder; Cretan qtr.; *P. Princ.* II 46.6.

40 ACOUS; Oct 8; doc. pr. Oxy. - Little Oasis; *OD Pisa* 1.6.

ACUSILAUS; see DION( ).

41 ADMETUS; ch. Dionysius; 93; Enteiis; addr. for s.; *P. Princ.* II 42 V ii 21, iii 30.

42 ADRASTUS; April 71; Oxy.; bro. of Spartacus; XXXIV 2725 V.

43 ---; Jan/Feb 75; II 362 (descr.).

44 ---; sp. Tanaroous; ch. Thamunion; 94; Oxyrhynchite; Oxy.; addr. for d.; I 73.11.

45 ---; m. Eudaemonis; sp. Aphroditous alias Demarous; 99/100 or 118/119; Philonicus, Heracleopolite; Oxy.; age 32; wife from Oxy.; III 504.[6], 48.

46 ---; ch. Adrastus; i; Sesphtha, L. Top.; addr. for s.; *P. Ryl.* II 199.11.

47 ---; s. of Adrastus; i; farmer; Sesphtha, L. Top.; *P. Ryl.* II 199.11.

48 ---; s. of Chaeremon, s. of Adrastus; m. Philotera, d. of Origenes; 133; property owner; Alex., Nilanabateius, Althaieus; Oxy.; buys lot w. Dionysius alias Papontos in Cretan qtr or Jewish St.; I 100.3.

49 ---; ch. Chaeremon; 133; Alex., Nilanabateius; Althaieus; Oxy.; addr. for gs. Adrastus; I 100.4.

50 ---; ii; XLII 3063.5.

51 A]EIS; ii?; name restored *BL* III; *P. Harris* 103.2

AELIUS; see HORION.

52 AGATHANGELUS; Oct 111; slave; formerly of Ti. Julius Theon, now of Ti. Julius Theon, ex-strategus; XLIV 3197.9.

53 ---; Oct 111; slave; formerly of Tiberius Julius Theon, now of Ti. Julius Theon, games victor; XLIV 3197.14.

54 AGATHEINUS; sp. Tseei; ch. Diodorus; (1) March 97; (2) 138-161; Oxyrhynchite?; Oxy.; address for gs. Diodorus; (1) IV 713.8; (2) IV 723.2.

55 ---; c. 129; joint trustee of property with Heradion; XII 1420.8, 10.

56 ---; s. of Theon; ch. Theon; 130; Oxyrhynchite; Oxy.; addr. for s.; III 492.22.

57 AGATHEMERUS; Oct 111; slave; of Ti. Julius Theon, games victor; XLIV 3197.14.

58 AGATHOCLES; ii; III 611 (descr.).

59 AGATHODAEMON; (1) 127/8; (2) Jan/Feb 128; strategus; Oxy.; (1) XII 1452.1, 28; (2) XII 1422.3.

60 ---; alias DIONYSIUS; s. of Dionysius, s. of Dionysius; m. Hermione; 129; slave owner; Oxyrhynchite; Oxy.; I 95.4 etc.

61 ---; s. of Diogenes, s. of Theon; 129; Alex., Sosicosmius, Althaieus; Alexandria?; XXXVI 2774.1.

62 -] alias AGATHODAEMON; ii?; Pela, W. Top.; *P. Fuad I Univ.* 32.16.

63 AGATHOPOUS; Oct 111; slave; formerly of Ti. Julius Theon, now of Ti. Julius Theon, games victor; from Cussae; Oxy.; XLIV 3197.15.

64 AGATHUS; ii; Heracleopolis?; XXXVI 2787.9.

65 AGATHYS; Oct 111; slave; formerly of Ti. Julius Theon, now of Ti. Julius Sarapion; notary; XLIV 3197.11.

66 AGRON; sp Tamonnes; ch. Puoris; i-ii; *P. Harris* 72.15.

67 AISCHYRAS (=ISCHYRAS); ch. Tharion; 81-96; VI 984 R.

68 ALAB(?); n.d.; *SB* I 1403.1.

ALC.[..]; see THOONIS.

ALCIMUS; see NEMESION.

69 ALE[...]; ch. Chaeremon; c. 50; XXVII 2471.6.

70 ALEXANDRA; i; slave; of Claudia Dionysia, treated by Theon, physician; *P. Oslo* III 95.12.

71 ALE]XANDRUS; 44-37 BC; "one of first friends"; superintendent of land registers; XIV 1635.5.

72 ALEXANDRUS; ch. Dionysius; 19 BC; II 277.1.

73 ---; 23; in charge of grapheion of M. Top.; *P. Princ.* III 141.7.

74 ---; 30-35; strategus; II 282.1.

75 ---; ch. Menelaus; 31/2; Alex., Zeneius; Oxy.; deme and addr. for s.; *P. Ryl.* II 159.3.

76 ---; s. of Apollonius; c. 50; weaver; Oxyrhynchite; Thoeris St qtr; II 284.2.

77 ---; Mar/Apr 66; grammateus in Feb 65; *PSI* VIII 871.17.

78 ---; 77; banker, w. unnamed colleagues; Oxy.; II 242.31.

79 ALE[XANDRUS]; ch. Sarapion; Oct 80; Oxyrhynchite?; Oxy.?; II 248.5.

80 ALEXANDRUS; ch. Leonides; March 97; Oxyrhynchite; Oxy.; addr. for gd. Saraeus; IV 713.9.

81 ---; ch. Aristocles; Oct 98; Oxyrhynchite; *P. Genov.* II 62.1.

82 ---; 98-117; agoranomus with Theon; Oxy.; *P. Sel.* 24.2.

83 ---; ch. Dorion; i; Alex., Eileithyios; Sobthis; addr. for s.; VIII 1145.22.

84 ALEXANDRUS; gs. of Theon; m. Thaisous; d. of Epimachus; end i; slave owner; *P. Sel.* 23.8.

85 ---; m. Anabasis; Oct 111; slave of Ti. Julius Sarapion; XLIV 3197.12.

86 ---; m. Genella; Oct 111; slave of Ti. Julius Theon, games victor; XLIV 3197.15.

87 ---; ch. Callistratus; 117; Oxyrhynchite; Oxy.; addr. for gs. Pedon; III 489.24.

88 ---; ch. Demetrius; 126; *P. Harris* 142.15.

89 ---; ch. Diogenes; Aug 127; Pela?; addr. for s.; *P. Oxy. inv.*? 23.

90 TI. CLAUDIUS ALEXANDRUS; sp. Claudia Theanous (concubine?); ch. Ti. Claudius Ptolemaeus?; May 134; Roman; Oxy.; freedman of Tiberius; XXXVIII 2857.1 and passim.

91 ALEXANDRUS; ch. Asclas; ii; Oxyrhynchite; Oxy.; addr. for s.; III 498.3.

92 ---; sp. Dionysia; ch. Sarapion, Theon, Aristocleia; ii; XLVI 3313.22 and back.

93 ---; n.d. *SB* I 1961.

94 ALIA;alias DIOGENIS; early ii; property owner; Thoeris St qtr; *Coll. Pap.* I 50.8.

95 ALINE; d. of Dionysius; May 23; Alex.; Oxy.?; II 259.12.

96 ---; d. of Comon, s. of Dionysius; sp. Mnesitheus; m. Cleopatra, d. of Dionysius; ch. Comon, Charitous; (1) Aug 50; (2) Sept 64; (3) Aug 75; (4) July 85; (5) Aug 86; (6) Oct 86; (7) 2nd half i; landholder; property and slave owner; Oxyrhynchite; Sarapis St qtr; payment made in Kerkeura, M. Top., Sko for Kerkeura and in Senocomis, W. Top.; signalement; stemma in ed. pr.; (1) XXXVIII 2837.5; (2) 2839.3; (3) 2840.5-6; (4) 2841.6; (5) 2843.5; (6) I 48.8; XXXVIII 2846.5.

97 ---; sp Heracleides; ch. Theon; Aug 123; Pakerke distr.?, E. Top.; addr. for s.; XXXVIII 2864.1.

98 ALIS; sp. Hilarion (also bro.?); 1 BC; IV 744.1.

99 ---; d. of Apollophanes; ii; Oxy.; XII 1536.6.

100 ALLO[US; sp. Tachois; ch. Psois; 31/2; Oxy.; *P. Ryl*, II 159.4.

101 ALLOUS; sp. Tryphon; ch. Pyrrhias; Aug 133; *P. Köln* II 100.13.

102 ---; sp. Apollonius; ii; *P. Oslo* II 15.28

103 AM[-; ch. Amatis (or Amas?); ii; *P. Sel*, 22.6.

104 AMARANTUS; 79/80; slave; Lycians' Camp qtr?; formerly of Heracleides, now of his bro.; *P. Oxy. inv.* 20.3B.34/B.5.

105 ---; ii; I 113.27.

106 AMATIS (or AMAS?); s. of A-; ii; practor of money taxes, E. qtr, Oxy.; *P. Sel.* 22.6.

107 AMATOCUS; ii, practor of money taxes, E. qtr, Oxy.; *P. Sel.* 22.5.

108 AMENNEUS; i BC - i; *OD Pisa* 232.16.

109 ---; i BC - i; *OD Pisa* 510 + 568 Convesso i 14.

110 ---; s. of Harpaesis; i BC - i; *OD Pisa* 1264 Convesso 2.

111 ---; ch. Thais, Heraclous; 41-54; Oxyrhynchite; Oxy.; XXXIV 2720.2.

112 ---; ch. Pennamis; 80/81; Peeno, M. Top.; addr. for s.; *Coll. Pap.* I 21.5.

113 ---; i; *OD Pisa* 39 i X + 4.

114 ---; s. of Artemas; sp. Thacoris; ch. Artemidorus; ii; property owner; Oxyrhynchite; Pammenes' Garden qtr; addr. for s.; III 505.1.

115 ---; ch. Thacoris; ii; III 505.1.

116 ---; n.d.; *DO Colon. inv.* 39.

117 AMMENEUS; ii; flute player; XLII 3058.18.

118 AMITHONIS; ch. Thonis; 96; Oxyrhynchite; Oxy.; addr. for gd. Thaesis; II 266.3.

119 AMMAS; ch. Pecysis; ii; *P. Erl.* 44 ii 9.

120 AMMO( ); ch. Dioscorus; Apr/May 92; *PSI* VI 715.8.

121 AMMON; s. of Harpaesis; ch. Pisys; 87/88; Tanais?, M. Top.; addr. for s.; *Coll. Pap.* I 22.2.

122 ---; sp. Sambius; ch. Harphaesis; i - ii; *P. Harris* 72.14.

123 AMMONARION; d. of Ammonius, s. of Dionysius; sp. Heraclas (divorced); ch. Ophelous; 58; Ptolemais Hermiu; ex-husband Oxyrhynchite; II 268.2.

124 ---; alias THEOPOMPION; d. of Diogenes; sp. Heracleides; ch. Theopompion; end i; Oxyrhynchite; Oxy.; addr. for d.; *P. Sel.* 23.6.

125 ---; d. of Nicobulus; sp. Sarapion; ch. Areius, Anoup; i; Oxyrhynchite; Oxy.; addr. for sons; *P. Harris* 138 iii 12.

126 AMMONAS; c. 1; IV 736.69.

127 ---; s. of Theonas; m. Syras; c. 35; "brother" of Thaisous; II 295.12.

128 AMMONAS; 57; friend of Tryphon, s. of Dionysius; II 269 ii 1.

129 ---; Oct 111; slave; formerly of Ti. Julius Theon, now of Ti. Julius Theon, ex-strategus; notary; XLIV 3197.8.

130 AMMONIANUS; ch. Theon alias Anthus; 137/138; ex-gymnasiarch and agoranomus of Alexandria; Alex.; doc. pr. Oxy?; *PSI* IV 315.1.

131 AMMONIS; July, 72; episphragistes; Seryphis, W. Top.; XLIV 3163.18.

132 ---; s. of Heraclas, s. of Hermogenes; m. Senaias, d. of Naarophibis; 2nd half i; donkey seller; Sinary, L. Top.; XXXVIII 2846.1.

133 ---; s. of Heracleides, s. of Ptolemaeus; 117; Oxyrhynchite; witness; age 25; signalement; III 489.25.

134 AMMONIUS; s. of S[o]sipatrus; 73 or 44 BC; writes for Orsenouphis and Pecysis; XIV 1639.27.

135 ---; i BC - i; Petesis his dependant; *OD Pisa* 29 ii X + 11.

136 ---; i BC - i; *OD Pisa* 108 X + 3.

137 ---; c. 1; "brother" of Didymus and Apollonius; IV 791 (descr.).

138 ---; ch. Thoonis, Ammonius, Theon; (1) 19; (2) 19/20; (3) May 23; (4) 54; weaver?; Oxyrhynchite; Temgenuthis qtr; (1) II 253.[15]; (2) 252.2, 3; (3) 259.2; (4) 264.1.

139 ---; s. of Ammonius; (1) 19; (2) 19/20; (3) 54; weaver, property owner; Oxyrhynchite; Temgenuthis qtr; illiterate; (1) II 253.20; (2) 252.3; (3) 264.1.

140 ---; s. of Ptolemaeus; 26; farmer?; Isieum Tryphonos, L. Top.; VIII 1124.12.

141 ---; sp. Philumene; ch. [Ammoniu]s; 45; II 326 R 1.

142 [AMMONIU]S; s. of Ammonius; m. Philumene; 45; II 326 R [1].

143 AMMONIUS; ch. Pausiris; (1) Sept 49; (2) Aug/Sept 53; (3) Sept 58; (4) Oct 62; Oxyrhynchite; Knights' Camp qtr; (1) *P. Mich.* III 170.3; (2) *P. Wisc.* I 4.1-2. (3) *P. Mich.* III 171.15; (4) 172.2.

144 ---; s. of Pausiris, s. of Ammonius; Sept 49; apprentice weaver; Oxyrhynchite; Knights' Camp qtr; *P. Mich.* III 170.5.

145 ---; s. of Sarapion; June 52; Oxy.?; bro. of Hermodotus, Apollonia and Petusius; *SB* V 8034.4.

146 ---; ch. Ammonius; 54; livestock owner; II 297.1.

147 ---; s. of Ammonius; 54; livestock owner; II 297.1.

148 ---; 55; banker w. Epimachus; Sarapeum; II 304.4.

149 ---; s. of Antiphanes; ch. Antiphanes; (1) 58; (2) July 59; Oxyrhynchite; Oxy.; addr. for s.; (1) II 268.4; (2) 260.2.

150 AMMONIUS; ch. Dionysius; 59; Oxyrhynchite; Oxy.; addr. for s.; II 320.5.

151 TI. CLAUDIUS AMMONIUS; (1) Mar/Apr 59; (2) July 59; strategus; superintendent of revenues; Roman; Oxy.; (1) *P. Fouad* 28.1; (2) II 260.3-4.

152 AMMONIUS; s. of Sarapion; 60/61; Oxyrhynchite; Oxy.; II 250.12.

153 ---; July 64; banker, appointee of Sarapion and Sarapion; Oxy.; *P. Yale* 63.7.

154 ---; April 71; XXXIV 2725.15.

155 ---; 80 or 90; property owner; II 359 (descr.).

156 ---; ch. Philiscus; July 87; Senepta, M. Top.; addr. for gs. Peteesis; *PSI* III 203.2.

157 ---; ch. Ammonous; 90; Teis?, Thmois. Top.; addr. for gs. Plution; *P. Ryl.* IV 597 4-5.

158 ---; 91 or 107; Oxyrhynchite; Oxy.; gs. are Achilleus and Sarapas; IV 722.11.

159 ---; 92; comogrammateus of Psobthis and Pero ( ) or Peroth ( ); Psobthis, E. Top.; guarantor for Heracleides, s. of Heracleides; XVIII 2185.15-16.

160 ---; s. of Ptolemaeus; ch. Ptolemaeus; 94/95; Oxyrhynchite, gymnasial class; Heracles Place qtr; in graphe of AD 4-5; II 257.32, 36.

161 ---; ch. Ammonius; 99-117; XLVI 3274 i 7, ii 35.

162 ---; s. of Ammonius; 99-117; brings Demetria to trial re property taken by Dionytas, s. of Didymus; XLVI 3274 i 6-7, ii 35.

163 ---; s. of Ammonius; 2nd half i; banker;Sarapeum; *P. Oslo* III 130.10.

164 ---; ch. Ammonius; 2nd half i; Oxy.?; addr. for s.; *P. Oslo* III 130.10.

165 ---; ch. Ammonius; mid i; VII 1027.8.

166 ---; s. of Ammonius; ch. Theon, Pecysis; mid i; VII 1027.2.

167 ---; s. of Pancrates; end i; practor; Sesphtha, L. Top.; XXXVIII 2845.7.

168 ---; s. of Petechon; i; farmer?; Koba; corres. from s. of Petechon to Ammonius, s. of Petechon; VIII 1145.8.

169 ---; i - ii; belongs to group of "brothers"; XLII 3057.1.

170 ---; ch. Sarapion; Nov 103; Oxyrhynchite?; Oxy.?; addr. for gs. Ammonius; *P. Mert.* I 14.4.

171 AMMONIUS; s. of Sarapion, s. of Ammonius; Nov 103; farmer?; Oxyrhynchite; Oxy.; *P. Mert.* I 14.3.

172 ---; s. of Noeris; ch. Thoonis; Aug 106; Oxyrhynchite; Oxy.; dec.; *P. Wisc.* I 17 R 20.

173 ---; s. of Nicanor; ch. Diogenes, Nicanor; 115/116; Oxy.; I 97.20.

174 ---; s. of Paseis; Jan 121; property owner; Small Oasis; joint owner w. Tasionus of property in Metroon qtr.; *P. Fouad* 30.4.

175 ---; ch. Ammonius; Dec 127; Paomis, Thmois. Top.; addr. for s.; XXXIII 2670.11.

176 ---; s. of Ammonius; Dec 127; Paomis, Thmois. Top.; XXXIII 2670.11.

177 ---; s. of Pcaes?; ch. Ptolemaeus; 127/128; Oxyrhynchite, gymnasial class; Oxy.?; addr. for s. scrutinised in AD 4/5; XII 1452 ii 53.

178 ---; s. of Sarapion; sp. Tsenthotoumis; ch. Thatres; 130; Isieum Tryphonos; Lower Top., now living in Oxy.; addr. for d.; III 492.2.

179 ---; s. of Theon, s. of Sarapion; sp. Thaubarion, also sister, dec.; ch. Nilammon; 132/133; Alex., Propapposebasteius, Althaieus; Oxy.; became ephebus in 85; III 477.6.

180 ---; 132/133; unnamed d.; *PSI* I 53 xi 177.

181 ---; alias NICARIUS; Sept 135; sitologus; Psobthis, E. Top.; *P. Stras.* 127.2.

182 - alias AMMONIUS; ch. Ctesidemus; c. 136; Oxy.?; addr. for gs.; *P. Inst. Fran.* III 18.6.

183 AMMONI<U>S; s. of Apollonides; 137; farmer; sub-lessee of vineyard w. Ptollas, s. of Lucilo; illiterate; Ammonis in text; IV 729.35.

184 AMMONIUS; ch. Polydeuces; after 138/139; *PSI* IV 281 R i 4.

185 ---; s. of Theon; ch. Theon; Aug 148; dyke inspector in 140; Oxy.?; addr. for s.; *P. Iand.* VII 139.5.

186 ---; sp. Is]ido[te?; ch. Theon; Jan 139/Feb 140 and Aug 148(?); *P. Iand.* VII 139.8.

187 ---; ch. Theon; 148/149; Oxyrhynchite, gymnasial class; Pammenes' Garden qtr?; son listed in 34 Augustus 4/5; XLVI 3283.14.

188 ---; s. of Theon, s. of Ammonius; ch. Theon; 148/149; Oxyrhynchite, gymnasial class; Pammenes' Garden qtr?; s. listed in 5 Vespasian 72/73; XLVI 3283.12.

189 ---; s. of Pet[euri]s(?), s. of Apollonius; m. Heras, d. of Amois; 148/149; Oxyrhynchite, gymnasial class; Upper Camp qtr; enr. in 148/149; XLVI 3276.6.

190 AMMONIUS; s. of Neoptolemus; ii; practor of money taxes in E. (qtr?); *P. Sel.* 22.4.

191 ---; sp. Harasis; ch. Ammonius; ii; Oxyrhynchite?; Oxy?; addr. for s.; III 505.4.

192 ---; ii, has unnamed bros.; friend of Theon, called "brother"; addr. is house of Theon, s. of Apollonius, banker; XLI 2980.1, back.

193 ---; ch. Panteles; ii; *P. Oslo* III 108.3

194 ---; s. of Panteles, s. of Ammonius; ii; *P. Oslo* III 108.3.

195 ---; ch. Sarapion; ii; *P. Oslo* III 108.2.

196 ---; ii; sent greetings by Publius; XLI 2981.23.

---; see BESAS.

197 ---; alias DIONYSIUS; s. of Ammonius; m. Harasis; ii; Oxyrhynchite; Oxy.; guardian of Eudaemonis alias Plutarche; III 505.3.

198 ---; s. of Ptolemaeus; sp. Sinthonis; ch. Dionysia; ii; Oxy.?; addr. for d.; *P. Mil.* II 39.1.

199 ---; ch. Heracleides; ii; Oxy.; I 113.30.

200 ---; ch. Horion; ii; son owns corn transport vessel; III 522.12.

201 AMMONOUS; 85/86; slave, houseborn; II 336 (descr.).

202 ---; d. of Ammonius; sp. Dionysius; ch. Plution; 90; Teis, Thmois. Top.; addr. for s.; *P. Ryl.* IV 597.4.

203 ---; d. of Pecysis, s. of Hermes; m. Ptolema; 117-137; Oxyrhynchite; Cretan qtr; I 105.3 and passim.

204 ---; d. of Pausiris; sp. Sarapion; 119; landholder, lessor; Oxyrhynchite; Oxy.; leases out land nr Sko from Kleros of Antigonus; XXXVI 2776.7.

205 ---; sp. Panechotes; ch. Dionysius; 124; Oxy.; spouse freedman, son minor; III 490.4, 9.

206 ---; d. of Chaeremon; sp. Theon; early ii; Alex.; father Althaieus, sp. Proapposebasteius, Althaieus; III 497.3 and passim.

AMOINOMERIUS; see DIONYSIUS.

AMOIS; see DIONYSIUS.

207 ---; Aug 44; Hermaeum qtr, nr Sarapaeum; neighbour to house owned by Lugus and son; *P. Fouad* 44.31.

208 ---; s. of Phanias; 55-68; shepherd; Nemera; *P. Ross. Georg.* II 13.6.

209 AMOIS; s. of Dionysius; sp. Taseus; ch. Zois; Oct 62; Sesphtha, L. Top.; XXXVIII 2873 V 30.

210 ---; s. of Leucius junior; Dec 75/Jan 76; priest of Zeus, Hera, Apollo, Kore, Dionysus and assoc. gods; Oxyrhynchite; Oxy.; *P. Yale* 64.12.

---; see DIONYSIUS.

---; see PHANIAS.

211 ---; m. Demetria, d. of Sarapion; gs. of Prima; Oct 80; property owner; Oxy.; holds part house in Plateia qtr and property on Kleros of Ctesicles and Epimachus in W. Top.; II 248.7.

212 ---; s. of Apollonius, s. of Syrus; sp. Tecosis; m. Tecosis; Nov 83; Oxyrhynchite; Oxy.; X 1282.9.

213 ---; s. of Theon; ch. Papontos; Nov 83; Oxyrhynchite?; Oxy.?; addr. for s.; dec.; X 1282.20.

214 ---; s. of Theon; 90; Senepta, M. Top.; age c. 61; signalement; writes for Zoilus; I 72.23.

---; see DION( ).

215 ---; s. of Harpalus, s. of Theon; after 89; Oxy. nome?; addr. for father (dec.); father's debt claimed of him and Pamyris by Dionysius; *P. Lips.* 120.10.

---; see DIONYSIUS.

216 ---; early i; II 389 (descr.).

217 ---; i; XIV 1756.7.

218 ---; s. of Pasion; Jan 100; farmer; landholder?; Oxyrhynchite; Oxy.; bro. of Pasion; land in Nemerae; XLI 2960.5.

---; see STEPHANUS.

219 ---; s. of Ptollis; sp. Plutarche; ch. Ptollis; after 102; Oxy.?; addr. for s.; III 636.2.

220 ---; s. of Demetrius, s. of Dionysius; sp. Arsinoe (dec.); ch. Sambous; 104/105; Oxyrhynchite?; addr. for d.; XXXVIII 2852.2.

---; see DIONYSIUS.

221 ---; 126/127; Oxy.; has unnamed children; III 651 (descr.).

222 ---; ch. Tatriphis; 127/128; Oxyrhynchite?; Oxy.; addr. for d.; XII 1452 i 5.

223 ---; s. of Callias; m. Herais; 129; fisherman; Oxyrhynchite; Oxy.; *P. Cornell* 46.3.

224 ---; ch. Amois; 132/133; *PSI* I 53 i 6.

225 AMOIS; s. of Amois; sp. Theudous; ch. Ptollous; 132/133; *PSI* I 53 i 6.

226 ---; s. of Onnophris; 132/133 or 153/154; Oxy.; XII 1518.18.

227 ---; ch. Amois, Leon; 132/133 or 153/154; Oxy.; XII 1518.10.

228 ---; s. of Amois; 132/133 or 153/154; Oxy.; XII 1518.10.

229 ---; s. of Sarapion?; April 133; *PSI* I 53 vii 130.

230 ---; ch. Didymus; Jan 138; III 484.8.

231 ---; ch. Papentos (read Papontos); July 138; hamlet of Dositheus; doc. pr.?; addr. for s.; *P. Bad.* IV 74.13.

---; see DIONYSIUS.

232 ---; ch. Heras; 148/149; Oxyrhynchite, gymnasial class; Gymnasium St qtr; addr. for d.; XLVI 3276.7.

233 ---; s. of Terentius, s. of Diogenes; m. Thaesis, d. of Ptolemaeus; 148/149; Oxyrhynchite, gymnasial class; Upper Camp distr.; reg. in gymnasial class of 13 yr olds in above distr. this yr.; XLVI 3278.8.

234 ---; s. of Horus, s. of Pelus; m. Eirene; early ii; Oxyrhynchite; Oxy.; *P. Wisc.* I 13.4.

235 ---; s. of Sarapion; ch. Eudaemon alias Amois; early ii; Oxyrhynchite?; Oxy.?; addr. for s., witness to will; III 493.14.

---; see EUDAEMON.

236 ---; s. of Sarapion; ch. Amois, Onnophris; ii; hamlet of Cosmos?; doc. pr. Tebtynis?; *P. Mil. Vogl.* IV 211 a9, b5.

237 ---; s. of Amois, s. of Sarapion; ii; landholder; hamlet of Cosmos; doc. pr. Tebtynis?; *P. Mil. Vogl.* IV 211. a9, b5.

238 ---; sp. Tauris; ch. Apollonius; ii; Oxyrhynchite?; Oxy.?; addr. for s.; III 498.4.

239 ---; sp. Hermione; ch. Amois; ii; Oxyrhynchite; addr. for s.; *P. Hamb.* I 79.2.

240 ---; s. of Amois; m. Hermione; ii; slave owner; Oxyrhynchite; bought slave Hermeinus from Charmus; *P. Hamb.* I 79.2.

241 AMOITAS; s. of Pasion, s. of Horion; Sept 58; apprentice weaver; Oxyrhynchite; Thoeris St qtr; minor; father dec.; *P. Mich.* III 171.8.

---; see DIDYMUS.

242 ---; s. of Troilus (name?); 99; Oxy.; writes for Heras, s. of Heras; III 481.24.

243 AMPENDIS; ch. Harthotes (the elder, adopted); 100; Oxy.?; addr. for s.; I 46.7.

244 AMPHEION; ch. Theon; late i; Sesphtha?, L. Top.; addr. for s.; XXXVIII 2845.14.

AMPHION; see FAUSTUS.

245 AMYNTAS; s. of Promachus, s. of Aristion; m. Tauris, d. of Heniochus; Aug 72?; Oxyrhynchite?; Nemerae?, M. Top.; owns property in Nemerae; bro. of Heniochus and Aristion; XLI 2972.23.

246 ANABASIS; ch. Alexandrus; Oct 111; slave; m. of slave owned by Ti. Julius Sarapion; XLIV 3197.12.

247 ---; Oct 111; slave; of Ti. Julius Sarapion; may be same as Anabasis, m. of Alexandrus; XLIV 3197.13.

248 ANDROMACHUS; (1) 55; (2) April 60; agoranomus; Oxy.; assoc. with Diogenes (1) and w. Chaeremon and Sotades; (1) I 99.2; (2) *P. Mich.* III 192.30.

249 ---; 119/120; sitologus; Monimu, U. Top.; *P. Wisc.* II 39.2.

250 ---; ch. 136; of full age; *P. Inst. Fran.* III 18.14.

251 ANDRON; i BC - i; *OD Pisa* 99 i 8.

252 ANDRONICUS; 14-37; Oxy.; assoc. w. Menestheus; *P. Ryl.* IV 677.5.

253 ---; ch. Harbichis; 97; Oxyrhynchite; addr. for gs. Glaucias; II 371.2.

254 ---; ii; landholder; unnamed ch.; *P. Erl.* 44 ii 10.

255 ---; ch. Longius; ii; *P. Erl.* 44 iii 40.

256 ---; ii; "father" is Statilius Phanias, addressee; III 598 (descr.).

257 ANDROSTHENES; Oct 111; slave; of Ti. Julius Theon, ex-str.; XLIV 3197.9.

258 ---; Oct 111; slave; of Ti. Julius Sarapion; XLIV 3197.13.

259 ANICETUS; s. of Inaros; 83/84; landholder; Papsis?, Tychis Necotis; land there; II 290.31.

260 ANNIUS; ch. Tnepheros; 96; Oxyrhynchite; Oxy.; addr. for mat. gs. Sarapion; I 104.5.

261 ANOUP; s. of Sarapion, s. of Sarapion; m. Ammonarion, d. of Nicobulus; i; landholder, lessee; Oxyrhynchite; Oxy.; bro. of Areius?; catoecic land at Senepta?; *P. Harris* 138 iii 27.

262 ANRESIS; s. of Phatres; sp. Orseutes; ch. Onnophris; 81-96; child gymnasial class; VI 984 R (1).

263 ANTAEODORUS; n.d.; *SB* I 1938(a).

264 ANTAMON; 98/99; strategus; Oxy.; *P. Köln* II 86.2, 22.

265 ANTAS; (1) 2 BC; (2) 2 BC - 1; (3), (4) c.1; Oxy.; went to funeral of Athe..., fuller; (1) IV 742.1; (2) 811.1; (3) 736 [iii] 30, 36; (4) 745.3.

266 ---; m. Ptolema; 117-137; Oxyrhynchite; Cretan qtr; I 105.6.

267 ---; s. of Antigonus; m. Thermouthis; i-ii; age 40; *P. Harris* 72.12.

268 ANTEIS; s. of Panemgeus, s. of Dioscorus; m. Tauris, d. of Horus; 132/133; (joint) property owner; Oxyrhynchite; Hermaeum qtr, owns and lives in house at above addr. and has share with sisters Taamois and Tausoreus of unoccupied house in the Hermaeum qtr; tutors Onnophris and Heras; minor, no trade, signalement; *PSI* VIII 874 i 5, 15.

269 ANTEROS; s. of Lucretius; 10/9 BC; IV 817 (descr.).

270 ANTHESTIANUS; ii?; writes to Psois, potter, re outstanding debts; XLI 2996.1.

ANTHESTIUS; see GEMELLUS.

ANTHUS; see THEON.

271 ANTIAS; ch. Heracleides; 130; lessor; III 517.8.

272 ANTIGONUS; sp. Thermuthis; ch. Antas; i-ii; *P. Harris* 72.12.

273 ANTIOCHUS; i BC; bro. Onnophris; *PSI* IX 1079.1.

274 ---; ch. Theon; 55; Alex., Auximetoreius, Leneius; Oxy.; addr. for s.; II 261.6.

275 ---; ch. Apollonia; 77-83; I 170.6-7.

276 ANTIPATER; ch. Onnophris; 36; II 267.2.

277 ---; ch. Zois; 98-102; Oxyrhynchite?; Oxy.?; addr. for gd. Thaesis; *P. Mert.* I 13.3.

278 ANTIPHANES; s. of Ammonius, s. of Antiphanes; (1) 58; (2) July 59; property owner; Oxyrhynchite; Oxy.; involved in court case in Alexandria; (1) II 268.5; (2) 260.2.

279 ---; ch. Heraclas, Ammonius; 58; Oxyrhynchite?; Oxy.?; addr. for s.; II 268.9.

280 ---; s. of Heraclas; ch. Antiphanes; (1) 59; (2) 59; (3) July 59; property owner; Oxyrhynchite; Oxy.; sold property in which s. resident (2); in court case (3); (1) II 306.5; (2) 318.[3], 8; (3) 260.8.

281 ---; s. of Antiphanes, s. of Heraclas; 59; Oxyrhynchite; Oxy.; resident in property in Shepherds' qtr; sold by father to Tryphon; II 318.13.

282 L. OFILIUS ANTISTIUS; ch. Lucius; 95; Roman, Oufentina tribe; Oxy.; II 273.8.

283 ANTIPHANES; s. of Lucius; 95; Roman, Oufentina tribe; guardian of Julia Heracla; Oxy.; II 273.8.

284 ANTISTIUS (ANTHESTIUS in text); c. 136; Oxyrhynchite?; Oxy.?; bro. of Philinus; IV 707 ii 12.

ANTIT( ); see PETSIRIS.

ANTONIA; see ASCLEPIAS.

285 ANTO(NIA); c. 1; IV 736.54.

286 ANTONIA; d. of Drusus; 23; slave owner; II 244.2.

287 ---; s. of Pro[.]ius; sp. Procope; ii; perhaps res. in Coptos; *P. Wurz.* 21 R A 1.

288 CLAUDIUS ANTONIUS; (1) 77; (2), (3) 77-83; (4) 79; (5) c. 81-83; (6) 83; Roman; Oxy.; reg. land for Demetria, d. of Theon (2); appointee of Sarapion (3); Didymus (5) and Chaeremon (6) his appointees; (1) II 242.[1], 30; (2) I 170.1; (3) II 330 (descr.); (4) 243.2; (5) 334 (descr.); (6) 331 (descr.).

289 ANTONIUS; ch. Heliodorus; 132/133; *PSI* I 53 i 10.

290 ---; s. of Ptolemaeus; ii; writes from Poteoli, Italy; has family; (1) III 523.1; (2) XVIII 2191.[1], V.

---; see M. ANTONIUS ASCLEPIADES, DIUS, PALLAS, PTOLEMAEUS, SPENDON, VALENS.

291 ANOUBAS; i; involved in tax collecting; II 298.32.

292 ANUBAS; ii; messenger of Cornelius to his s. Hierax; III 531.16, 19, 20.

ANUBION; see HERMAEUS.

293 ANUBION(?); ch. Apollonides; 135; Oxy.?; possible addr. for gs. Hermaeus; name possibly this, but traces "hardly identifiable"; IX 1195.9.

294 ANUBION; s. of Julius; ii; ex-grammateus dioikeseos; III 642 (descr.).

295 ANUBIS; ch. Harpaesis; i BC - i; *OD Pisa* 779 + 242 Convesso X + 4.

296 APAROUS; d. of Aristion, s. of Promachus?; m. Hagnes?, d. of Ptolemaeus?; gd. of Tauris?; Aug 72; property owner; Oxyrhynchite?; Nemerae, M. Top.; father Oxyrhynchite; see intro. to text; XLI 2972.26.

297 APEIS; s. of Lucas; 119/120; landholder, farmer; has land at Monimu, U. Top. and Sinary, L. Top.; *P. Wisc.* II 39.3.

298 APEI; ch. Sarapion; ii; III 530.14.

299 APELL[AS]; ch. Taagrellsa; 60/61; Oxyrhynchite?; Oxy.?; addr. for d.; II 250.15.

300 APELLES; ch. Apelles; 135/136; Talao?, L. Top.; doc. pr.?; addr. for gs. Apelles and Di[....]es; *P. Iand.* VII 136.18.

301 ---; s. of Apelles; ch. Apelles, Di[....]es; 135/136; landholder; Talao?, L. Top.; doc. pr.?; addr. for s.; *P. Iand.* VII 136.17.

302 ---; s. of Apelles, s. of Apelles; 135/136; landholder; Talao?, L. Top.; doc. pr.?; land held w. bro. Di[....]es; *P. Iand.* VII 136.17.

303 APELLION; ch. Apellion; 135/136; Talao?, L. Top.; doc. pr.?; addr. for gs. Apellion; *P. Iand.* VII 136.9.

304 ---; s. of Apellion; ch. Apellion; 135/136; Talao?, L. Top.; addr. for s.; *P. Iand.* VII 136.9.

305 ---; s. of Apellion, s. of Apellion; 135/136; landholder; Talao, L. Top.; doc. pr.?; land at above addr.; *P. Iand.* VII 136.9.

306 APEROS; ch. Harpochration; 20; Oxy.?; addr. for s.; II 305.7.

307 ---; s. of Diogenes; sp. Thaesis; m. [...]ce, d. of Atreus or Hatres; Dec 75/Jan 76; Oxyrhynchite; Oxy.; Persian of Epigone; see also Peros; *P. Yale* 64.6.

308 ---; ch. Gaius; 77-83; I 170.10.

309 ---; ch. Heras; 117-138; Oxyrhynchite?; Oxy.?; addr. for gs. Heras; I 178.1.

310 ---; ch. Totoes; 132/133; *PSI* I 53 i 2.

311 APE[ROS; s. of [-i]on?; ch. Aperos; 148/149; Oxyrhynchite, gymnasial class; Knights' Camp qtr; addr. fors. scrutinised as above age in 56-58; XLIV 3279.17.

312 APEROS; s. of Aperos, s. of [-i]on?; gs. Pausirion; 148/149; Oxyrhynchite, gymnasial class; Knights' Camp qtr; scrutinised among those over age in 56-58; XLVI 3279.2-3, 17.

313 APEṬẸ[ ]; ch. Euporus; i-ii; Oxyrhynchite; addr. for s.; *P. Princ.* II 25.2.

314 APHRO[DI...]; 100; slave?; Oxy.; I 50.3.

315 APHRO[D......; m. Hermione; c. 130; Oxy.; sister of Dionysia and another; III 472 ii 41.

316 APHRODISIAS; 1 BC; IV 744.11.

317 - alias APHRODITE; i; slave; doc. pr.?; signalement; P. Mil. Vogl. IV 325.8.

318 APHRODITE; ii. *P. Harris* 104.14.

319 APHRODITOUS; alias DEMAROUS; d. of Epicrates (adoptive), s. of Epicrates; sp. Adrastus; m. Thaisous alias Thaesis (adoptive), d. of Heracleides; 100/101 or 119.120; freed-

woman of Epicrates; landholder; Oxyrhynchite; Oxy.; sells catoecic land at Psobthis, E. Top., in Kleros of Ptolemaeus, s. of Theodotus.... s. of Artemon; III 504.3.

320 APHRODITOUS; Oct 111; slave; of T. Julius Theon, ex-strategus; XLIV 3197.9.

321 APHYNCHIS; ch. Horus; Sept/Oct 3 BC; farmer; lessee?; livestock owner; XLI 2979.1.

322 ---; alias ZOILUS; ch. Papontos; 56; Oxyrhynchite?; Oxy.; addr. for s.; II 271.4.

323 ---; ch. Taseus; i; *P. Harris* 144.1.

324 ---; m. Didyme; April 133; bro. of Sarapion; *PSI* I 53 vii 112.

325 ---; ii; granary guard; III 522.9.

326 ---; ii; landholder, farmer; Tychis Necotis; leases land from Didymus; property nr village of Leon from Kleros of Apollonius; *P. Palau. Rib. inv.* 150.3.

327 ---; s. of Hermias; ii; Tacona, L. Top.; Oxy.; *P. Inst. Fran.* I 4.2.

328 APHYNCH[IU]S; ii; fruiterer; XXXVI 2781.5.

329 APHYNCHI[US; ii?; Senocomis?, W. Top.; *P. Fuad I Univ.* 32.10.

330 APIA; d. of Protas; sp. Teos; ch. Diogas, Publius; Oct 80; Oxyrhynchite?; Oxy.; addr. for sons who own property in Pammenes' Garden qtr; II 249.3-4.

331 ---; d. of Pheremphis; Jan 121; property owner; Metroon qtr; jointly owns property with Philon and bros. Dionytas, Tapontos, Arsous, Demetrous and Sarapion, about to collapse; cf. complaint by Tasionus; *P. Fouad* 30.11.

332 ---; alias DIONYSIA; d. of Dionysius; Nov 139; slave owner? Oxyrhynchite; Oxy.; Ophelas alias Corax her freedman; X 1279.3.

333 ---; ii; Zoilus her "brother"; XII 1581.1, V.

334 APIAṆỤṢ; ch. - nus; ii; *SB* VI 9024.30.

335 APIMENES (Ḥp-mn?); ch. Pausiris; late i BC - early i; *OD Pisa* 35 Convesso 16.

336 APION; ch. Heracleius; Jan 26; Pela?, W. Top.; addr. for s.; II 245.4.

337 ---; ch. Saraeus; (1) 36; (2) 36-50; (3) 49/50; (4) 59; (5) Sept 66; Oxyrhynchite?; Oxy.?; addr. for d.; (1) II 267.1; (2) 321.2; (3) I 38.4; (4) II 320.7; (5) 275.8.

338 ---; 45; Alexandria; bro. Callidamas is guardian; II 283.10.

339 APION; s. of Tryphon, s. of Dionysius; m. Saraeus, d. of Apion; (1) 49/50; (2) June 56; apprentice weaver; Oxyrhynchite; Temgenuthis qtr; (1) I 38.13; (2) II 310.3.

340 ---; 52/53; unnamed son sells groceries in Sarapis St qtr; *PSI* VI 692.6.

341 ---; ch. Stratonicus; 55; Oxy.?; addr. for s.; II 304.30.

342 ---; ch. Teseuris, Syrus (= Lucius); 64; children owned property in Hermaeum qtr; *SB* XII 10788.10, 61.

343 ---; s. of Leonides, s. of Ptolemaeus; 66-72/73; Alex., Althaieus?; Oxy.?; deme of father; IX 1203 + *SB* IV 7339.16.

344 ---; s. of Herodes; ch. Heracleides; (1) 70; (2) 79/80; Oxyrhynchite?; Lycians' Camp qtr (2); addr. for s.; (1) XXII 2349.6, 32; (2) *P. Oxy. inv.* 20.3B.34/B.2.

345 ---; late i; II 299.1.

346 ---; i; XLII 3070.1.

347 ---; s. of Nigaeus (Nicaeus?); i; landholder?, farmer; Koba; land at Theon village, M. Top.; VIII 1145.3.

348 FLAVIUS APION; 100/101 or 119/120; landholder; Roman; age 55; has children; buys into Kleros of Ptolemaeus at Psobthis, E. Top.; buys catoecic land nr Psobthis; III 504. [7], 14.

349 APION; ch. Apion; March 102; Oxyrhynchite; Oxy.; addr. for s.; XXII 2342.2.

350 ---; s. of Apion; March 102; wine merchant; Oxyrhynchite; Oxy.; partner of Pasion, s. of Sarapion; XXII 2342.2.

351 ---; (1) June c. 103-110; (2) 104/5; strategus; Oxy.; (1) XLVI 3275.1; (2) XXXVIII 2852.1.

352 ---; s. of Demetrius; 104/5; Oxyrhynchite; Oxy.; XXXVIII 2852.6.

353 ---; 104; pastophorus of Temple of Isis; VIII 1155.1, 18.

354 ---; ch. Syrus; Aug 114 or 133; Hermaeum qtr; addr. for s.; *SB* VIII 9824.4.

355 ---; s. of Syrus, s. of Apion; Aug 114 or 133; property owner; Hermaeum qtr; bro. of Nilus now called Polem[archus]?, Syrus, Sarapion, and Thais; *SB* VIII 9824.2.

356 ---; ch. Heracles alias Apion; 117; Oxy.?; addr. for s.; III 489.20.

357 ---; alias HERACLES; s. of Apion; 117; signalement; III 489.20.

358 ---; 124; Oxyrhynchite?; Oxy.?; has s. and gs. (Apion); addr. for gs. III 490.20.

359 ---; gs. of Apion; Oxyrhynchite; Oxy.; witness; III 490.19.

360 APION; ch. Thermuthis; 129; Oxyrhynchite?; Oxy.?; addr. for d.; I 75.3.

361 ---; ch. Sarapion; 130; Ibion Ammonii, L. Top.; addr. for gs. Horion alias Theon; III 492.16.

362 ---; ch. Zoilus; 130; Oxyrhynchite?; Oxy.?; addr. for gs. Apion; III 492.18.

363 ---; s. of Zoilus, s. of Apion; m. Neilarous; 130; Oxyrhynchite; Oxy.; signalement; witnesses will; age 44; III 492.18.

364 ---; Nov/Dec 132; doc. pr. Sinary, Oxy.; unnamed s. writes for d. of Castor and her unnamed guardian; *PSI* I 53 viii 146.

365 ---; ch. Apion; Aug 133; Oxyrhynchite; Oxy. nome; addr. for gs. Heracleides; *P. Köln* II 100.32.

366 ---; s. of Apion; ch. Heracleides; Aug 133; Oxyrhynchite; Oxy. nome; addr. for s.; *P. Köln* II 100.32.

367 ---; ii; writes to "sister" Hexaconous; VI 967.1.

---; see EPICRATES.

368 ---; ii; episkeptes of riverside estates; III 589 (descr.).

369 ---; ii; brother of Hermatois; III 530.24.

370 APIS; Sept/Oct 3 BC; landholder, lessor; Oxyrhynchus; addressee of letter; XLI 2979.1, back.

371 ---; late i BC; advocate; Alexandria; XII 1479.4

372 ---; s. of Harpaesis, s. of A or HA; m. Taysorapis, d. of Harthoonis; 77; priest of Thoeris, Isis, Sarapis and assoc. gods; property owner; Oxy.; bought w. others property in Hermaeum qtr; II 242.3 etc.

373 ---; March 154; property owner; Oxy.; house in tenth qtr, E. of property of Thonis; firekindler of Athena Thoeris; XXXIV 2722.25.

374 APOL( ); s. of Hera( ); Nov.42 BC; witness; Oxy.; *P. Ryl.* IV 582.22

375 ---; s. of Ie( ) or Hie( ); Nov 42 BC; witness; Oxy.; *P. Ryl.* IV 482.22.

376 ---; ch. Diosco( ); 119/120; *P. Wisc.* II 39.4.

377 APOLINARIUS; 1; merchant; *P. Erl.* 14 V 3.

378 ---; (1) 136; (2) 137; (3) Jan 138; (4) c. 138; strategus; Oxy.; (1) XII 1472.1; (2) *PSI* XII 1262 ii 8, iii 10-11; (3) III 484.2; (4) III 379 (descr.).

379 CLAUDIUS APOLL(ONIUS?); m. Isidora, d. of Apollonius; gs. of Dionysius alias -onius (by adoption); c. 47-54; Roman; adoptive gf. Alexandrian, Gamma distr.; XLVI 3271.2.

380 APOLL[-]; s. of Trig-?; ii; unnamed d. buried in the Hermopolite; *PSI* IV 281 V 62.

381 APOLL[...]US; 132/133; Oxy.; *PSI* I 53 ix 158.

382 APOLLO..[.]; sp. Taseus; ch. Heraclas; March 66; s. apprenticed to weaver; XLI 2971.6.

383 APOLLO[ ]; after 138/139; Chysis; gives name to measure of grain; *PSI* IV 281 R i 6.

384 ---; m. Siag( ); 119/120; landholder, farmer; has land at Monimu, U. Top. and Sinary, L. Top.; *P. Wisc.* II 39.4.

385 ---; ch. Theon; ii; s. banker; XLI 2980 back.

386 APOLLO; s. of Comon; m. Tapotamon; ii. landholder; Cretan qtr; *P. Princ.* II 46.9.

387 ---; sp. Harthosis; ch. Cerdon; ii; Thoeris St qtr; *P. Princ.* II 46.15.

388 APOLLOGENES; ii; vineyard manager; manages v. of Diogenes, his friend, at Phai and Chalothis; XLII 3063.1.

389 APOLLON; s. of Apollonius, s. of Apollonius; m. Diogenis; Aug 133; Oxyrhynchite; Oxy. nome; guardian to sister Taarpaesis; illiterate; *P. Köln* II 100.3.

390 ---; s. of Diogenes, s. of Theon; early ii; Oxyrhynchite; Oxy.; witness to will; III 493.14.

391 APOLLONARION; 1 BC; IV 744.2-3.

392 ---; July/Aug 67; freedwoman of Themistocles, an Alexandrian; II 377 (descr.).

---; see ISIDORA.

393 APOLLONIA; d. of Sarapion; sp. Cendeas; sister of Ammenius, Hermodotus and Petusius; June 52; Oxy.?; *SB* I 8034.6.

394 ---; d. of Antiochus; sp. Theon; ch. Demetria; 77-83; I 170.6.

395 ---; 79/80; landowner, Sinary, L. Top.; her guardian Themistocles, Alexandrian; II 373 (descr.).

396 ---; sp. Heracleodorus; ch. Hierax; 81-96; addr. for s.; VI 984 R (3).

397 ---; 81-96; formerly owner of Panesneus, now freedman; VI 984 R init.

398 ---; ii; XXXI 2593.1.

399 APOLLONIDES; i?; *P. Erl.* 14 V 16.

400 ---; s. of Petosiris, s. of Thoonis; m. Taps[ois?], d. of Paulus; 119; stonecutter; North St qtr; unmarked; age 21; XII 1547.19.

401 APOLLONIDES; s. of [Anubi]on(?); ch. Hermaeus; Jan/Feb 135; Oxy.?; possible addr. for s. Hermaeus alias Anubion, whose opponent from Herm. Magna; IX 1195.9.

402 ---; ch. Ammoni[u]s; Sept/Oct 137; IV 729.35.

403 APOLLONIS; s. of Tareinus; ii; landholder; bro. Epimachus; *P. Erl.* 44 iii 36.

404 APOLLONIUS; s. of Dionysius; m. Arsinoe, d. of Ptolemaeus; 63/62 BC; Macedonian of catoecic cavalry; Cleopatra Aphrodite St; XIV 1644.5.

405 ---; alias HARBICHIS; ch. Apollonius alias Harbichis; July 44 BC; Oxyrhynchite?; Cleopatra Aphrodite St?; addr. for s.; XIV 1629.6.

406 ---; alias HARBICHIS; s. of Apollonius alias Harbichis; July 44 BC; farmer, lessee; Oxyrhynchite; Cleopatra Aphrodite St; Persian of Egigone; rents land at Païmis from Theon, s. of Theon; XIV 1629.5.

407 ---; Aug 35 BC; *P. Ryl.* IV 593.1.

408 ---; July 23 BC; grapheion official, in charge w. Dorion; Oxy.; *P. Inst. Fran.* I 13.31.

409 ---; s. of Ptolemaeus; 22 BC; comogrammateus; landholder; Tholthis, Thmois. Top.; bro. of Dionysius alias Amois; staying nr Theon, s. of Ischyrion; VII 1061.3-4, V.

410 ---; 2 BC; descr. as the Libyan; IV 743.37.

411 AP]OLLONIUS; i BC; *OD Pisa* 55 ii 11.

412 APOLLONIUS; i BC - i; *OD Pisa* 29 ii X + 2.

413 ---; s. of Horus; i BC - i; *OD Pisa* 510 + 568 Convesso ii 6.

414 ---; s. of Petesis; i BC - i; *OD Pisa* 5 i X + 8.

415 ---; s. of Psencales; i BC - i; *OD Pisa* 228 X + 6.

416 ---; c. 1; Cynus village? or Cynopolis?; IV 739.1.

417 ---; c. 1; "brother" of writer Didymus and Ammonius; IV 791 (descr.) V.

418 ---; 9; *DO Colon. inv.* 286.1.

419 ---; ch. Hatres; 14-37; Thmois. Top.?; addr. for gs., name lost; *P. Cornell* 54.6.

420 ---; 22; archistator of prefect's court; Alexandria; II 294.18.

421 ---; s. of Achilleus; ch. Herodes; 25-37; landholder; addr. for s.; land in Thmois. Top. ceded to him by Herodes; *PSI* X 1118.1.

422 ---; 27; toparch; II 356 (descr.).

423 APOLLONIUS; ch. Apollonius, Dionysius; June 29; *SB* VIII 9827 (a) 3, (b) 3.

424 ---; s. of Apollonius; June 29; guardian to niece Didyme; *SB* VIII 9827 (a) 3, (b) 3.

425 ---; (1) 41-54; (2) Sept 49; topogrammateus; comogrammateus; Oxy.; assoc. w. Didymus; ?also restored in II 251.1 and in 255.2; (1) XXXIII 2669.1; (2) *P. Mich.* III 170.1, 20.

426 ---; s. of Ptolemaeus; 41-79; XLII 3061.19.

427 ---; 41-79; grammateus (to Theon, eisagogeus); XLII 3062.114.

428 ---; ch.]on; 43/44; Pela?, W.Top.; s., descr. as Persian of Epigone, leases land there; II 368.2.

429 APO(LLONIUS?); ch. Phatres; July 44, Pela, W. Top.; addr. for gd. Ar..; XII 1447.4.

430 [APOLLO]NIUS; Nov 45; strategus; perhaps also in II 283.1 as T.C. Apollonius; X 1258.7.

431 APOLLONIUS; ch. Isidora; c. 47-54; child adopted by Dionysius alias ....onius, Alexandrian; XLVI 3271.3.

432 ---; s. of Sotades; 48; guardian of Thermutharion; II 255.5.

433 ---; ch. Menodorus; 48; son is Alex., Althaieus; *P. Fouad* 37.1.

434 ---; s. of Apollonius; (1) 49; (2) Aug/Sept 53; master weaver; Oxyrhynchite; Knights' Camp qtr; (1) *P. Mich.* III 170.10; (2) *P. Wisc* I 4.2.

435 ---; ch. Apollonius; (1) 49; (2) Aug/Sept 53; Oxyrhynchite; Knights' Camp qtr; addr. for s.; (1) *P. Mich.* III 170.11; (2) *P. Wisc.* I 4.2.

436 APOL(LONIUS); ch. Alexandrus; c. 50; Oxyrhynchite; Thoeris St qtr; addr. for s., weaver; II 284.2.

437 APOLLO(NIUS); c. 52/53, date of R; *PSI* IX 1029 V 3.

438 APOLLONIUS; June 56; Oxy.; II 310.6.

439 ---; 58; registers document; II 268.20.

440 ---; 59; agoranomus; Oxy.; formerly reg. as Secundus; II 320.25.

441 ---; s. of Menches; ch. Tauris; July 64; Oxyrhynchite; Knights' Camp qtr; addr. for s.; *P. Mich.* III 179.3.

442 ---; July 66; assistant to strategus Papiscus; Oxy.; II 246.28.

443 ---; Aug 69; doc. pr.?; *PSI* XIV 1433.9.

444 ---; Jan/Feb 75; guardian for cousin Sarapous; II 362 (descr.).

445 APOLLONIUS; s. of Dionysius, s. of Dionysius alias Didymus; sp. Heliodora, d. of Heliodora; April 77; guardian of wife; II 263.7.

446 ---; after 79; had twin bro.; may not be Oxyrhynchite; XXXVI 2757 i 3.

447 ---; after 81; Oxyrhynchite; Oxy.; II 369.[1], 18.

448 ---; c. 81-83; rep. of Didymus, rep. of Claudius Antoninus; II 334 (descr.).

449 ---; ch. Apollonius; 81-95; Oxyrhynchite; gr. gf. (mat.) of Sarapous; probably dec.; II 265.9.

450 ---; s. of Apollonius; 81-95; Oxyrhynchite; gf. (mat.) of Sarapous, being married; probably dec.; II 265.9.

451 ---; alias -; 83; banker w. Chaeremon; II 289 ii 12.

452 ---; s. of Syrus; sp. Tecosis; ch. Amois; Nov 83; Oxyrhynchite?; Oxy.?; addr. for s.; X 1282.9.

453 ---; 86; city grammateus; Oxy.; w. Theon; VII 1028.4.

454 ---; ch. Apollonius; 87/88; Oxyrhynchite?; addr. for s.; *P. Princ.* III 147.4.

455 ---; s. of Apollonius; sp. Hierakiaena; 87/88; Oxyrhynchite; acts as wife's guardian in land lease; *P. Princ.* III 147.3-4.

456 ---; s. of Ptollion; sp. Ptolema; ch. Zoilus; 90; Senepta?, M. Top.; Oxy.; addr. for s.; I 72.2.

457 ---; Feb 91; practor (of weavers' tax)?; Oxy.; XLI 2957.29.

458 ---; s. of Chaeremon; sp. Herais; ch. Heracleides; 94; Oxyrhynchite; Oxy.?; II. 270.10.

459 ---; (1) Mar 97; (2) 99; bibliophylax, w. Demetrius and Diogenes; Oxy.; (1) IV 713.2; (2) *P. Harris* 74.1.

460 ---; alias SECUNDUS; s. of Epimachus; Dec 99; farmer; landholder?; Oxyrhynchite; Oxy.; farms land in Chysis and Athychis; XLI 2958.2.

461 ---; ch. Apollonius; early i; Oxyrhynchite; Oxy.; addr. for s.; *P. Mert.* III 104.1.

462 ---; s. of Apollonius; sp. Charitos; early i; Oxyrhynchite; Oxy.; claim against Sinth( ) re mortgage; *P. Mert.* III 104.1.

463 ---; s. of Herodes; late i; unnamed sons, students in Alex.; XVIII 2190.22-23.

464 ---; s. of P_3-tj-jm(*Peteiomis?); i; *OD Pisa* 318.5.

465 APOLLO(NIUS); m. Ta...ri[; i; Oxy.?; age 24; guardian of m.; *P. Ryl.* II 145.[28], V.

466 APOLLONIUS; i; agoranomus; Oxyrhynchite; *P. Mil. Vogl.* IV 235.3.

467 ---; i; II 399 (descr.).

468 ---; ch. Petechon; i; Koba; addr. for s.; VIII 1145.9.

469 ---; ch. Selene; i; *P. Harris* 144.5.

---; see ATHENAEUS.

470 ---; ch. Apollonius, Pausanias; i; VIII 1153.1.

471 ---; s. of Apollonius; i; Alexandria; staying in Alex.; VIII 1153.1.

472 ---; i; farmer; *P. Ryl.* II 199.25.

473 ---; sp. Taareotis; ch. Heracles; i - ii; *P. Harris* 72.28.

474 APOLLO(NIUS)?; ch. Apollonius; i - ii; XLII 3057 back.

475 APOLLONIUS; s. of Apollonius?; i - ii; surveyor; belongs to group of "brothers"; XLII 3057.1 and V.

476 ---; ch. -us; 101; landholder; doc. pr. Oxy.?; doc. dated 197/198; s. held catoecic land in A[ ]; *P. Bour.* 16.15.

477 ---; (1), (2), May/June 102; (3) 116; (4) Feb 122; (5) 132/133; city secretary w. Didymus (1-3) and w. Diogenes alias Hermaeus (5); ex-exegetes (4); Oxy.; (1) *PSI* VIII 952.13; (2) 952.12; (3) XII 1550.1; (4) IV 714.6; (5) *PSI* VIII i [1], ii 20.

478 ---; ch. [..]eia; after 102; Oxyrhynchite; Oxy.?; addr. for gd.; III 636.7.

479 ---; 107/108; comogrammateus; U. Top.; c. of Monimu estate and other villages; XII 1434 i 1.

480 ---; s. of Epimachus; 107-116; Oxy.?; known as the younger; leases land nr Kerkethyris from bro. Apollonius; *P. Stras.* 244.4

481 ---; s. of Epimachus; 107-116; landowner; Oxy.; leases land nr Kerkethyris to bro. Apollonius the younger; *P. Stras.* 244.1.

482 ---; May 109; perhaps non-Oxyrhynchite; case against by Arius and Sarapion; bro. or relative of Athenodorus?; XLII 3015.8.

483 ---; (1) 115/116; (2) and (3) 116; (4) April 116; (5) 117/118; strategus; Oxy.; (1) I 97.10; (2) 74.3; (3) *P. Cair. Preis.* 32.4; (4) XXXVI 2759.4; (5) IX 1189.3.

484 ---; ch. Diogenes?; Oxyrhynchite?; Oxy.?; readings uncertain; III 489.21.

485 ---; m. Philumene?; (1), (2) 117-138; (3) n.d.; bro. of Asinnius Secundus and Theon; doc. 3 prov.?; (1) X 1293.23, 32; (2) *P. Brem.* 56 a 2; (3) *SB* I 4630.1.

486 APOLLONIUS; s. of Horus; 121; farmer; lessee; Senepta, M. Top.; Persian of Epigone; III 499.3.

487 ---; March 122; property owner; slave owner; Oxyrhynchite; W. Quay qtr?; reg. 13 yr old slave of houseborn female slave; in 12 dr. tax class; IV 714.8.

488 ---; 124; Oxyrhynchite?; Oxy.?; has s. and gs.; addr. for s., witness; III 490.15.

489 ---; Aug 127; bibliophylax?; Oxy.; I 34 iv 1.

490 ---; 127 or 128; secretary to sitologi of Sinkepha; *P. Lips.* 113.2.

491 ---; s. of Heliodorus, s. of Apollonius; m. Thais, d. of Chaeremon; Nov 129; farmer; lessee; Oxyrhynchite; Oxy.; leases land at Ophis, E. Top., in Kleros of Apollonius; age c. 78; signalement; VII 1024.13-14.

492 ---; ch. Heliodorus; 129; Oxyrhynchite?; Oxy.?; addr. for gs. Apollonius; VII 1024.14-15.

493 ---; ch. Asclepiades; 130; Oxyrhynchite?; Oxy.?; addr. for gs. Apollonius; III 492.21.

494 ---; s. of Asclepiades, s. of Apollonius; 130; Oxyrhynchite; Oxy.; age 70; signalement; witnesses will; III 492.21.

---; see THEON.

495 ---; ch. Valerius; 130; son leases land Senepta, M. Top.; IV 730.3.

496 ---; ch. Ese[-; 132/133; Oxy.?; addr. for d.; *PSI* VIII 874 ii 24.

497 --- alias D[..]; m. Didyme (dec.); 132/133; unmarked; *PSI* VIII 874 ii 32.

498 ---; ch. Apollonius, Abau, Horus; Aug 133; Oxyrhynchite; addr. for gd. Taarpaesis alias Isidora; *P. Köln* II 100.3.

499 ---; s. of Apollonius; sp. (1) Tsenamunis, (2) Diogenis; ch. Taarpaesis alias Isidora (by 1), Apollon (by 2); Aug 133; Oxyrhynchite; Oxy.; addr. for d.; *P. Köln* II 100.3.

500 ---; s. of Horus, s. of Apollonius; Aug 133; cousin Taarpaesis witness to will; age 41; signalement; *P. Köln* II 100.[30], 37.

501 ---; s. of Demetrius; 133; ousia of Seneca; to receive grain from a/c of Demetrius; *P. Lips.* 115.5.

502 ---; s. of Eutychides; ch. Eutychides alias Horion; (1) 133; (2) ii; to receive grain from a/c of Demetrius; name in (2) restored from *Chrest. Wilck.* 217; (1) *P. Lips.* 115.8; (2) P. Sel. 22.2 and note.

503 ---; 134; grammateus (of sitologi); Oxy.; III 515.3.

504 APOLLONIUS; s. of Ptolemaeus; 135; hyperetes; Oxy.; assistant of strategus Demetrius; I 106.2-3.

505 ---; c. 135; rhetor; perhaps not an Oxy.; XVII 2111 i 21.

506 ---; s. of Diogenes; sp. Tanechotarion alias Euterpe; ch. Apollonius; Dec 134/Jan 135; Oxyrhynchite?; Oxy.?; addr. for s.; IV 726.5.

507 ---; s. of Apollonius, s. of Diogenes; m. Tanechotarion alias Euterpe, d. of Diogenes; Dec 134/Jan 135; Oxyrhynchite; Oxy.; unable to attend inquiry before prefect; IV 726.5.

508 ---; 135; judge; appt. by Petronius Mamertinus; case involves party from Hermopolis Magna and party from Oxy.; IX 1195.1.

509 ---; ch. Tsintotoes; 137; Mermertha; addr. for d.; *PSI* XII 1262 iii 4.

510 ---; Jan 139; city grammateus; *P. Oslo* III 105.2.

511 ---; s. of Peteuris, s. of Eubion; ch. Pet[euri]s(?); 148/149; Oxyrhynchite, gymnasial class; Gymnasium St qtr; scrutinised there in 72/73; XLVI 3276.2.

512 ---; s. of Pasion, s. of Sarapion; m. Berenice; early ii; Oxyrhynchite; Oxy.; bro. of Sarapas, Diogenes and another; III 493.6.

513 ---; s. of Gaius; early ii; summoned; VI 969 (descr.).

514 ---; early ii; VI 969 (descr.).

515 ---; sp. Taotous (Taos?); ch. [....]n; ii; Oxy.; s. married to Dionysia; addr. for s.; *SB* VI 9372.1.

516 ---; ii; tax collector?; XXXVIII 2861.1.

517 ---; ii; carpenter; hamlet of Ctesis, Senepta; *P. Med. inv.* 12.2.

518 ---; ii; friend of Eirene; I 115.8.

519 ---; s. of Besas alias Ammonius; sp. Taamois; ch. Ptolema; ii; Oxy.?; addr. for s.; *P. Mil.* II 51.2-3.

520 ---; ch. Pausiris; ii; s. owns corn transport vessel; III 522.13.

521 ---; sp. Didyme?; ii; bro. of Theonas;? "brother" of Didyme; XLII 3059.1.

522 ---; ii; grammateus; to Flavius and partner; XLII 3058.7-8.

523 ---; s. of Claudius Deme[trius; ii; slave owner; Thoeris St qtr; III 574 (descr.)R.

524 ---; ii; Oxy.; guardian of Antonia Asclepias alias Cyria; III 498.2.

525 APOL(LONIUS); ii; livestock owner; I 113.2.

526 APOLLONIUS; s. of Amois; m. Tauris; ii; stone cutter; Oxyrhynchite; Oxy.; III 498.4.

527 ---; ch. Sarapion; ii; III 609 (descr.).

528 ---; sp. Allous; ii; *P. Oslo* II 15.31.

529 ---; ii; *P. Oslo* II 49.10-11.

530 ---; ii; III 611 (descr.).

531 ---; s. of Eutychides; ch. Eutychides alias Horion; ii; name restored on analogy of *Chrest. Wilck.* 217; *P. Sel.* 22.2.

532 ---; s. of Demetrius; mid. ii; farmer; XLIV 3165.3.

533 ---; ii; writes to Dionysia re supply roses for wedding of Sarapion; XLVI 3313.1.

534 ---; s. of Zoilus; ii; I 164 (descr.).

535 ---; ii; reg. doc.?; *P. Oslo* III 108.6.

536 ---; ii; "brother" of writer Publius; XLI 2981.1.

537 ---; ii; XLI 2981.24.

538 APOLLONOUS: d. of S[ ]; sp. Glaucias; m. Saraeus, d. of Nechthenibis; 81/82; nurse; Oxyrhynchite; Oxy.; *P. Mert.* III 118.4.

539 ---; 91 or 107; slave; of Achilleus, Sarapas and others, ransomed by Heraclas, s. of Tryphon; c. 26 yrs; signalement; IV 722.15.

540 ---; i; has brother; II 298.43.

541 ---; sp. Luci(u)s; ch. Luci(u)s; i; Sobthis; addr. for s.; VIII 1145.20.

542 ---; d. of Sarapion; 98-117; landowner; guardian is nephew Horion; leases land nr Nesla to Ptolemaeus; *PSI* VII 772.1.

543 ---; sp. Sarapas; ch. Ophelas alias Besas; ii; Oxyrhynchite; Oxy.; addr. for s.; III 505.1.

544 ---; sp. Sarapion; ch. Pausanias; 129; Oxyrhynchite; Oxy.; addr. for s.; XXXVI 2774.3.

545 APOLLOPHANES; ch. ..]ros; 6-35; Oxy.; II 256.4.

546 ---; (1) c. 50; (2) 50; ex-practor of tax on weavers; Oxy.; practor in 47-48; charged w. extortion; (1) II 284.6; (2) 285.5.

547 ---; Feb 61; slave; weaver; Temgenuthus qtr; died away from Oxy.; slave of Sarapion; II 262.3.

548 APOLLOPHANES; (1) 62; (2) Mar/Apr 66; (3) 72/73; (4) 79/80; topogrammateus and comogrammateus w. Diogenes (1, 2, 4) and w. Ap (3); Oxy.; (1) *SB* XII 10788.24; (2) *PSI* VIII 871.2, 20; (3) *P. Genov.* I 12.2; (4) *P. Oxy. inv.* 20.3B.34/B.1.

549 ---; 63/64; city secretary (?) w. A[...]n[; *P. Gen. inv.* 222.2.

550 ---; ch. Alis; ii; Oxy.; XII 1536.6.

551 ---; s. of Th[]; m. Arsinoe; Jan 93; Alex., Neocosmius, Genearcheius?; age 30; signalement; catoecic land from Kleros of Heracles nr Sinary, L. Top., ceded to him by Sarapion; neighbours to south, catoecic land of Dionysius; *PSI* VIII 897.61, 94.

552 ---; ch. Sosibius; Aug 102; Oxyrhynchite?; Oxy.?; addr. for gs. Stephanus alias Amois; III 508.6.

553 APOLLOS; s. of Theon; 30; X 1291.10-11.

554 ---; m. Se( ); i - ii; slave? of Ision; age 28; *P. Harris* 72.34.

555 ---; s. of Heracleus; m. Berous; i - ii; age 41; *P. Harris* 72.7.

556 ---; s. of Heracleus; sp. Tamystha; m. Berous; ch. Heracles; i - ii; bro. of Mysthas, Heracles and Nemion; age 41; *P. Harris* 72.6.

557 ---; Aug 106; *P. Wisc.* I 17 V 7.

558 ---; s. of Heracleides; c. 110-112; Oxyrhynchite; Oxy.; charged w. attack on Taamois, sp. of Heraclas; XXXVI 2758.6.

559 ---; d. of Paesis; sp. (1) Dio[genes; (2) Apollos; ch. Didymus (1); 117/118; landowner; leaves property at Kerkemorinis, U. Top.; unnamed ch. by 2; IV 837 (descr.).

560 ---; s. of Ophelas; sp. Apollos; 117/118; children left property at Kerkemorinis, U. Top., by m.; IV 837 (descr.).

561 APOULES; i - ii; clerk in merchant's office; going to Pakerke; *P. Harris* 96.3, 16, 30, 36.

562 [AP]YNCHIUS?; s. of A( ); 60/61; property owner; farmer in Kleros of Nicanor and Drimax; Oxy.; II 250.25.

563 AR...; s. of Phatres, s. of Apo(llonius?); July 44; farmer; landholder; Pela, W. Top.; acts through Heras; XII 1447.4.

564 AR...? or HAR[or DIOGENES; 72/73; topogrammateus and comogrammateus w. Apollophanes; *P. Genov.* I 12.2.

565 ARAEUS; ch. Ptolemaeus; 92; landholder?; Peroth( )?; addr. for s.; XVIII 2185.21.

566 ARASIS; d. of Vettius; sp. Philiscus; ch. Peteesis; July 87; Senepta, M. Top.; addr. for s.; *PSI* III 203.2.

567 ARCHELAUS; 13/14; landholder?; applies to buy land in Thmois. Top. from idios logos; IV 721.2, 10.

568 ---; s. of Heraclas; 41-79; grammateus to Theon, strat. of Panopolite; Panopolis; "brother" of Sarapion; (1) XLII 3061.1; (2) 3062.1.

569 AURELIUS ARCHELAUS; ii?; Roman; beneficiarius; Latin doc.; I 32.2.

570 ARCHIAS; ch. Narcissus; c. 50; XXVII 2471.10.

571 ---; c. 110-112; strategus; Oxy.; XXXVI 2758.1.

572 ARCHIBIUS; 10-11?; banker; XXXVI 2772.1.

573 ---; s. of Archibius; 57; banker; Sarapeum; II 269.3.

574 ---; ch. Archibius; 57; Oxy.?; addr. for s.; II 269.3.

575 AR]CHION; s. of Lyc<a>rion, s. of Hermogenes; 117; Oxyrhynchite; Oxy.; witness of will of Dionysius; III 489.23.

576 AREIA; sp. Zenas; m. [..]ticus; ch. Heras alias Gaius, Zenas; (1) after 88/89; (2) c. 107-112; (3) before 123; Oxyrhynchite; Heracles Place qtr; addr. for s.; claims to be d. of Roman soldier; (1) *PSI* VII 731.7; (2) *PSI* V 450 R 1, 23; (3) XVIII 2199.14.

577 AREIONIS; ch. Tausorapis; 71; addr. for mat. gs. Theon; *P. Med. inv.* 71.70.9.

578 AREIUS; ch. Harpocration; 44; Pammenes' Garden qtr; addr. for s.; *P. Fouad* 27.5.

579 ---; 45; Alexandria; II 283.9.

580 ---; after 79; nomikos; Oxyrhynchite?; XXXVI 2757 ii 5.

581 ---; s. of Sarapion, s. of Sarapion; m. Ammonarion, d. of Nicobulus; i; catoecic landholder; lessor; Oxyrhynchite; Oxy.; leases land at Senepta to Nechthosiris, s. of Sarapion; *P. Harris* 138 iii 11.

582 ---; s. of Ariston; i - early ii; borrows from Aristandrus; *P. Oslo* III 114.15.

583 ---; s. of Ptolemaeus; May 109; Oxyrhynchite?; contra Athenodorus and Apollonius re will; bro. of Sarapion; XLII 3015.6.

584 CLAUDIUS AREIUS; (1) 92; (2) 93/94; strategus; Roman; Oxy.; (1) XVIII 2185.1; (2) *PSI* X 1109.1.

585 ARIEUS; ch. Smj; Sept 6; *OD Pisa* 431.4.

586 ---; i BC - i; dependant of P_3-tš; *OD Pisa* Convesso i 11.

587 ARISTANDRUS; s. of Ariston; 23; practor of taxes; villages of Apion, W. Top.; tax collector for above; II 287.5.

588 ARISTANDRUS; ch. Aristandrus; (1) 66-72/73; (2) 2nd half i; practor; Oxyrhynchite; Sesphtha (or Psenorisis?), L. Top.; descr. as the younger, bro. of A. the elder and Theon; (1) IX 1203 + *SB* IV 7339.3; (2) XXXVIII 2845.12.

589 ---; s. of Aristandrus; 66-72/73; Oxyrhynchite; Oxy.; descr. as the elder, bro. of A. the younger and Theon; IX 1203 + *SB* IV 7339.2.

590 ---; ch. Theon, Aristandrus (elder), Aristandrus (younger); (1) 66-72/73; (2) 2nd half i; landowner; Oxyrhynchite?; Sesphtha? (or Psenosiris?), L. Top.; addr. for s.; mortgaged land in Senepta, Kleros of Damon; (1) IX 1203 + *SB* IV 7339.3-4; (2) XXXVIII 2845.12.

591 ---; early i; *P. Wisc.* I 23.8.

592 ---; s. of Sarapion, s. of Sarapion; m. Arsinoe, d. of Theon; i - early ii; Oxyrhynchite; makes loan to Areius; *P. Oslo* III 114.14.

593 ---; s. of [ ]minis; ch. Tryphon; (1) 121; (2) 137; Oxyrhynchite?; Oxy.?; addr. for s.; (1) III 499.1; (2) *PSI* XII 1262 ii 1.

594 ARISTAS; s. of Plutus; 49/50; weaver; Oxyrhynchite; Knights' Camp qtr; complains re Damis; II 393 (descr.) 3.

595 ARISTION; s. of Promachus, s. of Aristion; m. Tauris, d. of Heniochus; sp. Hagnes; ch. Promachus; Aug 72; property owner; Oxyrhynchite; Oxy.; guardian of wife; XLI 2972.5.

596 ---; ch. Promachus; Aug 72; Oxyrhynchite?; Oxy.?; addr. for gs. Aristion; XLI 2972.6.

597 ---; Jan 119; reg. in South Quay qtr; assoc. w. Didymus in census return; IV 786 (descr.).

598 ARISTIUS; 98-117; agoranomus w. Alexandrus, Theon, etc.; Oxy.; *P. Sel.* 24.10.

599 ARISTOCLEIA; d. of Alexandrus; ii; unnamed children; stepmother? Dionysia; sister of Sarapion and Theon; XLVI 3313.24.

600 ARISTOCLES; 49; advocate; I 37.4.

601 ---; s. of Alexandrus; Oct 98; Oxyrhynchite; Epaphroditus freedman; *P. Genov.* II 62.1.

602 ---; ch. Didymus; late i; res. in Alexandria; XVIII 2190.8.

603 ARISTON; 4/3 BC; tax farmer (6 dr. tax on asses); Oxy.; farms tax in Oxy. w. Ptolemaeus; XII 1457.1.

604 ---; ch. Aristandrus; 23; villages of Apion?, W. Top.; addr. for s.; II 287.5.

605 ---; ch. Ariston; late i; Oxyrhynchite; Oxy.; addr. for gs. Heliodorus; *P. Sel.* 23.11.

606 ARISTON; s. of Ariston; sp. Tryphaena; ch. Heliodorus; late i; Oxyrhynchite. Oxy.; addr. for s.; *P. Sel.* 23.11.

607 ---; ch. Areius; i - early ii; *P. Oslo* III 114.15.

608 ---; s. of Artemidorus; 124; Oxyrhynchite; Oxy.; witness; age 50; signalement; III 490.16.

609 ---; ii; possibly husband or guard of T[.......]; XXXVI 2787.13.

610 ARISTOPOUS; March 18; landowner; Kerkemunis, U. Top.; cedes land in Kleros of Philon nr Kerkemunis to Hermaphilus; *PSI* IV 320.3.

611 AVIDIUS ARRIANUS; 103; cornicularius of 3rd Ituraean cohort; Roman; VII 1022.27.

ARRIUS; see EUDAEMON.

612 ARSINOE; d. of Ptolemaeus; sp. Dionysius; ch. Pasion, Ptolemaeus, Apollonius, Berenice; 63/62 BC; Cleopatra Aphrodite St; dec.; addr. for sons; XIV 1644.12.

613 ---; d. of Co[ ]; 60/61; II 250.4.

614 ---; sp. The[ ]; ch. Apollophanes; Jan 93; Alex., Neocosmius?, Genearcheius?; tribe and deme for s.; *PSI* 897.62.

615 ---; d. of Demetrius, s. of Dionysius; sp. Amois; ch. Sambous; 104/105; Oxyrhynchite?; Oxy.; addr. for d., now dec.; XXXVIII 2852.21.

616 ---; d. of Theon; sp. Sarapion; ch. Aristandrus; (1) 122/123; (2) Aug 123; (3) i - early ii; Oxyrhynchite; Pakerke distr.?, E. Top.; to receive grain from a/c of Dionysius and Theon (1) and from Pakerke (2); (1) *P. Lips.* 116.5, 13; (2) XXXVIII 2864.4; (3) *P. Oslo* III 114.14.

ARSINOE; see CLAUDIA HERACLEIA.

617 ---; d. of Sarapion; sp. Dionysius; 148/149; Oxyrhynchite, gymnasial class; unnamed s. enrolled this year; XLVI 3281.3.

618 ---; ii; XXXI 2613.3-4.

619 ARSOU[ ]; i; farmer; II 298.4-5.

620 ARTEM[....; ch. Petosiris; 71; Senekeleu, W. Top.; addr. for gs. Pane[ ]; *P. Med. inv.* 71.70.5.

621 ARTEMAS; c. 1; IV 745.2.

622 ---; ch. Amenneus; ii; Oxyrhynchite?; Oxy.?; addr. for gs.; III 505.1.

623 ARTEMIDORUS; s. of Artemidorus; 19 BC; farmer; lessee; Oxy.; leases land at Pamis in Kleros of Philon; descr. as Macedonian; II 277.2.

624 ---; ch. Artemidorus; 19 BC; Pamis?; s. descr. as Macedonian; addr. for s.; II 277.2.

625 ARTEMIDORUS; 5/4 BC; landowner; W. Top.; land at above address; *P. Oslo* II 26, 29.

626 ARTEMIDO[RUS; 96; I 104.34.

627 ARTEMIDORUS; 98-117; agoranomus w. Alexandrus, Theon et al.; Oxy.; *P. Sel.* 24.10.

628 ---; 101; loans money on security of Dionysius' property in Psobthis, E. Top.; III 510.18.

629 ---; May 109; nomikos; Oxy.; advises Sulpicius Similis; XLII 3015.9.

630 ---; ch. Ariston; 124; Oxyrhynchite?; Oxy.?; addr. for s., witness; III 490.16.

631 ---; after 138; banker; Sarapeum; has associates; *P. Yale* 65.12.

632 ---; ch. .]tetheus; ii; Oxy.?; addr. for d.; *P. Flor.* III 381.3.

633 ---; s. of Amenneus, s. of Artemas; m. Thacoris, d. of Amenneus; ii; property owner; Oxyrhynchite; Pammenes' Garden qtr; III 505.1.

634 ---; ii; doc. pr.?; receives letter from Theogenes, s. of Heraclianus in Antinoopolis; *P. Iand.* VI 107 V 3.

635 ---; ch. Sarapion; early ii; Alex., Auximetoreius; tribe for unnamed gs.; III 497.22.

636 ASCLAS; ch. Papechiris; early i; *OD Pisa* 320.2-3.

637 ---; ch. Charitos; early Roman period; Oxyrhynchite?; Oxy.?; addr. for d.; *P. Mert.* III 104.6.

638 ---; s. of Onnophris, s. of Osmolchis; m. Tesauris; 107; hieroglyp carver; Oxyrhynchite; Tenth qtr; only five h. carvers in Oxy.; VII 1029.3.

639 ---; s. of Alexandrus; ii; stonecutter; Oxyrhynchite; Oxy.; III 498.3.

640 ---; ch. Pecysis; ii; *P. Erl.* 44 iii 28.

641 ---; s. of Horion; m. Heras; ii; landholder; Gymnasium St qtr; *P. Princ.* II 46.12.

ASCLATARION; see DEMETRIA.

642 ASCLATAS; i; II 296.1.

643 JULIUS ASCLEPEINUS; i; strategus; Roman; *PSI Bartoletti Colombo* 2.1.

644 ASCLEPIADES; s. of Dionysius; 54/53 BC; landowner; lessor; Macedonian; Oxy.?; leases land nr Seryphis from Kleros of Alexander to Neracleides; *PSI* X 1097.1.

645 ---; 21/20 BC; banker; IV 806 (descr.).

646 ASCLE[PIADES; ch. [Ascle]piades; 4/5; Oxyrhynchite, gymnasial class; geometres; s. scrutinised this yr; *PSI* V 457.9-10.

647 ---; s. of [Ascle]piades; ch. Asclepiades; 4/5; Oxyrhynchite, gymnasial class; Oxy.; scrutinised this yr; *PSI* V 457.9-10.

648 ASCLEPIADES; ch. Dionysius; 23; doc. pr. Oxy.?; *P. Princ.* III 141.3-4.

649 TI. CLAUDIUS ASCLEPIADES; (1) July 60; (2) 62; strategus; Roman; Oxy.; (1) XXXVIII 2851.1; (2) *SB* XII 10788.23.

650 ASCLEPIADES; s. of Ascle[piades], s. of Ascle[piades]; ch. Origenes; 72/73; Oxyrhynchite, gymnasial class; Chenoboskan qtr; s. scrutinised this yr; *PSI* V 457.8-9.

651 AS]CLEPIADES; 81-96?; basilicogrammateus; Oxy.; I 44.2.

652 ASCLEPIADES; 85/86; seller of land from Kleros of Euphron nr Th.thothis; sells to Sinthonis vel sim. (reading uncertain); IV 794 (descr.).

653 ---; Apr/May 92; has unnamed d.; receives money, wine and oil from Sarapion; guardian is relative Dioscorus; paid via bank in Hiera St; *PSI* VI 715.7.

654 ---; ch. Triadelphis; i; Oxyrhynchite?; Oxy.?; addr. for gs. Diophantus alias Sarapion; *P. Harris* 138 iii 5.

655 ---; ch. Asclepiades, Ptolemaeus; 2nd half i; dec.; *P. Oslo* III 130.6.

656 ---; s. of Asclepiades; sp. Tan....is; 2nd half i; dec. bro. of Ptolemaeus; has unnamed children; *P. Oslo* III 130.5.

657 ---; sp. Sinthonis; ch. Asclepiades; c. 100; *P. Stras.* 266.21.

658 ---; s. of Asclepiades; m. Sinthonis; c. 100; signs doc. for m. as her guardian; *P. Stras.* 266.21.

659 M. ANTONIUS ASCLEPIADES; 122/123; Roman; Oxy.; III 592 (descr.)R 7.

660 ASCLEPIADES; (1) and (2) c. 129; (3) Nov 129; (4) Dec 129; strategus; Oxy.; (1) XII 1420.1; (2) *P. Cornell* 46.1; (3) VII 1024,1; (4) *SB* VI 9617.1.

661 ---; s. of Apollonius; ch. Apollonius; 130; Oxyrhynchite?; Oxy.?; addr. for s.; III 492.21.

662 ---; ch. Sarapion; 138-161; Oxy.?; addr. for s.; IV 723.4.

663 ---; ii; III 531.25.

664 ANTONIA ASCLEPIAS;alias Cyria; ii; property owner; Roman; Pammenes' Garden qtr; Apollonius is guardian; III 498.1.

665 ASIES; late i BC; bro. of Erasippus; IV 717.6.

666 ASINIS; ch. Ptolema; March 79; Hermaeum qtr; addr. for d.; II 243.19-20.

667 ASPIDAS; 81-96; VI 984 R fin.

668 ASTERIUS; i BC - i; *OD Pisa* 510 + 568 Convesso i 17.

669 ASTYANAX; s. of Tryphon; ch. Pausanias alias Dionysius; 95; Alex., Phylaxithalassius, Heracleius; Oxy.?; addr. and deme for s.; II 273.12.

670 ATAREUS; ii; s. leases land at Antipera; *P. Erl.* 44 ii 17.

671 ATHE...; c. 1; fuller; dec.; IV 736.37.

672 ATHENA; sp. Ptollis; ch. Phaon; Jan 132; Oxyrhynchite; Thoeris St qtr; III 478.21.

673 ATHENẠ[ ]; ch. Theopompus; ii?; Senocomis?, W. Top.; *P. Fuad I Univ.* 32.8.

674 ATHENAEUS; s. of Heras; 21; livestock owner; reg; sheep pastured in Seryhphis, W. Top.; *SB* XII 10794.2.

675 ---; ch. Sarapion; 83/84; Tychis Necotis; addr. for g.g.ch.; II 290.19.

676 ---; alias Apollonius; i - ii; bibliophylax w. Herac[l?; PSI VII 731.4.

677 ---; after 138; Oxyrhynchite?; Oxy.?; addr. for gs. Athenaeus; son's name lost; *P. Yale* 65.4-5.

678 ---; gs. of Athenaeus; after 138; slave owner; Oxyrhynchite; Oxy.; guardian of Dionysia; Dionysius alias Amois his freedman; *P. Yale* 65.4.

679 ---; ii; Roman?; bro. of Aurelius Sarapion; XXXIII 2679.2.

680 ---; s. of Sarapion; ch. Sarapas; ii; XLVI 3268.5.

681 ---; ch. Theon; ii; XLII 3059.8.

682 ATHENAIS; d. of Lycarion; sp. Dionysius; ch. Didyme; 99; Oxyrhynchite; Oxy.; *P. Harris* 74.4.

683 ---; ii; XLVI 3312.5.

684 ATHENAROUS; d. of Diogenes; 22 BC; VII 1061.25.

685 ---; d. of Eunomus, s. of ..mus; sp. Synistor (1), Petsiris (2); ch. Synistor (1), Hermaeus (2); Sept 103; landholder; lessor; Toka, M. Top.; s. guardian; XLI 2973.3.

686 ---; d. of Cerdon; ii; III 529 V.

687 ATHENODORUS; May 109; Oxyrhynchite?; case against by Areius and Sarapion re will; bro. or relative of Apollonius?; XLII 3015.7.

688 ---; ch. Harpachtes; n.d.; *SB* I 1987 (b).

689 ATREUS; ch. -- ce; Dec 75/Jan 76; Oxyrhynchite?; Oxy.?; name may be Hatres; addr. for gs. Aperos; *P. Yale* 64.7.

690 ---; sp. Spocis; ch. Psenosiris; 124; Oxyrhynchite?; Oxy.?; name may be Hatres; addr. for gs. Tastraton; III 490.2, 5.

691 ATRION; early i; pays poll tax; II 389 (descr.).

692 ATTINUS; 31; fisherman; Teis, Thmois. Top.; XIX 2234.11.

AUFENNIUS; see AUFENNIUS MACER.

693 AULEIU(S?); ch. Diophantus; early ii; Oxyrhynchite?; Oxy.?; addr. for gs. Diophantus who witnesses will; III 493.14.

694 AUNCHIS; d. of Isas; sp. Abascantus; 126; Oxy.; III 634 (descr.).

695 AUNES; ch. Apollonius; 87/88; Oxyrhynchite; addr. for gs. Apollonius; *P. Princ.* III 147.4.

AURELIUS; see under cognomen.

696 ---; n.d.; *SB* I 1938 (e).

AVIDIUS; see AVIDIUS ARRIANUS

697 B....; s. of Sambathaeus; 27/8; shepherd; reg. for census in Satyros' settlement, E. Top.; Pela, W. Top.; Pela, W. Top. is place of work; II 353.15.

698 BAAL; i; *OD Pisa* 129 X + 7.

699 BACCHE; d. of Hermon; April 77; slave owner; Alexandrian; is illiterate; II 263.2.

700 BACCHIUS; (1) 42/43; (2) 61; bibliophylax w. Teiron; (1) *PSI* XII 1235.2; (2) *SB* XII 10788.1.

701 ---; s. of Chaeremon; 107; Episemon, U. Top.; writes for lessee; XVIII 2188.29.

702 ---; Oct 111; slave; formerly of Ti. Julius Theon, now of Ti. Julius Theon, ex-strategus and archidikast; XLIV 3197.6.

703 BALLARUS; ch. Psammis; 98; Oxyrhynchite, gymnasial class; Oxy.; addr. for gs. Dionysius alias Amois; X 1266.7.

704 BALLOUS; ch. Petesouchus; i; Sesphtha?, W. Top.; addr. for s.; *P. Ryl.* II 199.18.

705 TI. JULIUS BASILIDES; 90; landholder; Roman; land at Petne, M. Top., sold to Marcus Porcius; I 72.16-17.

706 BASSUS; Aug 7 BC; *P. Ryl.* IV 603.1.

707 ---; ch. Bassus; 44; Oxyrhynchite; Oxy.?; addr. for s.; *P. Fouad* 27.3.

708 ---; s. of Bassus; 44; Oxyrhynchite; Oxy.; lent to Harpochration; *P. Fouad* 27.3.

709 BATRACHUS; ch. Didymus; i; Koba; addr. for s.; VIII 1145.14.

710 BE[ ]; 135/136; doc. pr. Talao, L. Top.?; *P. Iand* VII 136.18.

711 BECIS; sp. Tachecysis; ch. Horus; ii; Sento; addr. for s.; *P. Erl.* 44 iii 27.

712 BELAEUS; 31/32; Sinary, L. Top.; *P. Mich. inv.* 69.22.

713 BELLES; i BC - i; *OD Pisa* 137 Convesso 7.

714 ---; i BC - i; *OD Pisa* 755 Concavo X + 1.

715 ---; early i; *OD Pisa* 164.5.

716 ---; ch. Saron; 8; doc. pr. Little Oasis; *OD Pisa* 1.9.

717 ---; ch. Sarapion; 2nd half i; VI 985 (descr.).

718 ---; ch. Patous; i; *OD Pisa* 60 Convesso i 16.

719 ---; s. of Dionysius; i; Tacona, Oxy. nome; considered financially sound and fit for nomination to sitologus in Oxy. nome; Belles, s. of Patermuthis, nom. by mistake; XLVI 3273.5.

720 ---; s. of Patermuthis; i; Tacona, Oxy. nome; nominated by mistake to serve as sitologus in Oxy. nome; same name and addr. as Belles, s. of Dionysius; descr. as poor and unfit for service; XLVI 3273.7.

721 BEḶ[LES; ch. Harsiesis; i; *P. Ryl.* II 199.27.

722 BERENICE; d. of Dionysius; m. Arsinoe, d. of Ptolemaeus; ch. Moschion; 63/62 BC; Cleopatra Aphrodite St; dec.; addr. for s.; XIV 1664.6.

723 ---; d. of Heracleides; 5/4 BC; landholder, W. Top.; *P. Oslo* II 26.24.

724 ---; d. of Bitharion; sp. Herodes; 79/80; slave owner; Lycians' Camp qtr; death of slave Diogenes declared by husband; *P. Oxy. inv.* 20.3B.34/B.7.

725 ---; sp. Pasion; ch. Sarapion, Apollonius, Diogenes (minor), unnamed (minor); (1) early ii; (2) March 102; landholder; slave owner; Oxyrhynchite; Oxy.; (1) III 493.8; (2) XXII 2342.7.

726 ---; d. of Psenesis alias Ision, s. of Ptolemaeus; m. Taarpaesis alias Isidora; sp. Heracleides; ch. Ision; Aug 133; Oxyrhynchite; Oxy.; *P. Köln* II 100[5], 16.

727 BEROUS; (1) 1 BC; (2) c. 1; (1) IV 744.2; (2) 736.71.

728 ---; sp. Heracleus; ch. Apollos, Apollos, Mysthas, Heracles, Nemion; i - ii; *P. Harris* 72.6, 8.

729 BES[ ]; i BC - i; *OD Pisa* 755 Convesso X + 14.

730 BESARION; s. of Heras; 58; Ptolemais Hermiu; guardian of half sister Ammonarion; II 268.4.

731 BESAS; 16/15 BC; taxpayer; IV 832 (descr.) ii.

732 ---; ch. Thaesis; Dec 75/Jan 76; Oxyrhynchite; Oxy.; *P. Yale* 64.3

733 ---; ch. Pemnas; 126; Oxyrhynchite?; Oxy.?; addr. for s., witness to will; III 491.20.

---; see OPHELAS.

734 ---; alias Ammonius; ch. Apollonius; ii; Oxy.?; addr. for gd. Ptolema; *P. Mil.* II 51.3.

735 BESIS?; s. of Diogenes(?), s. of Apollonius (?); ch. Plution; 117; Oxyrhynchite?; Oxy.?; addr. for s.; readings uncertain; III 489.21.

736 B]E[SI]US; i?; "brother" of Ptolemaeus; name restored in *BL* III; *P. Harris* 102.1.

737 BILLUS; May 23; hyperetes to dioecetes; II 259.13.

738 BION; early i; *OD Pisa* 419.9.

739 ---; ch. Ti. Claudius Demetrius, Ti. Claudius Isidorus; c. 50; Roman?; Alexandria?; probably held some office; XXVII 2471.4.

740 BITHARION; ch. Berenice; 79/80; Lycians' Camp qtr?; addr. for d.; *P. Oxy. inv.* 20.3B.34/B.8.

BIUS; see SEVERUS.

741 BOETHUS; ch. Didymus; 36; II 267.36.

742 BRABIRIUS; Sept 77; centurion, 22nd legion; Roman; II 276.10.

743 BRICHIS; ch. Nectenibis; early i; *OD Pisa* 425.3.

744 CAECIL[IUS?]; ch. Taptollous; c. 1; IV 736.55.

CAECILIUS; see CAECILIUS CLEMENS.

745 CAESARIANUS; i BC - i; *OD Pisa* 502 X + 3.

746 CALAS; March 97; Oxyrhynchite?; Oxy.?; addr. for gd. Saraeus; IV 713.10.

747 CALES; i BC - i; *OD Pisa* 84.3.

748 ---; ch. Horus; i BC - i; *OD Pisa* 256.3.

749 ---; 31; fisherman; Teis, Thmois. Top.; XIX 2234.10.

750 ---; early i; *OD Pisa* 164.2.

751 CALLIAS; ch. Demetrius; 83/84; Sinary, L. Top.; addr. for s.; XII 1462 ii 25-26.

752 CALLIAS; ch. Callias; Jan 100; Oxyrhynchite?; Oxy.?; addr. for s.; XLI 2960.6.

753 ---; s. of Callias; Jan 100; farmer (landholder?); Oxyrhynchite; Oxy.; land at Nemerae; XLI 2960.5-6.

754 ---; s. of Spartalas; Jan 100; farmer (landholder?); Oxyrhynchite; Oxy.; land at Nemerae; has bro. Didymus; XLI 2960.3.

755 ---; sp. Herais; ch. Amois; c. 129; Oxyrhynchite?; Oxy.?; addr. for s.; *P. Cornell* 46.3.

756 ---; 148/149; Oxyrhynchite, gymnasial class; declares bro. Harthoonis is of same; XLVI 3284.2.

757 CALLICORNUS; ch. Pedon; 135; Oxyrhynchite?; Oxy.?; addr. for s.; I 106.22-23.

758 CALLIDAMAS; 45; Alexandria; guardian of bro. Apion; II 283.10.

759 CALLISTRATUS; s. of Alexandrus; ch. Pedon; 117; Oxyrhynchite?; Oxy.?; addr. for s.; III 489.24.

760 CALLISTUS; sp. Florentia?; ii; slave trader?; unnamed children; XXXVIII 2860.1.

761 CALLITYCHE; 127; slave; Oxy.; Thais gives to gd. Thais; III 496.5-6.

762 CALOCAERUS; ii; (1) I 116.2, passim; (2) III 526.1.

763 CALPURNIUS; ch. Hermi[ ]; 132/133; Oxy.; address for gs. Herodes; *PSI* VIII 874 ii 23.

CALPURNIUS; see L. CALPURNIUS GAIANUS, SENECA, SERENUS.

764 CALYCE; ii; Oxy.; XII 1583.7.

765 CAMES; alias HARMIYSIS; s. of Harmiysis; c. i BC?; Seryphis, W. Top.; being arrested; demanded by Thompecysis; *P. Inst. Fran.* I 36.2.

766 CAMES; ch. ....]toeius; Sept 31 BC; Tholthis, Thmois. Top.?; addr. for s.; *P. Wurz.* 5.2.

767 CANBAROUS; ch. Stephanus; 132/133 or 153/155; Oxy.; XII 1518.1.

768 CANDAEUS; ch. Candion; 168; gd. Herais alive in 168; XIV 1648.15.

769 CANOPUS; ii; sent greetings; XXXVIII 2860.19.

770 CAROUSIS; s. of Pecysis; m. Tausiris; ii; landholder; *P. Erl.* 44 iii 33.

771 CARPUS; Oct 111; slave; of Ti. Julius Theon, ex-strategus and archidikast; XLIV 3197.9.

772 C. JULIUS CARUS; 6-5 BC; veteran (cavalry); business man; Roman; Oxy.; *P. Yale* 60.2.

773 CAS[ ]; gs. of Cephalon; July 140; slave seller; Alex., Sosicosmius, Althaieus; Alexandria?; bro. Isidorus; *SB* XII 10894.5.

774 CASTOR; s. of Polydeuces; sp. Isarous; ch. Sarapion; after 81; Oxyrhynchite?; Oxy.; addr. for s.; II 369.4.

775 ---; 107-112; tabularius in court of Sulpicius Similis; *PSI* IV 281 R i 39.

776 CASTOR; 117-138; has bros.?; X 1293.38.

777 ---; ch. Thermutharion?; 132/133; d. illiterate; *PSI* I 53 viii 142.

778 M. LONGINUS CASTRESIUS; Dec 81; veteran; Roman; Oxy.; XII 1471.5.

779 CASYLLAS; ii; Coptos resident?; *P. Wurz.* 21 R A 25, B 13.

780 CASYLLOUS; ii; two unnamed ch.; Coptos resident; *P. Wurz.* 21 R B 14.

781 CATHYTES; ch. Horus; i BC; *OD Pisa* 149.3, 6.

782 ---; ch. Haris]esis; i BC; *OD Pisa* 55 i 6.

783 ---; i BC - i; *OD Pisa* 23 i X + 6.

784 ---; i BC - i; other information via Tenis; *OD Pisa* 477 Convesso 2.

785 ---; i BC - i; *OD Pisa* 451 Concavo 2, 5.

786 ---; s. of Menches; i BC - i; *OD Pisa* 25 i 11.

787 CATHYTES(?); i BC - i; *OD Pisa* 25 ii 7.

788 CATHYTES; Aug 3; bro. of Kpbs; *OD Pisa* 473 Concavo i 5.

789 CATILLIUS; Oct 111; slave; of Ti. Julius Sarapion; XLIV 3197.12.

790 CATO; ch. Dionysius; ii; Oxy.; former owner of Dionysia, now freedwoman; *SB* VI 9372.4, 8-9.

791 CE( ); Nov 42 BC; witness; Oxy.; *P. Ryl.* IV 582.22.

792 CLAUDIUS CELER; Sept 77; guard on corn transport; soldier 22nd legion, century of Brabirius; Roman; II 276.8.

793 P. PETRONIUS CELER; 117; veteran; Roman; Oxy.?; VII 1023.1-2.

794 CELOL (Ḳll$_{3}$); i BC - i; *OD Pisa* 543 X + 3.

795 ---; s. of W$_{3}$ḥ-p$_{3}$-$^{c}{}_{3}$; i BC - i; *OD Pisa* 543 X + 4.

796 CELOL; ch. Ḥwn; i; *OD Pisa* 60 Convesso 1.7.

797 CELSIANUS; 103; prefect of 3rd Ituraean coh.; Roman; VII 1022.2.

798 CENDEAS; ch. Cendeas; June 52; Oxy.?; addr. for s.?; *SB* V 8034.5.

799 ---; s. of Cendeas; sp. Apollonia; June 52; Oxy.?; lends money to Hermodotus and bros.; *SB* V 8034.5.

800 CENTAURUS; ch. Teos; Oct 80; Oxyrhynchite?; Pammenes' Garden qtr?; addr. for gss. Diogas and Publius; II 249.3.

801 CEPHALAS; 21/20 BC; goldsmith; mentions payments to priests of Thoeris and stone cutters; IV 806 (descr.).

802 ---; s. of Petechon, s. of Salvius; i; XIV 1756.5.

803 ---; s. of Sarapion; i; farmer; Sesphtha?, L. Top.; *P. Ryl.* II 199.19.

804 ---; ch. Ptolemaeus; i; Sesphtha?, L. Top.; addr. for s.; *P. Ryl.* II 199.12.

805 ---; ch. Psenosiris (restored); 2nd half i; Sesphtha, L. Top.; addr. for s.; XXXVIII 2845.3.

806 ---; s. of Plution; Jan 100; farmer (landholder?); Oxyrhynchite; Oxy.; land at Nemerae; XLI 2960.6.

807 CEPHALION; 2nd half i; writes to Comon re Nemesous; XXXVIII 2844.1.

808 ---; Nov/Dec 132?; writes for Dioscurides; *PSI* I 53 xii 196.

809 ---; ii; Oxy.; XII 1584.31.

810 CEPHALON; ch. Harpaesis; i BC - i; *OD Pisa* 288 X + 5.

811 ---; ch. Petechonsis; Aug 3; *OD Pisa* 473 Convesso 1, 5.

812 ---; 14-37; ?tax collector; E. Top.; *P. Inst. Fran.* I 40.2.

813 ---; s. of Harthoonis, s. of Eubulus; m. Thaesis; sp. Thermuthion; 77; Oxyrhynchite; Oxy.; guardian of wife; II 242.26.

814 ---; 93; landholder; Athychis, U. Top. and Thmoi(nepsobthis?), E. Top.; land there; *P. Princ.* II V ii 19, 22, 27, iii 36.

815 ---; ch. Horus; June 103-110; Senocomis?; addr. for s., priest of Ammon; XLVI 3275.2.

816 ---; s. of Demetrius?; sp. Tauris; ch. Faustus; c. 129; Oxyrhynchite?; Oxy.?; addr. for s.; *P. Cornell* 46.2.

817 ---; July 140; Alex., Sosicosmius, Althaieus; Alexandria; addr. for gss. Cas[...] and Isidorus; *SB* XII 10894.5.

818 CEPHALON; s. of Heracleus; m. Thaesis; ii; boundary marker; priest, of Isis, in Talao; Talao, L. Top.; arrested; XXXI 2573.1.

819 CERDON; m. Nicarous; 127; slave; Oxy.; slave of bridegroom Sarapion; bro. of Sarapous and Epicharmus; III 496.7.

820 ---; ch. Athenarous; ii; agent for Dionysius; III 529.2-3 and V.

821 ---; s. of Apoll(o); m. Harthosis; ii; landholder; Thoeris St qtr; *P. Princ.* II 46.15.

822 CERINTHUS; 23; slave of Antonia, d. of Drusus; Oxy.; writes in Latin; II 244.2.

823 CEROM( ); 60/61; Oxyrhynchite; Oxy.; addr. for unnamed s., aged 17; II 250.30.

824 CH[; ch. Pausis; i; *P. Ryl.* II 199.31.

825 CH ...[; ch. -].eibius; i - ii; *PSI* VII 814.29.

826 CHAERAS; ch. Phatres; ii; doc. pr. Oxy.?; sends grain to Heracleides; *SB* VI 9025.33.

827 CHAEREAS; (1) Feb 23; (2) 24/25; (3) 25/26; (4) Jan 26; (5) 27/28; (6) Jan 28; (7) Jan/Feb 28; (8) Jan 29; strategus; Oxy.; (1) II 244.1; (2) 350 (descr.); (3) 291.1; (4) 245.2; (5) 353.1; (6) 351.1; (7) 352 (descr.); (8) XXXVIII 2850.1.

828 CHAEREIS; s. of Harpaesion; ch. Didymus alias Amoitas; c. 81-86; Senocomis, W. Top.; Oxy.; I 47.13.

829 CHAEREMON; ch. Dionysius; 6/5 BC; Oxy.?; addr. for s., Persian of Epigone; (1) *P. Yale* 60.1; (2) *PSI* X 1099.1.

830 ---; s. of Ale ..; ch. Sarapion; (1) c. 50; (2) July 50; Tholthis, Thmois. Top.; addr. for s.w. land in Kleros of Pyrrhias; (1) XXVII 2471.6; (2) XXXVIII 2836.2.

831 ---; ch. Demetria; gf. of Chaeremon; 55; Alexandrian; Oxy.; addr. for d.; II 261.4.

832 ---; s. of Chaeremon, s. of Demetria; (1) 55; (2) March 79; Alex., Maroneius; Oxy.; nominee of Claudius Antoninus; (1) II 261.8; (2) 243.1.

833 ---; ch. Chaeremon, Demetria; m. Demetria; (1) 55; (2) March 79; Alex., Maroneius; Oxy.?; addr. for s.; (1) II 261.8; (2) 243.1.

834 ---; April 60; agoranomus; Oxyrhynchite?; Oxy.; assoc. w. Andromachus and Sotades; *P. Mich.* III 192.31.

835 ---; 65-83; by error(?) for Onnophris; II 289.3.

836 ---; (1) Sept 66; (2) 83; (3) 86; banker w. Dorion and Apollonius; Oxy.; (1) *CPR* V ii 1, 4; (2) II 289 i 1, ii 12; (3) I 48.1.

837 CHAEREMON; s. of Dionysius, s. of Sarapion; 83/84; landholder; Alex.?, Athenaeus?; Tychis Necotis; holds land there; bro. of Sarapion and Dionysia; II 290.18.

838 ---; 83; representative of Claudius Antoninus; II 331 (descr.).

839 ---; s. of Onnophris, s. of Sois; m. Taorseus, d. of Thompsemis; 86; pastophorus of Sarapis; Oxyrhynchite; Hippodrome qtr; age 14; VII 1028.15.

840 ---; 83; representative of Claudius Antoninus; II 331 (descr.).

841 ---; ch. Apollonius; 94; Oxyrhynchite; Oxy.; addr. for gs. Heracleides; II 270.11.

842 ---; sp. Tnepheros; ch. Sarapion; 96; Oxyrhynchite?; Oxy.?; addr. for s.; I 104.5.

843 ---; late i; kathegetes; Alexandria; XVIII 2190.7.

844 ---; s. of Horion; m. Thermuthis; i - ii; age 40; *P. Harris* 72.13.

845 ---; ch. Ptollarous; Aug 102; Oxyrhynchite?; Oxy.?; addr. for d.; III 508.7.

846 ---; ch. Bacchius; 107; Episemon, U. Top.; addr. for s.; XVIII 2188.30.

847 ---; ch. Dionysius; 117; Oxyrhynchite?; Oxy.?; addr. for gs. Hermaeus alias Hermaeon; *P. Harris* 85.4-5.

848 ---; ch. Thais; Nov 129; Oxyrhynchite?; Oxy.?; addr. for d. and gs. Apollonius; VII 1024.16.

849 ---; ch. Hermione; 131; Oxyrhynchite; Oxy.?; addr. for gd. Dionysia; III 486.2.

850 ---; sp. Hermione; ch. Dionysia; 131; Oxyrhynchite; Oxy.; III 486.2.

851 ---; ch. Chaeremon; Nov 132; property owner; Oxy.?; dec.; had part house w. Cleon in Myrobalanus qtr; III 480.20.

852 ---; s. of Chaeremon; Nov 132; property owner; Oxy.?; owns part house in Myrobalanus qtr; III 480.20.

853 ---; s. of Adrastus; sp. Philotera; ch. Adrastus; 133; Alex., Nilanabateius, Althaieus; Alexandria?; addr. for s.; I 100.3-4.

854 ---; s. of Heracleius; Oct/Nov 132; writes for Dionysius and Papontos; *PSI* I 53 x 170.

855 ---; 134; sitologus w. Papontos; Monimu distr.; III 515.1.

856 ---; Sept 135; sitologus; Psobthis, E. Top.; sit. w. Ammonius alias Nicarius; *P. Stras.* 127.1.

857 CHAEREMON; 138-161; Oxy.; IV 723.5.

858 ---; ch. Ammonous; early ii; Alex., Althaieus; marries d. to Theon; III 497.10, 15, passim.

859 ---; ch. Demetrius; ii?; Senocomis?, W. Top.; addr. for s.; *P. Fuad I Univ.* 32.9.

860 ---; ii; delivers letter of Dionysius to Tetheus; III 530.11.

861 ---; ch. Dionysius, T[....]?; ii; XXXVI 2787.3-4.

862 ---; ii; I 110.1.

863 CHAMAUS; s. of Lycus; 31/32?; Sinary, L. Top.; *P. Mich. inv.* 69.12.

864 CHARES; Nov 42 BC; landholder; farmer; Oxy.?; *P. Ryl.* IV 582[10], 13.

865 CHAREIS; 81/82; Oxyrhynchite; *P. Mert.* III 118.9.

866 CHARIDEMUS; n.d. (c. i BC - i); *DO Colon.* inv. 49.1.

867 CHARIT.( ); ch. Didymus; 3; s. dec.; IV 826 (descr.)1.

868 CHARITESIUS; ch. Heracleides; 33/34; Se[pho, Thmois. Top.; 354 (descr.).

869 CHARITOS; d. of Asclas; sp. Apollonius; early Roman period; landholder?; Oxyrhynchite; Oxy.; *P. Mert.* III 104.5-6.

870 CHARITOUS; Feb 62; has unnamed s.; XXXVIII 2838.10.

871 ---; d. of Petosius; sp. Sarapion; ch. Didymus; March 79; Oxyrhynchite?; Oxy.?; addr. for s.; II 243.5.

872 CHARMUS; ch. Hilarus; ii; Oxyrhynchite; addr. for gs. Charmus; *P. Hamb.* I 79.5.

873 ---; s. of Hilarus, s. of Charmus; m. Leontous; ii; slave owner; Oxyrhynchite; sells slave Hermeinus to Amois; *P. Hamb.* I 79.5.

874 CHEEPHEIBIS; ch. Hatres, Petsoronno(phris); 31/32; Sinary?, L. Top.; addr. for s.; *P. Mich. inv.* 69.13, 15.

875 CHEMENEUS; 81-96; VI 984 R fin.

876 CHENAMOU[NIS?; sp. Heracleus; 126; Sesphtha?, L. Top.; Doc. pr. Oxy.?; addr. for s.; *P. Harris* 142.3.

877 CHENPSOIS; sp. Horus; ch. Petosiris; 137/138; Sinageris in the Hermopolite; addr. for s. who leases land in Oxy.; *PSI* IV 315.4.

878 CHERES; ch. Nectenibis; i BC - i; *OD Pisa* 267.3.

879 CHIUS; 27 BC - 14; descr. on back as "Chio. Caesaris"; *XLIV* 3208.1.

880 CHONSIMEN? (Ḥnsw-mn); ch. Pausiris; i BC; *OD Pisa* 55 ii 9.

881 CHONSIS; i BC - i; *OD Pisa* 126 i 2.

882 ---; i BC - i; *OD Pisa* 451 + 540 Convesso 1.

883 ---; s. of Totoes; i BC - i; *OD Pisa* 127.1.

884 CHONSUTEPACHTE (Ḫns-tꜣe-[f-nḫt]); i BC - i; *OD Pisa* 755 Concavo X + 13.

CHRESIMUS; see DIONYSIUS.

885 CHYPSIS; i BC - i; *OD Pisa* 99 ii X + 1.

886 CINAS; ch. Heras alias Gaius; 130; Oxyrhynchite?; Oxy.?; addr. for s.; see Zenas; III 492.20.

887 CL....THOS; s. of Joseph; 20/21; livestock owner; Sepho, Thmois. Top.; livestock pastured at above addr.; *P. Inst. Fran.* III 43.3.

888 CLARA; d. of Narcissus; sp. Sarapion; ch. Sarapion alias Clarus; 94; Oxyrhynchite; Oxy.; addr. for s.; II 270.6.

889 CLARUS; ch. Dionysia; 66; II 272.27.

---; see SARAPION.

890 ---; sp. Didyme; 98-138; has 2 unnamed ch.; VI 968 (descr.).

CLAUDIA; see DIONYSIA; HERACLEIA: PTOLEMA: THEANOUS: ZOSIME alias HERMIONE.

891 ---; ii. after 137; greetings from Horeis via Horion; XIV 1757.25.

CLAUDIUS; see TI. CLAUDIUS AMMONIUS, ANTONINUS, ASCLEPIADES, CELER, DEMETRIUS, DI[ ], HERODES, ISIDORUS, SARAPION, THEON.

CLAUDIUS; see CLAUDIUS ALEXANDRUS, ANTONINUS, APOLL(ONIUS), AREIUS, DEMETRIUS, HERACLEIUS, MACEDONIUUS, MENANDER, MUNATIANUS, POTAMON, PTOLEMAEUS, SARAPION, --C]UNTIA[--.

892 TI. CLAUDIUS[; 54-68; strategus?; Oxy.; *P. Inst. Fran.* I 21.1.

893 CLAUDIUS ......; ch. Claudius (?) ......]inus; May 89; Roman; probably Antoninus; debt owed him by Petsiris alias Libo; XLII 3051.9-10.

894 CLAUDIUS(?) .....]INUS; s. of Claudius ....; May 89; steward of Ti. Claudius Theon; Roman; XLII 3051.1.

895 CLAUDIUS; s. of Heracleides; 93; Protar( )?; *P. Princ.* II 42 R 4.

896 CLEANDRUS; ch. Sarapion; 36; son a banker at Sarapeum Oxy.; II 267.4.

897 CLEITUS; ch. Pagonis; i BC - i; *OD Pisa* 377 Convesso 2, 9.

898 CLEITUS; i BC - i; *OD Pisa* 510 + 568 Convesso ii 5.

899 T. FLAVIUS CLEMENS; June/July 77; soldier, legio III Cyrenaica; II 376 (descr.).

900 CAECILIUS CLEMENS; (1) 98; (2) 98/99; (3) Aug 99; (4) 99/100; Roman; Oxy.; (1) II 241.1; (2) 340 (descr.); (3) III 581 (descr.); (4) II 338 (descr.).

901 CLEMES; i BC - i; *OD Pisa* 410 + 568 Concavo i X + 5.

962 CLEON; s. of Dionysius; Nov 132; property owner; Oxy.?; owned w. Chaeremon part house in Myrobalanus qtr; III 480.4.

903 CLEOPAS; 129; *P. Harris* 147.1.

904 CLEOPATRA; d. of Dionysius; sp. Comon; ch. Aline; Aug 86; Oxyrhynchite; Oxy.; XXXVIII 2843.6.

905 ---; d. of Heliodorus; m. Ptollous, d. of Amois; 132/33; age 20; *PSI* I 53 i 8.

906 ---; sp. Ptolemaeus; ch. Glaucias, Sarapion; ii; Gymnasium St qtr; addr. for s.; *P. Princ.* II 46.5.

907 CLEOPATRUS; s. of Didymus; ii; landholder; Thoeris St qtr; *P. Princ.* II 46.10.

908 CO( ); ch. Arsinoe; 60/61; II 250.4.

909 COLLUTHES; 8/7 BC; livestock owner; Oxy.?; *P. Inst. Fran.* I 5.7.

910 ---; April 4; *OD Pisa* 511 + 512 i 15.

911 COLLUTHUS; ch. Naris; Jan 26; Pela?, W. Top.; descr. as the elder; addr. for s.; II 245.4.

912 ---; 30; X 1291.6.

913 COL(LUTHUS); 47; banker w. partner; II 313.2.

914 COLLUTHUS; ch. Tapontos; i; Pakerke, M. Top.; doc. pr. Oxy.?; addr. for gd. Tausiris; *P. Harris* 138 i 20.

915 ---; 117-138; X 1293.41.

916 COL]LUTHUS; ch. Diemous; 144; Oxyrhynchite?; Oxy.; addr. for d.; X 1272.26.

917 COLOBUS; ii; procurer?; III 528.18.

918 COLCULIS; i; Sobthis; makes payment for Dorion, s. of Alexandrus; VIII 1145.22.

919 COLYLIS; ch. Ptolemaeus; 95; Korobis, Kleros of Menoetius; addr. for gd. Tapotamon; I 45.5.

920 COMOAPIS; July 85; farmer; Syron Kome, W. Top.; acting for Aline, d. of Comon; XXXVIII 2841.6-7.

921 COMOAPIS; ch. Thompeidisis; 126; Oxyrhynchite?; Oxy.; addr. for unnamed gs., witness to will; III 491.22.

922 COMON; ch. Tausorapis, Pecysis; 52/53; *PSI* IX 1029.1.

923 ---; s. of Dionysius; sp. Cleopatra; ch. Aline, Dionysius, Dioscorus; (1) Aug 50; (2) Sept 64; (3) Aug 75; (4) July 85; (5) Aug 86; (6) 86; (7) 93/94; (8) 2nd half i; Oxyrhynchite; Sarapis qtr Oxy.; gf. of Comon; addr. for d.; stemma at XXXVIII p. 38; (1) XXXVIII 2837.5; (2) 2839.3; (3) 2840.6; (4) 2841.6; (5) 2843.5; (6) I 48.8; (7) *PSI* X 1109.14; (8) XXXVIII 2846.5.

924 ---; s. of Mnesitheus, s. of Petesuchus; m. Aline, d. of Comon; (1) Feb 62; (2) Aug 86; (3), (4) and (5) 2nd half i; practor; Oxyrhynchite; Sesphtha, L. Top.; has unnamed sister; guardian of m.; signalement; (1) XXXVIII 2838.9; (2) 2843.9; (3) 2845.5; (4) 2844.1; (5) 2846.4.

925 ---; s. of Dioscorus, s. of Comon; gs. of Cleopatra; 86; Oxyrhynchite; Oxy.; guardian of aunt Aline; I 48.13.

926 ---; ch. Tapsois; Jan 90; Oxy.?; addr. for d.; *PSI* VIII 942.8.

927 ---; s. of Dionysius, s. of Comon; m. Tiouda; ch. Dionysius; 93/94; Oxyrhynchite; Hippodrome qtr; *PSI* X 1109.5, 14.

928 COM(ON); ch. Thracidas? (Thrakita); i; Koba?; addr. for s.; VIII 1145.12, 16.

929 COMON; sp. Tapotamon; ch. Apollo; ii; Cretan qtr; addr. for s.; *P. Princ.* II 46.9.

930 ---; ii; doc. pr. Oxy.?; *P. Mich. inv.* 3799.9.

931 COMONOS; s. of Joseph; 20/21; shepherd; Sepho, Thmois. Top.; reg. in Taruthinou distr.; *P. Inst. Fran.* III 43.17.

932 *COMORINUS (Gm-w-rn); n.d.; *DO Colon.* inv. 89.

933 CONUPHIS; ch. Pamun; early i; *OD Pisa* 164.6.

934 COPRES; i?; lists costs for Hierax; *P. Erl.* 14 V 8.

CORAX; see OPHELAS.

935 CORAXUS; c. 1; IV 736.4, 10.

936 CORBULO; ii; has son, bro. and nephew; I 113.1 and passim.

937 ---; ii; I 113.19, 29.

938 CORINTHUS; Oct 111; slave; formerly of Ti. Julius Theon, now of his s., Ti. Julius Sarapion; XLIV 3197.11.

939 ---; sp. Diogenis; ch. Dionysius alias Isidorus; Aug 133; Oxyrhynchite; Oxy. nome; addr. for s.; *P. Köln* II 100.30.

940 CORNELIUS; Oct 111; slave; formerly of Ti. Julius Theon, now of his s., Ti. Julius Theon, ex-strategus and archidikast; Berky, Oxy. nome?; XLIV 3197.7.

941 CORNELIUS; ch. Hierax; ii; property owner; III 531.1.

942 COSMUS; Aug 9; *OD Pisa* 429.2.

943 COTTES; ch. Petsiris; 31/32; *P. Mich. inv.* 69.3.

COTTUS; see DIOGENES.

944 CRATES; i BC - i; *OD Pisa* 25 i 11.

945 CRATINUS; ch. Hero(i)des; July 64; addr. for s.; *P. Mich.* III 179.6.

946 ---; s. of Demetrius; ch. Plution; early ii; Oxyrhynchite; Oxy.; addr. for s.; III 493.13.

947 CRIPIS; i; *OD Pisa* 60 Convesso ii 7.

948 L. HERENNIUS CRISPUS; ii; property owner; Roman; Pammenes' Garden qtr; III 505.1.

949 CRONIUS; 6-35; Oxyrhynchite?; Gooseherders' Lane qtr; addr. for sons, both under age, one 5 years; II 256.12.

950 CTESIDEM(US); s. of Sotades; 116; assistant (to strategus?); *P. Cair. Preis.* 32.2.

951 CTESIDEMUS; 127/128; misthotes of Usiac land of Julia Polla(?); doc. pr. Sinkepha, Oxy. nome; transfer grain to Petsiris; *P. Lips.* 113.1.

952 ---; s. of - alias Ammonius(?); ch. Ctesidemus; c. 136; Oxy.?; addr. for s.; *P. Inst. Fran.* III 18.5.

953 ---; s. of Ctesidemus; s. of - alias Ammonius; c. 136; ex-exegetes of Oxy.; Oxy.; *P. Inst. Fran.* III 18.5.

954 CLAUD[IUS C]UNTIA[-; i - ii (prob. i); centurion of 22nd legion; *PSI* VI 687.5.

955 CUPHATEUS; ch. Hatres; Sept/Oct 110; III 575 (descr.) V.

CURTIUS; see CURTIUS PAULINUS.

956 C. CUTIUS; s. of M. Cutius; July 50; farmer; lessee w. Mnesitheus; Roman; Tholthis, Kleros of Pyrrhias, Thmois. Top.; XXXVIII 2836.3.

957 M. CUTIUS; ch. C. Cutius; July 50; Roman; Tholthis?, Thmois. Top.; addr. for s.; XXXVIII 2836.3.

CYRIA; see ANTONIA ASCLEPIA.

958 CYRILLA; ii; Sebennyte, U. Top.; w. Sarapion, strategus there; VI 931.11.

959 ---; sp. Heraclammon?; ii; unnamed daughters; XXXVIII 2860.20.

960 CYRILLUS; ii; III 526.2.

961 CYRUS; s. of Didymus; ch. Cyrus; 126; Oxyrhynchite; Oxy.; addr. for s.; III 491.18.

962 ---; s. of Cyrus, s. of Didymus; 126; Oxyrhynchite; Oxy.; witness to will; III 491.18.

963 D[; ch. Sarapas; ii; Tacona?, L. Top.; Oxy.; *P. Inst. Fran.* I.4.2.

D- ; see APOLLONIUS.

DAEMON; see AGATHODAEMON.

964 DAMARION; i. pastophorus?; gives name to club of Pastophori; *P. Oslo* III 143.9.

965 ---; c. 115; freedman of Heracleides; IV 706.10.

966 DAMAS; 2 BC; IV 743.24.

---; see SOTER.

967 DAMIS; 49/50; ex-practor; accused of extortion by Aristas; II 393.8.

968 DEESOTE; d. of M[ ]?; (1) 19; (2) 19/20; property owner; Temgenuthis qtr?; former owner of part house in above qtr; (1) II 253.4; (2) 252[7].

969 D]EIU[S; ch. Is]ido[te?; Aug 148(?) and Jan/Feb 140; Oxy.; addr. for gs. (mat.) Theon; *P. Iand.* VII 139.8.

970 DEMAENETUS; ch. Diodotus; ii; *P. Flor.* III 381.14.

971 DEMAROUS; sp. Didymus; ch. Dionysia; after 138; Oxyrhynchite?; Oxy.; addr. for d.; *P. Yale* 65.2-3.

DEMAROUS; see APHRODITOUS.

972 DEMAS; Oct 111; slave; formerly of Ti. Julius Theon, now of his s., Ti. Julius Sarapion; amanuensis; XLIV 3197.10.

973 ---; ch. Demas; ii; *P. Erl.* 44 iii 31.

974 ---; s. of Demas; ii; landholder; *P. Erl.* 44 iii 31.

975 DEMES; sp. Harsiesis; ch. Epimachus; 118; Oxyrhynchite; Oxy.; addr. for s.; III 503.2.

976 DEMETRAS; Oct 111; slave; of Ti. Julius Sarapion; XLIV 3197.12.

977 DEMETRIA; d. of Chaeremon; ch. Chaeremon; g.ch. Demetria, Chaeremon; 55; Alex.; Oxy.; guardian is Theon, s. of Antiochus; II 261.4.

978 ---; d. of Chaeremon; sp. Theon, s. of Antiochus; gd. of Demetria; 55; Alex.; Oxy.; sister of Chaeremon; II 261.5.

979 ---; d. of Theon; sp. Gaius; m. Apollonia, d. of Antiochus; 77-83; property owner; I 170.4.

980 DEMETRIA; d. of Sarapion, s. of Theon; m. Prima; ch. Amois; Oct 80; Oxyrhynchite; II 248.3.

981 ---; d. of Didymus; sp. Neoptolemus; ch. Didymus; 91/92; Oxyrhynchite?; Oxy.?; addr. for s.; XXXVIII 2856.6.

982 DEME]TRIA?; d. of Theon; c. 99-117; Oxyrhynchite; Oxy.; sister of Dionytas and Didymus; XLVI 3274 i 3, ii 32.

983 DEMETRIA; sp. Heracleus; ch. Theon; i - ii; *P. Harris* 72.33.

984 ---; sp. Dionysius; ch. Dionysius; 104/105; Oxyrhynchite; Oxy.?; addr. for s.; XXXVIII 2852.8.

985 ---; ch. Ephar[mostus]; 109; Oxyrhynchite; Heracleopolis; s. landowner; *P. Rein.* II 98.6.

986 ---; c. 136; landholder (vineyard and orchard); lessor; Oxyrhynchite?; Oxy.?; leases land at Seryphis; IV 707.8,9, 27.

987 ---; ch. Theon; early ii; Alex., Propapposebasteius, Althaieus; tribe and deme for s., groom; III 497.20.

988 ---; alias ASCLATARION; d. of Heracleides; sp. Harpocration; ch. Sarapion; 148/149; Oxyrhynchite, gymnasial class; Tenth qtr?; addr. for s. enr. this yr; XLVI 3282.3.

989 DE]METR[IA or OUS?; April 133; *PSI* I 53 vii 115.

990 DEMETRIS; d. of Dioscorus; 31/32 Sinary, L. Top.; *P. Mich. inv.* 69.6.

991 DEMETRIUS; 30 BC - 14; Oxy.; *P. Rein.* II 99.5.

992 ---; ch. Diogenes; 22 BC; VII 1061.6.

993 ---; s. of Theon; Oct 4 BC; landowner; leases land to Thoonis?; *SB* XII i 10942. 5, 38 et al.

994 ---; i BC - i; *OD Pisa* 8.22.

995 ---; i BC - i; *OD Pisa* 451 + 540 Convesso 3.

996 ---; i BC - i; *OD Pisa* 460 Convesso ii X + 1.

997 ---; i BC - i; *OD Pisa* 5 ii X + 9.

998 ---; i BC - i; *OD Pisa* 72 ii X + 8.

999 ---; i BC - i; *OD Pisa* 127.2.

1000 ---; i BC - i; Nechotes his dependant; *OD Pisa* 502 X + 7.

1001 ---; i BC - i; *OD Pisa* 25 ii 20.

1002 ---; i BC - i; *OD Pisa* 23 i X + 10.

1003 ---; ch. Pasenis; i BC - i; *OD Pisa* 84.2.

1004 DEMET[RIUS; i BC - i; *OD Pisa* 228 X + 1.

1005 DEMETRIUS; end i BC - early i; *OD Pisa* 35 Convesso 1.

1006 ---; May 23; prison governor; II 259.3.

1007 ---; 26?; *P. Rein.* II 104.4.

1008 ---; ch. Hermon; 31; Teis, Thmois. Top.; addr. for s.; XIX 2234.2.

1009 ---; s. of Pausanias; 37-41; wine merchant; XIV 1672.1.

1010 TI. CLAUDIUS DEMETRIUS; s. of Bion; c. 50; gymnasiarch; priest; banker; Roman, Quirina tribe; also Alex.; Alexandria; exempt from tax; member of museum; XXVII 2471.3.

1011 DEMETRIUS; ch. Thaisous; gs. Sarapion; gd. Thermuthion; (1) Mar/Apr 66; (2) 91/92; Oxyrhynchite?; Oxy.?; addr. for gs.; (1) *PSI* VIII 871.31; (2) XXXVIII 2856.13.

1012 ---; s. of Didymus; 83/84; landholder; Papsis?, Tychis Necotis; land there; bro. Theon; II 290.12.

1013 ---; s. of Callias; 83/84; catoecic landholder; Sinary L. Top.; land ceded him by contract drawn via Nois record office, Alex. chora; XII 1462 ii 25.

1014 ---; (1) March 97; (2) 99; bibliophylax w. Apollonius and Diogenes; Oxy.; (1) IV 713.2; (2) *P. Harris* 74.1.

1015 ---; i; *OD Pisa* 318.4.

1016 ---; ch. Plutus; i - ii; gs. -utus; *PSI* VI 687.6.

1017 ---; ch. Apion; 104/105; Oxyrhynchite?; Oxy.?; addr. for s.; XXXVIII 2852.6.

1018 ---; alias DIOGENES; gs. of Demetrius; 104/105; property owner; Oxyrhynchite?; Oxy.?; cousin of Sambous, d. of Amois; XXXVIII 2852.11.

1019 ---; s. of Dionysius; ch. Amois; 104/105; Oxyrhynchite?; Oxy.; addr. for gd. Arsinoe; XXXVIII 2852.16.

1020 ---; Oct 111; slave; formerly of Ti. Julius Theon, now of his s., Ti. Julius Sarapion; XLIV 3197.11.

1021 ---; Oct 111; slave; formerly of Ti. Julius Theon, now of his gs., Ti. Julius Theon, games victor; L. Top.; XLIV 3197.15.

1022 ---; s. of Hermippus; 117-137; slave owner; Oxy.; Ptolema his freedwoman; I 105.5.

1023 ---; (1) July 118; (2) Jan 121; strategus; Oxy.; (1) XLII 3025.1; (2) *P. Fouad* 30.1.

1024 ---; s. of Theon, s. of Theon; Jan 121; Oxy.; guardian of Tasionus; *P. Fouad* 30.6.

1025 ---; s. of Alexandrus; ch. -us; 126; Sesphtha?, L. Top.; *P. Harris* 142.15.

1026 DEṂ[ETRIUS?; ch. Cephalon; c. 129; Oxyrhynchite; Oxy.; *P. Cornell* 46.2.

1027 DEMETRIUS; ch. Apollonius; 133; *P. Lips.* 115.5.

1028 ---; s. of Diogenes; 133; transfer of grain to a/c of Apollonius and Apollonius; *P. Lips.* 115.1.

1029 TI. CLAUDIUS DEMETRIUS; May 134; Oxy.; fellow freedman and beneficiary of Ti. Claudius Alexandrus; XXXVIII 2857.18.

1030 DEMETRIUS; April 135; strategus; Oxy.; I 106.5-6.

1031 ---; ch. Didymion; 139; Senao, M. Top.; addr. for s.; X 1279.14.

1032 ---; ch. Heliodorus; early ii; Oxyrhynchite?; Oxy.?; addr. for gs. Demetrius; *P. Wisc.* I 13.14.

1033 ---; s. of Heliodorus, s. of Demetrius; early ii; Oxyrhynchite; Oxy.; writes for Taptollion and Harmiysis; *P. Wisc.* I 13.14.

1034 ---; ch. Apollonius; mid ii; XLIV 3165.3.

1035 ---; s. of Lacon; ch. Theon; mid ii; Syron Kome?, W. Top.; addr. for s.; XLIV 3165.5.

DE[METRIUS]; see Dorion.

1036 DEMETRIUS; ii; XIV 1759.1.

1037 ---; s. of Chaeremon; ii?; Senocomis, W. Top.; *P. Fuad I Univ.* 32.9.

1038 ---; ii; "brother" of Heracleides; III 582 (descr.).

1039 ---; ch. Cratinus; early ii; Oxyrhynchite?; Oxy.?; addr. for gs. Plution who witnesses will; III 493.13.

1040 ---; ii; gymnasiarch; Oxyrhynchite; Oxy.; XLII 3063.4.

1041 CLAUDIUS DEMETRIUS; ch. Apollonius; ii; Thoeris St qtr; addr. for s.; III 574 (descr.) R.

1042 DEMETROUS; 22; ?relative of Sarapion and Dorion, sons of Dorion; II 294.31.

1043 ---; d. of Heracleides; sp. Tryphon (former); m. [The]namunis; (1) 30-35; (2) 37; Oxyrhynchite; Oxy.; accused of assaulting Saraeus; (1) II 282.5; (2) 315.9.

1044 ---; Jan 49; slave; bought from Metrophanes, s. of Heras, of Taamechis in Heracleopolite by Pasion, s. of Harthonis; Oxy.; age 25; signalement; XXXI 2582.6.

1045 ---; m. Sarapous; Oct 62; slave, houseborn; Sesphtha?, L. Top.; age c. 24; XXXVIII 2873 V 34.

1046 ---; 81-96; II 379 (descr.).

1047 DEMETROUS; ch. Euphrosyne; (1) Aug 86; (2) 86; slave of Aline, d. of Comon; (1) XXXVIII 2843.14; (2) I 48.4-5.

1048 ---; d. of Sarapion; 89-97; property owner; Oxy.; w. nephew Sarapion alias Diogenes; II 274.5.

1049 ---; m. Demetrous; end i; slave owner; age c. 21; *P. Sel.* 23.8.

1050 ---; ch. Demetrous; end i; addr. for d.; *P. Sel.* 23.8.

1051 ---; sp. Heraclas; ch. Heraclas; Aug 102; Oxyrhynchite?; Oxy.?; addr. for s.; III 508.9.

1052 ---; d. of Mnesitheus, s. of Theon; sp. Ptollis; m. [..]eia, d.]heme.[....]; after 102; property owner; Oxy.; property in Temgẹnuthis qtr gained from Pausiris left to husband; III 636.6.

1053 ---; d. of Dionysius; Jan 121; property owner; Metroon qtr; property there w. Apia and others; *P. Fouad* 30.13.

1054 ---; 138-161; slave; Oxy.; unnamed d. freed by Diodorus; IV 723.3.

1055 ---; early ii; buys catoecic land, Monimu distr., from Kleros of Nicander et al.; under age; III 633 (descr.).

1056 ---; early ii; letter from Diogenes; III 576 (descr.) V.

1057 ---; ch. Dionysius; ii; Apollonopolite nome; addr. for s.; XXXI 2559.15.

1058 ḌẸP̣Ḥ..SIO(N); ch. Ptolemaeus; n.d.; II 309 i 3, ii 2.

1059 DEX[ITHEUS?; ch. Polydeuces, Leon; 132/133 or 153/154; XII 1518.8, 14.

1060 DI[.]....[.]US; Oct 62; son wine-dresser of Ischyrion, s. of Dionysius; XLI 2970.2.

1061 DI[...; s. of Epimachus; ch. Dionysia alias Taamois; 77; Oxy.?; addr. for d.; II 242.9.

1062 DI[.....; sp. Nechthenicis; ch. Harmiysis; early ii; Phthochis?, E. Top.; addr. for niece Taptollion; *P. Wisc.* I 13.2.

1063 DI[.; ch. .]e alias Dionysia; ii?; Senocomis?, W. Top.; addr. for d.; *P. Fuad I Univ.* 32.11.

1064 ḌỊ[....]ES; s. of Apelles, s. of Apelles; 135/136; landholder; Talao?, L. Top.; bro. of Apelles; *P. Iand.* VII 136.17.

1065 ḌỊ[c. 10]; s. of Ptolemaeus, s. of P[ ]; 148/149; Oxyrhynchite, gymnasial class; Upper Camp qtr; enrols unnamed s. in g. class of 13 yr olds in above qtr in this yr.; XLVI 3277.2.

1066 TI. CLAUDIUS DI.[ ]; c. 136; has unnamed ch.; *P. Inst. Fran.* III 18.12.

1067 DIALLUS; ch. Ptollion; 99; form of name?; VI 975.16.

1068 DID[.....; 98-117; may not be Oxy.; case against by Tryphon; XLII 3015.14.

1069 DIDAS; s. of Dionysius; 129; shepherd?; doc. pr. Tholthis, M. Top.; pastures animals nearby; Didas may be scribe; *PSI* I 40.17.

1070 DIDOUS; ch. Heras; 127; Oxyrhynchite; Oxy.; addr. for gs. Sarapion, being married; III 496.2.

1071 DIDYM[(f); i; *P. Med. inv.* 71.47.2.

1072 DIDYMAS; Sept 32; XXII 2353.3.

1073 ---; ii; dec.; relative of Eirene; I 115.4.

1074 ---; ii; has unnamed children; XIV 1758.1.

1075 DIDYME; 27; property owner?; "sister" of Dionysius; II 293.1.

1076 ---; d. of Dionysius, s. of Apollonius; June 29; property owner; Gooseherders' qtr; *SB* VIII 9827 (a) 2, (b) 2.

1077 ---; d. of Dionysius; Aug 44; Oxy.; will live in part of house of L. Pompeius' father in Sarapeum, Hermaeum qtr; guardian Epimachus; *P. Fouad* 44.3.

1078 ---; d. of Diogenes; sp. Petosiris; ch. Harmiysis; July 66; Phthochis?, E. Top.; addr. for s.; II 246.7.

1079 ---; d. of Horion; 83/84; landholder; Papsis?, Tychis Necotis; holds land there; II 290.14.

1080 ---; sp. Sarapion (present), Clarus (former); 98-137; unnamed children; leaves property to s. of previous marriage and husband; provision for Harasis; VI 968 (descr.).

1081 ---; sp. Dionysius (dec.); ch. Dionysius; 99; Oxyrhynchite?; Oxy.?; doc. pr. Oxy.?; addr. for s.; *P. Harris* 74.16.

1082 ---; d. of Dionysius, s. of Dionysius; sp. Polydeuces; m. Athenais, d. of Lycarion; gd. of Didyme; 99; landholder; Oxyrhynchite; Oxy.; land at Seryphis and Thosbis; *P. Harris* 74.3.

1083 ---; d. of Rufion; sp. Diocles; ch. Rufus, Diocles; Aug 102; Oxyrhynchite; Oxy.; III 508.16.

1084 ---; d. of Euphranor; sp. Sarapion; ch. Diogenes alias Sarapion; Nov 103; Oxyrhynchite?; Oxy.?; addr. for s.; *P. Mert.* I 14.2.

1085 ---; d. of Philotas; sp. Hermes; ch. Pecysis; 117-137; Oxyrhynchite?; Cretan qtr; addr. for s.; I 105.2.

1086 ---; ch. Ọ[....]ṣ[...; c. 129; Oxyrhynchite?; Oxy.?; addr. for s.; *P. Cornell* 46.5.

1087 ---; ch. Apollonius alias D-; 132/133; dec.; *PSI* VIII 874 ii 33.

1088 ---; sp. Heliodorus; 132/133; unnamed d., age 20; *PSI* I 53 i 10.

1089 ---; 132; sister of Tne-; *PSI* I 53 iv 54.

1090 ---; ch. Sarapion, Aphynchis; April 133; *PSI* I 53 vii 109.

1091 ---; ch. Pausirion; 148/149; Oxyrhynchite, gymnasial class; Knights' Camp qtr; addr. for s.; XLVI 3279.3.

1092 ---; sp. Apollonius?; ii; calls A. her "brother and sun"; XLII 3059.1, V.

1093 DIDYMION; s. of Demetrius; 139; landholder; Senao, M. Top.; Oxyrhynchite; owns land at Senao; X 1279.14.

1094 DIDYMUS; i BC; mentions Mouchis, in Ars(P.)?; IV 784 (descr.).

1095 ---; c. 1; "brother" of Ammonius and of addressee Apollonius; IV 791 (descr.).

1096 ---; s. of Charit( ); 3; weaver; IV 826 (descr.) 1.

1097 ---; Sept/Oct 6; lessor; II 374 (descr.).

1098 ---; ch. Tryphon; (1) 12/13; (2) 25; Oxyrhynchite; Hippodrome qtr; (1) II 314.2; (2) 288.36.

1099 ---; s. of Tryphon, s. of Didymus; m. Timos; (1) 12/13; (2) 25; weaver; Oxyrhynchite; Hippodrome qtr; age 37 in 41 Augustus; (1) II 314.3; (2) 288.37.

1100 ---; s. of Heracleides; 13; applies to idios logos to buy wood from Kerkeura and Peeno, M. Top.; IX 1188.3.

1101 ---; s. of Sarapion; Mar 18; landholder; w. Hermaphilus in Kleros of Philon nr Kerkemunis, ceded by Aristopous; *PSI* IV 320.4.

1102 ---; s. of Dioscourides; 31/32; Sinary, L. Top.; *P. Mich. inv.* 69.11.

1103 ---; s. of Ptolemaeus; 31/32; Oxy.?; witness to contract; signalement; *P. Ryl.* II 159.41.

1104 ---; ch. Abarus; 36; Oxyrhynchite?; Oxy.?; addr. for s.; II 322.4.

1105 ---; s. of Abarus, s. of Didymus; 36; II 322.44.

1106 ---; s. of Boethus; 36; writes for Saraeus, d. of Apion; II 267.36.

1107 ---; (1) 41-54; (2) Jan 44; (3) 48; (4) Sept 49; topogrammateus and comogrammateus, assoc. w. Apollonius (1, 3, 4) and w. H .... (2); XXXIII 2669.1; (2) II 251.1; (3) 255.2; (4) *P. Mich.* III 170.1, 16.

---; see SARAPION.

1108 DIDYMUS; ch. Didymus; April 60; Oxy.; addr. for s.; *P. Mich.* III 192.10.

1109 ---; s. of Didymus; April 60; property owner; Hippodrome qtr; part house there; *P. Mich.* III 192.10.

1110 ---; s. of Thoonis?, s. of Onnophris?; m. Teteo(us) or Tetoeo(us)?; 65-83; perhaps bro. of Thoonis, s. of Thoonis, perh. his agent; II 289 ii 7.

1111 ---; s. of Sarapion; sp. Dionysia; ch. Sarapion; (1) 66; (2) March 79; Oxyrhynchite?; Oxy.?; addr. for gs. Didymus; (1) II 272.26; (2) 243.4.

---; see DIONYSIUS.

1112 ---; ch.[....]nis; 71; Senekeleu, W. Top.; addr. for mat. gs. Pane[ ]; *P. Med. inv.* 71.70.5-6.

1113 ---; s. of Sarapion, s. of Didymus; m. Charitous, d. of Petosius; March 79; Oxyrhynchite; Oxy.; II 243.4.

1114 ---; 81/82; Oxyrhynchite; Oxy.?; possible addr. for gs. married to Tereus, d. of Ptolem( ); *P. Mert.* III 118.9.

1115 ---; c. 81-83; rep. of Claudius Antoninus; Apollonius his rep.; II 334 (descr.).

1116 ---; alias AMOITAS; s. of Chaereis, s. of Harpasion; 81-86; landholder; Senocomis?, W. Top.; Oxyrhynchite; cedes to Teos land at S. in Kleros of Zenodorus; I 47.12-13.

1117 ---; ch. Demetrius, Theon; 83/84; Papsis?, Tychis Necotis; addr. for s.; II 290.13.

---; see HATRES.

1118 ---; ch. Thepseis?; 86/87?; Oxyrhynchite; Shepherds' qtr; II 258.4, 11.

1119 ---; s. of Neoptolemus, s. of Neoptolemus; m. Demetria, d. of Didymus; 91/92; Oxyrhynchite; Oxy.; slave buyer; XXXVIII 2856.4.

1120 ---; ch. Demetria; 91/92; Oxyrhynchite; Oxy.; addr. for gs. Didymus; XXXVIII 2856.7.

1121 ---; ch. Herais; 94; Oxyrhynchite; Oxy.; addr. for mat. gs. Heracleides; II 270.11.

1122 ---; s. of Theon; 99-117; dec. sister has half estate confiscated to compensate D. whose property was stolen by another bro.; accuser Ammonius; XLVI 3274 i 9, ii [41].

1123 ---; s. of Aristocles; late i; teacher; Alexandria; XVIII 2190.8 and passim.

1124 ---; i; estate manager; asked by Eudaemon to assess tax; *P. Bon.* 43.1.

1125 ---; s. of Batrachus; i; farmer; Koba; VIII 1145.14.

1126 DIDYMUS; i; agent of Julius Musaeus w. Numenius; II 349.1.

1127 ---; s. of Spartalas; Jan 100; farmer (landholder?); Oxyrhynchite; Oxy.; land in Nemerae; XLI 2960.2.

1128 ---; (1) May/June 102; (2) 116; city secretary w. Apollonius; (1) *PSI* VIII 952.11; (2) XII 1550.1.

1129 ---; s. of Sarapion; 103; public official; Aphroditopolis; III 511.2.

1130 ---; Aug 106; *P. Wisc.* I 17 V 9.

1131 ---; Aug 106; *P. Wisc.* I 17 V 19.

1132 ---; ch. Achillas; Feb/Mar 108; Kleros of Zenodorus, E. Top.?; addr. for s.; III 483.31.

1133 ---; Oct 111; slave; of Ti. Julius Theon, games victor; XLIV 3197.16.

1134 ---; s. of Sotades; April 116; assistant to str. Apollonius; XXXVI 2759.2.

1135 ---; 117; Oxyrhynchite; Oxy.; guardian of unnamed sister; *P. Harris* 85.2-3.

1136 DIDYM[US; ch. Ammonianus (reg. 161/162); gs. of Origenes; 117/138; Oxyrhynchite; gymnasial class; addr. may be Pammenes' Garden qtr; unnamed father's is North Quay qtr; scrutinised in this year; *PSI* V 457.11-12.

1137 DIDYMUS; s. of Dio[genes]; m. Apollos, d. of Paesis; step-f. Apollos, s. of Ophelas; 117/118; property left him by m. in Kerkemunis, U. Top; IV 837 (descr.).

1138 ---; Jan 119; reg. in Knights' Camp qtr; assoc. w. Aristion in census return; IV 786 (descr.).

1139 ---; 119/120; bibliophylax w. Ptolemaeus; *PSI* XIII 1322.1.

1140 ---; 121; landholder; Senepta, M. Top.; III 499.12.

1141 ---; 122/123?; property owner; "brother" of Hephaeston and Phabanon; *P. Wisc.* II 73.1.

1142 ---; s. of Ptolemaeus, s. of Ptolemaeus; m. Prima; 123; wheat from Claudius Munatianus; *P. Lips.* 112.4.

1143 ---; s. of Dionysius alias Phatres; m. Matrina, d. of Heracleus alias Matreus; Oct 123; landholder; Oxyrhynchite; Oxy.; mother guardian; land at Oasis; VI 898.3.

1144 ---; ch. Leontas; Aug 123; Phoboou distr., E. Top.; addr. for s.; XXXVIII 2863.1.

1145 ---; ch. Cyrus; 126; Oxyrhynchite; Oxy.; addr. for gs. Cyrus who witnesses will; III 491.18.

1146 ---; sp. Demarous; ch. Dionysia; after 138; Oxyrhynchite?; Oxy.?; addr. for d.; *P. Yale* 65.2.

1147 DIDYMUS; s. of Amois; ch. Didymus; Jan 138; III 484.7-8.

1148 ---; s. of Didymus, s. of Amois; Jan 138; allegedly defrauded by Pausiris, wheat seller; III 484.10-11.

1149 ---; ch. Thaesis; 148/149; Oxyrhynchite, gymnasial class; Knights' Camp qtr?; addr. for d.'s sp. Theon; XLVI 3283.7.

1150 DIDY(MUS); 168; Alex.; gs. Diogenes alive in 168; XIV 1648.19.

1151 DIDYMUS; ch. Cleopatrus; ii; Thoeris St qtr; addr. for s.; *P. Princ.* II 46.10.

1152 ---; s. of Sarapion; ii; III 610 (descr.).

1153 ---; gs. of [-]nius; ii; landowner; lessor; leases land to Aphynchis; property nr Leon from Kleros of Apollonius; *P. Palau. Rib. inv.* 150.1.

1154 ---; ii; banker; XXXIV 2726.24.

1155 DIEMOUS; d. of Colluthus; Nov 144; property owner; Oxyrhynchite; Oxy.; guardian Sarapion; neighbour Heras, s. of Calathus; X 1272.25.

1156 DIEUCHES; m. Euterpe; i - ii, probably i; *PSI* VI 687.6.

1157 ---; s. of Panouphis; sp. Tetheus; ch. Panouphis; 131; Talao, L. Top.; addr. for s.; *SB* VI 9190.6.

1158 ---; ch. Diogenes; after 136-141; Oxy.; addr. for gs. Theon; *PSI* IV 281 R ii 29.

1159 ---; s. of Theon; s. of Diogenes; after 136-141; Oxy.; addr. for father; *PSI* IV 281 R ii 30.

1160 DIEUS; d. of Soceus; sp. Horus; ch. Zoilus; Sept 66; Oxy.?; addr. for s. who writes for Ptolemaeus; II 275.42.

1161 ---; d. of Papont[os; sp. Harbichis; ch. Glaucias; 97; Oxyrhynchite; II 371.2.

1162 DINCHON; ch. Tachois; 31/32; Oxy.?; addr. for d.; *P. Ryl.* II 159.3.

1163 DIO[; i. *P. Ryl.* II 199.26.

1164 DIỌ[ ]; ch. Sarapion; 128/129; Oxyrhynchite; Hermaeum qtr; addr. for gs. Sarapion; perhaps Diọ[scorus], name of one of gs.'s freedmen; X 1263.5.

1165 DIO[GENIS; ii; Oxy.; not Diogenis of line 1; XII 1584.24-25.

1166 DIOCLES; ch. Diocles; Aug 102; Oxy.?; addr. for gs. Rufus and Diocles; III 508.15.

1167 ---; s. of Diocles; sp. Didyme; ch. Rufus, Diocles; Aug 102; Oxyrhynchite; Oxy.; III 508.14, 15.

1168 ---; s. of Diocles, s. of Diocles; m. Didyme; Aug 102; property owner; Oxy.?; borrows from Heraclas, s. of Heraclas; III 508.22.

1169 DIODORA; sp. Sarapion; ch. Sarapion alias Heraclas; ii; ref. to village of Taampemou; *P. Oslo* III 108.2.

1170 DIODORUS; s. of Agatheinus; m. Tseei, d. of Theon; ch. Diodorus and another; (1) March 97; (2) 138-161; property owner; Oxyrhynchite; Oxy.; 2nd s. frees Demetrous; (1) IV 713.5; (2) 723.2.

1171 ---; s. of Diodorus, s. of Agatheinus; sp. Saraeus; ch. Leonides, Diodorus and Thais; March 97; property owner; Oxyrhynchite; Oxy.; dec.; married in 52; IV 713.3, 7.

1172 ---; s. of Diodorus, s. of Diodorus; m. Saraeus, d. of Leonides; gs. of Isidora; March 97; landowner; Oxyrhynchite; Oxy.; inherited m.'s land in Nesla and Peeno; bro. of Leonides and Thais; IV 713.21.

1173 ---; ch. Pecysis; i; Sobthis; addr. for s.; VIII 1145.21.

1174 ---; s. of Ptolemaeus, s. of Ammonius; ch. Plution; 127/128; Oxyrhynchite, gymnasial class; Gymnasium St qtr; addr. for s.; over age in 72/73; his father reg. in 4/5; XII 1452 i 4.

1175 ---; s. of Plution, s. of Diodorus; m. Tatriphis, d. of Amois; 127/128; Oxyrhynchite, gymnasial class; Gymnasium St qtr; father reg. there; XII 1452 i 3.

1176 ---; Nov 140; Oxyrhynchite; Oxy.; *P. Inst. Fran.* I 14.3.

1177 ---; sp. Dionysia; ch. Syrus; ii; Shepherds' qtr; addr. for s.; *P. Princ.* II 46.13.

---; see PAPONTOS.

1178 DIODOTUS; s. of Demaenetus; ch. -]us; ii; *P. Flor.* III 381.14.

1179 DIOGAS; April 71; XXXIV 2725.10.

1180 ---; s. of Teos, s. of Centaurus; m. Apia, d. of Protas; Oct 80; property owner; Oxyrhynchite; Pammenes' Garden qtr; inherits part house there; II 249.2.

1181 ---; s. of Heracleus; Nov 82; property owner; weaver?; Oxy.?; lends to Heraclas, s. of Ptolemaeus; XXXVI 2773.4-5.

1182 ---; 83; slave; of M. Antonius Ptolemaeus; Oxy.; age c. 30; I 94.10.

1183 ---; alias NILUS; 83; slave; of M. Antonius Ptolemaeus; Oxy.; age c. 40; I 94.9.

1184 ---; Feb 91; slave; weaver; Temgenuthis qtr; dec.; was of Sarapion, s. of Diogenes; XLI 2957.8.

1185 ---; c. 100; *P. Yale* 77.28.

1186 ---; Oct 111; slave; formerly of Ti. Julius Theon, now of Ti. Julius Theon, ex-strategus and archidikast; XLIV 3197.7.

1187 DIOGAS; s. of Theon?; late i; student; Alexandria; from Oxy.?, studies in Alex.; bro. of Nilus; XVIII 2190.54-55.

1188 ---; i; blanket-maker?; VIII 1153.21.

1189 ---; ii; guard; Sento, M. Top.; IX 1212.2.

1190 DIOGENES; May 37 BC; ed. identifies w. Diogenes of VII 1061; *Coll. Pap.* I 17.1.

1191 ---; ch. Athenarous; 22 BC; landholder; has other children; VII 1061.1.

1192 ---; s. of Demetrius; 22 BC; VII 1061.6.

1193 ---; 22; friend of Dorion; II 294.26.

1194 ---; (1) 22/23; (2) 25; banker; Oxy.; (1) II 311.2; (2) 288.8.

1195 ---; 31/32; landholder; Pela, W. Top.; *P. Ryl.* II 159.12.

1196 ---; 55; agoranomus w. Andromachus; Oxy.; I 99.2.

1197 ---; s. of Sarapion; 57; Oxy.; X 1316 (descr.).

1198 ---; s. of Pasion; sp. Plutarche; (1) April 60; (2) March 61; Oxyrhynchite; Oxy.; guardian of step-d. Thermuthion; (1) *P. Mich.* III 192.6; (2) 194.6.

1199 ---; (1) 62; (2) Mar/Apr 66; (3) 79/80; city secretary, topogrammateus and comogrammateus w. Apollophanes; Oxy.; (1) *SB* XII 10788.25; (2) *PSI* VIII 871.2, 23; (3) *P. Oxy. inv.* 20.3B.34/B.1.

1200 ---; Sept 64; sitologus? w. associate; Kerkeura; M. Top.; XXXVIII 2839.2.

1201 DIOGE(NES); s. of Dionysius; ch. Seuthes; March 66; XLI 2971.3.

1202 DIOGENES; ch. Didyme; July 66; Phthochis?, E. Top.; addr. for mat. gs. Harmiysis; II 246.7.

1203 ---; ch. Isis; Sept 66; Oxy.; addr. for d. and gs. Theon; *CPR* V ii 1, 5.

1204 D]IOGENES; s. of Sarapion; ch. Diogenes; April 70; Oxyrhynchite; *P. Oxy. inv.* 50.4B. 24B.(3-4)2.

1205 DIOGENES; s. of Diogenes, s. of Sarapion; (1) April 70; (2) 80/81; dyke superintendent, Peeno, M. Top.; landholder; Oxyrhynchite; replaced Theogenes; (1) *P. Oxy. inv.* 50.4B. 24B.(3-4)2; (2) *Coll. Pap.* II 21. 10.

1206 ---; July 72; sitologus; Seryphis, W. Top.; XLIV 3163.4.

1207 ---; sp. [....]ce; ch. Aperos; Dec 75/Jan 76; Oxyrhynchite; Oxy.; *P. Yale* 64.6.

1208 ---; ch. Dionysodorus; c. 78/79; grammateus?; Oxyrhynchite; Oxy.; may be Diogenes of AD 62; XLI 2987 back.

1209 DIOGENES; ch. Dionysodorus; c. 78/79; Oxyrhynchite; Oxy.; addr. for s.; XLI 2987.3.

1210 ---; 79/80; slave; Lycians' Camp qtr; minor; dec.; former slave of Berenice; *P. Oxy. inv.* 20.3B.34/B.6.

1211 ---; alias HERACLEIDES; sp. Tausiris alias Thallous; ch. Heracleides; 89-97; Oxy.?; addr. for g.gd. Dionysia and Heras; II 274.48-49.

---; see SARAPION.

1212 ---; s. of Dionysius, s. of Dionysius; sp. Tapsois; m. Heraclous; ch. Dionysius; Jan 90; Oxyrhynchite; *PSI* VIII 942.3.

1213 ---; ch. Sarapion; (1) Feb 91; (2) Nov 103; Oxyrhynchite?; Oxy.?; s. dec., owned slave weaver; addr. for gs. Diogenes alias Sarapion; (1) XLI 2957.10; (2) *P. Mert.* I 14.1.

1214 ---; sp. Tsenuaris; ch. Onnophris; Jan 93; Oxyrhynchite; addr. for s.; *PSI* VIII 897.5.

1215 ---; s. of Theogenes, s. of Philiscus; sp. Ptolema; gs. of Sinthoonis; 94/95; Oxyrhynchite; Heracles Place qtr; unnamed s.'s sp. is Isidora, d. of Ptolemaeus; II 257[1], 16.

1216 ---; s. of Ptolemaeus, s. of Ptolemaeus; m. Tecosis, d. of Harthoonis; (1) 95; (2) 109; landholder, property owner, farmer; Oxyrhynchite?; Oxy.?; dec. by 109; unnamed s.; land (ceded) at Korobis in Kleros of Menoetius; part house at Senemeleu; (1) I 45.3; (2) III 482.22.

1217 ---; alias HERMAEUS; (1) 95; (2) n.d.; (3), (4), (5) c. 95-100 (n.d.?); (6) 100; (7) 128/129; (8) 132/133; superintendent of land distribution w. Phanias (1 - 4), w.[Phanias] and Heraclas; city secretary w. Apollonius (8); (1) I 45.1; (2) 175 (descr.); (3) II 341 (descr.); (4) 342 (descr.); (5) 347 (descr.); (6) I 46.1; (7) X 1263.1; (8) *PSI* VIII 874 i 1, ii 20.

1218 ---; (1) March 97; (2) 99; (3) 129; bibliophylax w. Demetrius, Apollonius, and Theon alias Ptolemaeus; Oxy.; (1) IV 713.3; (2) *P. Harris* 74.2; (3) I 75.1.

1219 ---; s. of Pak[---], s. of Senth(eus); 98/99; livestock owner; Tholthis, L. Top.; reg. of animals shepherded by Hatres; *P. Köln* II 86.4.

1220 ---; s. of Thonis; sp. Zois; ch. Thaesis; 98-102; Oxyrhynchite?; addr. for d.; *P. Mert.* I 13.2.

1221 ---; s. of Theogenes; 2nd half i; practor; Sesphtha (or Psenosiris?), L. Top.; XXXVIII 2845.15.

1222 ---; ch. Philiscus; 2nd half i; Sesphtha, L. Top.; addr. for s.; XXXVIII 2845.6.

1223 ---; ch. Sarapias; end i; addr. for gs. Diogenes, Alex.; *P. Sel.* 23.14.

1224 DIOGENES; ch. Ammonarion alias Theopompion; end i; Oxyrhynchite; Oxy.?; addr. for gd. Theopompion; *P. Sel.* 23.6.

1225 ---; s. of Theon, s. of Heracleides; m. Sarapias, d. of Diogenes; ch. Agathodaemon; (1) end i (or 55-68?); (2) Oct 111; (3) 129; slave owner; Alex., Propapposebasteius, Althaieus; Alexandria?; son is Sosicosmius, Althaieus; (1) *P. Sel.* 23.13; (2) XLIV 3197.6; (3) XXXVI 2774.1.

1226 ---; i?; *P. Harris* 102.8.

1227 ---; alias SARAPION; s. of Sarapion, s. of Diogenes; m. Didyme, d. of Euphranor; Nov 103; exegetes; property owner; Oxyrhynchite; Oxy.; Persian of Epigone; *P. Mert.* I 14.1.

---; see DEMETRIUS.

1228 ---; ch. Theon, Pecysis; c. 107-112; *PSI* V 450 R 1, 8, 15, 17.

1229 ---; Oct 111; slave; formerly of Ti. Julius Theon, now of his s., Ti. Julius Sarapion; cook; XLIV 3197.10.

1230 ---; s. of Ammonius, s. of Nicanor; 115/116; slave owner; age c. 40; signalement; I 97.20, 26.

1231 ---; s. of Apollonius(?); ch. Besis(?); 117; Oxyrhynchite?; Oxy.?; addr. for gs. Plution; readings uncertain; III 489.21.

1232 DIO[GENES]; sp. Apollos; ch. Didymus; 117/118; dec.; sp. remarried; IV 837 (descr.).

1233 DIOGENES; ch. Dionysius; 117-137; Oxyrhynchite?; Oxy.?; addr. for gs. Dionysius; I 105.19.

1234 ---; s. of Papontos; ch. Papontos; 117-137; Oxyrhynchite; Oxy.; addr. for s.; I 105.15.

1235 ---; s. of Sarapion; 118; weaver?; Oxyrhynchite; *SB* I 5678.3.

1236 ---; 118; owed money by Philumene, claims from her gss; *PSI* IV 281 R 42.

1237 ---; Aug 123; sitologus; Phoboou distr., E. Top.; XXXVIII 2863.1.

1238 ---; 126; slave owner; III 634 (descr.).

1239 ---; s. of Alexandrus; Aug 127; Pela; *P. Oxy. inv.*? 22.

1240 ---; s. of Hierax; 127; grammateus; Oxyrhynchite; Oxy.; III 496.16.

1241 ---; alias PHALANX; s. of Harpalus; ch. Phalanx; 130; Oxyrhynchite; Oxy.; addr. for s.; III 492.19.

1242 ---; m. Herais; Aug 133; signs will of Taarpaesis; *P. Köln* II 100.32.

1243 ---; ch. Demetrius; 133; *P. Lips.* 115.1.

1244 DIOGENES; s. of Philiscus; Oct 133; *P. Lips.* 114.4.

1245 ---; Oct 133; misthotes of Korobis distr.; *P. Lips.* 114.4.

1246 ---; ch. Tanechotarion alias Euterpe; Dec 134/Jan 135; Oxyrhynchite?; Oxy.?; addr. for d. and gs. Apollonius; IV 726.7-8.

1247 ---; ch. Apollonius; Dec 134/Jan 135; Oxyrhynchite?; Oxy.?; addr. for gs. Apollonius; IV 726.6.

1248 ---; Aug/Sept 136; lessor; leases land to two persons; IV 838 (descr.).

1249 ---; s. of Heracleides, s. of Mincion; 136; farmer; lessee; Oxyrhynchite; Oxy.; XII 1472.15.

1250 ---; ch. Diogenes; c. 136; *P. Inst. Fran.* III 18.8.

1251 ---; s. of Diogenes; c. 136; *P. Inst. Fran.* III 18.8.

1252 ---; s. of Dieuches; ch. Theon; after 136/141; Oxy.?; addr. for s.; *PSI* IV 281 R ii 29.

1253 ---; s. of Miccalus; sp. Thaesis; ch. Terentius; 148/149; Oxyrhynchite, gymnasial class; Upper Camp qtr?; called the elder; addr. for s.; scrutinised in 72/73; XLVI 3278.1.

1254 ---; early ii; III 576 (descr.) V.

1255 ---; s. of Theon; ch. Apollon; early ii; Oxyrhynchite?; Oxy.?; addr. for s. who witnesses will; III 493.14.

1256 ---; s. of Pasion, s. of Sarapion; m. Berenice; early ii; Oxyrhynchite; Oxy.; minor; bro. of Sarapas, Apollonius and another; III 493.7.

1257 ---; ch.]renorius?; ii; Oxyrhynchite; child witnesses will; III 647.14.

1258 ---; -us; ii; Psobthis?; addr. for s.; *P. Erl.* 59 R 7.

1259 ---; alias COTTUS; s. of Isa(s?); sp. Sarapous; ch. Is?]as; ii; landholder; Oxyrhynchite; Oxy.; XII 1536.2.

1260 ---; ii; property owner; Pammenes' Garden qtr; III 505.4.

1261 ---; ch. Ptolema; ii?; *PSI* XIV 1414.31.

1262 ---; ii; Oxy.; unnamed d., age 1; XXXVI 2791.1.

1263 ---; ii; greeted by Isidorus; XLI 2981.27.

1264 ---; ii; landholder; vineyard owner; farmer; owns land in Phai and Chalothis; XLII 3063.1.

1265 ---; ii; Oxy.; writes to Dioscoras; XII 1583.1.

1266 ---; ii; ref. to village of Taampemou; *P. Oslo* III 108.4.

1267 DIO(GENES?); n.d.; *SB* I 1938(f).

1268 DIOGENIS; d. of Sarapi( ); sp. Heracleides; ch. Heracleides; 92; Oxyrhynchite?; Oxy.?; addr. for s.; XVIII 2185.8.

1269 ---; d. of Ptolemaeus; sp. Dionysius; 117; Oxyrhynchite; North Quay qtr; unnamed children; III 489.5.

1270 ---; alias TAPONTOS; d. of Sarapion; sp. Theon; ch. Theon; 129; Oxyrhynchite; Shepherds' qtr; addr. for gs. Theon; I 75.8.

1271 ---; d. of Theon, s. of Theon; m. Thermuthis, d. of Apion; gd. of Diogenis alias Tapontos; 129; Oxyrhynchite; Shepherds' qtr; died childless 84-129; I 75.30.

1272 ---; sp. Apollonius; ch. Apollon; Aug 133; Oxyrhynchite; Oxy.; *P. Köln* II 100.4.

1273 ---; sp. Corinthus; ch. Dionysius alias Ididorus; Aug 133; Oxyrhynchite; *P. Köln* II 100.30.

1274 ---; d. of Heracleides; Sept 135; Psobthis, E. Top.; *P. Stras.* 127.6-7.

---; see ALIA.

1275 ---; ii; landowner; tenant Hatres; XIV 1758.1.

1276 ---; ii; "sister" of Eteocleia, Theon and Pannus(?); XII 1584.1.

1277 DIOGENOUS; d. of Dionysius; sp. Theon; ch. Theon; 148/149; Oxyrhynchite, gymnasial class; Pammenes' Garden qtr; addr. for sp. scrutinised in 91/92; XLVI 3283.3.

1278 DIOGNETUS; s. of Dionysius; April 77; Alex., Epiphaneius; guardian of Bacche, d. of Hermon; II 263.3.

1279 DIOMUS; 130; grammateus of Ptollas; lessor of Heracleides, s. of Antias; possibly Senepta or Sinkepha; III 517.17.

1280 DION( ); s. of Theon; July 72; landowner in Seryphis, W. Top.; bro. of Mnesitheus; XLIV 3163.6.

1281 ---; alias AMOIS; ch. Dius; after 89; Oxy. nome?; addr. for gs. Dion( ) alias Acusilaus; *P. Lips.* 120.2.

1282 ---; alias ACUSILAUS; s. of Dius, s. of Dion( ) alias Amois; after 89; Oxy. nome; claims debt from Amois and Pamyris incurred by Harpalus, their father; *P. Lips.* 120.2.

1283 DIONYSAMMON; s. of Dionysius, s. of Dionysius; ii?; *PSI* XIV 1414.18.

1284 DIONYSARION; ii; Oxy.; XLVI 3312.7.

1285 DIONYSAS; ii; "brother" of Nice; III 644 (descr.).

1286 DIONYSIA; Nov 42 BC; landholder; Oxy.?; *P. Ryl.* IV 582.10.

1287 ---; d. of Clarus; sp. Didymus; ch. Sarapion; 66; II 272.27.

1288 DIONYSIA; alias TAAMOIS; d. of Di[.... s. of Epimachus; 77; property owner; Oxy.; sold property in Hermaeum qtr; II 242.9 etc.

1289 ---; c. 79; slave; sold w. her 2 ch.; age 35; II 375 (descr.).

1290 ---; d. of Theon; ch. Dionysius; 81-95; Oxyrhynchite; son being married; II 265.2.

1291 ---; d. of Dionysius, s. of Sarapion; sister of Sarapion and Chaeremon; 83/84; landholder; Alex.?, Athenaeus?; Papsis?, Tychis Necotis; holds land there; II 290.18.

1292 ---; d. of Pausiris, s. of Sarapion; m. Saraeus, d. of Heracleides; sp. Dius; 89-97; Oxy.; II 274.12.

1293 ---; d. of Petosi(ris); 93; landholder; Athychis?, U. Top.; land there, at Protar( ), Enteiis and in E. Top.; *P. Princ.* II 42 R 2.

1294 FLAVIA DIONYSIA; Nov 99?; farmer; landholder?; Roman; land in Kerkemunis; no guardian; may have another name; XLI 2959.2.

1295 CLAUDIA DIONYSIA; April 96; slave owner; of Alexandra; *P. Oslo* III 95.13.

1296 DIONYSIA; sp. Sarapion; ch. Ptolemaeus, Eusebes alias Germanus, unnamed d.; end i; Oxyrhynchite; Oxy.; addr. for s.; *P. Sel.* 23.16.

1297 ---; alias SAMBOUS; sp. -us; 117; Oxyrhynchite?; Oxy.?; addr. for unnamed s.; III 489.29.

---; see TASIONYS.

1298 ---; d. of Chaeremon; m. Hermione, d. of Chaeremon; (1) c. 130; (2) 131; landholder; farmer; vineyard owner; sister of Aphrod[ ]and another; (1) III 472 ii 41; (2) 486.2.

1299 ---; d. of Dionysius alias Chresimus, s. of Dionysius; Jan 132; Oxyrhynchite; Lycians' Camp qtr; addr. for father; freedwoman Dionysous; III 478.4.

1300 ---; sp. Straton; ch. Ptolema; April 135; Oxyrhynchite?; Oxy.?; addr. for d.; I 106.7.

1301 ---; d. of Didymus; m. Demarous; after 138; Oxyrhynchite; Oxy.; guardian Athenaeus; *P. Yale* 65.2.

---; see APIA.

1302 -]e alias DIONYSIA; d. of Di[-]; ii?; Senocomis, W. Top.; *P. Fuad I Univ.* 32.11.

1303 ---; d. of Ammonius, s. of Ptolemaeus; m. Sinthonis; ii; Oxy.; unnamed guardian to write will on her behalf; *P. Mil.* II 39.1.

1304 DIO]NYSIA; alias PTOLEMAIS; ii?; Senekeleu?, W. Top.; *P. Fuad I Univ.* 32.20.

1305 DIONYSIA; sp. -]n, s. of Apollonius; m. Eudaemon; ii; freedwoman; Oxy.; Theon foster father; m. the freedwoman of Dionysius; *SB* VI 9372.7-8.

1306 ---; sp. Diodorus; ch. Syrus; ii; Shepherds' qtr; addr. for s.; *P. Princ.* II 46.13.

1307 ---; sp. Alexandrus; ch. Sarapion?, Theon, Aristocleia? (may be step-children); ii; XLVI 3313.1.

1308 DIONYSIUS; sp. Arsinoe; ch. Pasion, Ptolemaeus, Apollonius, Berenice; 63/62 BC; Cleopatra Aphrodite St?; addr. for sons; XIV 1644.5.

1309 ---; ch. Asclepiades; 54/53 BC; Macedonian; son holds land nr Seryphis; *PSI* X 1097.1.

1310 ---; (1) May 37 BC; (2) 22 BC; measurer of land dues; (1) *Coll. Pap.* I 17.2; (2) VII 1061.8.

1311 ---; alias AMOIS; s. of Ptolemaeus; 22 BC; landholder; bro. Apollonius comogram. of Tholthis; VII 1061.1, V.

1312 ---; s. of Alexandrus; 19 BC; landholder; lessor; land at Pamis in Kleros of Philon; descr. as Macedonian; II 277.1 and passim.

1313 ---; s. of Chaeremon; ch. Onnophris; 6/5 BC; property owner; Oxy.?; Persian of Epigone; borrows price of grain from Nemeria Stlaccia; (1) *P. Yale* 60.1; (2) *PSI* X 1099.1.

1314 ---; 6/5 BC; banker w. Zoilus; Sarapeum; (1) *P. Yale* 60.5; (2) *PSI* X 1099.4-5.

1315 ---; 5/4 BC; exegetes; W. Top.; *P. Oslo* II 26.15.

1316 ---; s. of Tryphon, s. of Didymus; m. Timos; sp. Thamunis; ch. Tryphon, Thoonis, Onnophris; (1) 12/13; (2) 22/23; (3) 22-25; (4) 30-35; (5) 36; (6) 36-50; (7) 36; (8) 37; (9) 37; (10) 44; (11) 49/50; (12) 50; (13) 50; (14) 50/51; (15) 52; (16) 54; (17) 55; (18) 55; (19) 57; (20) 59; (21) 59; (22) 59; (23) 66; weaver; Oxyrhynchite; Hippodrome qtr (3); Temgenuthis qtr (10), addr. for s.; age 33 in 12/13; may be dec. by 44 as sp. has guardian; (1) II 314.4; (2) 311.3; (3) 288.2 and passim; (4) 282.2-3; (5) 267.1; (6) 321.1; (7) 322.3; (8) 319.[3], 12; (8) 315.[2]; (10) 251.7; (11) 1 38.2; (12) II 308.2; (13) 324.9; (14) 316.2; (15) I 39.8; (16) II 264.1; (17) 304.1; (18) I 99.2; (19) II 269.2; (20) 320.6; (21) 318.[4]; (22) 306.6; (23) 275.1.

1317 ---; 13; comogrammateus; Peeno, M. Top.; IX 1188.7.

1318 ---; ch. Dionysius; 17; Oxy.; addr. for s.; II 278.37.

1319 ---; s. of Dionysius; 17; Oxy.; writes for Heracleius, s. of Soterichus; II 278.37.

1320 ---; s. of Asclepiades; 23; doc. pr. M. Top.?; writes for Taseus; *P. Princ.* III 141.3.

1321 ---; ch. Aline; 23; Oxyrhynchite?; Oxy.?; addr. for d.; II 259.12.

1322 DIONYSIUS; s. of Phanias; 23/24 or 49/50; Oxy.; IV 789 (descr.).

1323 ---; 24/25; shepherd for Thais; Talao; II 350 (descr.).

1324 ---; 25; agent for Dionysius, s. of Tryphon; Oxy.; II 288.22.

1325 ---; s. of Hippalus; ch. Straton the younger; Feb 26; livestock owner; Pela, W. Top.; addr. for s.; II 245.16.

1326 ---; s. of Theon; 26; landholder; lessor; land at Isieum Tryphonos; VIII 1124.3, 22.

1327 ---; 27; "brother" of Didyme; II 293.1.

1328 ---; s. of Apollonius; ch. Didyme; June 29; property owner; Gooseherders' qtr; addr. for d.; *SB* VIII 9827 (a) 2, (b) 2.

1329 ---; s. of Hippodamus; ch. Dionysius, Sarapion; 41/42; *PSI* XII 1235.12.

1330 ---; s. of Dionysius, s. of Hippodamus; 41/42; *PSI* XII 1235.13.

1331 ---; s. of Ptolemaeus; 41/42; *PSI* XII 1235.15.

1332 ---; ch. Didyme; Aug 44; Oxy.?; addr. for d.; *P. Fouad* 44.2.

1333 ---; alias ...ONIUS; ch. Isidora (adopt.); c. 47-54; property owner; Alex.; householder in Gamma distr.; XLVI 3271.4.

1334 ---; s. of Comon; sp. Tiouda; ch. Comon; (1) Aug 50; (2) 93/94; Oxyrhynchite; Hippodrome qtr; addr. for s.; dec. by 93/94; (1) XXXVIII 2837.7; (2) *PSI* X 1109.14.

1335 ---; 50; banker w. Dorion; Oxy.; II 308 i 2, ii 2.

1336 ---; ch. Heracleides; 54; son writes for Ammonius; II 264.18.

1337 ---; June 56; Oxy.; II 310.5.

1338 ---; ch. Ammonius; 58; Ptolemais Hermiu?; addr. for gd. Ammonarion; II 268.2.

1339 ---; s. of Ammonius; sp. Isidora; 59; Oxyrhynchite; Oxy.; guardian of Tryphaena; II 320.5.

1340 ---; ch. Is]chyrion; Oct 62; XLI 2970.1.

1341 ---; s. of Ptollis, s. of Orthonoos; (1) Oct 62; (2) 2nd half i; farmer; practor; lessee; Sesphtha, L. Top.; leased part of estate of Seneca, Kleros of Diotomus, from Ti. Claudius Theon; (1) XXXVIII 2873.2; (2) 2845.11.

1342 ---; ch. Amois; Oct 62; Sesphtha?, L. Top.; XXXVIII 2873 v 30.

1343 ---; ch. Dionysius alias Didymus; 66; addr. for gs. Dionysius; II 272.23.

1344 DIONYSIUS; s. of Dionysius alias Didymus, s. of Dionysius; m. Ptolema, d. of Hermippus; ch. Apollonius; (1) 66; (2) April 77; (1) II 272.22; (2) 263.7.

1345 ---; alias DIDYMUS; s. of Dionysius; sp. Ptolema; ch. Dionysius; (1) 66; (2) April 77; (1) II 272.22; (2) 263.7-8.

1346 ---; ch. Diogenes; March 66; gs. Seuthes, weaver; XLI 2971.4.

1347 ---; alias THEOPOMPUS; 70; freedman and agent of C. Julius Satornilus; Oxy.; XXII 2349.6.

1348 ---; April 71; XXXIV 2725.8.

1349 ---; ch. Senamunis; Aug 72?; Nemerae, M. Top.; addr. for gd.; XLI 2972.8.

1350 ---; s. of Theon, s. of Theon; m. Sinthoonis alias Ophelous, d. of Sarapion; Aug 72?; property owner; Oxyrhynchite; Oxy.; bro. of Mnesitheus; owns part house in Nemerae; XLI 2972.3.

1351 ---; ch. Diognetus; April 77; Alex., Epiphaneius; deme for s.; II 263.3.

1352 ---; s. of Thoonis; sp. Teseuris; ch. Thermuthion; 77; Oxyrhynchite; Oxy.; II 242.24.

1353 ---; ch. Zenarion; March 79; Oxyrhynchite?; Oxy.?; addr. for d.; II 243.8.

1354 ---; alias AMOIS; s. of Phanias alias Amois, s. of Phanias; m. Zenarion, d. of Dionysius; March 79; property owner; Oxyrhynchite; Hermaeum qtr; part owner house there; II 243.7.

1355 ---; m. Dionysia, d. of Theon; sp. Sarapous; 81-95; Oxyrhynchite; Oxy.; being married; II 265[2], 6.

1356 ---; ch. Theon; 83; Oxyrhynchite?; Oxy.?; addr. for gs. Dionysius the elder; I 94.5.

1357 ---; s. of Dorion; 83; bibliophylax w. Heracleides; Oxy.; *P. Fam. Teb.* 15.99.

1358 ---; s. of Theon, s. of Dionysius; 83; slave seller; Oxyrhynchite; Oxy.; descr. as the elder; I 94.4.

1359 ---; ch. Sambous; 83/84; Tychis Necotis; addr. for d.; II 290.17.

1360 ---; s. of Sarapion; ch. Sarapion, Chaeremon, Dionysia; 83/84; Alex.?, Athenaeus?; Tychis Nechotis; addr. for children?; II 290.19.

1361 ---; 86; gymnasiarch; Oxyrhynchite; Oxy.; VII 1028.2.

1362 ---; ch. Cleopatra; Aug 86; Oxyrhynchite; Oxy.; XXXVIII 2843.6.

1363 ---; ch. Conon; (1) Aug 86; (2) 86; Oxyrhynchite?; Oxy.?; (1) XXXVIII 2843.6; (2) I 48.9.

1364 DIONYSIUS; (1) Aug 86; (2) 94; agoranomus w. Theon and Dius (1), w. 2 Sarapions and Pasion (2); (1) XXXVIII 2843.4; (2) I 73.7.

1365 ---; s. of Leon; sp. Isione; ch. Theon; (1) Aug 86; (2) 93/94; (3) i; Oxyrhynchite; Oxy.; addr. for s.; age c. 30 (3); signalement; (1) XXXVIII 2843.16-17; (2) *PSI* X 1109.2; (3) *P. Ryl.* II 156.28.

1366 ---; July 87; addr. for gs. Papontos; has unnamed s.; *PSI* III 203.3.

1367 ---; July 87; slave; foundling ch. owned by Papontos, suckled by Philotera; *PSI* III 203.4.

1368 ---; s. of Dionysius; 88/89; property owner; petition to prefect re Vegetus' boundary complaint; XLV 3240.9.

1369 ---; ch. Dionysius; 88/89; XLV 3240.9.

1370 ---; s. of Pausirion; ch. Dionysius; 88/89; Oxyrhynchite; Oxy.; addr. for s. who leases out land nr Tychis Necotis II 280.1.

1371 ---; s. of Dionysius, s. of Pausirion; 88/89; landholder; lessor; Oxyrhynchite; Oxy.; leases out land nr Tychis Necotis; II 280.1.

1372 ---; s. of Harpocration, s. of Sarapion; m. Esorsois; sp. Diogenis; (1) 88/89; (2) 117; farmer; property and slave owner; lessee; Oxyrhynchite; North Quay qtr; has children; illiterate; signalement; leases land at Tychis Necotis; (1) II 280.3; (2) III 489.3 and passim.

1373 ---; 89; rep. of Zenon; (1) II 332 (descr.); (2) 337 (descr.).

1374 ---; s. of Heracleus; sp. Ammonous; ch. Plution; 90; Teis, Thmois. Top.; addr. for s.; *P. Ryl.* IV 597.2-3.

1375 ---; ch. Dionysius; Jan 90; Oxy.?; addr. for gs. Diogenes; *PSI* VIII 942.4.

1376 ---; s. of Dionysius; sp. Heraclous; ch. Diogenes; Jan 90; Oxyrhynchite; addr. for s.; *PSI* VIII 942.3.

1377 ---; s. of Diogenes, s. of Dionysius; m. Tapsois; Jan 90; Oxyrhynchite; under age; father declares his catoecic land nr Nesla(?) from Kleros of Eudoxus?; *PSI* VIII 942.7.

1378 ---; s. of Sarapion; Jan 93; has catoecic land nr Apollophanes'; *PSI* VIII 897.68.

1379 DIONY(SIUS); ch. Herac(leides); 93; Enteiis; addr. for s.; *P. Princ.* II 42 R 5.

1380 DION(YSIUS); s. of Adme(tus); 93; landholder; Enteiis, U. Top.; land there; *P. Princ.* II 42 V ii 21, iii 30.

1381 DIONYSIUS; 93/94; Oxyrhynchite; Thoeris St qtr; died 86/87; has unnamed d. and mat. gs. Dionysius; *PSI* X 1109.18.

1382 DIONYSIUS; s. of Comon, s. of Dionysius; gs. of Tiouda and Dionysius; 93/94; Oxyrhynchite; Hippodrome qtr; tutor Theon; enr. in 93/94, age 11; *PSI* X 1109.5.

1383 ---; s. of Harpocration; m. Tausarapis, d. of Petosorapis; sp. Thamunion; 94; Oxyrhynchite; Oxy.; age c. 52; signalement; I 73.16.

---; see PAUSANIAS.

1384 ---; alias AMOIS; s. of Psammis, s. of Ballarus; ch. Psammis; June 98; palaestra guard; Oxyrhynchite, gymnasial class; enr. in 73?; X 1266.6-7.

1385 ---; s. of Theon (the elder); sp. Didyme; ch. Dionysius; 99; Oxyrhynchite; addr. for gd. Didyme; *P. Harris* 74.4.

1386 ---; s. of Dionysius, s. of Theon; m. Didyme; sp. Athenais; ch. Didyme; 99; landholder in Seryphis and Thosbis; Oxyrhynchite; died in 99; *P. Harris* 74.3.

1387 ---; s. of Harpocration; 99-117; Oxyrhynchite; agent (husband?) of Demetria; has unnamed child; XLVI 3274 14 ii 33.

1388 D]ION(YSIUS); 127/128; strategus (in 99/100); XII 1452 ii 58.

1389 DIONYSIUS; s. of Harpaesis; early i; Psobthis, M. Top.; *P. Wisc.* I 23.4.

1390 ---; early i; II 389 (descr.).

1391 ---; late i; "brother" to Sarapion; II 396 (descr.).

1392 ---; late i; addressee; II 400 (descr.).

1393 ---; late i; writes to Dionysius; II 400 (descr.).

1394 ---; late i; has partners; II 329 (descr.).

1395 ---; late i; res. in Alexandria; XVIII 2190.57.

1396 ---; late i; village headman; Nemerae, M. Top.; II 299.4.

---; see DIOSCORUS.

1397 ---; ch. Harpaesis; (1) 2nd half i; (2) i; Sesphtha?, L. Top.; addr. for s.; (1) XXXVIII 2845.10; (2) *P. Ryl.* II 199.13.

1398 ---; s. of Ptollis; 2nd half i; practor; Sesphtha?, L. Top.; XXXVIII 2845.11.

1399 ---; ch. Heracleides; i. Sesphtha; addr. for s.; *P. Ryl.* II 199.7.

1400 ---; ch. Belles; i; Tacona; addr. for s. nom. as sitologus in Tacona; XLVI 3273.5.

1401 ---; i; II 399 (descr.).

1402 DIONYSIUS; ch. Sarapion; i; XIV 1756.1, 13.

1403 ---; s. of Sarapion; i; property owner; Oxyrhynchite?; Sarapeum; part owner house there; *P. Ryl.* II 156.[5], 24.

1404 ---; ch. Tapontos; i; Senepta, M. Top.; addr. for mat. gs. Papontos; *P. Harris* 138 i 12.

1405 ---; i - ii; landholder (or name of Cleruchy); VI 971.1.

1406 ---; alias AMOIS; 100; epiteretes and cheiristes of land distributions of the Oxy.; II 346 (descr.).

1407 DIO[NYSIUS]; 100; cedes catoecic land; cf. II 346; III 641 (descr.).

1408 DIONYSIUS; 101; landholder; property owner in Psobthis; Psobthis, E. Top.; guardian of unnamed wife, d. of Tausiris; III 510.3.

1409 DION(YSIUS); 102; practor of poll tax; Oxy., 10th qtr; has associates; XII 1520.3.

1410 DIONYSIUS; ch. Demetrius; 104/105; Oxyrhynchite?; Oxy.?; addr. for g.gd. Arsinoe; XXXVIII 2852.16.

1411 ---; sp. Demetria; ch. Dionysius (Dionysis in text); 104/105; Oxyrhynchite?; Oxy.?; addr. for s.; XXXVIII 2852.7.

1412 ---; s. of Dionysius; m. Demetria; 104/105; Oxyrhynchite; Oxy.; name given as Dionysis; XXXVIII 2852.7.

1413 ---; Aug 106; Oxyrhynchite; Oxy.; unnamed child; *P. Wisc.* I 17 R 23.

1414 ---; Aug 106; *P. Wisc.* I 17 V 2.

1415 ---; Aug 106; *P. Wisc.* I 17 V 6.

1416 ---; s. of D[ ]; Aug 106; *P. Wisc.* I 17 V 17.

1417 ---; Aug 106; *P. Wisc.* I 17 V 23.

1418 DIONYS(IUS); s. of Prometheus; Sept/Oct 110; farmer; lessee; III 575 (descr.) V.

1419 DIONYSIUS; alias AMOINOMERIUS; ch. Panechotes; 117; Oxyrhynchite?; Oxy.?; addr. for s.; III 489.27.

1420 ---; s. of Diogenes; ch. Dionysius; 117-137; Oxyrhynchite?; Oxy.?; addr. for s.; I 105.19.

1421 ---; s. of Dionysius, s. of Diogenes; 117-137; Oxyrhynchite; Oxy.; age 46; witnesses will; signalement; I 105.19.

1422 ---; ch. Sarapion; (1) 117-137; (2) Aug 127; (3) 133-137; Oxyrhynchite?; Oxy.?; addr. for s. who holds land nr Seryphis; gs. is Sarapion; (1) I 105.13; (2) XXXVIII 2867.8; (3) *P. Flor.* III 319.2.

1423: ---; s. of Chaeremon; sp. Theolympion; ch. Hermaeus alias Hermaeon; (1) 117; (2) ii; surveyor(?) of Heracleopolis;

Oxyrhynchite?; Oxy.?; addr. for s.; (1) *P. Harris* 85.4; (2) XXXVI 2787.1.

1424 DIONYSIUS; sp. Eseremphis; ch. Hatres; 117/118; Sinkepha; *PSI* V 475.2.

1425 ---; ch. Epimachus; 118; Oxyrhynchite; Oxy.; addr. for gd. Sepsarion; gf. of Sepsarion, Dionysius and Harsiesis; III 503.4.

1426 ---; s. of Epimachus; sp. Thatres; ch. Epimachus (the younger), Petosiris; (1) 118; (2) c. 141; Oxyrhynchite; Oxy.; addr. for sons; (1) III 503.3; (2) *PSI* IV 281 R ii 28.

1427 ---; s. of Petosiris; sp. Mieus; ch. Petosiris; 119; North St qtr; addr. for s.; XII 1547.2.

1428 ---; s. of Sarapion, s. of Hierax; sp. Julia; ch. ....aros; (1) 119/120; (2) 122/123; (3) 123; Oxyrhynchite; Oxy.; guardian to wife who has land in M. Top.(1); addr. for s.; (1) *PSI* XIII 1322.4, 11; (2) *P. Lips.* 116.9; (3) I 107.1.

1429 ---; ch. Tasionys; Jan 121; Oxyrhynchite; Metroon qtr? addr. for d.; *P. Fouad* 30.3.

1430 ---; ch. Philon; Jan 121; Metroon qtr; addr. for s.; *P. Fouad* 30.10.

1431 ---; ch. Demetrous; Jan 121; Metroon qtr; addr. for d.; *P. Fouad* 30.13-14.

1432 ---; alias SARAS; Jan 121; hyperetes; delivers summons to Aria et al.; *P. Fouad* 30.31.

1433 ---; Feb 122; bibliophylax; epicrisis officer; Oxy.; IV 714.3.

1434 ---; Feb 122; bibliophylax; epicrisis officer; Oxy.; called "the other Dionysius"; IV 714.4.

1435 ---; 122/123; unnamed child; III 592 (descr.) V 1.

1436 ---; 122/123; unnamed child; III 592 (descr.) V 6.

1437 DION(YSIUS); s. of Doro.., s.? of Harpo(cration?); 122/123; III 592 (descr.) V 4.

1438 DIONYSIUS; s. of Sarapion; 122/123; unnamed child; III 592 (descr.) V 5.

1439 ---; 122/123; sitologus; Senepta, M. Top.; XXXVIII 2866.2.

1440 ---; alias PHATRES; sp. Matrina; ch. Didymus; Oct 123; Oxyrhynchite; Oxy.; addr. for s.; dec.?; VI 898.3.

1441 ---; s. of Panechotes; m. Ammonous; 124; Oxy.; minor; father freedman; III 490.4.

1442 ---; sp. Thaesis; ch. Dionysius; Aug 127; Lenon nr Pela?; addr. for s.; *P. Oxy inv.?* 2.

1443 DIONYSIUS; s. of Dionysius; m. Thaesis; Aug 127; Lenon nr Pela; leases land nr Paeimis from Eudaemon; *P. Oxy. inv.?* 2.

1444 ---; ch. Didas; Feb 129; Tholthis, M. Top.; *PSI* I 40.17.

1445 ---; ch. Dionysius; 129; Oxyrhynchite; Oxy.; addr. for gs. Agathodaemon alias Dionysius; I 95.5.

1446 ---; s. of Dionysius; sp. Hermione; ch. Agathodaemon alias Dionysius; 129; Oxyrhynchite; Oxy.; addr. for s.; I 95.5.

---; see AGATHODAEMON.

1447 ---; 131; property owner; bro. Sarapion; I 68.9.

1448 ---; ch. Dionysius alias Chresimus; Jan 132; Oxyrhynchite; Lycians' Camp qtr; addr. for s.; III 478.5.

1449 ---; alias CHRESIMUS; s. of Dionysius; ch. Dionysia; Jan 132; Oxyrhynchite; Lycians' Camp qtr; rated at 12 dr. tax in 104; III 478.4-5.

1450 ---; ch. Cleon; Nov 132; Oxy.; addr. for s.; III 480.4.

1451 DION]YSIUS; s. of Heliodorus; m. -psersois; 132/133; no trade; age 20; *PSI* I 53 i 4.

1452 DIONYSIUS; s. of Horus; 132/133; bro. Papontos; illiterate; *PSI* I 53 x 167.

1453 ---; alias ISIDORUS; s. of Corinthus: m. Diogenis; Aug 133; Oxyrhynchite; Oxy.; age 24; signs will of Taarpaesis; *P. Köln* II 100.30.

1454 ---; ch. Dionysius; Oct 133; *P. Lips.* 114.1.

1455 ---; alias PAPONTOS: s. of Horus; m. Taarpaesis, d. of Pertax; gs. of Tapsois; 133; property owner; Oxyrhynchite; Oxy.; minor; buys lots in Cretan qtr and Jewish St; I 100.5.

1456 ---; s. of Dionysius; Oct 133; a/c in Syron Kome, W. Top.; *P. Lips.* 114.1.

1457 ---; 133/137; property owner; orphan; owns w. uncle Sarapion land nr Seryphis; *P. Flor.* III 319.3.

1458 ---; 134; ex-sitologus of Mem( ) distr.; Oxy.; III 515.2.

1459 DIONY(SIUS); 134/135; III 617 (descr.).

1460 DIONYSIUS; 135/136; Talao, L. Top.; *P. Iand.* VII 136.12.

1461 ---; ch. Epimachus the younger; after 136/141; *PSI* IV 281 R 28.

1462 ---; alias AMOIS; after 138; freedman; Oxy.; f. of Athenaeus; *P. Yale* 65.6-7.

1463 ---; ch. Apia alias Dionysia; Nov 139; Oxyrhynchite; Oxy.; addr. for d.; X 1279.4.

1464 PETR[ONIUS D]IONYSIUS; Nov 139; strategus; Roman; X 1279.1.

1465 DIONYSIUS; alias PLUTION; gs. of Dionysius; Nov 140; Oxyrhynchite; Oxy.; borrows from Diodorus; *P. Inst. Fran.* I 14.1.

1466 ---; Nov 140; Oxyrhynchite; Oxy.; addr. for gs. Dionysius alias Plution; *P. Inst. Fran.* I 14.2.

1467 ---; ch. Dionysius alias Amois; 148/149; Oxyrhynchite, gymnasial class; Oxy.; addr. for gs. Dionysius; XLVI 3281.2-3.

1468 ---; alias AMOIS; s. of Dionysius; sp. Arsinoe; ch. Dionysius; 148/149; Oxyrhynchite, gymnasial class; Oxy.; addr. for s.; XLVI 3281.2.

1469 ---; s. of Dionysius alias Amois, s. of Dionysius; m. Arsinoe; 148/149; Oxyrhynchite, gymnasial class; Oxy.; reg. unnamed s. in g. class this yr; XLVI 3281.2.

1470 ---; ch. Diogenous; 148/149; Oxyrhynchite, gymnasial class; Oxy.; addr. for mat. gs. Theon; XLVI 3283.3.

1471 ---; s. of Dionysius; m. Thermuthis?, d. of Plution?; ch. Dionysammon; II?; landholder; land nr Terythis from Kleros of Cratidemus and other reg. in name of Ptolema; *PSI* XIV 1414.1, 29.

1472 ---; sp. Thermuthis?; ch. Dionysius; ii?; *PSI* 1414.29.

1473 ---; ii; landholder; lessor; VIII 1125.6-7.

1474 ---; s. of Epithynch(anon); m. E-; ii; landholder; Broad St; *P. Princ.* II 46.11.

1475 ---; m. Demetrous; ii; strategus; Apollonopolite nome; XXXI 2559.1.

1476 ---; ii; *P. Cair. Preis.* 48.1.

1477 ---; s. of Chaeremon; ii; epis(keptes?) in Heracleopolis; XXXVI 2787.1 V.

1478 ---; ii; XIV 1760.3.

1479 ---; ii; XX 2281 ii 1.

1480 ---; s. of Hermogenes; ii; Sinary, L. Top.; arrested; XXXI 2574.2.

1481 ---; ii; sent money by Eirene; I 116.3.

1482 ---; m. Tetheus; ii; landholder; III 530.1.

1483 ---; ii; has children who are marrying; III 524.1.

1484 ---; ii; III 529.3.

1485 ---; ii. friend and "agent" of Anthestianus; XLI 2996.35-36.

1486 ---; ii; assoc. supervisor of fish for city and nome of Oxy.; Oxy.; XLVI 3268.1.

1487 DIONYSIUS; ch. Onnophris; ii; *P. Sel.* 22.6

---; see AMMONIUS.

1488 ---; ii; overseer; Oxy.; XVIII 2191.1 and V.

1489 ---; s. of Cato; ii; Oxyrhynchite; *SB* VI 9372.4.

1490 DIONYSODORUS; s. of Diogenes; c. 78/79; Oxyrhynchite; Oxy.; XLI 2987.3.

1491 POMPEIUS DIONYSODORUS; 83; strategus; Roman; Oxyrhynchite; *P. Fam. Teb.* 15.98.

1492 DIONYSOUS; sp. Phaon; ch. Ptollis; Jan 132; freedwoman; Thoeris St qtr; f. of Dionysia; illiterate; III 478.3.

1493 DIONYTAS; s. of Theon; 97-117; accused of taking property of bro. Didymus; sister Demetria taken to court; XLVI 3274 ii 39.

1494 ---; s. of Pheremphis; Jan 121; property owner; Metroon qtr; owns property there w. sibs. Apia and Tapontos; *P. Fouad* 30.12.

1495 ---; s. of Ptolleros; ch. Ptolleros; early ii; Oxyrhynchite; Oxy.?; addr. for s.; *P. Wisc.* I 13.19.

1496 ---; m. Tetheus; (1) early ii; (2) ii; bro. Theonas; sent greetings by Dionysius via m.; (1) XII 1481.8; (2) III 530.25, 31.

1497 DIOPHANTUS; ch. Sarapion; (1) 92; (2) i; Peeno?, M. Top.; addr. for gs. Sarapion; (1) *PSI* VI 715.6; (2) *P. Harris* 138 iii 1, 2.

1498 ---; alias SARAPION; s. of Diophantus, s. of Sarapion; m. Triadelphis, d. of Asclepiades; i; property owner; Oxyrhynchite; Oxy.; buys vacant lot in Peeno from Sarapion, s. of Sarapion; *P. Harris* 138 iii 1.

1499 ---; s. of Sarapion; sp. Triadelphis; ch. Diophantus alias Sarapion; i; Oxyrhynchite?; Oxy.?; addr. for s.; *P. Harris* 138 iii 3.

1500 ---; s. of Ptolemaeus; c. 135; property owner assoc. w. Heracleius, s. of Heracleius; Oxyrhynchite?; XVII 2111 i 20.

1501 ---; s. of Auleius; ch. Diophantus; early ii; Oxyrhynchite?; Oxy.?; addr. for s. who witnesses will; III 493.14.

1502 ---; s. of Diophantus, s. of Auleius; early ii; Oxyrhynchite; Oxy.; witness of will; III 493.14.

1503 ---; ch. Heracleius; ii; Oxyrhynchite; Oxy.; addr. for gs. Diophantus; XXXI 2583.2.

1504 ---; s. of Heracleius, s. of Diophantus; ii; landholder; farmer; Oxyrhynchite; Oxy.; XXXI 2583.1.

1505 DIOSCO( ); s. of Apol( ); 119/120; landholder; farmer; land at Monimu. U. Top. and Sinary, L. Top.; *P. Wisc.* II 39.4.

1506 DIOSCORAS; ii; III 522.26.

1507 ---; ii; Oxy.; addressee of letter; XII 1583.1, 14 V.

1508 DIOSCOROUS; 129; slave; Oxy.; age c. 25; sold to C. Julius Germanus by Agathodaemon alias Dionysius; I 95.16.

1509 DIOSCORUS; ch. Demetris (sic); 31/32?; Sinary, L. Top.; *P. Mich. inv.* 69.6.

1510 ---; s. of Pausirion; 41-43; banker; *PSI* XII 1235.7.

1511 ---; April 48/Jan 49; Oxy.; X 1321 (descr.).

1512 ---; s. of Zenodorus; 57; Oxy.?; Persian of Epigone; illiterate; II 269.1.

1513 ---; ch. Orsenouphis; 80/81; Peeno, M. Top.; addr. for s.; *Coll. Pap.* II 21.3.

1514 DIOS[CORUS]; s. of Heracleides; 83/84; Alex., Zeneius?; Sinary, L. Top.; d. has land there; XII 1462.4.

1515 DIOSCORUS; s. of Comon, s. of Dionysius; m. Cleopatra; ch. Comon; (1) 86; (2) mid i; Oxyrhynchite; Oxy.; dec. by 86; bro. Dionysius, sis. Aline, bro.-in-law Mnesitheus; (1) I 48.12-13; (2) XXXVIII 2835.1.

1516 ---; s. of Ammo( ); April/May 92; guardian for d. of Asclepiades (related); *PSI* VI 715.8.

1517 ---; late i; II 300.7-8.

1518 ---; alias DIONYSIUS; late i; slave; II 327 (descr.).

1519 ---; before 123; tutor?; XVIII 2199.13.

1520 ---; Oct 123; Small Oasis; married to freedwoman of Matrina; VI 898.10.

1521 ---; 128/129; freedman; river worker; Hermaeum qtr; f. of Sarapion, s. of Sarapion; X 1263.3.

1522 ---; ch. Panemgeus; 132/133; Hermaeum qtr; addr. for g. children Anteis and Taamois; *PSI* VIII 874 i 6.

1523 ---; 134/135; lessee; leases royal land in Kleros of Xenon, nr Sinary, from Claudia Ptolema; IV 810 (descr.).

1524 ---; ii; doc. pr. Oxy.?; *PSI* VI 710.5.

---; see SARAPION.

1525 ---; sp. Tanenteris; ch. Dioscorus; ii; Upper Parembole qtr; addr. for s.; *P. Princ.* II 46.8.

1526 ---; s. of Dioscorus; m. Tanenteris; ii; landholder; Upper Parembole qtr; *P. Princ.* II 46.8.

1527 DIOSCOUS; s. of Pausiris, s. of Ammonius; sp. Thermuthion; (1) Aug/Sept 53; (2) April 60; (3) March 61; weaver; property owner; Oxyrhynchite; Oxy.; divorced by 61; (1) *P. Wisc.* I 4.4; (2) *P. Mich.* III 192.4 etc.; (3) 194.7 etc.

1528 ---; s. of Petearsenth ( ); i; sibling of Horus and Papontos?; *P. Harris* 144.2.

1529 DIOSCURIDES; Aug 7 BC; basilicogrammateus; *P. Ryl.* IV 603 V.

1530 ---; 13; basilicogrammateus; Oxy.; (1) IX 1188.2, 7, 13; (2) XX 2277.10.

1531 ---; ch. Didymus; 31/32?; Sinary?, L. Top.; addr. for s.; *P. Mich. inv.* 69.11.

1532 ULPIUS DIOSCURIDES; before 107/112; nomikos; *PSI* V 450 R ii 37.

1533 DIOSCU[RIDES?; Nov/Dec 132(?); *PSI* I 53 xii 194.

1534 DIOSCURIDES; ii; *P. Stras.* 299 V 18.

1535 ---; ii; tax-collector?; XXXVIII 2861.1.

1536 DIUS; 22 BC; son of agent; VII 1061.6.

1537 ---; s. of Sarapion; 20; writes for Heracleius; II 305.27.

1538 ---; Aug 86; agoranomus w. Theon and Dionysius; Oxyrhynchite; Oxy.; XXXVIII 2843.4.

1539 ---; s. of Dion( ) alias Amois; ch Dion( ) alias Acusilaus; after 89; Oxy. nome?; addr. for s.; *P. Lips.* 120.2.

1540 DI]US(?); ch. Ptollion; 89-97; Oxy.?; addr. for gs. Dius; II 274.9.

1541 DIUS; s. of Ptollion, s. of Dius(?); m. Thermous, d. of Sarapion; sp. Dionysia; 89-97; Oxy.; II 274.9.

1542 ---; (1) Nov 99; (2) Dec 99; (3) March 102; strategus; Oxy.; (1) XLI 2959.1; (2) 2958.1; (3) XXII 2342.17.

1543 ---; 113; practor of metropolitan money taxes; South Quay qtr; XII 1521.3.

1544 M. ANTONIUS DIUS; 133; ex-strategus of Alex.; neocorus of the Great Sarapis; property owner; Roman; Alexandria?; property in Cretan qtr and Jewish St, Oxy.; I 100.1.

1545 DOGYMIS(?); sp. Plution; ch. Sarapion, Tnephersois; 127/128; Oxyrhynchite; Cretan qtr; XII 1452 i 12, ii 39.

1546 C. JULIUS DOMITIANUS; ch. C. Julius Germanus; 129; Roman; Oxy.; addr. for s.; I 95.7.

1547 JULIUS DOMITIUS; ii?; mil. trib. of legion; Roman; I 32.1.

1548 DORCON; ch. Sarapion; 59; *P. Fouad* 28.9.

1549 DORION; July 23 BC; grapheion official w. Apollonius; Oxy.; *P. Inst. Fran.* I 13.31.

1550 ---; ch. Sarapion, Dorion; 22; II 294.32.

1551 ---; s. of Dorion; 22; II 294.2.

1552 ---; 37; banker w. Ptolemaeus; II 312.2.

1553 ---; 48; strategus; II 255.1.

1554 ---; 50 banker w. Dionysius; Oxy.; II 308 ii 2.

1555 ---; (1) Sept 66; (2) 83; banker w. Chaeremon; Oxy.; (1) *CPR* V ii 1, 3; (2) II 289 i 1.

1556 ---; ch. Dionysius; Oxy.; addr. for s.; *P. Fam Teb.* 15.99.

1557 ---; s. of Alexandrus; i; farmer; Alex., Eileithyios; Sobthis; VIII 1145.22.

1558 ---; Sept 103; clerk of archidikastes Isidorus?; reg. document; XLI 2973.33.

1559 ---; ii; XXXI 2613.6.

---; see DEM[ETRIUS].

1560 DORO..; s. of Harpoc(ration); ch. Dion(ysius); 122/123; III 592 (descr.) V 4.

1561 DOROTHEUS; ch. Papontos; 130; III 517.11.

1562 DOSITHES; s. of Stephanus, s. of Canbarous; 132/133 or 153/154; Oxy.; XII 1518.6.

1563 DROPIDES; sp. Tecosis; ch. Heras; 137; Oxyrhynchite; Oxy.?; addr. for s.; *PSI* XII 1262 iii 1.

1564 DRUSUS; ch. Antonia; 23; imperial family?; slave Cerinthus acts for A.; II 244.2.

1565 Ẹ.[..]; sp Epitynch(anus) or (anon); ch. Dionysius; ii; Broad St?; addr. for s.; *P. Princ.* II 46.11.

1566 E.EMOTHUS?; sp. Tasooue?; ch. P[e]neuaes?; i - ii; *P. Harris* 72.2.

1567 ECYSIS; Aug 3; *OD Pisa* 473 Concavo i 1.

1568 EIRENAEUS; 56; loans money to Pnepheros, s. of Papontos; II 271.19.

1569 EIRENE; ii; I 113.25.

1570 ---; sp. Horus; ch. Harmiysis alias Pelux, Amois; early ii; Oxyrhynchite?; Oxy.; addr. for sons; *P. Wisc.* I 13.4.

1571 ---; ch. (or close relative) Didymas; ii; has workman; (1) I 115.1; (2) 187 (descr.) ii; (3) 116.1.

1572 EIRENES; c. 100; property owner; Oxy.; "brother" of Epaphrys; *P. Yale* 77.1.

1573 ELIS; Oct 111; slave; formerly of Ti. Julius Theon, ex-hypom. and gym., now of his s., Ti. Julius Theon, ex-strategus and archidikast; XLIV 3197.8.

1574 EMECHUS; sp. Sintheus; ch. Panetbes; i - ii; *P. Harris* 72.24.

1575 EPAGATHUS; Oct 111; slave; formerly of Ti. Julius Theon, ex-hypom. and gym., now of his s., Ti. Julius Theon, ex-strategus and archidikast; XLIV 3197.6.

1576 EPAG[ATHUS; ch. ..rsis; ii; Oxyrhynchite; III 647.16.

1577 EPAPHRAS; 30 BC - 14; XLIV 3208.3.

1578 EPAPHRODITUS; 2 BC; Alexandria?; IV 743.25.

1579 ---; Oct 98; Oxyrhynchite; freedman of Aristocles, s. of Alexandrus; *P. Genov.* II 62.1.

1580 ---; i; XLII 3070.2.

1581 ---; ii; friend of Eirene; I 115.7.

1582 EPAPHRYS; c. 100; Oxy.; "brother" of Eirenes; has family; *P. Yale* 77.1.

1583 ---; Oct 111; slave; formerly of Ti. Julius Theon, now of his s., Ti. Julius Sarapion; tall; XLIV 3197.10.

1584 ---; Oct 111; slave; formerly of Ti. Julius Theon, now of his s., Ti. Julius Sarapion; notary; XLIV 3197.11.

1585 ---; Oct 111; slave; formerly of Ti. Julius Theon, now of his gs., Ti. Julius Theon, games victor; XLIV 3197.15.

1586 EPHAR[MOSTUS]; m. Demetria; 109; property owner; Oxyrhynchite; Heracleopolite; holds land in the Coites above Memphis in the H.; signalement; *P. Rein.* II 98.5.

1587 EPHONICUS; s. of Petechonsis; April 5 BC; *OD Pisa* 936 Concavo 8, 9.

1588 [EPICH]ẠRMUS; m. Nicarous; 127; slave; Oxy.; slave and groom of Sarapion; bro. of Sarapous and Cerdon; III 496.7.

1589 EPICRATES; alias APION; s. of Epicrates, s. of Heracleides; sp. Thaisous alias Thaesis; ch. Aphroditous alias Demarous (adopt.); early ii; Oxyrhynchite?; Oxy.?; addr. for d.; dec.; half bro. of Heracleides; Aphroditous his freedwoman; III 504.[3], 5, and passim.

1590 ---; s. of Heracleides; ch. Epicrates alias Apion; step ch. Heracleides; early ii; Oxyrhynchite?; Oxy.?; addr. for adopt. gd. Aphroditous alias Demarous; III 504.4.

1591 EPIMACHUS; s. of Lucius; Aug 44; Oxy.; guardian to Didyme; *P. Fouad* 44.4.

1592 EPIMACHUS; (1) June 52; (2) March 61; agoranomus; Oxyrhynchite?; Oxy.; (1) *SB* I 8034.38; (2) *P. Mich.* III 194.32.

1593 ---; 55; banker, w. Ammonius; Sarapeum; II 304.4.

1594 ---; s. of Polydeuces; July 55; II 261.10.

1595 ---; ch. Epimachus; 63/64; Oxyrhynchite; Knights' Camp qtr; addr. for gs. Ischyrion; *P. Gen. inv.* 222.6.

1596 ---; s. of Epimachus; ch. Ischyrion; 63/64; Oxyrhynchite; Knights' Camp qtr; *P. Gen. inv.* 222.5.

1597 ---; ch. Heracleia; Sept 66; Psobthis?, L. Top.; addr. for mat. gs. Epimachus; II 239.3.

1598 ---; s. of Pausiris, s. of Ptolemaeus; m. Heracleia, d. of Epimachus; Sept 66; Psobthis, L. Top.; was headman of village; II 239.2.

1599 ---; ch. Di[...; 77; Oxy.?; addr. for gd. Dionysia alias Taamois; II 242.10.

1600 ---; (1), (2) Oct 80; (3) 80 or 90; (4) 86-88; (5) Jan 90; (6) March 90; (7), (8) 90; bibliophylax w. Theon; Oxy.; (1) II 248.1; (2) 249.1; (3) 359 (descr.); (4) *PSI* XII 1235.2; (5) *PSI* VIII 942.[2]; (6) II 247.2; (7) I 72.1; (8) *P. Ryl.* 597.1.

1601 ---; ch. Heron; 98-102; Oxy?; addr. for s. dec.; *P. Mert.* I 13.8.

1602 ---; ch. Apollonius alias Secundus; Dec 99; Oxyrhynchite?; Oxy.?; addr. for s.; XLI 2958.3.

1603 ---; ch. Thaisous; end i; addr. for gs. Alexandrus; *P. Sel.* 23.9.

1604 ---; Aug 106; Oxy.; *P. Wisc.* I 17 V 10.

1605 ---; ch. Apollonius, Apollonius the younger; 107-116; Kerkethyris; addr. for s.; *P. Stras.* 244.2.

1606 ---; sp. Thatres; ch. Harsiesis, Dionysius, Sepsarion; 118; Oxyrhynchite; Oxy.; addr. for gs. Epimachus; III 503.2.

1607 ---; s. of Harsiesis, s. of Epimachus; m. Demes; 118; property owner; Oxyrhynchite; Oxy.; part owner property in Kerkethyris; III 503.2.

1608 ---; s. of Dionysius, s. of Epimachus; m. Thatres; (1) 118; (2) after 136/141; property owner; ex-exegetes of the Oxy.; Oxyrhynchite; Oxy.; bro. Petosiris; part owner property in Kerkethyris; accuses guardian Theon and son of stealing from his inheritance; had been ordered, in a *cognitio* before Heliodorus, to leave the country for three years; called the younger; (1) III 503.2; (2) *PSI* IV 281 R i [2], ii 28.

1609 ---; s. of Tareinus; ii; landholder; bro. Apollonis; *P. Erl.* 44 iii 36.

1610 EPIMACHUS; ii; landholder; cleruch; barley seller; has children; XII 1482.1.

1611 ---; s. of Plution; ii; camel stall owner; XLI 2981.19.

1612 EPIMAS; i; assoc. w. Apion; XLII 3070.2.

1613 EPINICUS; s. of Theon; sp. Helene; (1) Sept 58; (2) Oct 62; weaver; Oxyrhynchite; Hermaeum qtr; guardian of wife; (1) *P. Mich.* III 171.5; (2) 172.8.

1614 M. PORCIUS EPITYNCHANON; 90; landholder; Roman or freedman; Senepta, M. Top.; owns land at Petne, M. Top.; I 72.7.

1615 EPITYNCHANON; Oct 111; slave; of Ti Julius Theon, ex-strategus; XLIV 3197.8.

1616 EPITYNCH(ANON?); sp. E[; ch. Dionysius; ii; Broad St; addr. for s.; *P. Princ.* II 46.11.

1617 EPIX[ENUS; Aug 106; *P. Wisc.* I 17 V 4.

1618 ERASIPPUS; late i BC; bro. of Asies; IV 717.6.

1619 ERGEO(TES?); gd. of Tsenyris; 83/84; Papsis?, Tychis Necotis; addr. for d.; II 290.26.

1620 ERION; sp. Thaesis; ch. Harphaesis; i - ii; *P. Harris* 72.3.

1621 EROS; s. of Harpochras; Sept 32; XXII 2353.6.

1622 ---; i; property owner; Oxyrhynchite?; Sarapeum; part owner house there; *P. Ryl.* II 156.5.

1623 EROTARION; sp. Harbichis; ch. Harbichis; ii; *P. Erl.* 44 iii 34.

1624 ESARSENUPHIS; i BC - i; *OD Pisa* 38 i X + 7.

1625 ESE[-]; s. of Apollonius; sp. Hermi[ ]; ch. Herodes; 132/133; Oxyrhynchite; property owner; formerly held property in Hermaeum qtr; *PSI* VIII 874 ii 23, 27.

1626 ESENEUS; sp. Thonis; ch. Tecosis; Nov 83; Oxyrhynchite?; Oxy.?; addr. for d.; X 1282.12.

1627 ESEREMPHIS; sp. Dionysius; ch. Hatres; 117/138; Sinkepha; *PSI* V 475 21.

1628 ESERSOIS; sp. Harpocration; ch. Dionysius; 117; Oxyrhynchite?; Oxy.?; addr. for s.; III 489.4.

1629 ESTHOTES; i BC - i; *OD Pisa* 779 + 242 Convesso X + 3.

1630 ---; i BC - i; *OD Pisa* 502 X + 4.

1631 ESTHOTEUS; d. of Harpaesis; i BC - i; *OD Pisa* 460 Convesso ii X + 15.

1632 ETEOCLEIA; ii; "sister" of Diogenis, Theon and Pannus(?); XII 1584.5-6 V.

1633 EUBION; s. of Ptollion; ch. Peteuris; 148/149; Oxyrhynchite, gymnasial class; Gymnasium St qtr; listed in 4/5; addr. for gs. Apollonius; XLVI 3276.15.

1634 EUBULIA; s. of Sarapion; ch. Sarapion; 131; property owner; Oxyrhynchite; Oxy.; died c. 125/126; I 68.16-17.

1635 EUBULUS; ch. Harthoonis; 77; Oxyrhynchite; Oxy.; addr. for gs. Cephalon; II 242.26.

1636 EUCAERUS; Oct 111; slave; formerly of Ti. Julius Theon, now of his s., Ti. Julius Theon; bro. of Gemellus, Euporas; XLIV 3197.8.

1637 ---; Oct 111; slave; notary; formerly of Ti. Julius Theon, now of his gs., Ti. Julius Theon, games victor; XLIV 3197.15.

1638 EUCARPIA; n.d.; *SB* I 1933.

1639 EUDAE[M]; i; farmer?; II 298.6-7.

1640 EUDAEMON; 18; appointee of Theon, his bro.; in charge of reg. of land grants; *PSI* IV 320.7.

1641 ---; ch. Theon; July 50; Tholthis, Thmois. Top.; s. former part owner of Kleros of Pyrrhias; XXXVIII 2836.10.

1642 ---; ch. Heraclas (or g.ch.); 55-68; *P. Ross Georg.* II 13.15.

1643 ---; s. of Lycus, s. of Horus; 81-96; phronistes (= guardian?); lives in half house of Sennophris; makes decl. for Heracles; minor; VI 984 R init.

1644 ---; ch. Tetoe(us) or Tetoeo(us); 83; II 289 i 3.

1645 ---; s. of Thoonis, s. of Onnophris; m. Teteo(us) or Tetoeo(us), d. of Eudaemon; 83; livestock owner: bro. of Thoonis; II 289 i 4.

1646 ---; i; his d. is sp. of Philinus, s. of Philinus; *P. Med. inv.* 60.09.2.

1647 ---; i; slave?; of M. Antonius Spendon, phorologus; XLVI 3273.2.

1648 ---; i; animal owner; writes to Didymus; *P. Bon.* 43.1.

1649 ---; ch. Pausirion; after 102; Oxyrhynchite; Oxy.?; addr. for gs. Pausiris; III 636.16.

1650 ---; s. of Sarapion; 113; South Quay qtr; pays poll tax; XII 1521.4.

1651 ---; ch. Eudaemon; April 116; Oxyrhynchite?; Oxy.?; addr. for gs. Potamon alias Maximus; XXXVI 2759.6.

1652 ---; s. of Eudaemon; ch. Potamon alias Maximus; April 116; Oxyrhynchite?; Oxy.?; addr. for s.; name restored; XXXVI 2759.5-6.

1653 EUDAEMON; s. of Thonasychis, s. of Thonis; m. Thaesis; sp. Ta...; ch. Thonis, Horus, Eudaemon; 126; property and slave owner; pastophorus of Thoeris, Isis and Sarapis at Mouchinor; Oxyrhynchite; Oxy.; age 61; signalement; III 491.2.

1654 ---; s. of Eudaemon, s. of Thonasychis; m. Ta..., d. of Harpaesis alias Horus; gs. of Thaesis; 126; Oxyrhynchite; Oxy.; bro. of Thonis and Horus; III 491.4.

1655 ---; ch. Eudaemon; Aug 127; Oxy.?; addr. for s.; *P. Oxy. inv.?* 1.

1656 ---; s. of Eudaemon; Aug 127; Lenon, nr Pela; leases land nr Paeimis to Dionysius; *P. Oxy. inv.?* 1.

1657 ---; s. of Theon; sp. Heras; ch. Sarapion; 127; Oxyrhynchite; Oxy.; addr. for s. who is being married; III 496.2.

1658 ---; Dec 127; ex(?)-sitologus; Paomis, Thmois. Top.; XXXIII 2670.2.

1659 ---; s. of Menoetes; Jan 132; Oxyrhynchite; Oxy.; guardian of Dionysous, freedwoman; III 478.7.

1660 ---; alias AMOIS; s. of Amois, s. of Sarapion; early ii; Oxyrhynchite; Oxy.; witnesses of will; III 493.13-14.

1661 EUDẠ[E]MỌṆ; ch. Theon; ii; XIV 1759.11.

1662 ---; ii; once owned Isidorus, now freedman; *P. Erl.* 44 iii 29.

1663 ---; ii?; *P. Harris* 103.10-11.

1664 ARRIUS EUDAEMON; ii; Roman; unnamed wife and children; calls Dionysius, str. Antaeopolis, his "brother" XXXI 2559.1.

1665 EUDAEMON; ch. Adrastus; 100/101 or 119/120; Philonicus, Heracleopolite; doc. pr. Oxy.?; addr. for s.; III 504.7.

1666 ---; ch. Dionysia; ii; freedwoman of Dionysius; Oxy.?; addr. for d.; *SB* VI 9372.8.

1667 EUDAEMONIS; alias PLUTARCHE; m. Sinthonis, d. of Pecysis; gd. of Teencegous; ii; property owner; Tanais, M. Top.; buys courtyard at Pammenes' Garden qtr; III 505.2.

1668 EUGENETOR; ii; IV 741.1-2.

1669 EUMOERUS; s. of Philon; m. Taonnophris; ii; Oxy.; child, just died; I 115.4.

1670 EUNOMUS; s. of ..mus; ch. Athenarous; Sept 103; Toka, M. Top.; addr. for d.; XLI 2973.3.

1671 EUPHRANOR; ch. Didyme; Nov 103; Oxyrhynchite?; Oxy.?; addr. for gs. Diogenes alias Sarapion; *P. Mert.* I 14.2.

1672 EUPHROSYNE; m. Demetrous; (1) Aug 86; (2) 86; slave, houseborn, of Aline, d. of Comon, now freed; Oxy.; age c. 35;

signalement; (1) XXXVIII 2843.12; (2) I 48.2-3.

1673 EUPHROSYNE; ii; Oxy. nome?; *P. Warren* 13.22.

1674 EUPLIA; ii; sent greetings from Diogenes; XII 1583.12.

1675 EUPORAS; Oct 111; slave; of Ti. Julius Theon, ex-strategus and archidikast; bro. of Gemellus and Eucaerus; XLIV 3197.8.

1676 EUPORUS; i BC - i; *OD Pisa* 80.5.

1677 ---; 45; slave; Alexandria; arrested at Memphis; II 283.10.

1678 ---; Oct 111; slave; formerly of Ti. Julius Theon, now of his s., Ti. Julius Sarapion; XLIV 3197.12.

1679 ---; s. of Apeṭẹ[ ]; i - ii; Oxy.; *P. Princ.* II 25.2

1680 EURITAS; after 137; delivers letter from Horeis to Horion; XIV 1757.12.

1681 EUSEBES; s. of Sarapion, s. of Ptolemaeus; m. Dionysia; end i; Oxyrhynchite; Oxy.; name alias, real name lost; bro. Ptolemaeus alias Germanus; buys slave for full sister and wife; *P. Sel.* 23.16.

1682 EUTERPE; ch. Dieuches; probably i; *PSI* VI 687.6.

---; see TANECHOTARION.

1683 EUTRAPELUS?; Oct 111; slave; formerly of Ti. Julius Theon, now of his s., Ti. Julius Sarapion; XLIV 3197.12.

1684 EUTYCH( ); 83/84; catoecic landholder; ceding land to Demetrius at Nois via record office, Alex. chora; XII 1462 ii 39.

1685 EUTYCHES; Oct 111; slave; of Ti. Julius Sarapion; XLIV 3197.13.

1686 ---; ii; grammateus; landholder; *P. Erl.* 44 iii 38.

1687 EUTYCHIDES; 19/20; topogrammateus and comogrammateus (w. Theon); Oxy.; (1) II 252.1; (2) 254.1.

1688 ---; early i; IV 839 (descr.).

1689 ---; ch. Hermogenes; Nov 132; *PSI* I 53 iv 67.

1690 ---; ch. Apollonius; 133; *P. Lips.* 115.8.

1691 ---; ch. Apollonius; ii; Oxyrhynchite?; Oxy.?; addr. for gs.; *P. Sel.* 22.3.

1692 ---; alias HORION; s. of Apollonius, s. of Eutychides; ii; secretary; Oxyrhynchite; Oxy.; *P. Sel.* 22.2.

1693 EVANGELIUS; i or ii; doc. pr.?; *P. Princ.* III 188.9.

1694 EVANGELUS; ii; XLII 3058.20.

1695 EXACON; s. of Herodes, s. of Exacon; m. Caecilia Polla; ch. Herodes; (1) 103/104; (2) 108/109; (3) Sept 109; (4) 116; Oxyrhynchite?; Oxy.; name appears as Exacon, Exagon, Exaconn; leases olive garden at Psobthis, M. Top., to Horus (1); w. bro. Exacon, leases olive press to Heras(3); pastures sheep nr Psobthis (4); addr. for gs. Sarapion; also in III 506 (of 143); (1) III 639 (descr.); (2) *P. Med. inv.* 71.69.2; (3) *PSI* IX 1030.1; (4) I 74.5.

1696 EXACONOUS; ii; letter from "brother" Apion; VI 967.1.

1697 EXAGON (for EXACON); ch. Heros (for Herodes); Sept 109; Oxy.?; addr. for gs. Exagon and Sarapion; *PSI* IX 1030.2.

FABIUS; see FABULLUS.

1698 Q. FABIUS FABULLUS; i; centurion; Roman; Oxy.; *PSI* XIII 1356.1.

1699 FAUSTUS; 2 BC; Nekle; IV 742.1.

1700 ---; i; wine press operator; VI 985 (descr.).

1701 ---; alias AMPHION; Aug 126; sitologus; Pakerke distr., E. Top.; also in III 516.1-2 (of 160) w. Dionysius; XXXVIII 2864.1-2.

1702 ---; s. of Cephalon, s. of Demetrius?; m. Tauris; 129; fisherman; Oxyrhynchite; Oxy.; *P. Cornell* 46.2.

1703 FLAVIA; d. of Sinthonis; sp. Plutarchus; ch. Julia; 119/120; Oxyrhynchite; *PSI* XIII 1322.3.

---; see FLAVIA DIONYSIA.

FLAVIUS; see FLAVIUS APION; T. FLAVIUS CLEMENS, HERACLEIDES.

1704 ---; ii; wheatseller; "brother" of Morus; has unnamed partner, and secretary Apollonius; XLII 3058.1.

1705 FLOṚẸ[N]Ṭ[IA; sp. Callistus?; ii; unnamed children; XXXVIII 2860.18.

1706 FUSCUS; s. of L. Pompeius Niger; 48; apprentice weaver; doc. pr. Oxy.?; apprenticed to Menodorus; *P. Fouad* 37.2.

1707 C. ANNIUS FUSCUS; 92; solider?; Roman; loan to Psenamunis; *P. Michael* 9.12-13.

1708 G̣Ạ[...; ii; bro. of Pisas; XII 1584.14.

1709 GAIA; alias SARAPIAS; d. of Pausanias alias Dionysius, s. of Astyanax; sp. Theon (see intro.); m. Julia Heracla; 95; catoecic landholder; Alex., Phylaxithalassius, Heracleius; under age; land nr Seryphis; II 273.11.

1710 ---; ii; has husband and children; XLVI 3312.9.

1711 L. CALPURNIUS GAIANUS; s. of L. Calpurnius Seneca; 167; slave owner; Roman; Oxy.; bro. of L. Calpurnius Serenus; has unnamed slave; epicrisis 150-153; *PSI* V 447.8.

[G]AION; see SARAPION.

GAIUS; see C. CUTIUS, C. JULIUS, QUINTUS C. PASSER, C. RUSTICUS, C. THEON; C. JULIUS[- [, DOMITIANUS, GERMANUS, MAXIMUS, SATORNILUS, SATURNINUS, THEON: C. LONGIUS PRISCUS; C. MARCIUS APION alias DIOGENES, APOLLINARIS alias JULIANUS; C. VETURIUS GEMELLUS.

1712 ---; s. of Aperos; sp. Thermuthion; ch. Gaius, Heracleides; (1) 77-83; (2) 89; Oxy.?; addr. for s.; (1) I 170.9; (2) *P. Fouad* 48.4.

1713 ---; s. of Gaius, s. of Aperos; m. Thermuthion, d. of Heracleides; sp. Demetria; (1) 77-83; (2) 89; Oxy.; lends bro. Heracleides and wife money and grain; (1) I 170.9; (2) *P. Fouad* 48.4.

1714 ---; 86; basilicogrammateus; Oxy.; bg. of Claudius Macedonius str.; VII 1028.2.

---; see HERAS.

1715 ---; ch. Teros; 132/133; *PSI* I 53 i 12.

1716 ---; 132; unnamed ch.; *PSI* I 53 vi 96.

1717 ---; ch. Sarapion; 132/133; *PSI* I 53 xi 184.

1718 ---; ch. Apollonius; early ii; VI 969 (descr.).

1719 ---; ch. Sarapion; ii; ref. to Antipera and Sento; *P. Erl.* 44 iii 39.

1720 GALATE: 97; landholder?; freedwoman?; doc. pr. Oxy.?; palmgrove at Psinachis given by s. of Sarapion; *P. Bour.* 16.10.

1721 GALATI[US; 44/45; basilicogrammateus; II 279.1.

1722 GALES; ch. Psentres; i BC - i; *OD Pisa* 1023 Convesso i 7.

1723 GEMELLA; ch. Alexander; Oct 111; slave; of Ti. Julius Theon; XLIV 3197.15.

1724 GEMELLUS; c. 1; unnamed wife; IV 736.12.

1725 ---; i?; merchant; *P. Erl.* 14 V 3.

1726 C. VETURIUS GEMELLUS; ch. C. Veturius Gemellus; 103; soldier in 3rd Ituraean cohort, then veteran; Roman; Oxy.?; age 21 in 103; without signalement; ref. to s. in VII 1035 of 143; VII 1022.11.

1727 GEMELLUS; Oct 111; slave; formerly of Ti. Julius Theon, now of his s., Ti. Julius Theon; bro of Euporas and Eucaerus; XLIV 3197.8.

1728 ANTHESTIUS GEMELLUS; c. 117/118; Roman; Ars (P); appt. geometres of Oxy.; *P. Fam. Teb.* 18.7.

1729 GEMINUS; Oct 111; slave; formerly of Ti. Julius Theon, now of his gs., Ti. Julius Theon, games victor; barber; XLIV 3197.14.

GERMANUS; see PTOLEMAEUS.

1730 ---; ii?; *P. Harris* 104.14.

1731 C. JULIUS GERMANUS; s. of C. Julius Domitianus; 129; slave owner; Roman; Oxy.; I 95.6-7.

1732 ---; 132/133; illiterate; *PSI* I 53 v 74.

1733 GEṚ[MANUS; April 133; *PSI* I 53 vii 108.

1734 GHEMAPIS (Gm-Ḥp); s. of Petemunis; i BC - i; *OD Pisa* 69 Concavo 5.

1735 ---; s. of Harthotes; i BC - i; *OD Pisa* 755 Concavo X + 8.

1736 GHEMUBASTIS (Gmw-B_3st.t); i BC - i; *OD Pisa* 1023 Convesso i 3.

1737 GLAPHYRA; early i; II 397 (descr.).

1738 GLAUCE; sp. Heracles; ch. Heracles; i - ii; *P. Harris* 72.29.

1739 GLAUCI[AS; sp. Apollonous; 81/82; Oxyrhynchite; Oxy.; *P. Mert.* III 118.7.

1740 GLAUCIAS; s. of Harbichis, s. of Andronicus; m. Dieus, d. of Papontos; 97; Oxyrhynchite; II 371.2.

1741 GLAUCIAS; s. of Ptolemaeus; m. Cleopatra; ii; landholder; Gymnasium St qtr; bro. of Sarapion; *P. Princ.* II 46.4.

1742 GORSE[NOUPHIS; i; probably variant of Orsenouphis; *P. Med.* inv. 71.47.5.

1743 HADRION; Jan 132; bibliophylax w. Zoilus; Oxy.; III 478.1.

1744 HAGNES; d. of Ptolemaeus, s. of Ptolemaeus; m. Senamunis, d. of Dionysius; ch. Promachus; Oct 72(?); property owner; Oxyrhynchite?; Oxy.?; husband's addr., her family from Nemerae; XLI 2972.7.

1745 HAR[ ]; ii; landholder; land in Oxy.?; *P. Inst. Fran.* III 15.16.

1746 HARASIS; 98-137; nurse; in will of Didyme; VI 968 (descr.).

1747 ---; sp. Ammonius; ch. Ammonius; ii; Oxyrhynchite?; Oxy.?; addr. for s.; III 505.4.

1748 HARBELLES; ch. Patous; i BC - i; *OD Pisa* 308 X + 5.

1749 ---; i BC - i; *OD Pisa* 513 + 514 + 515 i X + 2.

HARBICHIS; see APOLLONIUS.

1750 ---; ch. Taurus (or Tauris?); 19/20; Myrobalanus qtr; addr. for s.; II 254.7.

1751 HARBICHIS; ch. Menander, Hierax; 41-54; Oxy.; property in Gooseherders' Lane; addr. for sons; XXXIII 2669.4.

1752 ---; s. of Andronicus; sp. Dieus; ch. Glaucias; 97; Oxyrhynchite; II 371.2.

1753 ---; sp. Thaisous; ch. Pecysis; ii; *P. Erl.* 44 ii 6.

1754 ---; sp. Erotarion; ch. Harbichis; ii; *P. Erl.* 44 iii 34.

1755 ---; s. of Harbichis; m. Erotarion; ii; landholder; *P. Erl.* 44 iii 34.

1756 HARCALES; i BC - i; *OD Pisa* 451 + 540 Convesso 5.

1757 HARCHEMIS; ch. Horus; i BC - i; *OD Pisa* 25 i 15.

1758 HARCHONSIS; s. of Herieus; i BC - i; *OD Pisa* 99 i 10.

1759 HARCHYPSIS; s. of Ptolemaeus; (1) i BC - i; (2) early i; (1) *OD Pisa* 510 + 568 Convesso 11 i 11; (2) 424.15.

1760 ---; ch. Nechutes; i BC - i; bro. of Pausiris; *OD Pisa* 25 i 26.

1761 ---; s. of Petemunis; i BC - i; (1) *OD Pisa* 127.6; (2) 541 Convesso i 1.

1762 ---; i BC - i; *OD Pisa* 755 Convesso X + 10.

1763 ---; s. of Horus; i BC - i; *OD Pisa* 87 X + b.

1764 ---; s. of Pe]tetymis; i BC - i; *OD Pisa* 755 Convesso X + 8.

1765 ---; s. of Kmj; late i BC - early i; w. Petechonsis; *OD Pisa* 35 Convesso 13.

1766 ---; (1) Nov 8; (2) 8; (3) June 9; (4) Aug 9; (5) - (8) 9; (9), (10) early i; (1) *OD Pisa* 421.1; (2) *DO Colon. inv.* 78.1; (3) *OD Pisa* 246.1; (4) 429.1; (5) *DO Colon. inv.* 95.1; (6) 85.1; (7) 286.1; (8) 300.1; (9) *OD Pisa* 435.1; (10) 423.1.

1767 ---; early i; *OD Pisa* 450B Convesso ii X + 4.

1768 HAREMPHOIS; s. of Wḥj; i BC - i; bro. of Jb; *OD Pisa* 22.4.

1769 ---; s. of Harpaesis; i BC - i; *OD Pisa* 1163 bis Concavo A1.

1770 ---; s. of Petechonsis; i BC - i; *OD Pisa* 1163 bis Convesso 4.

1771 ---; s. of P$_3$-Šrj-ḳns; i BC - i; bro. of Petamunis; *OD Pisa* 29 ii X + 7.

1772 ---; s. of Sgn(j)s; i BC - i; *OD Pisa* 23 i X + 11.

1773 ---; i BC - i; Sarapianus his dependant; *OD Pisa* 228 X + 8.

1774 ---; i BC - i; dependant of Pausiris; *OD Pisa* 228 X + 2.

1775 ---; i BC - i; *OD Pisa* 290 + 290A Concavo X + 3.

1776 HAREMPHOIS; s. of Psenpetimuthes; i BC - i; *OD Pisa* 460 Convesso i X + 3.

1777 HAR]EMPHOIS(?); i BC - i; *OD Pisa* 755 Convesso X + 19.

1778 HAREMPHOIS; ch. Harpaesis; i BC - i; *OD Pisa* 8. 15.

1779 ---; ch. Petechonsis; i BC - i; (1) *OD Pisa* 137 Convesso 4; (2) 460 Convesso i X + 6; (3) 1264 Concavo 3; (4) 755 Convesso X + 11; (5) 755 Convesso X + 15; (6) 510 + 568 Concavo i X + 8.

1780 ---; i BC - i; *OD Pisa* 454.3.

1781 ---; ch. Totoes, Petosiris; i BC - i; (1) *OD Pisa* 1264 Concavo 4; (2) 69 Convesso i 2.

1782 HAREMPHOIS(?); s. of Kmj; i BC - i; *OD Pisa* 29 ii X + 9.

1783 HAREMPHOIS; s. of P_3-...[; i BC - i; *OD Pisa* 25 ii 21.

1784 ---; ch. Petosorapis; i BC - i; *OD Pisa* 25 i 18.

1785 ---; Sept 6; dependant of Ḏd?; *OD Pisa* 814 Convesso 5.

1786 ---; s. of Psenpabis; Aug 9; *OD Pisa* 429.1.

1787 ---; early i; *OD Pisa* 42.1.

1788 ---; i; *OD Pisa* 39; i X + 3.

1789 HAREMPHOIS(?); i; *OD Pisa* 129 X + 12.

1790 HAREMPHOIS; i; *OD Pisa* 60 Convesso i 13.

1791 ---; ch. Patous; i; *OD Pisa* 60 Convesso i 5.

1792 HARENDOTES; i BC; pastophorus; *OD Pisa* 55 ii 3.

1793 ---; s. of Wḥj; i BC - i; *OD Pisa* 513 + 514 + 515 i X + 5.

1794 ---; i BC - i; has dependant; *OD Pisa* 510 + 568 Concavo i X + 4.

1795 ---; ch. Patous; i BC - i; *OD Pisa* 510 + 568 Convesso i 3.

1796 ---; i BC - i; (1) *OD Pisa* 25 ii 18; (2) 25 ii 24.

1797 ---; s. of Petosiris; i BC - i; *OD Pisa* 25 i 20.

1798 ---; ch. Petosiris; i BC - i; (1) *OD Pisa* 541 Convesso i 4; (2) 377 Convesso l. 7, 10 and Concavo 2, 8, 10, 12.

1799 ---; i BC - i; *OD Pisa* 561 + 562 + 795 ii X + 6.

1800 ---; ch. Pabis; i BC - i; *OD Pisa* 451 + 540 Convesso 7.

1801 ---; Aug 3; *OD Pisa* 473 Concavo i 6.

1802 ---; early i; *OD Pisa* 425.2.

1803 HARENDOTES; s. of Ptolemaeus; 102; Oxy., 10th qtr; pays poll and pig tax; XII 1520.4.

1804 HAREOTES; s. of Hatres; m. Soeris; gd. of Teraus alias Thaubastis; 96; Oxyrhynchite; Knights' Camp qtr; I 104.10.

1805 HARIMUTHES; ch. Teous; i BC - i; *OD Pisa* 228 X + 3, X + 12.

1806 ---; ch. Onnophris; i BC - i; (1) *OD Pisa* 460 Convesso i X + 4; (2) 451 + 540 Convesso 12.

1807 HARMAEIS; s. of Panetbes, s. of Harmaes; m. T..aete; i - ii; age 17; *P. Harris* 72.27.

1808 HARMAES; sp. Thermuthis; ch. Panetbes; i - ii; *P. Harris* 72. 25.

1809 HARMELLES; ch. Dd; i BC - i; *OD Pisa* 87 X + 7, X + 9.

1810 HARMENIS; early i; *OD Pisa* 450B Concavo ii X + 4.

1811 HARMIYSIS; ch. Cames alias Harmiysis; i BC?; Seryphis?, W. Top.; addr. for s.; *P. Inst. Fran.* I 36.3.

---; see CAMES.

1812 ---; s. of Ptollis; June 29; Gooseherders' qtr; *SB* X 9827 (a) 2.

1813 ---; s. of Heracleius; July 60; livestock owner; Syron Kome, W. Top.; XXXVIII 2851.4.

1814 ---; s. of Petosiris, s. of Peotsiris; m. Didyme, d. of Diogenes; July 66; livestock owner; Phthochis, E. Top.; II 246.5.

1815 ---; s. of Mylon; ch. Heras; 87/88; Syron Kome, W. Top.; doc. pr.?; addr. for s.; *P. Princ.* III 147.5.

1816 ---; s. of Pnepheros; m. Techonsis; i - ii; age 44; *P. Harris* 72.5.

1817 ---; ch. Panetbeus; Jan 100; Nemerae, M. Top.; addr. for s.; XLI 2960.11-12.

1818 ---; alias HERACLAS; 103; III 511.1.

1819 ---; s. of Nechthenicis, s. of Ptollion; m. Di[.....; early ii; Phthochis?, E. Top.; cousin and guardian of Taptollion; unmarked; *P. Wisc.* I 13.2, 13.

1820 ---; alias PELUX; s. of Horus, s. of Pelux; m. Eirene; early ii; Oxyrhynchite; Oxy.; bro. of Amois; *P. Wisc.* I 13.4, 10.

1821 ---; early ii; Oxyrhynchite; Oxy.?; has unnamed children; witnesses will of Taptollion; addr. for unnamed gs.; signalement; *P. Wisc.* I 13.15.

1822 ---; s. of Plution; ii; landholder; leases land at Antipera and Sento; *P. Erl.* 44 iii 24.

1823 HAROUSOIS; 81-96; VI 984 R fin.

1824 HARPACHTES; s. of Athenodorus; n.d.; *SB* I 1987 (b).

1825 HARPAERIS; ch. Horus; i BC - i; *OD Pisa* 460 Convesso i X + 9.

1826 ---; i BC - i; *OD Pisa* 25 i 8.

1827 HARPAESION; ch. Chaereis; c. 81-96; Senocomis, W. Top.; addr. for gs. Didymus alias Amoitas; I 47.14.

1828 HARPAESIS; ch. Thonis; 30/29 BC; Oxy.; s. writes for Paapis, temple lamplighter; XII 1453.32.

1829 ---; 8-7 BC; livestock owner; Oxy. nome?; *P. Inst. Fran.* I 5.4.

1830 ---; i BC; *OD Pisa* 323 X + 4.

1831 ---; i BC - i; *OD Pisa* 454.3.

1832 ---; s. of Horus; i BC - i; *OD Pisa* 72 ii X + 5.

1833 ---; i BC - i; dependant of Pasis; *OD Pisa* 111 Convesso 9.

1834 ---; i BC - i; *OD Pisa* 196 ii X + 4.

1835 [HAR]PAESIS; April 5 BC; *OD Pisa* 936 Convesso 12.

1836 HARPAESIS; ch. Ḥtws; (1) i BC; (2) i BC - i; (1) *OD Pisa* 55 ii 10; (2) 38 i X + 5.

1837 ---; Ḥr-mn; i BC - i; *OD Pisa* 5 ii X + 13.

1838 ---; ch. Prgs; i BC - i; *OD Pisa* 5 ii X + 12.

1839 ---; i BC - i; via Ḥlgj; *OD Pisa* 111 Concavo 1.3.

1840 ---; s. of Psenesis; i BC - i; Elephantine; *OD Pisa* 111 Concavo 8.

1841 ---; ch. Teos; i BC - i; *OD Pisa* 477 Convesso 7.

1842 ---; ch. Petechonsis; i BC - i; *OD Pisa* 243 + 472 i 7.

1843 ---; i BC - i; *OD Pisa* 667.1, 6.

1844 ---; ch. Ammoneus; i BC - i; *OD Pisa* 1264 Convesso 2.

1845 ---; s. of Kmj; i BC - i; *OD Pisa* 232.9.

1846 ---; i BC - i; *OD Pisa* 22.2, 4, 7.

1847 ---; ch. Haremphois; i BC - i; *OD Pisa* 1163 bis Concavo Al.

1848 ---; i BC - i; *OD Pisa* 38 i X + 1.

1849 ---; i BC - i; *OD Pisa* 243 + 472 i 15.

1850 ---; s. of P_3-sp; i BC - i; *OD Pisa* 502 X + 6.

1851 ---; s. of Thoteus; i BC - i; (1) *OD Pisa* 243 + 473 i 6; (2) 667.2.

1852 HARPAESIS; s. of P_3-sn(?); i BC - i; *OD Pisa* 25 ii 8.

1853 ---; s. of Petechonsis; i BC - i; *OD Pisa* 25 i 4.

1854 ---; s. of Cephalon; i BC - i; *OD Pisa* 228 X + 4.

1855 ---; ch. Esthoteus; i BC - i; *OD Pisa* 460 Convesso ii X + 15.

1856 ---; ch. Petubastis; i BC - i; *OD Pisa* 755 Concavo X + 6.

1857 ---; s. of P_3-spj (Pesphis?); (1) i BC - i; (2) i; (3) Sept 6; *OD Pisa* 23 ii 6; (2) 318.2; (3) 814 Convesso 8.

1858 ---; ch. Petechonsis; i BC - i; *OD Pisa* 137 Concavo 1, 5.

1859 ---; s. of Pa-mwt; i BC - i; *OD Pisa* 276 X + 2.

1860 ---; ch. D̲d; i BC - i; *OD Pisa* 217 Convesso X + 1.

1861 ---; alias Bw-nfr; i BC - i; *OD Pisa* 217 Convesso X + 2.

1862 ---; i BC - i; *OD Pisa* 779 + 242 Concavo 2.

1863 ---; s. of Anubis; i BC - i; *OD Pisa* 779 + 242 Convesso X + 4.

1864 ---; s. of P_3j-st$_3$(?); i BC - i; *OD Pisa* 779 + 242 Convesso X + 14.

1865 ---; ch. Petosiris; (1), (2) i BC - i; (3) July 7; (1) *OD Pisa* 561 + 562 + 795 i X + 4; (2) 779 + 242 Convesso X + 13; (3) 1131 Convesso 2.

1866 ---; s. of Petosiris; i BC - i; *OD Pisa* 451 + 540 Convesso 9.

1867 ---; s. of Haremphois; i BC - i; *OD Pisa* 8.15.

1868 ---; ch. Thoteus; i BC - i; *OD Pisa* 22.1.

1869 ---; s. of Pasis; i BC - i; *OD Pisa* 532 X + 5.

1870 ---; s. of Panrymis; Dec 20/Jan 21; linen weaver; property owner; Sinary, L. Top.; illiterate; X 1281.4.

1871 ---; ch. Plutarche; April 60; Oxyrhynchite?; Oxy.; addr. for d.; *P. Mich.* III 192.16.

1872 ---; s. of Papontos; 74; farmer; sub-lessee; XIV 1661.2.

1873 ---; s. of A or HA; sp. Tausorapis; ch. Apis; 77; Oxy.; addr. for s. who is priest; II 243.3.

1874 ---; ch. Horion; 84/84; Papsis?, Tychis Necotis; addr. for s.; II 290.6.

1875 ---; ch. Ammon; 87/88; Tanais?, M. Top.; addr. for gs. Pisys; *Coll Pap.* I 22.3.

1876 HARPAESIS; ch. Theon; (1) after 89; (2) April 96; (3) May 96; Oxy.; addr. for gs. Harpalus; son physician; (1) *P. Lips.* 120.5; (2) *P. Oslo* III 95.2; (3) *PSI Bartoletti Colombo* 2.2

1877 ---; ch. Thonis; 93; Athychis, U. Top.; addr. for ch.; (1) *P. Princ.* II 42 R 7; (2) *P. Princ.* II 42 V ii 2, 6.

1878 ---; ch. Petosiris; c. 98; Oxyrhynchite?; Oxy.; addr. for gs. (mat.) Thonis; II 241.8.

1879 ---; ch. Harpaesis; Oct 98; Oxyrhynchite; *P. Genov.* II 62.3.

1880 ---; s. of Harpaesis; sp. Tatreiphis; ch. Theon; Oct 98; Oxyrhynchite -cf. *P. Oslo* III 95, *PSI Bartoletti Colombo*.

1881 ---; s. of Petserothonis; sp. Petosiris; ch. Thonis, Thompyas; c. 98; Oxyrhynchite?; Oxy.?; II 241.5.

1882 ---; ch. Dionysius; early i; Psobthis, M. Top.; *P. Wisc.* I 23.4-5.

1883 ---; early i; dependant of P_3-ḥbs; *OD Pisa* 234 Convesso 1.

1884 ---; s. of Dionysius; (1) 2nd half i; (2) i; practor; farmer; Sesphtha, L. Top.; (1) XXXVIII 2845.10; (2) *P. Ryl.* II 199.13.

1885 ---; ch. Horus; i; Koba; addr. for s.; VIII 1145.11.

1886 ---; i; *OD Pisa* 129 X + 8.

1887 ---; ch. Heracles; i; farmer?; Koba; addr. for s.; VIII 1145.13.

1888 [HAR]PAESIS; s. of Harthoonis; i; farmer; Sesphtha, L. Top.; *P. Ryl.* II 199.14.

1889 HARPAESIS; ch. Tamonous; i; Pakerke, M. Top.; addr. for mat. gs. Horus; *P. Harris* 138 i 21.

1890 ---; ch. Tathotis; i; *P. Harris* 144.8.

1891 ---; s. of Ammon; m. Sambius; i - ii; Harphaesis in text; age 44; *P. Harris* 72.14.

1892 ---; s. of Erion; m. Thaesis; i - ii; Harphaesis in text; age 31; *P. Harris* 72.3.

1893 ---; alias HORUS; s. of Thonis; ch. Ta...; 126; Oxyrhynchite?; Oxy.?; addr. for d.; III 491.4-5.

1894 ---; s. of Harsiesis; ch. Papontos; ii; landholder; Hippodrome qtr; *P. Princ.* II 46.2, 3.

1895 ---; ii; doc. pr. Oxy.?; *PSI* VI 710 l.h. margin.

1896 HARPALUS; s. of Hermon; Nov/Dec 64; Oxy.; makes loan in Palosis, Thmois. Top.; IV 808 (descr.).

1897 HARPALUS; s. of Theon, s. of Harpaesis; ch. Amois, Pamyris; after 89, Oxy. nome; doc. pr. Oxy.?; dec.; was in debt to Dion( ) alias Acusilaus; *P. Lips.* 120.5.

1898 ---; ch. Theon; i; Oxy.?; addr. for s.; name Harpaesis?; *PSI Bartoletti Colombo* 2.2.

1899 ---; ch. Diogenes alias Phalanx; 130; Oxyrhynchite?; Oxy.?; addr. for gs. Phalanx; III 492.19.

1900 HARPAOSIRIS; ch. Pamun; early i; *OD Pisa* 42.1.

1901 HARCHEMIS; ch. Petosiris; (1) i BC - i; (2) i; (1) *OD Pisa* 755 Concavo X + 4; (2) 129 X + 3.

1902 ---; ch. Petubastis; i BC - i; *OD Pisa* 1023 Convesso i 6.

1903 ---; i BC - i; *OD Pisa* 8.4.

1904 HARPE-irt(?); early i; greeted by Petosiris; *OD Pisa* 164.1.

1905 HARPOCH( ); 92; basilicogrammateus; Oxy.; XVIII 2185.6.

1906 HARPOCHRAS; m. Sinthonis; Sept 32; XXII 2353.1.

1907 ---; ch. Eros; Sept 32; XXII 2353.4.

1908 ---; ch. Soeris; 96; Oxyrhynchite?; Knights' Camp qtr; addr. for d.; freedman of Sarapion, s. of Chaeremon; I 104.4.

1909 HARPOCRAS; Oct 111; slave; formerly of Ti. Julius Theon, ex-hypom. and gym., now of his gs. Ti. Julius Theon, games victor; XLIV 3197.14.

1910 ---; s. of Paoous; 116; *P. Cair. Preis.* 32.5.

1911 HARPOCRATES; i BC - i; Menches his dependant; *OD Pisa* 755 Convesso X + 5.

1912 ---; s. of Petesnes; i BC - i; *OD Pisa* 69 Convesso i 7.

1913 ---; s. of Šp; i; *OD Pisa* 60 Convesso i 10.

1914 HARPOCRATION; s. of Aperos; (1) 10/11?; (2) 20; banker, descr. as "private bank"; Sarapeum; (1) XXXVI 2772.3; (2) II 305.6

1915 ---; s. of Areius; 44; Pammenes' Garden qtr; borrowed from Bassus; *P. Fouad* 27.5.

1916 ---; s. of Sarapion; ch. Dionysius; 88/89; Oxyrhynchite; Oxy.; addr. for s.; II 280.3.

1917 ---; sp. Tausarapis; ch. Dionysius; 94; Oxyrhynchite; Oxy.; addr. for s.; I 73.17.

1918 ---; ch. Dionysius; 99-117; XLVI 3274 i 5, ii 33-34.

1919 ---; 2nd half i; *P. Oslo* III 130.6-7.

1920 ---; s. of Sarapion; sp. Esorsois; ch. Dionysius; 117; Oxyrhynchite?; North Quay qtr; addr. for s.; III 489.4.

1921 HARPOC(RATION); ch. Doro..; gf.? of Dion(ysius); 122/123; III 592 (descr.).

1922 HARPOCRATION; ch. Sarapion; 148/149; Oxyrhynchite, gymnasial class; 10th qtr; addr. for g.gs. Sarapion, scrutinised in 72/73; XLVI 3282.13.

1923 ---; s. of Sarapion, s. of Harpocration; sp. Demetria alias Asclatarion; ch. Sarapion; 148/149; Oxyrhynchite, gymnasial class; 10th qtr; addr. for s.; XLVI 3282.2.

1924 ---; s. of Saprion; ii; XLIV 3199.1.

1925 HARPSENTHOTES; i BC - i; *OD Pisa* 99 i 2.

1926 HARPSOIS; ch. Onnophris; Jan 93; Oxyrhynchite; Oxy.; addr. for gd. Tsenuaris; *PSI* VIII 897.3.

1927 HARPTU(?) (Ḥr-p$_3$-Dw); i BC - i; *OD Pisa* 84.4.

1928 HARSAOSIRIS; i BC - i; *OD Pisa* 561 + 562 + 795 i X + 17.

1929 HARSEIS; sp. Satyrus; ch. Acoris; ii; Cretan qtr; addr. for s.; *P. Princ.* II 46.6.

1930 HARSES (HARSIS); i BC; *OD Pisa* 55 ii 2.

1931 HARSETIUS; 117-138; Sinkepha?; *PSI* V 475.10.

1932 HARSI]ESIS; s. of Cathytes; i BC; *OD Pisa* 55 i 5.

1933 HARSIESIS; s. of Pạtous; i BC - i; *OD Pisa* 127.4.

1934 ---; ch. Patous; i BC - i; *OD Pisa* 276 X + 7.

1935 ---; i BC - i; *OD Pisa* 23 ii 2.

1936 ---; s. of Hermois; i BC - i; *OD Pisa* 256.1.

1937 ---; ch. Imouthes; i BC - i; *OD Pisa* 69 Convesso i 7.

1938 ---; ch. Pamun; i BC - i; *OD Pisa* 106.4.

1939 ---; ch. Slj; i BC - i; *OD Pisa* 1163 bis Convesso 2.

1940 ---; s. of Harthoonis; ch. Harthoonis; 54-68; s. is priest of Thoeris, Isis, and Sarapis; *SB* X 10256.1.

1941 ---; ch. .....is; May 96; *PSI Bartoletti Colombo* 2.11.

1942 ---; s. of Beḷ[les; i; farmer at Sesphtha?; *P. Ryl.* II 199.27.

1943 ---; s. of Epimachus; sp. Demes; ch. Epimachus; 118; Oxyrhynchite; Oxy.; addr. for s.; III 503.2.

1944 ---; ch. Harpaesis; ii; Hippodrome qtr; addr. for s.; *P. Princ.* II 46.3.

1945 HARSOUS; s. of Sarapion; Jan 121; property owner; Metroon qtr; owns property there w. Apia and others; *P. Fouad* 30.12.

1946 HARTHONIS; ch. Pasion; Jan 49; Oxyrhynchite; Oxy.; addr. for s.; XXXI 2582.2.

1947 ---; ch. Petosiris; 71/72; Oxy.?; doc. pr. Oxy.?; *P. Ryl.* II 95.3.

1948 ---; ch. Heraclas; Aug 102; Oxyrhynchite?; Oxy.?; addr. for gs.; III 508.9.

1949 ---; ch. Theon; 116; Oxy.; addr. for dec. gs. Harthonis, hierotekton of Thoeris, Isis, Sarapis, and assoc. gods and enrolled in Thoeris St qtr; XII 1550.12-13.

1950 ---; s. of Theon, s. of Harthonis; m. Thermuthion, d. of Pausiris; sp. [Taps]ois(?); 116; hierotekton of Thoeris, Isis, Sarapis and assoc. gods; died in 116; enrolled in Thoeris St qtr; XII 1550.3-4, 11-12.

1951 ---; 131 or 132; property owner; Oxy.; III 584 (descr.) V.

1952 HARTHOONIS; ch. Hermaphilus; 18; *PSI* IV 320.4.

1953 ---; ch. Harsiesis; 54-68; Sko, U. Top.; addr. for gs. Harthoonis; *SB* X 10256.1.

1954 ---; s. of Harsiesis, s. of Harthoonis; 54-68; priest and prophet of Thoeris, Isis, Sarapis and assoc. gods; land-owner; Sko, U. Top.; *SB* X 10256.1.

1955 ---; s. of Pausiris; 54-68; farmer; rents land at Sko, U. Top.; *SB* X 10256.3.

1956 ---; 74; XIV 1661.1.

1957 ---; 77; stolistes of Thoeris, Isis, Sarapis and assoc. gods; Oxy.; buys property; II 242.6.

1958 ---; ch. Tausorapis; 77; Oxy.?; addr. for d.?; II 242.4.

1959 ---; s. of Eubulus; sp. Thaesis; ch. Cephalon; 77; Oxyrhynchite; Oxy.; II 242.26.

1960 ---; s. of Harthoonis; 77; priest; property owner; Oxy.; buys land in Hermaeum qtr; pays encychon; II 242.32.

1961 ---; ch. Harthoonis; 77; Oxy.?; addr. for s.; II 242.32.

1962 ---; ch. Thoonis; 83/84; Papsis, Tychis Necotis; addr. for gs. Harthoonis; II 290.15.

1963 ---; s. of Thoonis, s. of Harthoonis; 83/84; landholder; Papsis?, Tychis Necotis; holds land there; II 290.14.

1964 ---; ch. Thoonis; 98-117; Oxyrhynchite; Oxy.; addr. for gd. Sinthoonis; *P. Sel.* 24.3.

1965 ---; s. of Thoonis, s. of Harthoonis; m. Tausorapis, d. of Tao( ); 98-117; priest of Thoeris, Isis, Sarapis and assoc. gods; Oxyrhynchite; Oxy.; age 30; signalement; sister Sinthoonis priestess; *P. Sel.* 24.4.

1966 HARTHOO(NIS); early i; II 389 (descr.).

1967 HARTHOONIS; s. of Harthoonis; i; Oxyrhynchite; called "Nothus" (or a natural son?); *PSI* XIII 1356.2.

1968 ---; ch. Harthoonis; i; Oxyrhynchite; addr. for s.; *PSI* XIII 1356.2.

1969 ---; ch. [Har]paesis; i; Sesphtha?, W. Top.; addr. for s.; *P. Ryl.* II 199.14.

1970 ---; ch. Tecosis; 109; Oxyrhynchite?; Oxy.?; addr. for gs. Diogenes; III 482.25.

1971 ---; ch. Harthoonis; Oct 112; Oxyrhynchite?; Oxy.?; addr. for gs. Phatres and Peteuris; XXII 2351.1-2.

1972 ---; s. of Harthoonis; ch. Phatres, Peteuris; Oct 112; Oxyrhynchite; Oxy.?; addr. for s.; XXII 2351.1.

1973 ---; s. of Peteuris, s. of Harthoonis; Oct 112; landholder; lessor; Oxyrhynchite; Oxy.?; owns part of Kleros of Niceus nr Tanais; addr. for uncle Phatres; XXII 2351.12.

1974 ---; ch. Sir[ ]; 135/136; Talao?, L. Top.; doc. pr.?; addr. for gs. Horus; *P. Iand.* VII 136.10.

1975 ---; 148/149; Oxyrhynchite, gymnasial class; Oxy.; bro. Callias declares status; XLVI 3284.5.

1976 ---; ch. C. Theon; ii; Oxy.?; addr. for s.; *P. Mil.* 51.4-5.

1977 HARTHOSIS; sp. Apollo(?); ch. Cerdon; ii; Thoeris St qtr; *P. Princ.* II 46.15.

1978 HARTHOTES; i BC - i; *OD Pisa* 25 ii 19.

1979 ---; i BC - i; *OD Pisa* 70.2.

1980 ---; ch. Ghemapis; i BC - i; *OD Pisa* 755 Concavo X + 8.

1981 ---; s. of Ḥr-mn; i BC - i; *OD Pisa* 5 i X + 13.

1982 ---; s. of Sambathaeus; 31/32?; Sinary, L. Top.; *P. Mich. inv.* 69.8.

1983 ---; s. of Peteesis; i; *OD Pisa* 60 Convesso ii 6.

1984 HARTHOTHES; ch. Petarbebecis; Jan 100; Oxy.?; addr. for gss. Harthothes (2); I 46.6.

1985 ---; s. of Petarbebecis, s. of Harthothes; Jan 100; priest of Thoeris, Isis, Sarapis and assoc. gods; landholder; Palosis, Thmois. Top.; adopted s. of Ampendis; called the elder; land at P. in Kleros of Andronicus ceded to him by H. the younger; I 46.5.

1986 ---; s. of Petarbebecis, s. of Harthothes; Jan 100; priest of Thoeris, Isis, Sarapis and assoc. gods; landholder; sealer of sacred calves; Oxy.; land at Palosis, Thmois. Top., in Kleros of Andronicus ceded by him to Harthothes the elder; called the younger; I 46.14.

1987 HARYOTES; ch. Patumis; i BC - i; *OD Pisa* 126 i 8.

1988 HARYOTES; ch. Teos; i BC - i; *OD Pisa* 668.3.

1989 ---; Feb 32; prophet; XII 1480.1, V.

1990 ---; i; *OD Pisa* 129 X + 11.

1991 ---; ch. [...]psamous; i; Sesphtha?; addr. for s.; *P. Ryl.* II 199.16.

1992 [HAR]YOTES; s. of Petsiris; i; farmer; Sesphtha, W. Top.; *P. Ryl.* II 199.17.

1993 HARYOTES; s. of Monius; m. Thaesis; i - ii; age 31; *P. Harris* 72.30.

1994 HATERIS; 81-96; VI 984 R fin.

1995 HATRES; ch. Kmj; i BC - i; *OD Pisa* 58.9.

1996 ---; i BC - i; *OD Pisa* 377 Concavo 15.

1997 ---; s. of Apollonius; 14-37; Thmois. Top.?; addr. for unnamed s.; *P. Cornell* 54.6.

1998 ---; s. of Cheepheibis; 31/32; Sinary, L. Top.; *P. Mich. inv.* 69.15.

1999 ---; sp. Heraclous; ch. Hatres; 41-54; Oxyrhynchite?; Oxy.?; addr. for s.; XXXIV 2720.7.

2000 ---; s. of Hatres; m. Heraclous, d. of Amenneus; 41-54; property owner; Oxyrhynchite?; Oxy.; age c. 18; signalement; ex-owner of house in Sarapeum, St of Ax..; XXXIV 2720.7.

2001 ---; alias DIDYMUS; s. of Horus; July 85; sitologus; Senocomis, W. Top.; XXXVIII 2841.9.

2002 ---; m. Teraus alias Thaubastis, d. of Phatres; sp. Soeris; ch. Tnepheros, Hareotes; 96; Oxyrhynchite; Knights' Camp qtr; I 104.6.

2003 ---; 98/99; shepherd; Tholthis, L. Top.; pays poll tax; sh. for Diogenes at above addr.; *P. Köln* II 86.17.

2004 ---; i; farmer; Koba; VIII 1145.15.

2005 ---; s. of Petenuphis; i; farmer; Koba; VIII 1145.17.

2006 ---; s. of Cuphateus; Sept/Oct 110; farmer; lessee; III 575 (descr.) V.

2007 ---; s. of Dionysius; m. Eseremphis; 117-137; Sinkepha; unnamed ch.; *PSI* V 475.2.

2008 ---; ii; owes money to Heracleides and partners; III 532.1.

2009 ---; ii; tenant farmer (of Diogenis); XIV 1758.10-11.

2010 HECATON; s. of Xenon; ch. Sarapion; (1) c. 52/53, date of R; (2) 117-137; Oxyrhynchite?; Oxy.?; addr. for gs. Hecaton; (1) *PSI* IX 1029 V 9; (2) I 105.14.

2011 HECATON; s. of Sarapion, s. of Hecaton; (1) 98-137; (2) 117-137; Oxyrhynchite; Oxy.; witnesses will; (1) VI 968 (descr.); (2) I 105.14.

2012 HEL[ ]; i; slave; doc. pr. Oxy.?; *P. Mil. Vogl.* IV 235-236.

2013 HELEIS; ch. Totoes; 132/133; *PSI* I 53 i 14.

2014 HELENE; d. of Horion; sp. Epinicus; Sept 58; bro. Pasion dec., apprentices nephew Amoitas; *P. Mich.* III 171.3.

2015 ---; d. of [...]us; sp. [...]chas; ch. N[...]lus; i; Senepta?, M. Top.; doc. pr. Oxy.?; addr. for s.; *P. Harris* 138 i 4.

2016 ---; sp. Theon alias Apollonius; ch. Theon; 130; Oxyrhynchite?; Oxy.?; addr. for gs. Theon; III 492.8.

2017 ---; ii; doc. pr. Oxy.?; greeted in letter to Horion; *SB* VI 9025.29.

2018 ---; ii; sent greetings by Publius; XLI 2981.24.

2019 HELENUS; 2 BC; IV 743.22-23.

2020 HELIODORA; ch. Helidora; April 77; II 263.6.

2021 ---; m. Helidora; sp. Apollonius; April 77; slave owner (Sarapous); II 263.5.

2022 HELIODORUS; ch. Heliodorus; 30/29 BC; Oxy.; addr. for s.; XII 1453.12.

2023 ---; s. of Heliodorus; 30/29 BC; temple overseer w. Heliodorus in Oxy. and Cynopolite nomes; Oxy.; XII 1453.11.

2024 ---; s. of Ptolemaeus; 30/29 BC; temple overseer in Oxy. and Cynopolite nomes; Oxy.; XII 1453.12.

2025 ---; 23; II 259.25.

2026 ---; s. of Ariston, s. of Ariston; m. Tryphaena; end i; Oxyrhynchite; Oxy.; buys slave for Potamon; *P. Sel.* 23.11.

2027 ---; i. Oxy.?; doc. pr. Oxy.?; age c. 35; signalement; *P. Ryl.* II 156.35.

2028 ---; ch. Straton; Oct 108; Oxyrhynchite; Oxy.; addr. for s.; XXXVIII 2874.1.

2029 ---; s. of Apollonius; sp. Thais; ch. Apollonius; Nov 129; Oxyrhynchite?; Oxy.?; addr. for s.; VII 1024.14.

2030 ---; sp. -pserois; ch. Dionysius; 132/133; *PSI* I 53 i 4.

2031 ---; sp. Ptollous; ch. Cleopatra; 132/133; *PSI* I 53 i 7.

2032 ---; s. of Antonius; sp. Didyme; 132/133; unnamed d., age 20; *PSI* I 53 i 10.

2033 HELIODORUS; s. of Heliodorus; 132/133; unnamed d.; *PSI* I 53 i 15, 24.

2034 ---; ch. Heliodorus; 132/133; *PSI* I 53 i 15, 24.

2035 ---; gf. of Heliodorus; 132/133; *PSI* I 53 i 25.

2036 ---; gs. of Heliodorus; 132/133; *PSI* I 53 i 24.

2037 ---; s. of Demetrius; ch. Demetrius; early ii; Oxyrhynchite?; Oxy.?; addr. for s.; *P. Wisc.* I 13.14.

2038 HELLENIS; d. of Pausirion; m. [...]n, d. of Leon; i; landholder; Oxyrhynchite; doc. pr. Oxy.?; under age; land at Peeno ceded to her; *P. Harris* 138 i 15.

2039]HEMẸ.[....]; sp. Theon; ch. Mnesitheus; after 102; Oxy.; addr. for gd.; III 636.22.

2040 HENIOCHUS; ch. Tauris; Aug 72(?); Oxyrhynchite?; Oxy.?; addr. for gs. Aristion; XLI 2972.6.

2041 ---; s. of Promachus; s. of Aristion; m. Tauris, d. of Heniochus; Aug 72 (?); property owner; Oxyrhynchite?; Nemerae?, M. Top.; owns property in Nemerae; father Oxy.; bros. Aristion and Amyntas; XLI 2972.25.

2042 HEPHAESTION; ch. Heracleides; Feb 91; Oxyrhynchite?; Oxy.?; addr. for gd. Zenarion; XLI 2957.4.

2043 ---; ch. Theon; 122/123; III 592 (descr.) V 3.

2044 ---; 122/123?; secretary to str. Philonicus; "brother"? of Didymus and Phabanon; *P. Wisc.* 73.1, 24.

2045 ---; 137; III 625 (descr.).

2046 ---; alias SARAPION; ii; notary; XXXIV 2726.2-3.

2047 HERA( ); ch. Apol( ); Nov 42 BC; Oxy.?; addr. for s.; *P. Ryl.* IV 582.22.

2048 HERACL[ ]; ch. Hermogenes; Feb 32; XII 1480 V.

2049 ---; i - ii; bibliophylax? w. Athenaeus alias Apollonius; *PSI* VIII 731.1.

2050 JULIA HERACLA; sp. Pausanias alias Dionysius; ch. Gaia alias Sarapias; 95; catoecic landholder; Roman; Oxy.; land at Seryphis in Kleros of Nicandrus; II 273.4.

2051 HERACLAMMON; sp. Tamochus; ch. Papontos; i - ii; *P. Harris* 72.1.

2052 ---; sp. Cyrilla?; ii; slave owner?; unnamed daughters?; XXXVIII 2860.1.

2053 HERACLAS; ch. Archelaus; 41-79; XLII 3061.1.

2054 ---; (1) 49; (2) 49/50; boy foundling, dead; (1) I 37.7-8; (2) 38.7.

2055 HERACLAS; s. (or gs.) of Eudaemon; 55-68; writes for Plution; *P. Ross Georg.* II 13.14.

2056 ---; s. of Antiphanes; sp. Ammonarion; ch. Ophelous, Antiphanes; (1) 58; (2) May/June 59; (3) June/July 59; (4) July 60; property owner; Oxyrhynchite; Oxy.; dec.; addr. for s.; (1) II 268.3, 9; (2) 318.3; (3) 306.5; (4) 260.8.

2057 ---; ch. Taseus, S....; March 66; XLI 2971.1-2.

2058 ---; s. of Apollo..[.]; m. Taseus, d. of Heraclas; March 66; apprentice weaver; not of age; XLI 2971.6.

2059 ---; April 71; grammateus; sec. of Sirion; called "Ischas"; XXXIV 2725.6.

---; see [PA]NISCUS.

2060 ---; s. of Tryphon; m. Taonnophris, d. of Panesies; 91 or 107; Oxyrhynchite; Oxy.; signalement; pays ransom for slave Apollonous; IV 722.21.

2061 ---; 95; superintendent of land distrib.; I 45.1, 18.

2062 ---; s. of Hermogenes; sp. Senaias; ch. Ammonis; 2nd half i; Sinary?, L. Top.; addr. for s.; XXXVIII 2846.1.

2063 ---; 2nd half i; wine press operator?; VI 985 (descr.).

2064 ---; late i; slave of Nilus(?) and Theon; XVIII 2190.41.

2065 ---; i; messenger, agent from Alex. for Apollonius, s. of Apollonius; VIII 1153.3.

2066 ---; i; boatman; VIII 1153.7.

2067 ---; s. of Harthonis; sp. Demetrous; ch. Heraclas; Aug 102; Oxyrhynchite?; Oxy.?; addr. for s.; III 508.8.

2068 ---; s. of Heraclas, s. of Harthonis; m. Demetrous; Aug 102; Oxyrhynchite; Oxy.; lends to Diocles and Rufus, sons of Diocles; III 508.8.

---; see HARMIYSIS.

2069 ---; s. of Pausirion; sp. Taamois; c. 110-112; property owner; Oxyrhynchite; Oxy.; XXXVI 2758.2.

2070 ---; Oct 111; formerly of Ti. Julius Theon, ex-hypom. and gym., now of Ti. Julius Theon, ex-strategus and archidikast; XLIV 3197.7.

2071 ---; alias HERACLEIDES; s. of Heraclas; (1) Nov 129; (2) 136; landholder; lessor; sitologus (1); Oxyrhynchite; Pakerke, E. Top.; leases to Diogenes, s. of Heracleides; (1) VII 1024.2; (2) XII 1472.2.

2072 ---; ch. Heraclas alias Heracleides; 136; Oxyrhynchite; Oxy.?; addr. for s.; XII 1472.2.

2073 ---; s. of Potammon; mid ii; farmer; XLIV 3165.1.

2074 HERACLAS; ch. Luci(u)s; ii?; s. holds land nr Nesla and Korobis; *P. Inst. Fran.* III 15.9.

2075 ---; ii; doc. pr. Oxy.?; *P. Mich. inv.* 3799.10.

---; see SARAPION.

2076 HERACLEIA; d. of Heracleides; 56; Alex.; Alexandria?; transfers debt to Papontos; II 271.3.

2077 ---; d. of Epimachus; sp. Pausiris; ch. Epimachus; Sept 66; Psobthis, L. Top.; addr. for s.; II 239.3.

2078 ---; 126; Heracleopolis; rents property in Sesphtha; may be same as Heracleia, d. of Onias in l. 16; has unnamed ch.; *P. Harris* 142.13.

2079 ---; d. of Onias; 126; Heracleopolis?; unnamed s.; may own land in Sesphtha, M. Top.; *P. Harris* 142.16.

2080 CLAUDIA HERACLEIA; alias ARSINOE; 136; heiress; *P. Inst. Fran.* III 18.7, 11.

2081 HERACLEIA; sp. Heracleides; ch. Thaisous alias Thaesis; early ii; Heracleopolis; addr. for d.; III 504.34.

2082 HERACLEIDES; s. of Nicias; i BC; landholder; Psobthis, M. Top.; doc. pr. Oxy.?; has bros.; *P. Ryl.* IV 579.2.

2083 ---; 73 or 44 BC; banker (private); Sarapeum; XIV 1639.5.

2084 ---; s. of ....]ius; 54/53 BC; lessee of land nr Seryphis, Kleros of Alexandrus, from Asclepiades; *PSI* X 1097.1.

2085 ---; s. of Totoes; 30/29 BC; templelighter; Oxy.; lampl. of Temple of Sarapis and Isieum; XII 1453.2.

2086 ---; s. of Tlep[olemus?]; 30 BC - 14; *P. Rein.* II. 99.11.

2087 ---; Oct/Nov 21 BC; basilicogrammateus; *P. Vindob. Worp* 2.1.

2088 ---; Aug 7 BC; grammateus?; Oxy.; ? same as Heras; *P. Ryl.* IV 603.1.

2089 ---; ch. Berenice; 5/4 BC; d. has land in W. Top.; *P. Oslo* II 26.[25].

2090 ---; ch. Leon; 5/4 BC; W. Top.; addr. for s.; *P. Oslo* III 26.4.

2091 ---; ch. Didymus; 13; s. applies to buy wood at Kerkeura and Peeno, M. Top.; IX 1188.3, 14 and passim.

2092 ---; (1) Sept 16; (2) 16/17; basilicogrammateus of Oxy. and Cynopolite nomes; Oxy.?; (1) IV 746.1 and V; (2) *P. Ryl.* IV 675.1.

2093 ---; c. 25; "brother" of Theon; II 292.3.

2094 ---; s. of Theon; May 26; writes for Taseus and Petsiris; *P. Rein.* II 103.35-36 and *P. Ryl.* II 178.

2095 HERACLEIDES; July 27; Oxy.; XVII 2148.8.

2096 ---; July 27; Oxy.; XVII 2148.V.

2097 ---; ch. Demetrous; 30-35; Oxyrhynchite?; Oxy.?; addr. for d.; II 282.5-6.

2098 ---; s. of Charitesius; ch. Heracleides (sometimes called ...tis); 33/34; Se[pho, Thmois. Top.; addr. for s.; II 354 (descr.).

2099 ---; s. of Heracleides, s. of Charitesius; 33/34; livestock owner; Se[pho, Thmois. Top.; sometimes called ...tis; II 354 (descr.).

2100 ---; ch. Sarapion alias Didymus; 43/44; II 368.1.

2101 ---; Aug 50; eclemptor, imperial estate; ousia of Tiberius Claudius Caesar; XXXVIII 2837.1.

2102 ---; June 52; agent of agoranomus Epimachus; *SB* I 8034.37.

2103 ---; s. of Dionysius; 54; writes for Ammonius, s. of Ammonius; II 264.17-18.

2104 ---; ch. Heracleia; 56; Alex.; Alexandria?; addr. for d.; II 271.3.

2105 ---; s. of Petosorapis; Mar/Apr 66; brass beater; Egzoeu qtr; Petechon his apprentice; *PSI* VIII 871.13.

2106 ---; s. of Apion, s. of Herodes; (1) 70; (2) 79/80; farmer; slave owner; lessee of land nr Senocomis; Oxyrhynchite; Oxy.; death of slave Amarantos decl. by bro. Herodes; (1) XXII 2349.6; (2) *P. Oxy. inv.* 20.3B.34/B.6.

2107 ---; 74; dioecetes (local?); XIV 1661.1.

2108 ---; ch. Thermuthion; (1) 77-83; (2) 89; (1) I 170.11-12; (2) *P. Fouad* 48.5.

2109 ---; s. of Philoxenus; March 79; property owner; Oxy.?; land in Hermaeum qtr; II 243.19.

2110 ---; sp. (?) Sarapous; 81-96; IV 795 (descr.).

2111 ---; ch. Heracleides; 82; may be non-Oxy.; II 286.26-27.

2112 ---; s. of Heracleides; 82; agent for ch. of Thaesis; may be non-Oxy.; II 286.26.

2113 ---; ch. Heras; Nov 83; Oxyrhynchite?; Oxy.?; addr. for gd. Thnas; X 1282.6.

2114 ---; 83; bibliophylax; *P. Fam. Teb.* 15.99.

2115 ---; ch. Dioscorus; 83/84; Alex., Zeneius?; Sinary, L. Top.; addr. for gd. Heraisce(?); XII 1462.5.

2116 ---; ch. Heracleides; 83/84; Tychis Necotis; addr. for s.; II 290.28.

2117 HERACLEIDES; s. of Heracleides; 83/84; landholder; Tychis Necotis; holds land there; II 290.28.

2118 T. FLAVIUS HERACLEIDES; (1) 86-88; (2) 87/88; (3) 88/89; strategus; Roman; Oxy.; (1) *PSI* XII 1235.1; (2) *Coll. Pap.* I 22; (3) XLV iv 3240.10.

2119 ---; s. of Gaius, s. of Peros; m. Thermuthion, d. of Heracleides; sp. Thaisous; 89; hamlet of Vestinus?; borrows from bro. Gaius; *P. Fouad* 48.5-6.

---; see DIOGENES.

2120 ---; s. of Diogenes alias Heracleides; m. Tausiris alias Thallous; ch. Saraeus; 89-97; slave owner; Oxy.?; addr. for gd. (mat.) Dionysia and Herais; has freedman; II 274.13, 48.

2121 ---; s. of Hephaestion; ch. Zenarion; Feb 91; Oxyrhynchite?; Temgenuthis qtr; addr. for d.; XLI 2957.3.

2122 ---; s. of Heracleides, s. of Ptolemaeus; m. Diogenis, d. of Sarapị( ); 92; farmer; lessee (ousia of Anticrates and Sostratus); Oxyrhynchite; Oxy.; has land at Psobthis; signalement; XVIII 2185.7.

2123 ---; s. of Ptolemaeus; sp. Diogenis; ch. Heracleides; 92; Oxyrhynchite?; Oxy.?; addr. for s.; XVIII 2185.7.

2124 ---; ch. Claudius; 93; Protar( )?; addr. for s.; *P. Princ.* II 42 R 4.

2125 ---; s. of Dionysius; 93; landholder; Enteiis; *P. Princ.* II 42 R 5.

2126 ---; ch. Heracleides; 94; Oxyrhynchite; Oxy.; addr. for gs. Heras; II 270.4.

2127 ---; s. of Heracleides; sp. Plutarche; ch. Heras; 94; Oxyrhynchite; Oxy.; addr. for s.; II 270.4.

2128 ---; ch. Sarapion; 94; Oxyrhynchite; Oxy.; addr. for gs. Sarapion alias Clarus; II 270.6.

2129 ---; s. of Apollonius, s. of Chaeremon; m. Herais, d. of Didymus; 94; Oxyrhynchite; Oxy.; II 270.10.

2130 ---; s. of Sarapion?, s. of Theon; ch. Diogenes; 97; landholder; Oxy.?; doc. pr. Oxy.?; doc. date 197/198; gs. holds palmgrove in Ars(P); *P. Bour.* 16.6.[10].

2131 ---; 98-117; agoranomus w. Alexandrus, Theon etc.; Oxy.; *P. Sel.* 24.10.

2132 ---; s. of Heracleides; ch. Polydeuces; 99; Oxyrhynchite?; Oxy.?; addr. for s.; *P. Harris* 74.8.

2133 ---; ch. Heracleides; 99; Oxyrhynchite?; Oxy.?; addr. for gs. Polydeuces; *P. Harris* 74.8.

2134 ---; sp. Ammonarion alias Theopompion; ch. Theopompion; end i; Oxyrhynchite; Oxy.; addr. for d.; *P. Sel.* 23.5.

2135 HERACLEIDES; ch. Theon; end i; Alex., Propapposebasteius, Althaieus; tribe and deme for gs. Diogenes; *P. Sel.* 23.13.

2136 ---; s. of Dion(ysius); i; farmer; Sesphtha, W. Top.; *P. Ryl.* II 199.7.

2137 ---; i; II 296.1.

2138 ---; i - ii; clerk (in merchant's office?); *P. Harris* 96.5.

2139 ---; s. of Epicrates; 100/101 or 119/120; age 68; bro. on m.'s side to Epicrates alias Apion; III 504.53.

2140 ---; s. of Olympus; sp. Heracleia; ch. Thaisous alias Thaesis; 100/101 or 119/120; Heracleopolis; addr. for d., adoptive m. of Aphroditous alias Demarous of Oxy.; III 504.5.

2141 ---; ch. Epicrates; 100/101 or 119/120; Oxyrhynchite?; Oxy.?; addr. for g.gd. Aphroditous alias Demarous; III 504.4.

2142 ---; ch. Apollos; c. 110-112; Oxyrhynchite?; Oxy.?; addr. for s.; XXXVI 2758.6.

2143 ---; c. 115; slave owner; Alex.(?); Alexandria?; has freedman Demarion; IV 706.2, 10.

2144 ---; ch. [ ]os; 117; Oxyrhynchite?; Oxy.?; addr. for gs.; III 489.29.

2145 ---; s. of Ptolemaeus; ch. Ammonis; 117; Oxy.; addr. for s.; III 489.25.

2146 ---; alias VALERIUS; c. 117/118; Ars (P.); appt. episkeptes of Oxy. by Apollonides, str. Ars (P.); *P. Fam. Teb.* 18.3-4.

2147 ---; s. of Horion; 117-138; I 188 (descr.).

2148 ---; s. of Sarapion; sp. Aline; ch. Theon; Aug 123; Parkerke?, E. Top.; addr. for s.; XXXVIII 2864.1.

2149 ---; 126; Heracleopolis; f.-in-law of Heracleia, d. of Onias; *P. Harris* 142.14.

2150 ---; alias THEON; s. of Machon; 129; slave owner; Alex., Sosicosmius, Althaieus; Oxy.; I 95.14.

2151 ---; s. of Antias; 130; landholder; lessor; of land nr Senepta or Sink(e)pha to Horus and Ptollas; III 517.7.

2152 ---; sp. Berenice; ch. Ision; Aug 133; Oxyrhynchite; Oxy.; *P. Köln* II 100.12-13.

2153 ---; s. of Apion, s. of Apion; Aug 133; Oxyrhynchite; Oxy.; signs will of Taarpaesis; seal is an Ibis; *P. Köln* II 100. 32.

2154 ---; 134; sitologus; Sinkepha; s. of Sinkepha distr.; III 575.2.

2155 HERACLEIDES; ch. Heracleides; Sept 135; Psobthis, E. Top.; doc. pr. Oxy.?; addr. for s.; *P. Stras.* 127.1.

2156 ---; s. of Heracleides; Sept 135; Psobthis, E. Top.; doc. pr. Oxy.?; pays grain to Diogenis; *P. Stras.* 127.1.

2157 ---; ch. Diogenis; Sept 135; Psobthis, E. Top.; doc. pr. Oxy.?; addr. for s.; *P. Stras.* 127.7.

2158 ---; ch. Pasion; 135/136; Alex.?, Althaieus?; Talao, L. Top.; doc. pr. Oxy.?; citizenship for s.; *P. Iand.* VII 136.11.

2159 HERACLEI(DES?); ch. Pen; 135/136; L. Top.; addr. for s.; *P. Iand.* VII 136.14.

2160 HERACLEIDES; s. of Mincion; ch. Diogenes; 136; Oxyrhynchite; Oxy.; addr. for s.; XII 1472.15.

2161 ---; ch. Theon; 138-161; Oxyrhynchite?; Oxy.?; addr. for gd. Tseei; IV 723.2.

2162 ---; ch. Demetria alias Asclatarion; 148/149; Oxyrhynchite, gymnasial class; 10th qtr; addr. for d.'s son, Sarapion; XLVI 3284.4.

2163 ---; early ii; XII 1481.7-8.

2164 ---; ch. Leonas; mid ii; Oxy.?; addr. for s.; *P. Stras.* 184.1.

2165 ---; ii; merchant?; doc. pr. Oxy.?; writes to Horion; *SB* VI 9025.1.

2166 ---; ii; greeted by Apollonia; XXXI 2593.2.

2167 ---; ii; "brother" of Demetrius; III 582 (descr.).

2168 ---; ii; has partners; owed money by Hatres; III 532.1.

2169 ---; ii; grammateus of str. of Oasis of Thebaid; *P. Cair. Preis.* 48.1.

2170 ---; ii; Oxy.; unnamed s.; greeted by Apia; XII 1581.15-16.

2171 ---; s. of Ammonius; ii; I 113.[1], 32.

2172 ---; ii; Oxy.; owner(?) of nomographeion; XXXIV 2726.27.

2173 ---; sp. Tbecis; ii; *P. Inst. Fran.* III 5.16.

2174 HERACLEID[ES; ii?; Pela, W. Top.; *P. Fuad I Univ.* 32.15.

2175 HERACLEIDES; n.d.; *SB* I 1938(d).

---; see HERACLAS.

2176 HERACLEIDION; Oct 111; slave; formerly of Ti. Julius Theon, ex-hypom. and gym., now of his s., Ti. Julius Theon, ex-strategus and archidikast; XLIV 3197.7.

2177 HERACLEIUS; s. of Soterichus; sp. Thermutharion; (1) Jan 17; (2) 20; miller?; property owner; Oxy.?; illiterate; Dius writes for him; leased mill from Isidorus; Persian of Epigone; (1) II 278.2; (2) 305.1.

2178 ---; s. of Horus; Dec 20/Jan 21; Sinary, L. Top.; writes for Harpaesis, s. of Panrymis; X 1281.11.

2179 ---; s. of Apion; Jan 26; livestock owner; Pela?, W. Top.; II 245.3.

2180 ---; ch. Thaesis, Thaesis; 48; *P. Fouad* 35.2.

2181 ---; ch. Harmiysis; July 60; Syron Kome, W. Top.; addr. for s.; XXXVIII 2851.4.

2182 ---; 66; II 272.14.

2183 CLAUDIUS HERACLEIUS; (1) Sept 77; (2) 80/81; strategus; Roman; Oxy.; (1) II 276.15; (2) *Coll. Pap.* II 21.7-8.

2184 ---; ch. Phribis; Sept 77; Dermeithae?, U. Top.; addr. for s.; II 276.10.

2185 ---; ch. Ptolemaeus, Senonnophris; 81-96; Oxy.; gs. Heracles of gymnasial class; VI 984 R init.

2186 ---; s. of Hierax; 81-96; owner of an enclosure?; VI 984 R (1).

2187 ---; ch. Diogas; Nov 82; Oxy.?; doc. pr. Oxy.?; addr. for s.; XXXVI 2773.5.

2188 ---; ch. Dionysius; 90; Teis?, Thmois. Top.; addr. for gs. Plution; *P. Ryl.* IV 597.3.

2189 ---; alias MATREUS; ch. Matrina; Oct 123; Oxyrhynchite?; Oxy.?; addr. for d.; VI 898.5.

2190 ---; s. of Sarapion; sp. Chenamu[nis?]; 126; Sesphtha?, L. Top.; doc. pr. Oxy.?; addr. for unnamed s.; *P. Harris* 142.3.

2191 ---; ch. Horus; 131; Talao?, L. Top.; addr. for gs. Horus; *SB* VI 9190.5.

2192 ---; ch. Chaeremon; 132/133; *PSI* I 53 x 170.

2193 ---; ch. Heracleius; c. 135; may not be an Oxy.; XVII 2111 i 20.

2194 ---; s. of Heracleius; c. 135; property owner w. s. of Diophantus; may not be an Oxy.; XVII 2111 i 20.

2195 ---; sp. Berous; ch. Apollos, Apollos, Mysthas?, Heracles?, Nemion; i - ii; *P. Harris* 72.6, 8.

2196 ---; sp. Tamochus; ch. Pylades; i - ii; *P. Harris* 72.21.

2197 ---; sp. Demetria; ch. Theon; i - ii; *P. Harris* 72.33.

2198 ---; sp. Thaesis; ch. Cephalon; ii; Talao, L. Top.; addr. for s.; XXXI 2573.2.

2199 HERACLEIUS; s. of Diophantus; ch. Diophantus, Horion (adopted); ii; landholder; farmer; lessor; Oxyrhynchite; Oxy.; land at Schoibis; addr. for s.; XXXI 2583.1.

2200 HERACLEODORUS; ch. Heracleodorus; 81-96; addr. for gs. Hierax; VI 984 R (3).

2201 ---; s. of Heracleodorus; sp. Apollonia; ch. Hierax; 81-96; addr. for s.; VI 984 R (3).

2202 HERACLES; ch. Xenon; c. 1; IV 785 (descr.).

2203 ---; ch. Heracles; 31/32; Sinary, L. Top.; addr. for s.; *P. Mich. inv.* 69.5.

2204 ---; s. of Heracles; 31/32 Sinary, L. Top.; *P. Mich. inv.* 69.5.

2205 ---; ch. Hermogenes; 31/32; Sinary, L. Top.; addr. for s.; *P. Mich. inv.* 69.11.

2206 ---; alias THOONIS; July 64; Oxy.; *P. Yale* 63.18.

2207 ---; s. of Ptolemaeus, s. of Heracleius; m. Senphois the elder, d. of Lycus; 81-96; member of gymnasial class; blackskinned; minor, aged 10+; Eudaemon makes decl. for him; VI 984 R init.

2208 ---; s. of Ptolemaeus; Nov 82; weaver?; Oxyrhynchite?; Oxy.?; bro. of Ptollas; Persian of Epigone; XXXVI 2773.1.

2209 ---; s. of Harpaesis; i; farmer; Koba; VIII 1145.13.

2210 ---; s. of Horus; m. Tammotus; ch. Heracles; i - ii; age 49; *P. Harris* 72.22.

2211 ---; s. of Apollonius; m. Taareotis; sp. Glauce; ch. Heracles; i - ii; age 44; *P. Harris* 72.28.

2212 ---; s. of Heracles, s. of Horus; gs. of Tammotus; i - ii; age 17; *P. Harris* 72.23.

2213 ---; s. of Heracleus?; m. Berous; i - ii; age 26; *P. Harris* 72.10.

2214 ---; s. of Apollos, s. of Heracleus; m. Tamystha; gs. of Berous; i - ii; age 15; *P. Harris* 72.7.

2215 ---; s. of Heracles, s. of Apollonius; m. Glauce; gs. of Taareotis; i - ii; age 15; *P. Harris* 72.29.

2216 ---; alias APION; s. of Apion; 117; Oxy.; writes will for Dionysius; age 37; signalement; III 489.20.

2217 ---; ii (year 20); archephodus; I 167 (descr.).

2218 ---; s. of Sarapas; ch. Sarapas, Petosarapis; early ii; Oxy.; III 649 (descr.).

2219 HERACLOUS; d. of Amenneus; sp. Hatres; ch. Hatres; 41-54; Oxyrhynchite?; Oxy.; addr. for s.; sister of Thais; XXXIV 2720.7.

2220 HERACLOUS; sp. Dionysius; ch. Diogenes; Jan 90; Oxy.; *PSI* VIII 942.4.

2221 ---; ch. Sarapion; June 91; Oxy.; X 1317 (descr.).

2222 ---; d. of Sarapion, s. of Sarapion; m. Tausiris alias Sarapous; sp. Sarapion; ch. Horion alias Theon, Thais; (1) 127; (2) 130; Oxyrhynchite?; Ibion Ammonii?, L. Top.; addr. for s.; d. is gm. of bride Thais; (1) III 496.5; (2) 492.3.

2223 ---; sp. Pecysis; ch. Syrus; ii; *P. Erl.* 44 iii 32.

2224 HERADION; c. 129; XII 1420.6.

2225 HERAIS; d. of Pausiris, s. of Sarapion; m. Saraeus, d. of Heracleides; 89-97; Knights' Camp qtr; sister of Dionysia; II 274.33.

2226 ---; d. of Didymus; sp. Apollonius; ch. Heracleides; 94; Oxyrhynchite; Oxy.; addr. for s.; II 270.11.

2227 ---; d. of Peteuris, s. of Sarapion; 122/123; Oxyrhynchite; (1) *SB* XII 10781.6; (2) III 592 (descr.) R 6.

2228 ---; 127; slave; Oxy.; bought from Isarion; *P. Bour.* 16.16.

2229 ---; sp. Callias; ch. Amois; 129; Oxyrhynchite?; Oxy.?; addr. for s.; *P. Cornell* 46.4.

2230 ---; d. of Teos; Aug 133; former property owner; Oxy.; her half house in North St qtr now owned by Taarpaesis; *P. Köln* II 100.12.

2231 ---; ch. Diogenes; Aug 133; Oxyrhynchite; s. witnesses will; *P. Köln* II 100.31.

2232 HERAIS[CE(?); d. of Dioscorus, s. of Heracleides; 83/84; catoecic landholder; Alex., Zeneius; Sinary, L. Top.; land there; bro. is guardian; under age; XII 1462.9-10.

2233 HERAS; Aug 7 BC; grammateus of Dioscurides, b.g.; same as Heracleides?; *P. Ryl.* IV 603 V.

2234 ---; ch. Athenaeus; 21; *SB* XII 10794.2.

2235 ---; s. of Onnophris; July 44; agent; Pela, W. Top.; agent for Ar..., d. of Phatres (Pela); XII 1447.4.

2236 ---; ch. Besarion, Ammonarion (step-d.); 58; Ptolemais Hermiu?; addr. for s.; II 268.4.

2237 ---; d. of Heracleides; sp. Petosorapis; ch. Thnas, Tecosis; Nov 83; Oxyrhynchite?; Oxy.?; addr. for d.; X 1282.5-6.

2238 ---; July 85; sitologus w. associates; Senocomis, W. Top.; XXXVIII 2841.4.

2239 ---; s. of Harmiysis, s. of Mylon; 87/88; Syron Kome; lessee of flooded land nr Nesla; *P. Princ.* III 147.4.

2240 ---; s. of Heracleides. s. of Heracleides; m. Plutarche, d. of Sarapion; 94; Oxyrhynchite?; Oxy.?; guardian of 2nd cousin Lucia alias Thaisas; II 270.4.

2241 HERAS; sp. Tnepheros; ch. Heras; 99; Oxyrhynchite?; Sarapis St qtr; addr. for s.; III 481.13.

2242 ---; s. of Heras; m. Tnepheros; ch. Heras; 99; property owner; Oxyrhynchite; Sarapis St qtr; died before reg. in 90; III 481.12.

2243 ---; s. of Heras; sp. Tha[esis?]; ch. [Heras]; 99; Oxy.; addr. for unnamed s.; *P. Princ.* II 32.1.

2244 ---; ch. Heras; 99; Oxy.; address for unnamed gs.; *P. Princ.* II 32.1.

2245 ---; s. of Heras, s. of Heras; gs. of Tnepheros; 99; property owner; Oxyrhynchite; Sarapis St qtr; illiterate; III 481.22.

2246 ---; ch. Zenas; (1) c. 107-112; (2) 117-137; (3) i - ii; Oxyrhynchite?; Heracles Place qtr; addr. for gs. Zenas; Heras alias Gaius another gs; (1) *PSI* V 450 R i 23; (2) I 105.18; (3) *PSI* VII 731.6.

2247 ---; alias GAIUS; s. of Zenas, s. of Heras; m. Areia; (1) c. 107-112; (2) 117-137; (3) 130; Oxyrhynchite; Oxy.; signalement; witnesses will; age 45, father's name Cinas (3); (1) *PSI* V 450 R i 23; (2) I 105.18; (3) III 492.20.

2248 ---; s. of Pausirion, s. of Pausiris; m. Teteuris; Sept 109; Psobthis, M. Top.; leases olive press from Sarapion and bro. Exagon; *PSI* IX 1030.2.

2249 ---; s. of Aperos; ch. Heras; 117-138; Oxyrhynchite?; Oxy.?; addr. for s.; I 178.1.

2250 ---; s. of Heras, s. of Aperos; 117-138; Oxyrhynchite; Oxy.; I 178.1.

2251 ---; c. 122/123; grammateus; of Julius Theon, gymnasiarch, for holdings in Phoboou distr., E. Top.; XXXVIII 2865.1.

2252 ---; m. Didous; sp. Eudaemon; ch. Sarapion; 127; Oxyrhynchite?; Oxy.?; addr. for s. being married; III 496.2.

2253 ---; s. of Horus, s. of Horus; m. Taamois; 132/133; tutor w. Onnophris to Anteis and Taamois; *PSI* VIII 874 i 3.

2254 ---; s. of Dropides; m. Tecosis; 137; Oxyrhynchite; guardian to Tsintotoes, d. of Apollonius; *PSI* XII 1262 iii 1.

2255 ---; s. of Pnepheros; sp. Thatres; ch. Pnepheros; 148/149; Oxyrhynchite, gymnasial class; Oxy.; addr. for s.; XLVI 3280.1.

2256 ---; d. of Amois; sp. Pet[euri]s(?); ch. Ammonius; 148/149; Oxyrhynchite, gymnasial class; Upper Camp qtr; addr. for sp.; XLVI 3276.7.

2257 HERAS; s. of Tryphon; ii; landholder; Ibiotapheum qtr; *P. Princ.* II 46.14.

2258 ---; sp. Horion; ch. Asclas; ii; Gymnasium St qtr; addr. for s.; *P. Princ.* II 46.12.

2259 ---; ii; has family; III 530.27.

HERENNIUS; see L. HERENNIUS CRISPUS.

2260 HERIEUS; April 5 BC; *OD Pisa* 936 Convesso 4.

2261 ---; ch. Petesis; i BC - i; *OD Pisa* 127.5.

2262 ---; ch. Harchonsis; i BC - i; *OD Pisa* 99 i 10.

2263 ---; ch. Pausiris; i BC - i; *OD Pisa* 8.11.

2264 ---; ch. Herieus; i BC - i; *OD Pisa* 510 + 568 Concavo i X + 11.

2265 ---; s. of Herieus; i BC - i; *OD Pisa* 510 + 568 Concavo i X + 11.

2266 ---; Aug 3; workman; *OD Pisa* 473 Convesso 6.

2267 ---; ch. Dd; Sept 6; *OD Pisa* 814.6 Convesso 3.

2268 HERIUBASTIS; ch. Patus; July 7; *OD Pisa* 1131 Concavo 7.

2269 HERM[......; Oct 111; slave; formerly of Ti. Julius Theon, now of his son Ti. Julius Sarapion; Arsinoite; XLIV 3197.11.

HERMAEON; see HERMAEUS.

HERMAEUS; see DIOGENES.

2270 ---; s. of Petsiris; m. Athenarous, d. of Eunomus; Sept 103; Oxyrhynchite; Oxy.; guardian of m.; m. from Toka; XLI 2973.4.

2271 ---; alias HERMAEON; s. of Dionysius, s. of Chaeremon; m. Theolympion, d. of Neoptolemus; 117; banker; Oxyrhynchite; Oxy.; *P. Harris* 85.4.

2272 ---; ch. Hermaeus alias Anubion; 135; Hermopolis Magna?; addr. for s. attending court in Oxy.; IX 1195.3.

2273 ---; alias ANUBION; s. of Hermaeus; 135; Hermopolis Magna; Hermaeus, the other party in the case, an Oxyrhynchite; IX 1195.3.

2274 ---; s. of Apollonides, s. of [Anubi]on?; 135; Oxy.?; IX 1195.9.

2275 HERMAPHILUS; s. of Harthoonis; March 18; landowner; land in Kleros of Philon nr Kerkemunis, U. Top., ceded to him and Didymus by Aristopous; *PSI* IV 320.4.

2276 HERMAS; c. 30; X 1292.9.

2277 HERMAS; ch. Hermas, Papontos; 98-117; Oxyrhynchite; *SB* XII i 10946.2.

2278 ---; s. of Hermas; ch. Hermes; 98-117; Oxyrhynchite; apprentices s. to bro. Papontos; *SB* XII i 10946.[1], 3.

2279 ---; 2nd half i; wineseller; VI 985 (descr.).

2280 ---; s. of Theon; 118; Oxyrhynchite?; Oxy.; guardian of Sepsarion, d. of Epimachus; III 503.5.

2281 ---; s. of Tarutillius; 119-120; landholder; farmer; land at Monimu, U. Top., and Sinary, L. Top.; *P. Wisc.* II 39.3.

2282 HERMATOIS; ii; bro. of Apion; III 530.25.

2283 HERME[....]; s. of Ischyrion; Feb 91; Oxyrhynchite?; Oxy.?; guardian of m.-in-law, Zenarion; XLI 2957.6.

2284 HERMES; s. of *Psenpalalis; i BC - i; *OD Pisa* 561 + 562 + 795 i X + 2.

2285 ---; 41-79; XLII 3062.8.

2286 ---; s. of Hermas, s. of Hermas; 98-177; apprentice; Oxyrhynchite; appr. to uncle Papontos; *SB* XII 10946.4.

2287 ---; i; assoc. w. Achilleus; XXXVI 2786.5.

2288 ---; s. of Pecysis; sp. Didyme; ch. Pecysis; 117-137; Oxyrhynchite; Cretan qtr; addr. for s.; I 105.[2], 8.

2289 ---; 139; nomographus; Oxy.?; X 1279.31.

2290 ---; ii; vineyard manager?; XIV 1673.1.

2291 HERMI[ ]; s. of Calpurnius; sp. Ese[-]; ch. Herodes; 132/133; Oxyrhynchite; Oxy.; addr. for s.; *PSI* VIII 874 ii 22.

2292 HERMIAS; c. 25; "brother" of Tyrannus; II 292.7.

2293 ---; July 28; Oxy.; XVII 2148.8.

2294 ---; sp. Tapontos; ch. Purois, Puoris the younger; i - ii; *P. Harris* 72.16, 20.

2295 ---; s. of Purois, s. of Hermias; m. Tnepheros; gs. of Tapontos; i - ii; age 26; *P. Harris* 72.17.

2296 JULIUS HERMIAS; Jan 100; strategus; Roman; XLI 2960.17.

2297 ---; ch. Aphynchis; ii; Tacona?, L. Top.; addr. for s.; *P. Inst. Fran.* I 4.2.

2298 ---; s. of Spartas; ii; III 591 (descr.).

2299 HERMINUS; ii; slave; Oxy.; bought by Amois from Charmus; *P. Hamb.* I 79.4.

2300 ---; ii; freedman of Caesar; probably a servus Caesaris who bought freedom; now in Rome; XLVI 3312.11.

2301 HERMIONE; sp. Dionysius; ch. Agathodaemon alias Dionysius; 129; Oxyrhynchite; Oxy.; addr. for s.; I 95.5.

2302 ---; d. of Chaeremon; sp. Chaeremon; ch. Dionysia, Aphrod[.......]; (1) c. 130; (2) 131; property owner; Oxyrhynchite; Oxy.; died rec.; has three d.; (1) III 472 ii 2; (2) 486.2.

---; see CLAUDIA ZOSIME.

2303 ---; sp. Amois; ch. Amois; ii; Oxyrhynchite; Oxy.; addr. for s.; *P. Hamb.* I 79. 2-3.

2304 ---; ii; Oxy.; assoc. w. Heracleides in greetings from Apia; XII 1581.15.

2305 HERMIPPUS; 2 BC - 1; IV 811.4.

2306 ---; ch. Ptolema; 66; II 272.23.

2307 ---; ch. Demetrius; 117-137; Oxy.; addr. for s. whose freedwoman Ptolema; I 105.5.

2308 HERMOCLES; late i; II 300.8.

2309 HERMODORUS; i; involved in tax collecting; II 298.25.

2310 ---; c. 100; agent; *P. Yale* 77.30.

2311 ---; (1) Feb 122; (2) Oct 123; basilicogrammateus; strategus, acting for Philonicus; Oxy.; (1) IV 714.2; (2) VI 898.1.

2312 HERMODOTUS; s. of Sarapion; bro. of Ammonius, Apollonia, Petusius; June 52; Oxy.?; borrows from Cendeas; *SB* V 8034.4.

2313 HERMOGENES; i BC; unnamed ch.; *PSI* I 64.1.

2314 ---; c. 30; "brother" of Ischyras (Ischyrion); X 1292.1.

2315 ---; s. of Tabynis; 31/32; Sinary, L. Top.; *P. Mich. inv.* 69.7.

2316 ---; s. of Heracles; 31/32; Sinary, L. Top.; ? same as XII.1480 n. 10; *P. Mich. inv.* 69.10.

2317 ---; ch. Petraeus; 31/32; Sinary?, L. Top.; addr. for s.; *P. Mich. inv.* 69.13.

2318 ---; Feb 32; comogrammateus; XII 1480.8.

2319 ---; s. of Heracl( ); Feb 32; has s.; friend of prophet Haryotes; XII 1480.1 V.

2320 ---; ch. Thracidas; Jan 93; Isieum Tryphonos?, L. Top.; addr. for gs. Sarapion; *PSI* VIII 798.60.

2321 ---; ch. Heraclas; 2nd half i; Sinary?, L. Top.; addr. for gs. Ammonis; XXXVIII 2846.1.

2322 ---; late i; superintendent of land distributions of Egypt; appointee, w. Panther, of Tiberius Claudius; II 344 (descr.).

2323 HERMOGENES; s. of Nilus; i; sib. of Papontos; *P. Harris* 144.7.

2324 ---; Aug 106; *P. Wisc.* I 17 V 24.

2325 ---; ch. Lycarion; 117; Oxyrhynchite?; Oxy.?; addr. for gs. [Ar]chion; III 489.23.

2326 ---; s. of Eutychides; Nov 132; illiterate; *PSI* I 53 iv 66-67.

2327 ---; ch. Dionysius; ii; Sinary, L. Top.; addr. for s.; XXXI 2574.2.

2328 HERMOIS; ch. Harsiesis; i BC - i; *OD Pisa* 256.1.

2329 HERMOLAUS; ch. Magrus; ii; hamlet of Sarapion, s. of Chaeremon?; addr. for gs. Rhynchis; *P. Erl.* 59 R 2.

2330 HERMON; s. of Demetrius; 31; landholder; Teis, Thmois. Top.; land there inherited from paternal gf.; XIX 2234.2.

2331 ---; ch. Harpalus; Nov/Dec 64?; Oxy.; addr. for s. who makes loan at Palosis, Thmois. Top.; IV 808 (descr.).

2332 ---; ch. Bacche; April 77; Alex.; II 263.2.

2333 ---; i; farmer; Sesphtha?, W. Top.; *P. Ryl.* II 199.24.

2334 HERMOPHANTUS; Nov 42 BC; tax farmer w. Hierocles; Oxy.; *P. Ryl.* IV 582.25.

2335 HERMOPHILUS; Sept 16; bearer of letter has business at Kerkemunis; IV 746.3.

2336 ---; 80/81; basilicogrammateus?; *Coll. Pap.* II 21.2.

2337 HERODES; s. of Apollonius; 25-37; landholder; Thmois. Top.?; cedes to Apollonius land nr Phna from Kleros of Diocles and Amotocus and nr Sepho from Kleros of Epimenes (both in Thmois. Top.); *PSI* X 1118.1, 8.

2338 HERO(I)DES; s. of Cratinus; July 64; Knights' Camp qtr; guardian of Tauris, d. of Apollonius; *P. Mich.* III 179.5.

2339 T. CLAUDIUS HERODES; (1) 66-72/73; (2) April 70; strategus; Roman; (1) IX 1203.1; (2) *P. Oxy. inv.* 50.4B.24B(3-4).

2340 ---; ch. Apion; 70; Oxyrhynchite?; Oxy.?; addr. for gs. Heracleides; XXII 2349.6.

2341 ---; s. of Apion; sp. Berenice; (1) 70; (2) 79/80; Lycians' Camp qtr; bro. Heracleides; land at Senocomis mortgaged to gs. Herodes; (1) XXII 2349.32; (2) *P. Oxy. inv.* 20.3B.34/B.2.

2342 ---; ch. Hieraciaena; 87/88; Oxyrhynchite; doc. pr.?; addr. for d.; *P. Princ.* III 147.1.

2343 ---; ch. Apollonius; late i; XVIII 2190.22-23.

2344 ---; s. of Exacon; sp. Caecilia Polla; ch. Sarapion, Exacon; (1) 108/109; (2) Sept 109; (3) 116; (4) 121; (5),

(6) 130; Oxyrhynchite; Oxy.?; addr. for s.; has sheep in Psobthis, M. Top.; land leased in Senepta; s. sub-lets domain land at Senepta; also in III 506 (of 143); (1) *P. Med. inv.* 71.69.2; (2) *PSI* IX 1030.1; (3) I 74.6; (4) III 499.2; (5) 517.10; (6) IV 730.1.

2345 HERODES; s. of Hermi[ ], s. of Calpurnius; m. Ese[-]; 132/133; landowner; Oxyrhynchite; owns empty plots in Hermaeum qtr, formerly m.'s; signalement; *PSI* VIII 874 ii 22.

2346 ---; 134; bibliophylax w. Philiscus; Oxy.; III 515.1.

2347 HERODIUS; i; *P. Ryl.* II 156.9.

2348 HEROIS; ii?; *P. Harris* 104.12.

2349 HERON; s. of Sarapion; 80/81; XIV 1648.43.

2350 ---; gs. of Heron; sp. Zenarion?; m. Philumene; 82; landholder; Oxy.; II 286.3.

2351 ---; ch. Philumene; 82; Oxy.; addr. for d.; II 286.4.

2352 ---; s. of Epimachus; sp. Thaesis; 98-102; Oxyrhynchite; Oxy.; dec.; *P. Mert.* I 13.8

2353 ---; i; IV 736.99.

2354 ḤẸṚỌ(N); i; farmer; Sesphtha?, W. Top.; *P. Ryl.* II 199.5.

2355 ḤẸṚON; i; Oxy.?; *P. Ryl.* II 156.27.

2356 ---; Oct 111; slave; formerly of Ti. Julius Theon, ex-hyp. and gym., now of his s., Ti. Julius Theon, ex-strategus and archidikast; grammateus; XLIV 3197.6.

2357 ---; 117/118; property owner w. Horion; sells property in Pammenes' Garden qtr to Zoilus; XIV 1648.27.

2358 ---; gs. of Philumene; 118; denies Diogenes' claim that gm. is in debt to him; *PSI* IV 281 R i 44.

2359 ---; 132; unnamed ch.; *PSI* I 53 vi 93.

2360 HERONIANUS; ii?; *P. Harris* 104.13.

2361 JUNIUS HESTIAEUS; 88/89; strategus; Roman; Oxy.; XLV iv 3240.8.

2362 HIERACIAENA; d. of Herodes; sp. Apollonius; 87/88; Oxyrhynchite; Oxy.; w. husband as guardian, leases land nr Nesla to Heras; *P. Princ.* III 147.1.

2363 HIERAX; (1) 20/21; (2), (3) 21; strategus; (1) *P. Inst. Fran.* III 43.2; (2) *P. Princ.* II 24.3 (corr. *BL* VI); (3) *SB* XII 10794.1.

2364 ---; s. of Harbichis; 41-54; property owner; lessor; Oxy.; property in Gooseherders' lane w. Menander, bro.; XXXIII 2669.3.

2365 HIERAX; July 50; landholder; Tholthis, Thmois. Top.; w. Theon, s. of Eudaemon, former owner of Kleros of Pyrrhias; XXXVIII 2836.9.

2366 ---; s. of Heracleodorus, s. of Heracleodorus; m. Apollonia; 81-96; proxenus of the Bouletae; VI 984 R (3).

2367 ---; ch. Heracleius; 81-96; VI 984 R (1).

2368 ---; s. of Thoonis; ch. Tbecis; 81-96; Oxyrhynchite; Sarapis St qtr; addr. for d.; VIII 1105.14.

2369 ---; i?; farmer?; *P. Erl.* 14 V 1.

2370 ---; ch. Sarapion; 119/120; Oxyrhynchite; Oxy.; addr. for gs. Dionysius; *PSI* XIII 1322.5.

2371 ---; ch. Diogenes; 127; Oxyrhynchite; Oxy.; addr. for s., grammateus; III 496.16.

2372 ---; (1) 127/128; (2) Nov 129; (3) Feb 130(?); basilicogrammateus; acting strategus (2, 3); Oxy.; (1) XII 1452 i 2; (2) VII 1024.7; (3) *P. Mich. inv.* 974.1.

2373 ---; Feb 130(?); basilicogrammateus, acting str.; *P. Mich. inv.* 974.1.

2374 ---; c. 138; basilicogrammateus to Apolinarius, str.; Oxy.; III 579 (descr.).

2375 ---; ii?; Senocomis, W. Top.; *P. Fuad I Univ.* 32.10.

2376 ---; s. of Cornelius; ii; III 531.1.

2377 ---; ii; donkey driver; *P. Harris* 95.14.

2378 HIEROCLES; Nov 42 BC; tax farmer; Oxy.; partner of Hermophantus; *P. Ryl.* IV 582.24.

2379 HILARION; Oct/Nov 21 BC; slave; Tacona; *P. Vindob. Worp* 2.5.

2380 ---; sp. Alis (also sister?); 1 BC; IV 744.1.

2381 HILAROUS; 117; slave; North St qtr; slave of Dionysius; has children; III 489.8.

2382 HILARUS; ii; s. of Charmus; sp. Leontous; ch. Charmus; ii; Oxyrhynchite; Oxy.; addr. for s.; *P. Hamb.* I 79.5.

2383 HIPPALUS; i BC - i; *OD Pisa* 377 Convesso 3, 12; Concavo 6.

2384 ---; ch. Dionysius; Feb 26; Pela?, W. Top.; addr. for gs. Straton; II 245.16.

2385 HIPPODAMUS; ch. Dionysius; 41/42; *PSI* XII 1235.12.

2386 HOMERUS; late i BC; Alexandria; XII 1479.9.

2387 HOR[ ]; ch. Sinthonis; c. 100; *P. Stras.* 266.14.

2388 HOR(E)IS; early ii; "brother" of Ptolemaeus; XLII 3060.1.

2389 HOREIS; ii after 137; "brother" of Horion; XIV 1757.1, 30.

2390 HORIMUS; Oct 111; slave; formerly of Ti. Julius Theon, now of his son, Ti. Julius Sarapion; XLIV 3197.10.

2391 HORION; s. of Petosiris; sp. Tasis; 19/20; priest of Isis, greatest goddess; property owner; Myrobalanus qtr; part owner house in temple of Duo Adelphi; II 254.2.

2392 ---; ch. Helene, Pasion; Sept 58; Hermaeum qtr; addr. for gs. Amoitas; *P. Mich.* III 171.3.

2393 [H]ORION?; ch. Tryphaena; 59; Oxyrhynchite; Oxy.; addr. for d.; has second d.; II 320.3.

2394 HORION; July 66; agent for Ptolemaeus, basilicogrammateus; Oxy.; II 246.32.

2395 ---; s. of Harpaesis; 83/84; landholder; Papsis?, Tychis Necotis; holds land there; II 290.11.

2396 ---; ch. Didyme; 83/84; Papsis?, Tychis Necotis; addr. for d.; II 290.14.

2397 ---; ch. Tanechotes; 83/84; Papsis?, Tychis Necotis; addr. for s.; II 290.16.

2398 ---; 83/84; overseer; Papsis?, Tychis Necotis; II 290.20.

2399 ---; s. of Ṗẹ[- ; 98-117; guardian to Apollonous; *PSI* VIII 772.2.

2400 ---; s. of Theon; sp. Zois; ch. Menalous; i - ii; property owner; Isieum Tryphonos?; owned land nr Talao (catoecic land, Kleros of Seuthes) inherited by d.; *PSI* VI 687.1.

2401 ---; sp. Thermuthis; ch. Chaeremon; i - ii; *P. Harris* 72.13.

2402 ---; 100; former slave; Oxy.; buys freedom from Sinthoonis, d. of Pecysis; I 49.3.

2403 ---; s. of Orsenouphis, s. of [Po]c[o]ous? or [Pe]c[o]ous?; Sept 103; farmer; lessee; Oxyrhynchite; Oxy.; leases land in Toka; XLI 2973.5-6.

2404 ---; 117/118; property owner w. Heron; sells property in Pammenes' Garden qtr to Zoilus; XIV 1648.27.

2405 ---; ch. Heracleides; 117-138; I 188 (descr.).

2406 ---; s. of Sarapion; (1) 117-138; (2) 123; grammateus (to agoranomoi); Oxy.; (1) I 178.2-3; (2) 107.2.

2407 ---; 120; landholder; lessor; Oxyrhynchite; Oxy.; unnamed s.; lets part of Nicanorian estate; XXIV 2410.2.

2408 ---; Aug 127; bibliophylax?; Oxy.; I 34 iv 1.

2409 ---; 129; comogrammateus; Tholthis, Mouchinaryo, L. Top.; c. of T. and M.; *SB* VI 9617.2.

2410 HORION; alias THEON; s. of Sarapion, s. of Apion; m. Heraclous, d. of Sarapion and Tausiris alias Sarapous; 130; Ibion Ammonii, L. Top.; age 40; guardian of m.'s cousin Thatres, d. of Ammonius; signalement; III 492.3, 16.

2411 ---; Nov/Dec 132; *PSI* I 53 ii 40.

2412 ---; 135/136; comogrammateus of Talao(?) and other villages in L. Top.; *P. Iand.* VII 136.1.

2413 ---; s. of Sarapion; 140/141; farmer; Lonemus distr.; I 89.6.

---; see EUTYCHIDES.

2414 ---; ii; doc. pr. Oxy.?; writes to Heracleides; *SB* VI 9025.1.

2415 ---; ii after 137; "brother" of Horeis; XIV 1757.1, 30.

2416 ---; s. of Heracleius (adopted), s. of Diophantus; ii; landholder; farmer; Oxyrhynchite; Oxy.; XXXI 2583.2.

2417 ---; ii; gretted by Publius; XLI 2981.22-23.

2418 ---; sp. Heras; ch. Asclas; ii; Gymnasium St qtr; addr. for s.; *P. Princ.* II 46.12.

2419 ---; s. of Ammonius; ii; shipowner; III 522.12.

2420 ---; ii; pilot; III 522.15.

2421 ---; ii; potter; XLI 2996.17.

2422 ---; ii; "brother" of Taeoucon(?); III 608 (descr.).

2423 ---; ii; III 582 (descr.).

2424 HOR[ION]; ii; I 113.2.

2425 HORION; n.d.; *SB* I 1938 (L).

2426 HOROCRATES; i BC - i; *OD Pisa* 816 X + 3.

2427 ---; early i; *OD Pisa* 249.2.

2428 HORUS; s. of Totoeus; 30/29 BC; writes for Heracleides; XII 1453.38.

2429 ---; s. of Aphynchis; Sept/Oct 3 BC; XLI 2979.2.

2430 ---; ch. Orsenouphis; i BC; *OD Pisa* 55 i 3.

2431 ---; s. of Petechonsis; i BC; *OD Pisa* 55 i 2, ii 7.

2432 HOR[US; ch. Petechonsis; i BC; *OD Pisa* 289.1.

2433 HORUS; s. of Cathytes; i BC; *OD Pisa* 149.7.

2434 ---; i BC - i; *OD Pisa* 58.4, 6.

2435 ---; i BC - i; *OD Pisa* 280 X + 2.

2436 ---; i BC - i; *OD Pisa* 755 Convesso X + 7.

2437 HORUS; ch. Harchypsis; i BC - i; *OD Pisa* 87 X + b.

2438 ---; i BC - i; *OD Pisa* 217 Concavo i X + 4.

2439 ---; i BC - i; *OD Pisa* 561 + 562 + 795 i X + 16.

2440 ---; ch. Onnophris; i BC - i; (1) *OD Pisa* 779 + 242 Convesso X + 17; (2) 510 + 568 Convesso i 9.

2441 ---; i BC - i; *OD Pisa* 1023 Convesso ii 4.

2442 ---; s. of P_3-šwtj; *OD Pisa* 451 + 540 Convesso 4.

2443 ---; s. of Petseous; i BC - i; *OD Pisa* 58.9, 11, 16.

2444 ---; s. of Totoes; i BC - i; (1) *OD Pisa* 58.10; (2) 510 + 568 Convesso i 10.

2445 ---; s. of Harpaeris; i BC - i; *OD Pisa* 460 Convesso i X + 9.

2446 ---; i BC - i; *OD Pisa* 460 Concavo X + 5.

2447 ---; s. of Cales; i BC - i; *OD Pisa* 256.3.

2448 ---; ch. Picos; i BC - i; *OD Pisa* 117.1.

2449 ---; ch. Pebrichis; i BC - i; *OD Pisa* 360 Concavo X + 7.

2450 ---; s. of Petosiris; i BC - i; (1) *OD Pisa* 290 + 290A Concavo X + 5; (2) 755 Concavo X + 9.

2451 ---; s. of Onnophris; i BC - i; (1) *OD Pisa* 5 ii X + 4; (2) 351 X + 2.

2452 ---; s. of Patous; i BC - i; sent a/c by Chonsis; (1) *OD Pisa* 360 Concavo X + 6; (2) 451 + 540 Convesso 1.

2453 ---; ch. Petosiris; i BC - i; (1) *OD Pisa* 360 Concavo X + 5; (2) 276 X + 3; (3) 232.6.

2454 ---; ch. Ḏd; i BC - i; (1) *OD Pisa* 5 i X + 16, X + 17; (2) 779 + 242 Concavo 5.

2455 ---; ch. Patous; i BC - i; (1) *OD Pisa* 72 ii X + 7; (2) 69 Concavo 1; (3) 69 Convesso i 10; (4) 127.6.

2456 ---; ch. Horus; i BC - i; (1) *OD Pisa* 196 i X + 3; (2) 5 ii X + 10.

2457 ---; ch. Harpaesis; i BC - i; *OD Pisa* 72 ii X + 5.

2458 ---; s. of Petesorapis; i BC - i; *OD Pisa* 127.4.

2459 ---; ch. Somtous; i BC - i; *OD Pisa* 127.2.

2460 ---; ch. Tenis, i BC - i; *OD Pisa* 243 + 472 i 4, 12.

2461 ---; s. of Horus; i BC - i; (1) *OD Pisa* 196 i X + 3; (2) 5 ii X + 10.

2462 ---; s. of Ḥtb; i BC - i; *OD Pisa* 68.3.

2463 HORUS; s. of Pa[...; i BC - i; *OD Pisa* 816 X + 6.

2464 ---; s. of Stotoetes; i BC - i; (1) *OD Pisa* 72 ii X + 3; (2) 69 Concavo 6; (3) 510 + 568 Convesso i 18; (4) 1264 Concavo 2.

2465 ---; i BC - i; *OD Pisa* 290 + 290A Concavo X + 7.

2466 ---; s. of Somtous; i BC - i; (1) *OD Pisa* 23 ii 5; (2) 532 X + 6.

2467 ---; s. of Patesis; i BC - i; *OD Pisa* 228 X + 5.

2468 ---; i BC - i; called the elder; *OD Pisa* 243 + 472 i 3, 13.

2469 ---; ch. Stotoetes; i BC - i; *OD Pisa* 228 X + 10.

2470 ---; s. of Harchemis; i BC - i; *OD Pisa* 25 i 15.

2471 HORUS(?); i BC - i; *OD Pisa* 25 i 24.

2472 HORUS; i BC - i; acts through Penaus; *OD Pisa* 510 + 568 Convesso ii 3.

2473 ---; ch. Pausiris; i BC - i; *OD Pisa* 532 X + 8.

2474 ---; ch. Apollonius; i BC - i; *OD Pisa* 510 + 568 Convesso ii 6.

2475 ---; Aug 3; *OD Pisa* 473 Concavo i 2.

2476 ---; s. of Premosiris; April 4; *OD Pisa* 511 + 512 ii 3.

2477 ---; ch. Totoes; (1) July 7; (2) i; (1) *OD Pisa* 1131 Convesso 5; (2) 318.6.

2478 ---; s. of Dd(?); Aug 7; *OD Pisa* 432.2.

2479 ---; ch. Heracleius; Dec 20/Jan 21; Sinary L. Top.; addr. for s.; X 1281.11.

2480 ---; ch. Petsiris; May 26; Tanais?, M. Top.; addr. for s.; *P. Rein.* II 103.4.

2481 ---; 41-54; weaver; property owner; Oxyrhynchite?; Sarapeum, house in Ax... St; XXXIV 2720.20.

2482 ---; ch. Thaesis; c. 45-47; Little Oasis; addr. for d.; XLII 3033.2.

2483 ---; s. of Zoilus; sp. Dieus; ch. Zoilus; (1) 57; (2) Sept 66; Oxy.; addr. for s. who writes for Ptolemaeus; (1) II 269.17; (2) 275.41.

2484 ---; ch. Lycus; 81-96; gs. Eudaemon; VI 984 R init.

2485 ---; July 85; episphragistes; Senocomis, W. Top.; XXXVIII 2841.12.

2486 ---; ch. Hatres alias Didymus; July 85; XXXVIII 2841.10.

2487 HORUS; ch. Tha[esis]?; 99; Oxy.?; addr. for d.; *P. Princ.* II 32.2.

2488 ---; ch. ..a..nus; 99; Oxy.?; addr. for gs. Paas; *P. Princ.* II 32.4.

2489 ---; early i; greets Sisois; *OD Pisa* 419.1.

2490 ---; ch. Petubastis; early i; called the ancient; *OD Pisa* 249.4.

2491 ---; ch. Thonis; early i; Psobthis?, M. Top.; addr. for s.; *P. Wisc.* I 23.3.

2492 ---; late i; II 299.1.

2493 ---; s. of Horus, s. of Porepomis; m. Tamonous, d. of Harpaesis; i; landholder; Pakerke, M. Top.; doc. pr. Oxy.?; land owned by Tausiris (g.m.) ceded to him; *P. Harris* 138 i 20.

2494 ---; s. of Porepomis; sp. Tamonous; ch. Horus; i; Pakerke?, M. Top.; doc. pr. Oxy.?; addr. for s.; *P. Harris* 138 i 21.

2495 ---; s. of Petearsenth( ); i; sib. of Dioscous and Papontos; *P. Harris* 144.3.

2496 ---; s. of Petechon; i; farmer; Koba; VIII 1145.8.

2497 ---; s. of Ptollis; i; farmer; Koba; VIII 1145.10.

2498 ---; ch. Pathebis; i; Peeno; addr. for s.; *P. Bon.* 43.7.

2499 ---; s. of Harpaesis; i; farmer; Koba; VIII 1145.11.

2500 ---; s. of Pamun; i; *OD Pisa* 60 Convesso i 6.

2501 ---; sp. Tammotus; ch. Heracles; i - ii; *P. Harris* 72.22.

2502 ---; 103/104; lessee of olive garden at Psobthis, M. Top.; III 639 (descr.).

2503 ---; ch. Panesneus; June 103-110; Senocomis?; addr. for s., priest of Ammon; XLVI 3275.3.

2504 ---; s. of Cephalon; June 103-117; priest of Ammon; Senocomis; illiterate; XLVI 3275.2.

2505 ---; s. of Menestheus; ch. Menestheus; 115/116; Seryphis, W. Top.; addr. for s.; I 97.7.

2506 ---; 116; banker; *P. Harris* 89.4.

2507 ---; ch. Mieus; 119; Oxy.; XII 1547.3.

2508 ---; s. of Apollonius; ch. Apollonius; (1) 121; (2) Aug 133; Senepta, M. Top.; addr. for s.; (1) III 499.4; (2) *P. Köln* II 100.30.

2509 ---; 126; Oxyrhynchite?; Oxy.?; has s. and gs.; gs. witness; age 36; signalement; III 491.25.

HORUS; see HARPAESIS.

2510 ---; s. of Eudaemon, s. of Thonasychis; m. Ta..., d. of Harpaesis alias Horus; gs. of Thaesis; 126; Oxyrhynchite; Oxy.; minor; bro. of Thonis and Eudaemon; III 491.4.

2511 ---; ch. Petsiris; 127/128; Patne; addr. for s.; *P. Lips.* 113.6.

2512 ---; 130; farmer?; lessee of Heracleides, s. of Antias; lives nr Senepta or Sink( )?; III 517.8.

2513 ---; s. of Heracleius; sp. Nephersous; ch. Horus; 131; Talao. L. Top.; addr. for s.; *SB* VI 9190.5.

2514 ---; s. of Horus, s. of Heracleius; m. Nephersous; 131; Talao, L. Top.; lends money to Panouphis; *SB* VI 9190.5.

2515 ---; ch. Horus; 132/133; gs. Heras; *PSI* VIII 874 i 4.

2516 ---; s. of Horus; sp. Taamois; ch. Heras; 132/133; *PSI* VIII 874 i 4.

2517 ---; ch. Tauris; 132/133; Oxy.?; addr. for d.; *PSI* VIII 874 i 7.

2518 ---; ch. Dionysius, Papontos; Oct/Nov. 132; *PSI* I 53 x 167.

2519 ---; m. Tapsois; sp. Taarpaesis; ch. Dionysius alias Papontos; 133; Oxyrhynchite; Oxy.; I 100.7.

2520 ---; s. of Sir[ ], s. of Harthoonis; 135/136; Talao, L. Top.; doc. pr?; *P. Iand.* VII 136.10.

2521 ---; ch. Horus; 135/136; Psobthis?, L. Top.; doc. pr.?; addr. for s.; *P. Iand.* VII 136.15.

2522 ---; s. of Horus; 135/136; landholder; Psobthis, L. Top.; doc. pr?; *P. Iand.* VII 136.15.

2523 ---; s. of Petosiris; sp. Chenpsois; ch. Petosiris; 137/138; Sinageris, Hermopolite; addr. for s. leasing land in Oxy.; *PSI* IV 315.3.

2524 ---; ch. Thompecysis; Jan 139; South St qtr; addr. for gs. Horus; *P. Oslo* III 105.4.

2525 ---; s. of Thompecysis, s. of Horus; m. Thaesis; sp. Sintotoes; ch. Thompecysis, Horus; Jan 139; pastophorus of Sarapis, greatest god; South St qtr; owns half house there; *P. Oslo* III 105.3.

2526 ---; s. of Horus, s. of Thompecysis; m. Sintotoes; gs. (pat.) of Thaesis; Jan 139; South St qtr; previously reg. at g.m.'s property, transferred by f. to his house; *P. Oslo* III 105.10.

2527 ---; s. of Pelux; sp. Eirene; ch. Harmiysis alias Pelux, Amois; early ii; Oxyrhynchite; Oxy.?; addr. for sons; *P. Wisc.* I 13.4.

2528 HORUS; sp. Sinth(oonis); ch. Sarap(ion?); ii; Cretan qtr; addr. for s.; *P. Princ.* II 46.7.

2529 ---; s. of Becis; m. Tachecysis; ii; landholder; leases land at Sento; *P. Erl.* 44 iii 27.

2530 ---; ii; III 587 (descr.) V.

2531 ---; s. of Sarapis; ii; landholder; leases land at Antipera; *P. Erl.* 44 ii 5.

2532 HORUS-Dd; ch. Peteuris; i BC - i; *OD Pisa* 460 Convesso ii X + 10.

2533 IE( ) or HIE( ); ch. Apol( ); Nov 42 BC; Oxy.?; addr. for s.; *P. Ryl.* IV 582.22.

2534 IMOUTHES; i BC - i; *OD Pisa* 232.1, 4.

2535 ---; i BC - i; *OD Pisa* 196 ii X + 7.

2536 ---; s. of Harsiesis; i BC - i; *OD Pisa* 69 Convesso i 7.

2537 ---; i BC - i; *OD Pisa* 532 X + 9.

2538 IMOU]THES; i BC - i; *OD Pisa* 755 Concavo X + 1.

2539 IMOUTHES; i BC - i; *OD Pisa* 755 Convesso X + 8.

2540 ---; s. of Petearpochrates; i BC - i; *OD Pisa* 281 + 94 X + 6.

---; see PATESIS-IMOUTHES.

2541 INARUS; i BC; *OD Pisa* 55 ii 5.

2542 ---; i BC - i; *OD Pisa* 38 i X + 4.

2543 ---; i BC - i; *OD Pisa* 360 Concavo X + 2.

2544 ---; ch. Dd; i BC - i; (1) *OD Pisa* 69 Convesso i 8; (2) 510 + 568 Convesso i 5; (3) 510 + 568 Concavo i X + 10.

2545 ---; ch. Petsiris alias Anicetus; 83/84; Tychis Necotis; addr. for s.; II 290.31.

2546 INDICE; late i; related to Thaisous, wife of Theon?; II 300.1.

2547 IS[.......; Sept 31 BC; ferryman; Tholthis, Thmois. Top.; has house there; *P. Wurz.* 5.6.

2548 ISAREUS; d. of Theon; sp. Theon (1), Theon (2); ch. Ptollion, Theon; 130; Oxyrhynchite?; Oxy.?; addr. for s.; III 492.5.

2549 ISARION; 127; slave owner; sells Herais; doc. date 197/198; *P. Bour.* 16.16.

2550 ISAROUS; d. of Sarapion; sp. Castor; ch. Sarapion; after 81; Oxyrhynchite; Oxy.; addr. for s.; II 369.4-5.

2551 ISAROUS; c. 92; landholder; Tacona, L. Top.; owns land there; *P. Michael* 9.17.

2552 ---; d. of Ptolemaeus; sp. Sarapion; ch. Plutarchus, Ptolemaeus; 119/120; Oxyrhynchite; Oxy.; *PSI* XIII 1322.8.

2553 ISAS; c. 1; (1) IV 736.32; (2) 739.1.

2554 ---; ch. Aunchis; 126; Oxy.; III 634 (descr.).

2555 ---; s. of Isidorus; m. Soeris or Soerous; ch. Sarapas, Sarapous; early ii; property owner; weaver; Oxyrhynchite?; Oxy.?; dec.; addr. for bro. Theonas; X 1269.10.

2556 IS?]AS; s. of Diogenes alias Cottus; s. of Isa(s?); m. Sarapous; ii; landholder; Oxyrhynchite; Oxy.; XII 1536.2.

2557 ISA(S?); ch. Diogenes alias Cottus?; ii, Oxyrhynchite; Oxy.; addr. for gs. Isas; XII 1536.3.

2558 ---; ii; may not be in Oxy.; XII 1488.24.

ISCHAS; see HERACLAS.

2559 ISCHYR( ); 98/99; hypogrammateus to str. Antamon; *P. Köln* II 86.22.

2560 ISCHYRAS; c. 30; "brother" of Hermogenes; may be Ischyrion of X 1291; X 1292.1 V.

2561 ---; Aug 44; nr Sarapeum, Hermaeum qtr; neighbour to house owned by Lucius and s.; *P. Fouad* 44.31.

---; see AISCHYRAS.

2562 ISCHYRION; ch. Theon; 22 BC; VII 1061 V.

2563 ---; 30; "brother" of Zois; may be Ischyras of X 1292; X 1291.1, 15.

2564 ---; Sept 58; tax farmer (weavers' tax); Oxy.; assoc. w. Panechotes; *P. Mich* III 171.1.

2565 IS]CHYRION; s. of Dionysius; Oct 62; vintner; lessee of vineyard; XLI 2970.1.

2566 ISCHYRION; s. of Epimachus, s. of Epimachus; 63/64; Oxyrhynchite; Knights' Camp qtr; left Oxy.; *P. Gen. inv.* 222.8.

2567 ---; ch. Ptolema; 90; Senepta, M. Top.; addr. for gs. Zoilus; I 72.4.

2568 ---; ch. Herme[....]; Feb 91; Oxyrhynchite?; Oxy.?; addr. for s.; XLI 2957.7.

2569 ---; ch. Plution; 117-138; Oxy.; III 646 (descr.).

2570 ---; ii; property owner; III 524.3.

2571 ISIDORA; d. of Apollonius (adoptive f. Dionysius alias ...onius); ch. Claudii Potamon and Apoll(onius?); c. 47-54; adopt. f. an Alex., resident in Gamma distr.; XLVI 3271.3.

2572 ---; sp. Dionysius; 59; Oxyrhynchite; Oxy.; niece of Tryphaena; II 320.3-4.

2573 ---; d. of Ptolemaeus, s. of Ammonius; ch. Theogenes; 94/95; Oxyrhynchite, gymnasial class; Heracles Place qtr; II 257.7.

2574 ---; d. of Calas; sp. Leonides; ch. Saraeus; March 97; Oxyrhynchite; Oxy.; addr. for d.; IV 713.10.

2575 ---; alias APOLLONARION; d. of Psenesis alias Ision; m. Taarpaesis alias Isidora; Aug 133; Oxy.; sister of Ptolemaeus and Berenice; *P. Köln* II 100.5.

---; see TAARPAESIS.

2576 -]E; alias ISIDORA; ii?; Paeimis?, W. Top.; *P. Fuad I Univ.* 32.2.

2577 ---; ii; Coptos resident?; *P. Wurz.* 21 R B 17.

2578 ---; sp. Serenus (also her "brother"); ii; III 528.1.

2579 ---; ii; unnamed bro.; XLVI 3312.4.

2580 ISIDORUS; 6/5 BC; Oxy.; IV 816 (descr.).

2581 ---; s. of Isidorus; Jan 17; mill owner; lessor; Oxy.; leased mill to Heracleius, s. of Soterichus; II 278.1.

2582 ---; ch. Isidorus; Jan 17; Oxy.; addr. for s.; II 278.1.

2583 ---; ch. -on; 1st half i; Oxy.?; addr. for banker gs.; *P. Inst. Fran.* III 30.4.

2584 T. CLAUDIUS ISIDORUS; s. of Bion; c. 50; banker; Roman, Quirina tribe; also Alex.; Alexandria; bro. Demetrius; XXVII 2471.3-4.

2585 ISIDORUS; s. of Nicanor, s. of Sostratus; m. .....atos, d. of Thaisas; 78/79; weaver; Oxyrhynchite; Thoeris St qtr; resides temp. in Alexandria; XXXVI 2756.11.

2586 ---; late i; Oxyrhynchite; res. in Alex.?; imprisons slave Heraclas; XVIII 2190.42.

---; see DIONYSIUS.

2587 ---; 139/161; livestock owner?; Mareotis?; *P. Oslo* III 84.12.

2588 ---; gs. of Cephalon; July 140; Alex., Sosicosmius, Althaieus; Alexandria?; bro. of Cas[...]; *SB* XII 10894.15.

2589 ---; sp. Soeris or Soerous; ch. Theonas or Theon, Isas; early ii; Oxyrhynchite?; Oxy.?; addr. for s.; X 1269.2, 13.

2590 ---; ii; in charge of men; XLIV 3199.9.

2591 ISIDORUS; ii; Oxy.; XII 1583.6.

2592 ---; ii; freedman; landholder; f. of Eudaemon; *P. Erl.* 44 iii 29.

2593 ---; ii; XLI 2981.25-26.

2594 ---; n.d.; *SB* I 1539.

2595 IS]IDO[TE?; d. of D]eiu[s; sp. Ammonius; ch. Theon; Jan 139/ Feb 140 and Aug 148(?); addr. for s.; *P. Iand.* VII 139.8.

2596 ISIERAX; ch. Pecysis; 97; Oxyrhynchite; II 371.3.

2597 ISION; i - ii; slave owner (of Apollos); *P. Harris* 72.34.

2598 ---; s. of Heracleides; m. Berenice; gs. (mat.) of Psenesis alias Ision and Taarpaesis; Aug 133; Oxyrhynchite; Oxy.; addr. for gm. who bequeathes him land nr Ophis; *P. Köln* II 100.[12], 15.

---; see PSENESIS.

2599 ISIONE; sp. Dionysius; ch. Theon; (1) Aug 86; (2) 93/94; Oxyrhynchite; Oxy.; addr. for s.; (1) XXXVIII 2843.17; (2) *PSI* X 1109.3.

2600 ISIS; d. of Diogenes; sp. Theon; ch. Theon; Sept 66; Temgenuthis qtr; addr. for s.; *CPR* V ii 1, 5.

---; see THAESIS.

2601 ISOCRATES; July 72; farmer; lessee; Seryphis, W. Top.; tenant of Mnesitheus and Dion( ), sons of Theon; XLIV 3163.8.

2602 JACOBUS; ch.]s; Sept 77; Dermeithai?, U. Top.; addr. for s., pilot; II 276.5.

2603 ---; ch. Thed(etus); 93; Enteiis, Athychis, U. Top.; addr. for s.; *P. Princ.* II 42 V ii 21, iii 32.

2604 JESOUS; 6/5 BC; IV 816 (descr.).

2605 JOSEPH; ch. Cl[.]thos, Comonos; 20/21; Sepho?, Thmois. Top.; addr. for Cl[.]thos; *P. Inst. Fran.* III 43.4.

2606 ---; Dec 20/Jan 21; Jewish; Sinary, L. Top.; loan to Harpaesis; X 1281,[1], 9.

2607 JULIA; d. of Plutarchus, s. of Sarapion; m. Flavia, d. of Sinthonis; gd. of Isarous; sp. Dionysius; 119/120; property owner; Oxyrhynchite; Oxy.; property nr Ieme, M. Top., from Kleros of Chares; *PSI* XIII 1322.2.

JULIA; see HERACLA.

2608 C. JULIUS; s. of C. Julius Theon; 107/108; landholder; Roman; Alexandria; father from Alex.; has land in Monimu distr., U. Top.; XII 1434.9.

2609 C. JULIUS [ ]; 44; strategus; Roman; *P. Fouad* 27.1.

JULIUS; see C. JULIUS CARUS, DOMITIANUS, GERMANUS, MAXIMUS, SATORNILUS, SATURNINUS; JULIUS ASCLEPEINUS, DOMITIUS, HERMIAS, LEPOS, MUSAEUS, SARAPION, THEON: M. JULIUS VALERIANUS: TI. JULIUS BASILIDES, PHILETUS.

2610 ---; ch. Anubion; ii; Roman?; III 642 (descr.).

2611 MALIA JULIA; ii; Roman; guardian is bro. Titus Malius Villus; *P. Flor.* III 381.12.

2612 JU]STUS; 22; sword-bearer (of str.?); Oxy.; in custody in Alex.; II 294.20.

2613 ---; s. of Sarapion; (1) i; (2) ii; Sinary, L. Top.; has bros.; (1) XXXVI 2786.1, V; (2) XXXI 2574.3.

2614 ---; n.d. *SB* I 1985 (b).

2615 LABANES(?) (Lbn_3); Sept 6; salt merchant; *OD Pisa* 1163.2.

2616 LACON; Oct 111; slave; formerly of Ti. Julius Theon, now of Ti. Julius Sarapion, his son; XLIV 3197.11.

2617 ---; ch. Demetrius; mid ii; Syron Kome, W. Top.; addr. for gs. Theon; XLIV 3165.6.

2618 LAGOUS; ch. [....]..rio(n); i; Sesphtha?, W. Top.; addr. for s.; *P. Ryl.* II 199.15.

2619 LAMPON; late i; mouse catcher; Toka?, M. Top.; II 299.2.

2620 LAODICE; c. 1; IV 736.95.

2621 L]AODICE; ii?; *P. Harris* 103 V.

2622 LASTAS; s. of Thonis; 41-79; Teis, Thmois. Top.; to be arrested for violence to Heraclas; XLII 3061.10.

2623 LATINUS; ch. -on; ii; Oxy.; *P. Stras.* 299 R 17.

2624 LEBIS (Lbj); i; has unnamed ch.; *OD Pisa* 55 ii 12.

2625 LEMYSUS; ch. Paṛias; 71/72; Oxy.?; addr. for s.; *P. Ryl.* II 95.4.

2626 LEON; s. of Heracleides; 5/4 BC; public farmer; W. Top.; Oxy.; farms nr Antilochou Ibion against Pelle (Pela?); *P. Oslo* III 26.4.

2627 ---; s. of .[..]eros; 36; writes for Tryphon, s. of Dionysius; II 267.26.

2628 ---; ch. Dionysius; (1) Aug 86; (2) 93/94; (3) i; Oxyrhynchite; Oxy.; addr. for s.; (1) XXXVIII 2843.17; (2) *PSI* X 1109.2; (3) *P. Ryl.* II 156.28, V.

2629 ---; ch. Leontas/Leon; i; Oxy.?; addr. for s.; *P. Ryl.* II 156.30.

2630 LEON/LEONTAS; s. of Leon; i; Oxy.?; age 19; witness; signalement; *P. Ryl.* II 156.30, 36.

2631 LEON; ch.[...]n; i; Oxyrhynchite?; Oxy.?; doc. pr. Oxy.?; addr. for gd. Hellenis; *P. Harris* 138 i 16.

2632 ---; s. of Amois; 132/133 or 153/154; Oxy.; XII 1518.12.

2633 ---; s. of Dexitheus; 132/133 or 153/154; former official; Oxy.; XII 1518.14.

2634 LEONAS; i - ii; XLII 3057.29.

2635 ---; s. of Heracleides; mid ii; woodseller; Oxy.; sells to Achilleus from the Hermopolite in Hermopolis; *P. Stras.* 184.1.

2636 LEONIDAS; 103-107; *PSI* IV 281 R i 20.

2637 LEONIDES; s. of Ptolemaeus; ch. Apion; 66-72/73; landholder; lessee; Alex., Althaieus; now res. in Alexandria; holds land at Senepta, M. Top., in Kleros of Damon, belonging to Aristandrus; IX 1203 + *SB* IV 7339.8.

2638 ---; s. of Alexandrus; sp. Isidora; ch. Saraeus; March 97; landholder; Oxyrhynchite?; Oxy.?; addr. for d., m. of Leonides; IV 713.9.

2639 ---; s. of Diodorus, s. of Diodorus; m. Saraeus, d. of Leonides; gs. (mat.) of Isidora; March 97; landholder; property owner; Oxyrhynchite; Oxy.; inherited m.'s land at Nesla and Peeno; has bro. Diodorus and sister Thais; IV 713.4.

2640 LEONTAS; s. of Didymus; (1) Aug 123; (2) 123; overseer; landholder; Phoboou distr.?. E. Top.; grain deposit there (1); o. for Claudius Munatianus (2); (1) XXXVIII 2863.1; (2) *P. Lips.* 112.8.

2641 ---; ii; has family; III 530.27.

---; see PAPONTOS.

2642 LEONTIAS; i; *SB* XII 10765.4.

2643 LEONTOUS; sp. Hilarus; ch. Charmus; ii; Oxyrhynchite; Oxy.; addr. for s.; *P. Hamb.* I 79.6.

2644 JULIUS LEPOS; 10/11; Roman; XXXVI 2772.1.

2645 LEUCIUS (sic.); ch. Amois; Dec 75/Jan 76; Oxyrhynchite?; Oxy.? addr. for s.; descr. as the younger; *P. Yale* 64.12.

2646 LIBANUS; i BC - i; acts via Petesis; *OD Pisa* 510 + 568 Concavo i X + 9.

LIBO; see PETSIRIS.

LICINNIUS; see LICINNIUS MARTIALIS.

2647 LOCHUS; ch. Sarapion; 54; Oxyrhynchus; addr. for s. having bank nr Sarapeum; II 264.7.

2648 ---; s. of Onnophris; April 96; hyperetes of Peisis; *P. Oslo* III 95.10-11.

2649 LOCHUS; s. of Sarapion; ch. Lochus; early ii; Oxyrhynchite?; Oxy.?; addr. for s. who witnesses will; III 493.13.

2650 ---; s. of Lochus, s. of Sarapion; early ii; Oxyrhynchite; Oxy.; witness to will; III 493.12.

2651 LOCRION; Oct/Nov 5 BC; IV 812 (descr.) 5.

2652 LONGINUS; late i; Roman?; II 300.10.

2653 ---; ch. Lucia; 100; Roman; Oxy.?; addr. for gd. Sinthoonis; I 49.7.

---; see M. LONGINUS CASTRESIUS.

---; see PAPONTOS.

2654 LONGIUS; s. of Andronicus; ii; landholder; *P. Erl.* 44 iii 40.

---; see C. LONGIUS PRISCUS.

2655 LOUS; i BC - i; *OD Pisa* 217 Convesso X + 5.

2656 ---; Nov 8; *OD Pisa* 421.1.

2657 LUCAS; ch. Apeis; 119/120; *P. Wisc.* II 39.3.

2658 LUCIA; c. 35; II 295.8-9.

2659 ---; alias THAISAS; d. of Lucius; m. Sinthoonis, d. of Theon; 94; landholder; Oxyrhynchite; Oxy.; land at Seryphis and Syron Kome in Kleros of Demetrius et al.; II 270.3.

2660 ---; d. of Longinus; sp. Pecysis; ch. Sinthoonis; 100; Oxyrhynchite; Roman; Oxy.; addr. for d.; I 49.6.

2661 LUCIUS; Oct/Nov 5 BC; IV 812 (descr.) 6.

2662 ---; ch. Epimachus; Aug 44; Oxy.?; addr. for s.; *P. Fouad* 44.4.

2663 ---; ch. Lucius Pompeius Niger; (1) Aug 44; (2) 62; property owner; Roman, Pollia tribe; w. son owns property at Sarapeum, Hermaeum qtr; (1) *P. Fouad* 44.5; (2) *SB* XII 10788.28, 48-49.

2664 ---; sp. Sinthonis; ch. Lucia alias Thaisas; 94; Oxyrhynchite; Oxy.?; addr. for d.; II 270.3.

2665 LUCI(U)S; sp. Apollonous; ch. Luci(u)s; i; Sobthis; VIII 1145.20.

2666 ---; s. of Luci(u)s; m. Apollonous; i; Sobthis; VIII 1145. 20.

2667 ---; s. of Petronius; i; farmer?; Sobthis; VIII 1145.21.

2668 LUCIUS; ch. Ptollas; Sept/Oct 137; IV 729.35.

2669 LUCIUS; ch. Cedilla; 168; Alex.; mat. gs. Diogenes alive in 168; XIV 1648.21.

2670 LUCI(U)S; s. of Heraclas; ii; landowner; nr Nesla and Korobis; *P. Inst. Fran.* III 15.9.

LUCIUS; see L. CALPURNIUS GAIANUS, SENECA, SERENUS: L. HERENNIUS CRISPUS: L. POMPEIUS NIGER; L. OFILIUS; L. PAMIGEUS; L. POMPEIUS; [.]L. SECUNDUS.

2671 LUCRETIUS; ch. Anteros; 10/9 BC; IV 817 (descr.).

2672]US LUCRETIUS; 92; soldier?; *P. Michael* 9 B3.

2673 LYCARION; ch. Athenais; 99; Oxyrhynchite?; Oxy.?; addr. for gd. Didyme; *P. Harris* 74.5.

2674 LYC(A)RION; s. of Hermogenes; ch. [Ar]chion; 117; Oxyrhynchite?; Oxy.?; addr. for s.; III 489.23.

2675 [L]YCARION(?); ch. Pasion; 2nd half i; Sesphtha?, L. Top.; addr. for s.; XXXVIII 2845.13.

2676 LYCAS; ch. Soterichus; May 91; *PSI* III 181.3.

2677 LYCOPHRON; ch. Orseutes; 81-96; gs. Onnophris decl.self as gymn. class; VI 984 R(1).

2678 LYCUS; ch. Chamaus; 31/32; Sinary?, L. Top.; addr. for s.; *P. Mich. inv.* 69.12.

2679 ---; ch. Totoes; 31/32; Sinary?, L. Top.; addr. for s.; *P. Mich. inv.* 69.16.

2680 ---; s. of Horus; ch. Senphois the elder, Eudaemon; 81-96; VI 984 R init.

2681 LY]ṢIMACHUS; 89-91; *PSI* XIV 1434.9.

2682 ---; c. 1; IV 822 (descr.).

2683 Ṃ[; ch. Plutus; i; *P. Ryl.* II 199.29.

2684 M[; m. Nicarion; ii; Oxy.; witnesses to will; III 647.12.

2685 M[; sp. Thatres; ch. Taarime; ii; Oxy.?; addr. for s.; III 647.18.

2686 M..IS; i; Oxy.?; age 35; *P. Ryl.* II 156 V.

2687 CLAUDIUS MACEDONIUS; 86; strategus; Roman; Oxy.; VII 1028.1.

2688 MACER (C)]ḶUFENNIUS or AUPHENNIUS; i - ii; soldier, legio XXII, century of Claudius Cuntia[ ]; *PSI* VI 687.5.

2689 MACHON; ch. Heracleides alias Theon; 129; Alex., Sosicosmius, Althaieus; I 95.15.

2690 MACRINUS; ii; workgang supervisor; XLI 2981.5, 8.

2691 MAGIANUS; May 23; II 259.12.

2692 MAGRUS; s. of Hermolaus; sp. Taonnophris; ch. Rhynchis; ii; hamlet of Sarapion?, s. of Chaeremon; addr. for s.; *P. Erl.* 59 R 2.

2693 MẠḶẠNX(?); ch. Mẹục̣ḥo( ); i; Sesphtha?, W. Top.; *P. Ryl.* II 199.2.

MALIA; see MALIA JUSTA.

MALIUS; see T. MALIUS VILLUS.

2694 MANOUS; c. 100; *P. Yale* 77.15.

MARCUS; see M. ANTONIUS DIUS, PALLAS, PTOLEMAEUS, SPENDON, VALENS; CASTRESIUS; M. CUTIUS; M. PORCIUS EPITYNCHANON; VALERIANUS.

2695 ---; ch. Saras; 117-138; X 1293.5.

2696 ---; ii. buys fleeces; VII 1062.1.

2697 MARINUS; ii?; *P. Harris* 104.5.

2698 MARRES; i BC - i; *OD Pisa* 29 ii X + 13.

2699 LICINIUS MARTIALIS; 137; banker w. partners; mentioned as banker in XXXIV 2722.9 of March 154; *PSI* XII 1262 ii 3-4, iii 6-7.

2700 MẠṬṚẠ; i; Oxy.?; age 20; *P. Ryl.* II 156 V.

2701 MATREAS; ii; wool seller?; VII 1062.1.

2702 MATRINA; d. of Heracleus alias Matreus; sp. Dionysius alias Phatres; ch. Didymus; Oct 123; Oxyrhynchite; Oxy.; guardian of s.; VI 898.5.

MATREUS; see HERACLEIUS.

2703 MATRIS; ii; has children; III 529.13.

2704 C. JULIUS MAXIMUS; Feb 103; recruit in 3rd Ituraean cohort; Roman; descr. as aged 25; no signalement; VII 1022.15.

MAXIMUS; see POTAMON.

2705 MELANOUS; d. of Horion, s. of Theon; m. Zois, d. of Tyrus; i - ii; property owner; Isieum Tryphonos; inherits catoecic land, Kleros of Seuthes, nr Talao; *PSI* VI 687.1.

2706 MELAS; June 9; *OD Pisa* 246.2.

2707 ---; 31; fisherman; Teis, Thmois. Top.; XIX 2234.11.

2708 ---; s. of Tryphon; m. Tanemeus; i - ii; *P. Harris* 72.31.

2709 ---; i; *OD Pisa* 129 X + 1.

2710 MENANDRUS; s. of Harbichis; 41-54; property owner; lessor of house?; Oxy.; property in lane of Gooseherders w. bro. Hierax; XXXIII 2669.3.

2711 CLAUDIUS MENANDRUS; (1) 107; (2) 108/9; (3) 118; basilicogrammateus (1 and 2; "former" in 3); Roman; Oxy.; (1) VII 1029.1; (2) *P. Med. inv.* 71.69.1; (3) *SB* I 5768.12.

2712 ---; ii; IX 1213.3 V.

2713 MENCHES; s. of Patesis; i BC; *OD Pisa* 149.1.

2714 ---; i BC - i; dependant of Harpochrates; *OD Pisa* 755 Convesso X + 4.

2715 ---; s. of Pr-Imnt.t; i BC - i; *OD Pisa* 22.9.

2716 ---; i BC - i; *OD Pisa* 127.1.

2717 ---; ch. Cathytes; i BC - i; *OD Pisa* 25 i 11.

2718 ---; July 7; labourer; *OD Pisa* 1131 Convesso 3, 7.

2719 ---; ch. Orsenouphis; 41-54; Oxyrhynchite; lane of Gooseherders?; addr. for s.; XXXIII 2669.7.

2720 ---; ch. Apollonius; 64; Oxyrhynchite; Knights' Camp qtr; addr. for gd. Tauris; *P. Mich.* III 179.4.

2721 MENELAUS; s. of Alexandrus; 31/32; landholder; Alex., Zeneius; Oxy.?; cedes land at Pela; age 32; signalement; *P. Ryl.* II 159, [3] passim.

2722 MENESTHEUS; 14-37; assoc. w. Andronicus; Senepta?, M. Top.; *P. Ryl.* IV 677.6.

2723 ---; ch. Horus; 115/116; Seryphis, W. Top.; addr. for gs. Menestheus; I 97.7.

2724 ---; s. of Horus, s. of Menestheus; 115/116; slave owner; Seryphis, W. Top.; I 97.7.

2725 MENODORUS; s. of Apollonius; 48; weaver; Alex., Althaieus; age 40; signalement; Fuscus his apprentice; *P. Fouad* 37.1.

2726 MENOETES; ch. Eudaemon; Jan 132; Oxyrhynchite?; Oxy.?; addr. for s.; III 478.7.

2727 MENON; i BC - i; *OD Pisa* 22.5.

2728 ---; ch. P_3-spj; i BC - i; *OD Pisa* 111 Convesso 7, Concavo 6.

2729 MESOESIS; i BC - i; *OD Pisa* 451 + 540 Convesso 17.

2730 MEUCHO( ); s. of Malanx(?); i; sitologus; farmer; Sesphtha, W. Top.; *P. Ryl.* II 199.2.

2731 MICCALUS; ch. Diogenes; 148/149; Oxyrhynchite, gymnasial class; Upper Camp qtr; addr. for gs. Terentius; s. scrutinised in 72/73; XLVI 3278.2.

2732 MIEUS; d. of Horus; sp. Dionysius; ch. Petosiris; 119; North St qtr; addr. for s.; XII 1547.3.

2733 MINCION; ch. Heracleides; 136; Oxyrhynchite; Oxy.; addr. for s.; XII 1472.16.

2734 MNESITHEON; July 87; agoranomus; *PSI* III 203.13.

2735 MNESITH[EUS; 13; landholder; Kerkeura, M. Top.; XX 2277.17.

2736 MNESITHEUS; ch. O[.]..[...]; July 42; lessor; XXXVIII 2834.1.

2737 ---; s. of Petesuchus; sp. Aline; ch. Comon; (1) July 42; (2) mid i; (3) July 50; (4) Aug 50; (5) Aug 86; (6), (7) 2nd half i; farmer; lessee; w. Gaius Cutius, at Tholthis, Thmois. Top., Kleros of Pyrrhias; Oxyrhynchite; Sarapis St qtr; stemma in intro (1); Dioscorus bro.-in-law? (2); tax exempt on ousia of Ti. Claudius Caesar (4); died Aug 50 (4); (1) XXXVIII 2834.1; (2) 2835.1, 20; (3) 2836.2; (4) 2837.8; (5) 2843.9; (6) 2845.5; (7) 2846.4.

2738 ---; s. of Theon, s. of Theon; m. Sinthoonis alias Ophelous, d. of Sarapion; (1) July 72; (2) Aug 72 (?); landholder; property owner; lessor; land in Seryphis, W. Top.; part house in Nemerae w. bro. Dionysius; (1) XLIV 3163.6; (2) XLI 2972.3.

2739 ---; i; landholder; II 296.5.

2740 ---; ch. Theon; after 102; III 636.22.

2741 ---; s. of Theon, s. of Mnesitheus; sp. [..]-eia; m.]Hemẹ.[....]; ch. Demetrous; after 102; Oxy.; addr. for d.; III 636.6, 22.

2742 ---; ch. Sarapion; 131; landholder; farmer and vineyard owner; Oxyrhynchite; Oxy.; sold land 127, died between 127 and 131; III 486.4.

2743 MODESTAS; ii; Oxy.; has unnamed s.; XII 1581.10-11.

2744 MONIUS; sp. Thaesis; ch. Haryotes; i - ii; *P. Harris* 72.30.

2745 MONTHIS; s. of W_3ḥ-p_3-pr-$^{c}{}_3$ (?); i BC - i; *OD Pisa* 541 Convesso ii 1.

2746 ---; s. of Tcales; i BC - i; *OD Pisa* 779 + 242 Concavo 4.

2747 MORUS; ii; "brother" of Flavius; XLII 3058.1.

2748 ---; ii; agent for Epimachus; XII 1482 R and V 1.

2749 MOSCHION; m. Berenice, d. of Dionysius and Arsinoe; 63/62 BC; Macedonian of catoecic cavalry; Cleopatra Aphrodite St; XIV 1644.7.

2750 CLAUDIUS MUNATIANUS; 123; landowner?; Roman; overseer Leontas; *P. Lips.* 112.1,8-9.

2751 MUNATIUS; 37-41; XIV 1672.16.

2752 JULIUS MUSAEUS; i; II 349.2.

2753 MYLON; ch. Harmiysis; 87/88; Syron Kome, W. Top.; doc. pr.?; addr. for gs. Heras; *P. Princ.* III 147.5.

2754 MYNIUS; sp. Philumene; ch. Tryphon; i - ii; *P. Harris* 72.32.

2755 MYRON; ii; money from Cornelius; III 531.24.

2756 MYSTHARAS; ii; Oxy.; XII 1584.28.

2757 MYSTHAS; d. of Heracleus?; m. Berous; i - ii; age 32; *P. Harris* 72.9.

2758 N[; ch. Pausiris; i; Sesphtha; addr. for s.; *P. Ryl.* II 199.22.

2759 N[...]LUS; s. of ...chas, s. of ...mis; m. Helene, d. of ...us; i; property owner; Senepta, M. Top.; doc. pr. Oxy.?; buys part court yard in Senepta; *P. Harris* 138 i 3.

2760 NAAROPHIBIS; ch. Senaias; 2nd half i; Sinary?, L. Top.; addr. for gs. Ammonis; XXXVIII 2846.2.

2761 NARCISSUS; s. of Archias; c. 50; banker; XXVII 2471.10.

2762 ---; ch. Narcissus; 71; Oxyrhynchite; Oxy.; addr. for gs. Theon; *P. Med. inv.* 71.70.8.

2763 ---; s. of Narcissus; sp. Tausorapis; ch. Theon; 71; Oxyrhynchite; Oxy.; addr. for s.; *P. Med. inv.* 71.70.8.

2764 ---; ch. Clara; 94; Oxyrhynchite; Oxy.; addr. for gs. Sarapion alias Clarus (mat.); II 270.7.

2765 NARIS; s. of Colluthus; Jan 26; livestock owner; Pela?, W. Top.; II 245.3.

2766 NECTHENIBIS; ch. Saraeus; 81/82; Oxyrhynchite?; Oxy.?; addr. for gd. Apollonous; *P. Mert.* III 118.5.

2767 ---; ch. Theon; 107; Episemon, U. Top.; addr. for s.; XVIII 2188.17.

2768 NE]CHTHENIBIS; ch. Thermuthion; 119; Oxy.; addr. for gs. (mat.) Theon; XII 1547.32.

2769 NECHTHENICIS; s. of Ptollion; sp. Di[.....; ch. Harmiysis; early ii; Phthochis?, E. Top.; addr. for niece Taptollion; *P. Wisc.* I 13.2.

2770 NECHTHESORIS; ch. Papontos; 19/20; Myrobalanus qtr; addr. for s.; II 254.8.

2771 NECHTHEUS; c. 1; baker; IV 739.3.

2772 NECHTHONSIS; i BC - i; *OD Pisa* 38 i X + 9.

2773 NECHTHOSIRIS; ch. Sarapion; i; Oxyrhynchite?; Oxy.?; addr. for gs. Nechthosiris; *P. Harris* 138 iii 14.

2774 ---; s. of Sarapion, s. of Nechthosiris; m.[....]nius; i; lessee of catoecic land; Oxyrhynchite?; Oxy.?; leases land at Senepta from Areius, s. of Sarapion; *P. Harris* 138 iii [13], 16.

2775 NECHUTES; ch. Nechutes; i BC - i; *OD Pisa* 28 X + 4.

2776 ---; s. of Nechutes; i BC - i; inhabitant? of Š^{c}r; *OD Pisa* 28 X + 4

2777 ---; ch. Tri$_{3}$s(?); i BC - i; *OD Pisa* 25 ii 1.

2778 ---; s. of Thotes; i BC - i; *OD Pisa* 25 i 16.

2779 ---; s. of Harchypsis; i BC - i; *OD Pisa* 25 i 26.

2780 ---; i BC - i; *OD Pisa* 25 ii 8.

2781 ---; ch. Pausiris; i BC - i; *OD Pisa* 668.1.

2782 ---; ch. Petechonsis; i BC - i; *OD Pisa* 281 + 94 X + 11.

2783 ---; i BC - i; dependant of Demetrius; *OD Pisa* 502 X + 7.

2784 ---; i BC - i; *OD Pisa* 477 Concavo X + 6.

2785 ---; s. of Snn; i BC - i; *OD Pisa* 755 Concavo X + 7.

2786 ---; i BC - i; *OD Pisa* 779 + 242 Convesso X + 5.

2787 ---; i BC - i; *OD Pisa* 58.3, 12.

2788 NECTENIBIS; s. of Cheres; i BC - i; *OD Pisa* 267.3.

2789 ---; ch. Pasis; i BC - i; *OD Pisa* 106.8.

2790 ---; s. of Patous; i BC - i; *OD Pisa* 1163 bis Convesso 5.

2791 ---; s. of Pamun; i BC - i; *OD Pisa* 504.5.

2792 ---; s. of P$_{3}$-rj.t; i BC - i; *OD Pisa* 504.6.

2793 ---; Aug 3; *OD Pisa* 473 Convesso 3.

2794 ---; s. of Petosiris; (1) April 4; (2) i; (1) *OD Pisa* 511 + 512 i 8; (2) 60 Convesso ii 5.

2795 ---; s. of Brichis; early i; *OD Pisa* 425.2.

2796 ---; s. of Petetymis; i; *OD Pisa* 60 Concavo 3.

2797 NEILAROUS; sp. Zoilus; ch. Apion; 130; Oxyrhynchite?; Oxy.?; III 492.18.

NEMERIA; see STLACCIA.

2798 NEMESIANUS; early ii; XVIII 2200.9.

2799 NEMESION; alias ALCIMUS; 112/113; paid opsonion to Socrates; III 586 (descr.).

2800 NEMESOUS; 2nd half i; shop owner; XXXVIII 2844.4.

2801 NEMION; s. of Heracleius; m. Berous; i - ii; age 24; *P. Harris* 72.11.

2802 NEOPTOLEMUS; ch. Neoptolemus; 91/92; Oxyrhynchite; Oxy.; addr. for gs. Didymus; XXXVIII 2856.5.

2803 ---; s. of Neoptolemus; sp. Demetria; ch. Didymus; 91/92; Oxyrhynchite; Oxy.; addr. for s.; XXXVIII 2856.5.

2804 ---; ch. Theolympion; 117; Oxyrhynchite?; Oxy.?; addr. for gs. Hermaeus alias Hermaeon; *P. Harris* 85.5.

2805 ---; ch. Ammonius; ii; *P. Sel.* 22.4.

2806 NEPHERSOUS; sp. Horus; ch. Horus; 131; Talao, L. Top.; addr. for s.; *SB* VI 9190.5.

2807 NEPHORSAIS; i BC - i; *OD Pisa* 267.1.

NICAEA; see NICAEA SIL[VA]NUS.

2808 NICANDRUS; (1) 72/73 (?); (2) 94/95; (3) 98; (4) 127/128; (5) to (9) 148/149; basilicogrammateus in 72/73 (2 to 9) w. Sutorius Sosibius, str., but descr. as "former" in 94/95 (2); (1) *P. Genov* I 12.1; (2) II 257.14; (3) X 1266.27; (4) XII 1452 ii 45; (5) XLVI 3276.11; (6) 3277.[9]; (7) 3279.[14]; (8) 3282.16; (9) 3283.11.

2809 NICAEUS (NIGAEUS?); ch. Apion; i; Koba; addr. for s.; VIII 1145.3.

2810 NICANOR; s. of Sostratus; sp.[..].[..]as; 78/79; Oxyrhynchite; Thoeris St qtr; XXXVI 2756.3.

2811 ---; i; now in Alexandria; VIII 1153.5 and passim.

2812 ---; ch. Ammonius; 115/116; gf. of Nicanor; I 97.21.

2813 ---; s. of Ammonius, s. of Nicanor; slave owner; age 32; I 97.3 and passim.

2814 NICARION; ch. M.....; ii; Oxyrhynchite; III 647.12.

NICARIUS; see AMMONIUS

2815 NICAROUS; ch. Sarapous, Cerdon, Epicharmus; 127; slave; Oxy.; s. of bridegroom, Sarapion; III 496.7.

2816 NICE; ii; re buying slave; VIII 1149.4.

2817 Ṇ[I]CE; ii; III 530.25-26.

2818 NICE; ii; "sister" of Dionysas; III 644 (descr.).

2819 NICIAS; ch. Heracleides; i BC; Psobthis (restored), M. Top.; doc. pr. Oxy.?; addr. for s.; has other sons; *P. Ryl.* IV 579.2.

2820 NICIPPUS; ch. Nicippus; (1) 56; (2) 95; Alex., Phylaxithalassius, Althaieus; Alexandria? (1), Oxy.? (2); deme for gs. Theon; addr. for s. (1), gs. (2); (1) II 271.3; (2) 273.9.

2821 NICIPPUS; s. of Nicippus; ch. Theon; (1) 56; (2) 95; Alex., Phylaxithalassius, Althaieus; Alexandria? (1), Oxy.? (2); guardian of Heracleia, d. of Heracleides; deme and addr. (2) for s.; (1) II 271.3; (2) 273.8.

2822 NICOBULUS; ch. Theon; late i; II 300.7, V.

2823 ---; ch. Ammonarion; i; Oxyrhynchite?; Oxy.?; addr. for gs. (mat.) Areius and Anoup; *P. Harris* 138 iii 12.

2824 NICOSTRATUS; ch. ...euris; Jan 28; Pela?, W. Top.; addr. for s.; II 351.2-3.

2825 ---; s. of ...euris, s. of Nicostratus; Jan 28; shepherd; Pela, W. Top.; minor; II 351.13-14.

2826 ---; ch. Ptollas; Sept 77; Oxy.; addr. for s., pilot; II 276.6.

2827 L. POMPEIUS NIGER; s. of Syrus (= Lucius), s. of Apion; ch. Fuscus; (1) Aug 44; (2) 48; (3) 61; (4) 62; (5) 64; veteran of 22nd legion; property owner; Roman, Pollia tribe; Oxy.?; doc. pr. Oxy.? (2-5); s. apprenticed as weaver to Menodorus; inherited quarter house (3, 4) from f. and owns w. Teseuris (5); (1) *P. Fouad* 44.5; (2) 37.1; (3) *SB* XII 10788.2; (4) 10788.27; (5) 10788.48.

2828 NILAMMON; s. of Ammonius, s. of Theon; m. Thaubarion; 132/133; Alex., Propapposebasteius, Althaieus; Oxy.?; being reg. this year; III 477.15.

2829 NILUS; i BC - i; *OD Pisa* 510 + 568 Convesso i 16.

---; see DIOGAS.

2830 ---; ?s. of Theon; late i; student; Alexandria; from Oxy.?; XVIII 2190 [1], V.

2831 ---; ch. Papontos, Hermogenes; i; *P. Harris* 144.6, 7.

2832 ---; i - ii; XXXI 2592.1.

2833 ---; s. of Syrus, s. of Apion; Aug 114 or 133; soldier; property owner; now called Polem[archus](?); bro. of Apion, Syrus, Sarapion and Thais; *SB* VIII 9824.3.

2834 NISUS; ii; *P. Harris* 106.8.

2835 NOERIS; ch. Ammonius; Aug 106; Oxyrhynchite; 10th qtr; *P. Wisc.* I 17 R 20.

2836 NỌMUS?; ch. Eunomus; Sept 103; Toka, M. Top.; addr. for gd. Ạthenarous; XLI 2973.2.

NOTHUS; see HARTHOONIS.

2837 [NU]MENIUS; i; agent of Julius Musaeus; II 349.1.

2838 O[.]..[...; s. of Mnesitheus; July 42; lessor; XXXVIII 2834.1.

2839 Ọ[....]S[...; c. 129; fisherman; Oxyrhynchite; Oxy.; *P. Cornell* 46.4.

OFILIUS; see L. OFILIUS ANTISTIUS.

2840 OHAPIM; 30 BC - 14; public banker; Oxy.; XLIV 3208.1.

2841 OLYMPUS: ch. Heracleides; 100/101 or 119/120; Heracleopolis; addr. for gd. Thaisous alias Thaesis, adoptive m. of Aphroditous alias Demarous of Oxy.; III 504.34.

2842 ON( ); ch. Seuthas; Nov 42 BC; Oxy.?; addr. for s.; *P. Ryl.* 582.22.

2843 ONESIMUS; ii; XXXIII 2679.1.

2844 ONIAS; ch. Heracleia; 126; Heracleopolis?; doc. pr. Oxy.?; *P. Harris* 142.16.

2845 ONNOPHRIS; i BC; "brother" of Antiochus; Oxy.; *PSI* IX 1079.1.

2846 ---; s. of Dionysius, s. of Chaeremon; 6/5 BC; *PSI* X 1099.1.

2847 ---; s. of Petosiris; April 5 BC; *OD Pisa* 936 Convesso 7.

2848 ---; 5/4 BC; topogrammateus of W. Top.; *P. Oslo* III 26.2.

2849 ---; i BC - i; *OD Pisa* 510 + 568 Convesso i 10.

2850 ---; ch. Horus; i BC - i; (1) *OD Pisa* 351 X + 2; (2) 5 ii X + 4.

2851 ---; s. of Horus; i BC - i; see also Onnophrius; *OD Pisa* 799 + 242 Convesso X + 17.

2852 ---; ch. Pecmius (P_3-gmws); i BC - i; *OD Pisa* 280 X + 3.

2853 ---; s. of Harimuthes; i BC - i; (1) *OD Pisa* 460 Convesso i X + 4; (2) 451 + 540 Convesso 12.

2854 ---; ch. Onnophris; i BC - i; *OD Pisa* 25 ii 15.

2855 ---; s. of Onnophris; i BC - i; *OD Pisa* 25 ii 15.

2856 ONNOPHRIS(?); s. of Tbt; i BC - i; *OD Pisa* 243 + 472 i 9.

2857 ONNOPHRIS; i BC - i; addr. Pr-Sg_3; *OD Pisa* 132 X + 4.

2858 ---; s. of Ḥr-Ḥbj; i BC - i; *OD Pisa* 196 ii X + 5.

2859 ---; s. of Totoes; i BC - i; (1) *OD Pisa* 5 i X + 7; (2) 5 ii X + 8.

2860 ---; i BC - i; *OD Pisa* 477 Convesso 5.

2861 ---; s. of Patous; late i BC - early i; *OD Pisa* 35 Concavo ii 17.

2862 ---; s. of Petetymis; late i BC - early i; *OD Pisa* 35 Concavo ii 16.

2863 ---; Jan/Feb 21; II 386 (descr.).

2864 ONNOPHRIS; s. of Antipater; 36; guardian of Saraeus, d. of Apion; illiterate; II 267.2.

2865 ---; ch. Thamunion; (1) 36; (2) 37; (3) Jan 44; (4) Sept 66; Oxyrhynchite?; Oxy.?; addr. for gs. Tryphon; (1) II 322.[2]; (2) 319.1; (3) 251.4; (4) 275.3.

2866 ---; Nov 41; II 325.1.

2867 ---; ch. Heras; July 44; Pela, W. Top.; addr. for s.; XII 1477.4.

2868 ---; s. of Dionysius; m. Thamunion, d. of Onnophris; (1) 36; (2) 59; apprentice weaver in (1); Oxyrhynchite; Oxy.; descr. as Persian of Epigone; (1) II 322.8; (2) 320.6.

2869 ---; ch. Theon; (1) July 59; (2) 66-72/73; Oxy.?; addr. for s., hyperetes to Ti. Claudius Herodes, str.; (1) II 260.19; (2) IX 1203 + *SB* IV 7339.31.

2870 ---; m. Taorse[us; Dec 75/Jan 76; Oxyrhynchite; Oxy.; addr. for unnamed gs.; *P. Yale* 64.5.

2871 ---; s. of Orseutes, s. of Lycophron; m. Anresis, d. of Phatres; 81-96; Oxyrhynchite, gymnasial class; Oxy.; age 40; VI 984 R (1).

2872 ---; ch. Thoonis; 83; Oxy.; addr. for gss. Thoonis, Eudaemon, Didymus(?); II 289 i 5.

2873 ---; ch. Totoeus; 83/84; Tychis Necotis; addr. for s.; II 290.23.

2874 ---; ch. Tasentheus; 83/84; Tychis Necotis; addr. for d.; II 290.25.

2875 ---; s. of Sois; sp. Taorseus; ch. Chaeremon; 86; Oxyrhynchite; Hippodrome qtr; died in 80; VII 1028.16.

2876 ---; s. of Diogenes; m. Tsenouaris, d. of Onnophris; Jan 93; Oxyrhynchite; Oxy.; age 50; guardian of m.; *PSI* VIII 897.5, 56.

2877 ---; s. of Harpsois; ch. Tsenouaris; gs. Onnophris; Jan 94; Oxyrhynchite; Oxy.; addr. for s., aged 70; *PSI* VIII 897.3.

2878 ---; ch. Lochus; April 96; *P. Oslo* III 95.11.

2879 ---; s. of Pammenes; sp. Taarthonis; ch. Onnophris; 96; Oxyrhynchite?; Oxy.?; addr. for s.; II 266.4.

2880 ---; s. of Onnophris, s. of Pammenes; m. Taarthonis; sp. Sintheus; 96; Oxyrhynchite; Oxy.; guardian of step-d. Thaesis; II 266.4.

2881 ---; ch. Ptolemaeus; 98-117; Isieum Panga; addr. for s.; *PSI* VII 772.3.

2882 ---; late i; II 396 (descr.).

2883 ---; i; "brother" of Antiochus; *PSI* IX 1079.1.

2884 ONNOPHRIS; s. of Osmolchis; sp. Tesauris; ch. Asclas, Osmolchis; 107; Oxyrhynchite?; 10th qtr?; addr. for s.; VII 1029.3, 13.

2885 ---; s. of Teos; sp. Taseus; ch. Onnophris, Teos; 107; Oxyrhynchite?; 10th qtr?; addr. for s.; VII 1029.2.

2886 ---; s. of Onnophris, s. of Teos; m. Taseus; 107; hieroglyph carver; Oxyrhychite; 10th qtr; only 5 h. carvers in Oxy.; VII 1029.13.

2887 ---; ch. Thermuthion; 132/133; gs. Onnophris; *PSI* VIII 874 i 3.

2888 ---; s. of Theon, s. of Sarapion; m. Thermuthion, d. of Onnophris; 132/133; tutor of Anteis and Taamois (w. Heras); *PSI* VIII 874 i 2.

2889 ---; s. of Thonis; ch. Theon; Aug 133; *P. Köln* II 100.29.

2890 ---; ch. [A]mois; 132/133 or 153/154; Oxy.; XII 1518.18.

2891 ---; ii; camel driver; of Apollonius; I 113.4, passim.

2892 ---; s. of Amois, s. of Sarapion; ii; hamlet of Cosmos?; doc. pr. Tebtynis; addr. for bro. Amois; *P. Mil. Vogl.* IV 211 b 8.

2893 ---; s. of Dionysius; ii; practor of money taxes in E. (qtr?); Oxyrhynchite; *P. Sel.* 22.6.

2894 ---; ii; III 531.12-13.

2895 ---; ii; descr. as the younger; XXXI 2593.3.

2896 ONNOPHRIUS; s. of Horus; i BC - i; *OD Pisa* 510 + 568 Convesso i 9.

2897 ONTHONOBIS; c. 1; IV 815 (descr.).

2898 OPHELAS; ch. Apollos; 117/118; IV 837 (descr.).

2899 ---; alias CORAX; 139; freedman; farmer; lessee; Oxyrhynchite?; Oxy.; f. of Apia alias Dionysia; leases land in Senao, M. Top., from Kleros of Heracleides and Heracleides; X 1279.2.

2900 ---; ii; Oxy.; III 647.10.

2901 ---; ii; *P. Mert.* III 109.9 and passim.

2902 ---; alias BESAS; s. of Sarapas; m. Apollonous; ii; Oxyrhynchite; Oxy.; appt. rep. of Artemidorus; III 505.1.

2903 OPHELOUS; d. of Heraclas, s. of Antiphanes; m. Ammonarion, d. of Dionysius; 58; property owner; Ptolemais Hermiu; II 268.3.

2904 ---; d. of Theon; sp. Pausirion; ch. Ptolemaeus; Sept 66; Oxyrhynchite; Oxy.; addr. for s.; II 275.4.

---; see SINTHOONIS.

2905 OPHIEUS; ch. Sisyphis; 81-96; gs. Sisyphis is 60; VI 984 R (2).

2906 ORIGAS; i; messenger; VIII 1153.13.

2907 ORIGENES; s. of [Ascle]piades, s. of Asclep[iades]; 72/73; Oxyrhynchite, gymnasial class; Chenoboskon qtr; unnamed s. lives in North Quay qtr; *PSI* V 457.8-9.

2908 ---; ch. Philotera; 133; Alex.; Alexandria; addr. for (mat.) gs. Adrastus; I 100.5.

2909 ORSENOUPHIS; s. of Petosiris; 73 or 44 BC; farmer; wheat seller; Oxy.?; descr. as Persian of Epigone; bro. of Pecysis; XIV 1639 i 24.

2910 ---; May 37 BC; pays crown tax; *Coll. Pap.* I 17.8.

2911 ---; s. of Horus; i BC; *OD Pisa* 55 i 3.

2912 ---; s. of Menches; 41-54; bronze-smith; Oxyrhynchite; Gooseherders' lane; XXXIII 2669.7.

2913 ---; s. of Dioscorus; 80/81; presbyteros; Peeno, M. Top.; *Coll. Pap.* II 21.3.

2914 ---; s. of [Po]c[o]ous? or [Pe]c[o]ous?; Sept 103; Oxyrhynchite?; Oxy.; XLI 2973.6.

2915 ORSES; i BC - i; *OD Pisa* 1163 bis Concavo B 4.

2916 ORSEUTES; s. of Lycophron; sp. Anreisis; ch. Onnophris; 81-96; s. aged 40 and of gymnasial class; VI 984 R (1).

2917 ORTHONOOS; ch. Ptollis; Oct 62; Sesphtha?, L. Top.; addr. for gs.; XXXVIII 2873.3.

2918 OSIR[ ]?; ch. Totoes; i BC - i; *OD Pisa* 561 + 562 + 795 ii 20.

2919 OSMOLCHIS; ch. Onnophris; 107; Oxyrhynchite?; 10th qtr; addr. for gs. Asclas and Osmolchis; VII 1029.4.

2920 ---; s. of Onnophris, s. of Osmolchis; m. Tesauris; 107; hieroglyph carver; Oxyrhynchite; 10th qtr; only 5 h. carvers in Oxy.; VII 1029.15.

2921 OSORAPIS; ii; priest; XXXIII 2679.7.

2922 OTHENYRIS; c. 107-112; unnamed m.; *PSI* V 450 R ii 38.

2923 P.[..]; ch. Tetoeris; Dec 81; Oxyrhynchite?; Oxy.?; addr. for d., descr. as Persian; XII 1471.7.

2924 P[-]; ch. Ptolemaeus; 148/149; Oxyrhynchite, gymnasial class; Upper Camp qtr; addr. for gs. Di[ ]; XLVI 3277.2.

2925 PA...; ch. Horus; i BC - i; *OD Pisa* 816 X + 6.

2926 PA-$_3$ll; ch. Petosiris; i BC - i; *OD Pisa* 126 i 9.

2927 PAAEIS; ch. Theon; 36; II 267.30.

2928 PAANUPHIS; 81-96; VI 984 R fin.

2929 PAAPIS; s. of Thonis; 30/29 BC; temple lamplighter; Oxy.; t. of Thoeris; XII 1453.6.

2930 ---; 25; Oxy.; Tryphon, s. of Dionysius pays via him; II 288.2.

2931 ---; s. of Philas; May 26; slave owner; provides slave Thermutharion for Taseus; *P. Rein.* II 103.5.

2932 ---; sp. Tecosis; ch. Thompachrates; Nov 83; Oxyrhynchite; addr. for s.; X 1282.8.

2933 PAAS; s. of ..a..nus, s. of Horus; m. Sinthoonis; 99; Oxyrhynchite; *P. Princ.* II 32.3-4.

2934 PABELLAS; early i; *OD Pisa* 450A Concavo i 10.

2935 PABIS (Pa-bj); ch. Dd; i BC - i; *OD Pisa* 127.3.

2936 ---; ch. C_3; i BC - i; *OD Pisa* 281 + 94 X + 5.

2937 ---; s. of Harendotes; i BC - i; *OD Pisa* 451 + 540 Convesso 7.

2938 ---; ch. Thoteus; i BC - i; *OD Pisa* 755 Convesso 10.

2939 ---; i; *OD Pisa* 60 Convesso ii 3.

2940 PACHNUBIS; 87/88; Tanais?, M. Top.; doc. pr. Oxy.?; unnamed d.; gs. (mat.) Pisys; *Coll. Pap.* I 22.4.

2941 ---; d. of Totoes, s. of Tryphon; sp. Thaesis; ch. Totoes alias Plutarchus, Pachnubis; (1) Oct 108; (2) Oct 112; farmer; lessor; Tanais, M. Top.; descr. as Persian of Epigone; name (in 2) Pachnumis; stemma at *BASP* 5 (1968) 142; (1) XXXVIII 2874.2; (2) XXII 2351.5.

2942 PACHNUBIS; s. of Pachnubis, s. of Totoes; m. Thaesis; Oct 112; farmer; lessee; Tanais, M. Top.; Persian of Epigone; rents part of Kleros of Nicaeus; XXII 2351.5.

2943 ---; s. of Pecysis; m. Teencegous; ii; Tanais?, M. Top.; guardian of sister Sinthonis; III 505.4.

2944 PACHOIS; 81-96; part owner house South Quay qtr; II 379 (descr.).

2945 PAEIS; 77; stolistes; Oxy.; s. of Thoeris, Isis, Sarapis and assoc. gods; II 242.7.

2946 PAERIS; s. of Psenthotes; i; *OD Pisa* Convesso i 12.

2947 PAESIS; ch. Paesis; 47; II 313.3.

2948 ---; s. of Paesis; 47; landholder; livestock owner; II 313.3.

2949 ---; ch. Apollos; 117/118; Kerkemunis, U. Top.; addr. for d.; IV 837 (descr.).

2950 PAGONIS; i BC - i; *OD Pisa* 510 + 568 Convesso i 13.

2951 ---; s. of Cleitus; i BC - i; *OD Pisa* 377 Convesso 9.

2952 ---; i BC - i; *OD Pisa* 72 i X + 5.

2953 ---; i BC - i; *OD Pisa* 454.2.

2954 ---; i BC - i; *OD Pisa* 460 Convesso ii X + 4, 5.

2955 ---; i BC - i; *OD Pisa* 561 + 562 + 795 i X + 8.

2956 ---; ch. Petechonsis; i BC - i; (1) *OD Pisa* 72 ii X + 6; (2) 470.6; (3) 8.10.

2957 PAK[- ; s. of Senth(eus); ch. Diogenes; 98/99; Tholthis, L. Top.; *P. Köln* II 86.4

2958 M. ANTONIUS PALLAS; Feb 91; Roman; house and slave at Temgenuthis qtr(?) pledged to Pallas; XLI 2597.12, 16.

2959 PAMIAS; i BC - i; dependant of Snmns; *OD Pisa* 502 X + 5.

2960 L. PAMISEUS; 59; veteran; farmer; Roman; *P. Fouad* 28.2.

2961 PAMM[; ch. Thonis; 126; Oxyrhynchite; Oxy.; addr. for s., witness to will; III 491.23.

2962 PAMMENES; ch. Onnophris; 96; Oxyrhynchite?; Oxy.?; addr. for gs. Onnophris; II 266.4-5.

2963 PAMONTIS; i BC - i; *OD Pisa* 196 ii X + 8.

2964 PAMPHILUS; s. of Sarapion; 35; banker; see Plutarchus; II 323[11], 18.

2965 ---; 98; basilicogrammateus in 74/75; X 1266.2.

2966 PAMUN; s. of Thoteus; i BC - i; *OD Pisa* 1023 Convesso i 5.

2967 ---; x. of Wrš; i BC - i; *OD Pisa* 460 Convesso ii X + 3.

2968 ---; i BC - i; *OD Pisa* 72 i X + 4.

2969 ---; i BC - i; *OD Pisa* 126 i 10.

2970 ---; ch. Petosiris; i BC - i; *OD Pisa* 126 ii 1.

2971 ---; s. of *Psenpebos (P_3-šrj-p_3-$_3b_3$); (1) i BC - i; (2) i; (1) *OD Pisa* 25 i 7; (2) 129 X + 10.

2972 ---; i BC - i; bro. of Psensnes; *OD Pisa* 25 i 3.

2973 ---; ch. Nectenibis; i BC - i; *OD Pisa* 504.5.

2974 ---; ch. Phatres; i BC - i; *OD Pisa* 106.7.

2975 ---; s. of Harsiesis; i BC - i; *OD Pisa* 106.4.

2976 PAMUN; i BC - i; *OD Pisa* 196 i X + 5.

2977 ---; ch. Petechonsis; (1), (2) i BC - i; (3) i; (1) *OD Pisa* 755 Concavo X + 11; (2) 540 + 568 Convesso i 6; (3) 60 Concavo 4.

2978 ---; s. of Conuphis; early i; *OD Pisa* 164.6.

2979 ---; s. of Harpaosiris; early i; *OD Pisa* 42.1.

2980 ---; April, early i; *OD Pisa* 423.1.

2981 ---; ch. Horus; i; *OD Pisa* 60 Convesso i 6.

2982 ---; s. of Pebos; i; *OD Pisa* 129 X + 4.

2983 ---; s. of Somtous; i; *OD Pisa* 318.3.

2984 ---; ii; Oxy.; *P. Erl.* 59 V.

2985 PAMYRIS; s. of Harpalus, s. of Theon; after 89; Oxy.?; doc. pr. Oxy.?; addr. for father (dec.); bro. Amois; *P. Lips.* 120.10.

2986 PANARES; early ii; X 1269.24.

2987 ---; ii; assists Morus in winnowing barley for Epimachus; XII 1482 R and V 8, 13.

2988 PANAS; Aug 106; *P. Wisc.* I 17 V 20.

2989 PANCRATES; ch. Ammonius; 2nd half i; Sesphtha?, L. Top.; addr. for s.; XXXVIII 2845.7.

2990 PANE[- ; s. of Petosiris, s. of Artem [....; m. ....]nis, d. of Didymus; 71; Senekeleu, W. Top.; *P. Med. inv.* 71.70.4.

2991 PANECHOTES (P_3-nḫt); s. of Petechonsis; i BC - i; *OD Pisa* 68.4.

2992 ---; i BC - i; dependant of Psenmonthes; *OD Pisa* 1023 Convesso i 4.

2993 ---; s. of Pausiris; 26?; slave owner; *P. Rein.* II 104.5.

2994 ---; s. of Petemunis; Jan 29; shepherd; Kerkemunis, U. Top.; minor, working in K.; XXXVIII 2850.14-15.

2995 ---; ch. Theon; 44/45; g.sons farm domain land nr Nesla, U. Top.; II 279.8-9.

2996 ---; Sept 58; tax farmer (weavers' tax); Oxy.; assoc. w. Ischyrion; *P. Mich.* III 171.1, 21.

2997 ---; ch. Petsiris alias Libo; May 89; unnamed gs. leases part of Estate of Seneca; XLII 3051.3.

2998 ---; ch. Tsenammonas; March 90; Oxyrhynchite?; Oxy.?; addr. for d.; II 247.7.

2999 PANECHOTES; ch. Pausiris; March 90; Oxyrhynchite?; Oxy.?; addr. for gs. Panechotes; II 247.5.

3000 ---; s. of Pausiris, s. of Panechotes; m. Tsenammonas, d. of Panechotes; March 90; Oxyrhynchite; Oxy.; bro. owns property in Knights' Camp qtr; II 247.4.

3001 ---; s. of Dionysius alias Amoinomerius; 117; Oxyrhynchite; Oxy.; age 32; witness; signalement; III 489.27.

3002 ---; ch. Zoilus; 117-137; Oxyrhynchite; Oxy.; addr. for gs. Zoilus; I 105.16.

3003 ---; sp. Ammonous; ch. Dionysius; 124; freedman; Oxy.; f. of Petosiris; III 490.4, 9.

3004 ---; ch.[c.5]ris(f); 148/149; Oxyrhynchite, gymnasial class; Knights' Camp qtr; addr. for d.; mat. gs. Sarapion enrolled this yr; XLVI 3279.9.

3005 ---; ii; XXXIV 2726.1.

3006 PANEMGEUS; alias .EO..; s. of Psenosiris; 2nd half i; practor; Sesphtha, L. Top.; XXXVIII 2845.8.

3007 ---; sp. Thermuthion; ch. Papotnos alias Leontas; Feb 130?; Sesphtha, L. Top.; addr. for s.; *P. Mich. inv.* 974.5.

3008 ---; s. of Dioscorus; sp. Tauris; ch. Anteis, Taamois, Tausoreus; 132/133; property owner; Oxy.; his property in Hermaeum qtr now owned by ch.; *PSI* VIII 874 i 5.

3009 PANESIES; ch. Taonnnophris; 91 or 107; Oxy.; addr. for gs. Heraclas; IV 722.22.

3010 PANESNEUS; sp. Tanouris; ch. Thaesis, Senpanesneus, Senparaithis, Petarpochration (dec.); 81-96; freedman; weaver; dwells in Temple of Ares greatest god; aged 45; f. of Apollonia; 2 s. by Tatnagous; VI 984 R init.

3011 ---; s. of Horus; June 103-110; priest of Ammon; Senocomis village; illiterate; XLVI 3275.3.

3012 PANETBES; s. of Emechus; m. Sintheus; i - ii; *P. Harris* 72.24.

3013 ---; s. of Harmaeis; m. Thermuthis; sp. Taorsenouphis (1), T..aete (2); ch. Pnepheros, Harmaeis; i - ii; aged 41; *P. Harris* 72.25.

3014 PANETBEUS; s. of Harmiysis; Jan 100; farmer; landholder?; Nemerae, M. Top.; XLI 2960.11.

3015 ---; n.d.; *DO Colon inv.* 50.1.

3016 [PA]NISCUS; [alias HERAC]LAS?; 81-96; strategus; Oxy.; I 44.1.

3017 PANISC[US; c. 107-112; advocate?; *PSI* IV 281 i 24.

3018 PANI[SCUS; Aug 107; *P. Wisc.* I 17 V 1.

3019 PANNUS; ii; bro.? of Theon; "brother" of Diogenis and Eteocleia; XII 1584.9, 32 V.

3020 PANOUPHIS; s. of Peret; 8; *OD Pisa* 1.10.

3021 ---; ch. Dieuches; 131; Talao, L. Top.; addr. for gs. Panouphis; *SB* VI 9190.6.

3022 ---; s. of Dieuches, s. of Panouphis; m. Tetheus; 131; landholder; Talao, L. Top.; borrows from Horus on security of land in catoecic holding of Conon; *SB* VI 9190.6.

3023 PANRYMIS; ch. Harpaesis; 21; Sinary?, L. Top.; addr. for s.; X 1281.4.

3024 PANTAUCHES; ch. Poccaous; 132/133; Oxyrhynchite; Oxy.; addr. for s.; *PSI* VIII 874 i 8.

3025 PANTELES; s. of Ammonius; ch. Ammonius; ii; ref. to village of Taampemou; *P. Oslo* III 108.3.

3026 PANTHER; late i; appointee, w. Hermogenes, of Ti. Claudius, superintendent of land distributions of Egypt; II 344 (descr.).

3027 PAOOUS; ch. Harpocras; 116; *P. Cair. Preis.* 32.5.

3028 PAOPETES; s. of Papnoutis, s. of Pnepheros and Tembius; m. Tapetouris; i - ii; age 15; *P. Harris* 72.19.

3029 PAOR; s. of Phatres; Oct 5; *OD Pisa* 427.2.

3030 PAOS; s. of Peteuris, s. of Saras; m. Taaphynchis; ch. [Taps?]ois; 116; tekton and pyraethes of Isis, Thoeris, Sarapis and assoc. gods; Gymnasium St qtr; dec. this yr; XII 1550.5, 17.

3031 PAPECHIRIS; s. of Asclas; early i; *OD Pisa* 320.2.

3032 PAPIRIS; i; XXXVI 2786.3.

3033 ---; s. of Totoes; sp. Tachnoumis; ch. Totoes, Thoonis alias Alc. ..; Oct 112; Tanais?, M. Top.; addr. for s.; XXII 2351.7, 83.

3034 PAPISCUS; July 66; strategus; ex-cosmetes of Alex.; Oxy.; II 246.1.

3035 PAPNOUTIS; s. of Pnepheros; sp. Tapetouris; m. Tembius; ch. Paopetes; i - ii; age 47; *P. Harris* 72.18.

3036 PAPONTOS; s. of Nechthesoris; 19/20; property owner; Myrobalanus qtr; owns part house in Temple of Duo Adelphi; II 254.8.

3037 ---; s. of Socrates; 31/32?; Sinary, L. Top.; *P. Mich. inv.* 69.9.

3038 ---; 41; II 325.17.

3039 PAPONTOS; s. of Aphynchis alias Zoilus; ch. Pnepheros, Tausiris; (1) 55; (2) 56; Oxyrhynchite; Oxy.; addr. for s.; sells house in Temgenuthis qtr; (1) I 99.4; (2) II 271.4, 10.

3040 ---; 74; XIV 1661.3.

3041 ---; Aug 75; sitologus; Sko, U. Top.; XXXVIII 2840.4.

3042 ---; s. of Amois, s. of Theon; sp. Thnas; Nov 83; property owner; Oxyrhynchite; Oxy.; dec.; X 1282.19-20.

3043 ---; m. Taier [ ]; gs. of Dionysius; July 87; slave owner; Oxy.?; slave child Dionysius; *PSI* III 203.[3] and passim.

3044 ---; 92; sitologus; Pakerke, E. Top.; has associates; XVIII 2185.2.

3045 PAPONṬ[OS; 97; Oxyrhynchite; Oxy.; addr. for mat. gs. Glaucias; II 371.2.

3046 PAPONTOS; s. of Hermas; 98-117; Oxyrhynchite; apprentice is nephew Hermes; *SB* XII i 10946.[1], 9.

3047 ---; ch. -yris (f); i; hamlet of Nomos?; doc. pr. Oxy.?; addr. for d., married to a s. of Theon; *P. Harris* 138 i 1.

3048 ---; s. of Nilus; i; *P. Harris* 144.6.

3049 ---; s. of Petearsenth ( ); i; sib. of Dioscous and Horus; *P. Harris* 144.4.

3050 ---; s. of ...on; sp. Tapontos; ch. Papontos; i; Senepta, M. Top.; addr. for s.; *P. Harris* 138 i 11.

3051 ---; s. of Papontos, s. of ...on; m. Tapontos, d. of Dionysius; i; landholder; Senepta, M. Top.; doc. pr. Oxy.?; cedes land nr Peeno to Hellenis, d. of Pausirion; *P. Harris* 138 i 11.

3052 ---; s. of Heraclammon; m. Tamochus; i - ii; age 41; *P. Harris* 72.1.

3053 ---; ch. Diogenes; 117-137; Oxyrhynchite?; Oxy.?; addr. for gs. Papontos; I 105.15.

3054 ---; s. of Diogenes, s. of Papontos; 117-137; Oxyrhynchite; Oxy.; witness; I 105.15.

3055 ---; ch. Thaisous; 119; Oxy.; addr. for mat. gs. Papontos; XII 1547.22.

3056 ---; s. of Thoonas, s. of Petosiris; m. Thaisous, d. of Papontos; 119; stone cutter; landowner; North St. qtr; bro. of Tetoeus and Petosiris; age 57; absent from home; XII 1547.11-12, 22.

3057 ---; ch. Papontos; Dec 127; Paomis, Thmois. Top.; addr. for s.; XXXIII 2670.12.

3058 PAPONTOS; s. of Papontos; Dec 127; epiploos w. Ammonius; Paomis, Thmois. Top.; XXXIII 2670.12.

3059 ---; alias LEONTAS; s. of Panemgeus; m. Thermuthion; Feb 130; Sesphtha, L. Top.; liturgist (appropriation of private donkeys); illiterate; *P. Mich. inv.* 974.4.

3060 ---; s. of Dorotheus; 130; farmer; pays to a/c of Sarapion, s. of Herodes, at Psobthis from grain held at Senepta; III 517.11.

3061 ---; s. of Horus; 132/133; bro. of Dionysius; illiterate; *PSI* I 53 x 167-168.

3062 ---; s. of Abau, s. of Apollonius; Aug 133; cousin to Taarpaesis; signs her will; *P. Köln* II 100.29.

---; see DIONYSIUS.

3063 ---; 134; sitologus w. Chaeremon; Monimu; s. of M. distr.; III 515.1.

3064 PAPENTOS (read PAPONTOS?); s. of Amois; July 138; hamlet of Dositheus; doc. pr.?; elder of above hamlet; *P. Bad.* IV 74.13.

3065 PAPONTOS; alias DIODORUS; Aug 148; comogrammateus of Teis and other villages of Thmois. Top. in Jan/Feb 140; surnamed Longinus; *P. Iand.* VII 139.13.

3066 PAPONTOS; ch. Pausorapis; ii; *P. Erl.* 44 iii 35.

3067 PAPONT(OS); s. of Harpaesis, s. of Harsiesis; ch. Petes(uchus); ii; landholder; Hippodrome qtr; *P. Princ.* II 46.1, 2.

3068 PAPSIOUS; 31; fisherman; Teis, Thmois. Top.; unnamed bro.; XIX 2234.10.

3069 PAR( ); early i; II 389 (descr.).

3070 PARAIS; July 72; assoc. of sitologus; Seryphis, W. Top.; XLIV 3136.12.

3071 PARAMMON; ii; workman of Eirene; (1) I 116.6; (2) 187 (descr.).

3072 PARECHATES; 81-96; VI 984 R fin.

3073 PARET(?); ch. Patous; (1) i BC - i; (2) early i; (1) *OD Pisa* 779 + 242 Convesso X + 16; (2) 234 Concavo 5.

3074 PARIAS; s. of Lemysus; 71/72; tax farmer; Oxy.?; doc. pr. Oxy.?; connection w. Oxy. via others in doc.; *P. Ryl.* II 95.4.

3075 PARIS; 67 BC?; grave digger; Oxy.?; *P. Ryl.* II 65.1.

3076 PASEIS; ch. Ammonius; Jan 121; Small Oasis?; addr. for s.; *P. Fouad* 30.4.

3077 PASENIS; s. of Demetrius; i BC - i; *OD Pisa* 84.2.

3078 PASES (PASEIS?); 41-79; agent for Heraclas, father of Archelaus; XLII 3061.3.

3079 PASION; s. of Dionysius, s. of Ptolemaeus; m. Arsinoe; 63/62 BC; Macedonian of catoecic cavalry; Oxyrhynchite; Cleopatra Aphrodite St; XIV 1644.4.

3080 ---; s. of Harthonis; Jan 49; slave owner; Oxyrhynchite; Oxy.; age c. 52; signalement; purchases slave Demetrous in Taamechis, Heracleopolite; XXXI 2582.2.

3081 TI. CLAUDIUS PASION; (1) 49; (2), (3) 49/50; (4), (5) c. 50; (6) 50/51; strategus; Roman; Oxy.; descr. as former str. in 2; (1) I 37.1; (2) 38.12; (3) II 393 (descr.); (4) 285.1; (5) 284.1; (6) 316 (1).

3082 PASION; s. of Horion; ch. Amoitas; Sept 58; Oxyrhynchite?; Hermaeum qtr; addr. for s.; now dec.; sister Helene; *P. Mich.* III 171.7.

3083 ---; ch. Diogenes; (1) April 60; (2) March 61; Oxyrhynchite; Oxy.; (1) *P. Mich.* III 192.6; (2) 194.6.

3084 ---; July 60; Oxy.; agent of Ptolemaeus, basilicogrammateus; XXXVIII 2851.25.

3085 ---; 94; agoranomus w. Dionysius, Theon and two Sarapions; Oxy.; I 73.9.

3086 ---; s. of [L]ycarion; 2nd half i; practor; Sesphtha? (or Psenosiris?), L. Top.; XXXVIII 2845.13.

3087 ---; i - ii; clerk (in merchant's office); *P. Harris* 96.12.

3088 ---; ch. Pasion, Amois; Jan 100; Oxyrhynchite?; Oxy.?; addr. for s.; XLI 2960.5.

3089 ---; s. of Pasion; Jan 100; farmer; landholder?; Oxyrhynchite; Oxy.; land at Nemerae; bro. of Amois; XLI 2960.4.

3090 ---; s. of Thonis; Jan 100; farmer; landholder?; Nemerae, M. Top.; XLI 2960.10.

3091 ---; s. of Sarapion, s. of Pasion; sp. Berenice; ch. Sarapas, Apollonius, Diogenes, and two minors; (1) March 102; (2) early ii; wine merchant; landholder; slave owner; Oxyrhynchite; Oxy.; died in Alex. (1); partner and debtor of Apion, s. of Apion; (1) XXII 2342.4; (2) III 493.15.

3092 ---; s. of Heracleides; 135/136; landholder; Alex.?, Althaieus?; Talao, L. Top.; doc. pr.?; *P. Iand.* VII 136.11.

3093 ---; ch. Sarapion; early ii; Oxyrhynchite?; Oxy.?; addr. for gs. Sarapion; III 493.1, 13, 15.

3094 PASIS; May 37 BC?; donkey driver; *Coll. Pap.* I 17.7.

3095 ---; ch. Harpaesis; i BC - i; *OD Pisa* 532 X + 5.

3096 ---; s. of Spj; i BC - i; Patus his agent; *OD Pisa* 451 + 540 Convesso 8.

3097 PASIS; s. of Pasis; i BC - i; (1) *OD Pisa* 360 Concavo X + 6; (2) 106.2.

3098 ---; s. of Nectenibis; i BC - i; *OD Pisa* 106.8.

3099 ---; s. of Petechonsis; i BC - i; Harpaesis his dependant; (1) *OD Pisa* 69 Convesso i 12; (2) 111 Convesso 9.

3100 ---; ch. Pasis; i BC - i; (1) *OD Pisa* 360 Concavo X + 6; (2) 106.2.

3101 ---; i BC - i; *OD Pisa* 779 + 242 Concavo 1.

3102 ---; s. of Šmr (Simarus?); (1) i BC - i; (2) i; (1) *OD Pisa* 502 X + 10; (2) 60 Concavo 1.

3103 ---; s. of T_3-ḳt(?); late i BC - early i; *OD Pisa* 35 Convesso 5.

3104 ---; s. of Kmj; (1) late i BC - early i; (2) i; acts through T_3-ḳt; (1) *OD Pisa* 35 Convesso 2; (2) 39 i X + 8.

3105 ---; late i BC - i; (1) *OD Pisa* 35 Convesso 15; (2) Concavo ii 11; (3) Concavo ii 15.

3105 ---; late i BC - i; (1) *OD Pisa* 35 Convesso 15; (2) Concavo ii 11; (3) Concavo ii 15.

3106 ---; c. 1; unnamed d., dec.; IV 736.85.

3107 ---; s. of Pe-; early i; *OD Pisa* 450B Concavo ii X + 6.

3108 ---; ch. -isis; i; *OD Pisa* 60 Convesso i 3.

3109 ---; ch. Totoes; i; *OD Pisa* 60 Convesso i 14.

3110 ---; ch. Petosiris; i; *OD Pisa* 60 Convesso ii 1.

3111 PASOIS; 31; fisherman; Teis, Thmois. Top.; XIX 2234.11.

3112 Q. GAIUS PASSER; 31; centurion; Roman; XIX 2234.1.

3113 PASTOUS; ch. Achilleus; April 60; Oxyrhynchite; Oxy.; addr. for s. Achilleus, now dec.; *P. Mich.* III 192.19.

3114 PATAS; ii; sailor; XII 1488.5.

3115 PATBEUS; ch. Thoonis; 20; II 305.3.

3116 PATCALAE; i BC - i; *OD Pisa* 117.3.

3117 PATEBIS; 81-96; VI 984 R fin.

3118 PATEPHIS; i BC - i; *OD Pisa* 58.7.

3119 PATERMUTHIS; ch. Belles; i; Tacona?; addr. for s. who incorrectly nom. as sitologus of Tacona; XLVI 3273.7, 8.

3120 PATES; s. of Patesis-Imouthes; i BC; *OD Pisa* 55 ii 8.

3121 ---; s. of Totoes; i BC; *OD Pisa* 227.1.

3122 PATES; i BC; pastophorus; *OD Pisa* 55 i 4.

3123 ---; i BC; *OD Pisa* 118.1.

3124 ---; s. of Petechonsis; (1) i BC; (2) i BC - i; (1) *OD Pisa* 55 ii 4; (2) 38 i X + 3.

3125 ---; ch. Peteuris; i BC - i; *OD Pisa* 460 Convesso i X + 7.

3126 ---; ch. Plenis; i BC - i; *OD Pisa* 106.3.

3127 ---; i BC - i; *OD Pisa* 460 Convesso ii X + 11.

3128 ---; i BC - i; *OD Pisa* 137 Concavo 2.

3129 ---; i BC - i; *OD Pisa* 25 i 8.

3130 ---; ch. Petosiris; i BC - i; *OD Pisa* 28 X + 5.

3131 ---; Oct 5; *OD Pisa* 427.2.

3132 PATESIS; ch. Menches; i BC; *OD Pisa* 149.2.

3133 ---; ch. Horus; i BC - i; *OD Pisa* 228 X + 5.

3134 ---; s. of Petechonsis; i BC - i; *OD Pisa* 5 i X + 9.

3135 ---; s. of Petemestous; i BC - i; *OD Pisa* 99 i 3.

3136 ---; s. of Psen-lws; i BC - i; *OD Pisa* 25 i 14.

3137 ---; i BC - i; *OD Pisa* 290 + 290A Convesso X + 9.

3138 ---; i BC - i; *OD Pisa* 38 i X + 2.

3139 ---; i BC - i; slave of Smtrw$_3$; *OD Pisa* 108 X + 2.

3140 PATESIS-IMOUTHES; ch. Pates; i BC; *OD Pisa* 55 ii 8.

3141 PATHEBIS; s. of Horus; i; practor?; Peeno; *P. Bon.* 43.7.

3142 PATHOOL( ); 119/120; unnamed s. has land at Monimu and Sinary; *P. Wisc.* II 39.4.

3143 PATHOS; ii; donkey driver; *P. Harris* 95.4.

3144 PATHOTES; i BC - i; *OD Pisa* 460 Convesso ii X + 7.

3145 ---; s. of Petubastis(?); i BC - i; *OD Pisa* 502 X + 10.

3146 PATIAPIS; i BC - i; *OD Pisa* 502 X + 2.

3147 PATIS; i BC - i; *OD Pisa* 470.1.

PATOIPHIS; see THONIS.

3148 ---; July 23 BC; ?father of Thonis; ?religious official; *P. Inst. Fran.* I 13.29.

3149 PATOUS; s. of Horus; i BC - i; (1) *OD Pisa* 72 ii X + 7; (2) 69 Convesso i 10; (3) Concavo i 1; (4) 127.6.

3150 PATOUS; s. of Kmj; i BC - i; *OD Pisa* 137 Convesso 2.

3151 ---; s. of Patous; i BC - i; *OD Pisa* 108 X + 1.

3152 ---; s. of Petechonsis; i BC - i; (1) *OD Pisa* 58.1; (2) 276 X + 5.

3153 ---; s. of Petubastis; i BC - i; Petechonsis his agent; (1) *OD Pisa* 510 + 568 Concavo i X + 8; (2) Concavo ii 1.

3154 ---; s. of Psenerieus; i BC - i; *OD Pisa* 29 ii X + 5.

3155 ---; s. of $S^{c}w$ (?); i BC - i; *OD Pisa* 228 X + 7.

3156 ---; i BC - i; *OD Pisa* 5 i X + 12.

3157 ---; i BC - i; *OD Pisa* 8.16.

3158 ---; i BC - i; *OD Pisa* 29 ii X + 6, 13.

3159 ---; i BC - i; *OD Pisa* 58.8.

3160 ---; ch. Psenyris; i BC - i; *OD Pisa* 69 Concavo 1.

3161 ---; ch. Petechonsis; (1) i BC - i; (2) 8; *OD Pisa* 1163 bis Convesso 6; (2) 1.16.

3162 ---; s. of Paret; (1) i BC - i; (2) early i; Petosiris his dependant; (1) *OD Pisa* 779 + 242 Convesso X + 16; (2) 234 Concavo 5.

3163 ---; s. of Petosiris; (1) i BC - i; (2) i; (1) *OD Pisa* 111 Convesso 4; (2) 60 Convesso i 9.

3164 ---; i BC - i; *OD Pisa* 228 X + 9.

3165 ---; i BC - i; *OD Pisa* 281 + 94 X + 9.

3166 ---; i BC - i; *OD Pisa* 290 + 290A Concavo X + 8.

3167 ---; i BC - i; *OD Pisa* 360 Concavo X + 2.

3168 ---; i BC - i; *OD Pisa* 126 i 11.

3169 ---; i BC - i; agent for Pasis; *OD Pisa* 451 + 540 Convesso 8.

3170 ---; i BC - i; *OD Pisa* 561 + 562 + 795 i X + 3.

3171 ---; i BC - i; *OD Pisa* 72 ii X + 2.

3172 ---; ch. Harsiesis; i BC - i; *OD Pisa* 127.4.

3173 ---; ch. Horus; i BC - i; (1) *OD Pisa* 360 Concavo X + 6; (2) 451 + 540 Convesso 1.

3174 ---; ch. Ḥḳws; i BC - i; *OD Pisa* 1163 bis Convesso 4.

3175 ---; ch. Nectenibis; i BC - i; *OD Pisa* 1163 bis Convesso 5.

3176 ---; ch. Patous; i BC - i; *OD Pisa* 108 X + 1.

3177 PATOUS; ch. Petosiris; i BC - i; (1) *OD Pisa* 25 i 21; (2) 779 + 241 Convesso X + 15; (3) 29 ii X + 14.

3178 ---; s. of Harbelles; i BC - i; *OD Pisa* 308 X + 5.

3179 ---; s. of Harendotes; i BC - i; *OD Pisa* 510 + 568 Convesso i 3.

3180 ---; s. of Harsiesis; i BC - i; *OD Pisa* 276 X + 7.

3181 ---; s. of Totoes; late i BC - early i; *OD Pisa* 35 Concavo ii 13.

3182 PATOUS(?); s. of Wḥj; late i BC - early i; *OD Pisa* 35 Convesso 11.

3183 PATOUS; ch. Peteesis; late i BC - early i; *OD Pisa* 35 Concavo ii 10.

3184 ---; ch. Onnophris; late i BC - early i; *OD Pisa* 35 Concavo ii 18.

3185 ---; late i BC - early i; *OD Pisa* 35 Concavo ii 19.

3186 ---; s. of Hrjw-B_3st.t; Sept 6; (1) *OD Pisa* 431.9; (2) 433.2, 4.

3187 ---; s. of Heriubastis; July 7; *OD Pisa* 1131 Concavo 7.

3188 ---; s. of Haremphois; i; *OD Pisa* 60 Convesso i 5.

3189 ---; s. of Belles; i; *OD Pisa* 60 Convesso i 16.

3190 PATUMIS; s. of Haryotes; i BC - i; *OD Pisa* 126 i 8.

3191 ---; ch. Petubastis; i BC - i; *OD Pisa* 126 i 8.

3192 PAUIS; ch. Pauis; 135/136; doc. pr. L. Top.; *P. Iand.* VII 136.16.

3193 ---; s. of Pauis; 135/136; doc. pr. L. Top.; *P. Iand.* VII 136.16.

3194 CURTIUS PAULINUS; (1), (2) 148/149; military tribune; Roman; in charge of epikrisis in 56/57 and 57/58; (1) X 1266.25; (2) XLVI 3279.20.

3195 P[AU]LUS?; Aug. 37 BC; slave supervisor; *P. Ryl.* IV 593.4.

3196 PAULUS; c. 85; property owner; Jewish; J. qtr, Oxy.; sells 1/6 house in J. qtr to Nicaea Sil[va]nus; II 335 (descr.).

3197 ---; ch. Taps[ois?]; 119; Oxy.; addr. for mat. gs. Apollonides; XII 1547.20.

3198 PAUPHOIS; 81-96; VI 984 R fin.

3199 PAUSANIAS; s. of Pausanias; 37-41; wine merchant; XIV 1672.1.

3200 ---; ch. Demetrius, Pausanias; 37-41; wine merchant; Pela?; W. Top.; XIV 1672.1.

3201 PAUSANIAS; alias DIONYSIUS; s. of Astyanax, s. of Tryphon; sp. Julia Heracla; ch. Gaia alias Sarapias; 95; Alex., Phylaxithalassius, Heracleius; Oxy.; II 273.11.

3202 ---; s. of Apollonius; i; bro. of Apollonius; VIII 1153.15.

3203 ---; c. 100; land from Kleros of Socrates ceded to him by Sinthonis; *P. Stras.* 266.3, 15.

3204 ---; s. of Sarapion, s. of Ammonius; Nov 103; Oxyrhynchite; Oxy.; bro. of Ammonius; dec.; *P. Mert.* I 14.17.

3205 ---; Aug 106; *P. Wisc.* I 17 V 21.

3206 ---; s. of Sarapion, s. of Sarapion; m. Apollonous; 129; property owner; Oxyrhynchite; Oxy.; lends to Agathodaemon, s. of Diogenes; XXXVI 2774.2.

3207 ---; ii; former city secretary; property owner; III 529 V.

3208 PAUSIRION; July 27; Oxy.; XVII 2148.7.

3209 ---; ch. Diosorus; 41/42; son banker; *PSI* XII 1235.7.

3210 ---; s. of Ptolemaeus; sp. Ophelous; ch. Ptolemaeus; Sept 66; Oxyrhynchite; Oxy.; addr. for s.; II 275.3.

3211 ---; ch. Dionysius; 88/89; Oxyrhynchite; Oxy.; addr. for gs. Dionysius; II 280.1-2.

3212 ---; i; farmer?; Oxy.; II 298.2.

3213 ---; s. of Zopyrus; m. Toutheus; ch. Hellenis (d. of -on); i; Oxyrhynchite; Oxy.; doc. pr.?; *P. Harris* 138 i 13.

3214 ---; s. of Eudaemon; sp. Sinthonia; ch. Pausiris; after 102; Oxyrhynchite; Oxy.; addr. for s.; III 636.16.

3215 ---; s. of Pausiris; sp. Teteuris; ch. Heras; Sept 109; Psobthis, M. Top.; addr. for s.; *PSI* IX 1030.2.

3216 ---; ch. Heraclas; c. 110-112; Oxyrhynchite?; Oxy.?; addr. for s.; XXXVI 2758.2-3.

3217 ---; gs. of Aperos; m. Didyme; sp. -ris; ch. Sarapion; 148/149; Oxyrhynchite, gymnasial class; Knights' Camp qtr; reg. s. this yr. in g. class in this qtr, same as his and father's; XLVI 3279.2.

3218 ---; ii; III 530.9.

3219 PAUSIRIS; sp. Tecosis; ch. Taseus; 42/41 BC; Oxyrhynchite; Oxy.; addr. for d.; *PSI* V 549.5.

3220 ---; s. of Chonsimen(?) (Ḫnsw-mn); i BC; *OD Pisa* 55 ii 9.

3221 ---; i BC - i; *OD Pisa* 8.10.

3222 ---; i BC - i; bro. of Harchypis; *OD Pisa* 25 i 27.

3223 ---; i BC - i; *OD Pisa* 29 ii X + 3.

3224 PAUSIRIS; i BC - i; Haremphois his dependant; *OD Pisa* 228 X + 2.

3225 ---; i BC - i; writes to Nephorsais; *OD Pisa* 267.1.

3226 ---; i BC - i; *OD Pisa* 308 X + 7.

3227 ---; i BC - i; *OD Pisa* 451 + 540 Convesso 16.

3228 ---; i BC - i; *OD Pisa* 477 Concavo X + 1.

3229 ---; i BC - i; *OD Pisa* 755 Convesso X + 2.

3230 ---; ch. Pausiris; i BC - i; *OD Pisa* 779 + 242 Concavo 6.

3231 ---; ch. Petosiris; i BC - i; (1) *OD Pisa* 196 ii X + 2; (2) 451 + 540 Convesso 2.

3232 ---; ch. Tenis; i BC - i; *OD Pisa* 477 Convesso 2.

3233 ---; s. of Herieus; i BC - i; *OD Pisa* 8.11.

3234 ---; s. of Chonsutephacte (Ḫns-t$_3$e-[f-nḫt); i BC - i; *OD Pisa* 755 Concavo X + 13.

3235 ---; s. of Horus; i BC - i; *OD Pisa* 532 X + 8.

3236 ---; s. of Kmj; i BC - i; *OD Pisa* 38 i X + 12.

3237 ---; s. of Nechutes; i BC - i; *OD Pisa* 668.1.

3238 ---; s. of Pausiris; i BC - i; *OD Pisa* 779 + 242 Concavo 6.

3239 ---; s. of Petosiris; i BC - i; (1) *OD Pisa* 25 ii 3; (2) 477 Concavo X + 7; (3) 132 X + 8; (4) 470.3.

3240 ---; s. of T$_3$-ḳt(?); i BC - i; *OD Pisa* 243 + 472 i 1.

3241 ---; s. of T$_3$-ḳt; i BC - i; *OD Pisa* 38 i X + 13.

3242 ---; s. of Apimenes; late i BC - early i; *OD Pisa* 35 Convesso 16.

3243 ---; ch. Panechotes; 26? (from *P. Rein.* II 103); *P. Rein.* II 104.5.

3244 ---; s. of Ammonius; ch. Ammonius, Dioscous, Pausiris; (1) Sept 49; (2) Aug/Sept 53; (3) Sept 58; (4) April 60; (5) March 61; (6) Oct 62; master weaver; Oxyrhynchite; Knights' Camp qtr; apprentices Ammonius to Apollonius, s. of Apollonius (1) and Dioscous to him also (2); Amoitas apprenticed to him (3); Pausiris a minor (6); (1) *P. Mich.* III 170.3; (2) *P. Wisc.* I 4.1; (3) *P. Mich.* III 171.15; (4) 192.4; (5) 194.7; (6) 172.2.

3245 ---; ch. Harthoonis; 54-68; *SB* X 10256.3.

3246 ---; s. of Pausiris, s. of Ammonius; Oct 62; apprentice weaver; Oxyrhynchite; Knights' Camp qtr; master is Epinicus, s. of Theon; minor; *P. Mich.* III 172.8-9.

3247 PAUSIRIS; s. of Petsiris; Nov/Dec 64; Palosis, Thmois. Top.; IV 808 (descr.).

3248 ---; s. of P]tole[maeus; sp. Heracleia; ch. Epimachus; Sept 66; Psobthis, M. Top.; addr. for s.; II 239.2.

3249 ---; s. of Sarapion; sp. Saraeus; ch. Dionysia, Herais; 89-97; Oxy.; addr. for d.; II 274.[12], 34.

3250 ---; s. of Panechotes; sp. Tsenammonas; ch. Panechotes; March 90; Oxyrhynchite?; Oxy.?; addr. for s.; two unnamed sons; sp. owned property in Knights' Camp qtr; II 247.5.

3251 ---; early i; greets Sisois; *OD Pisa* 419.1.

3252 ---; early i; *OD Pisa* 424.2.

3253 ---; s. of Petesiris; early i; Psobthis, M. Top.; *P. Wisc.* I 23.5.

3254 ---; i; *OD Pisa* 129 X + 8.

3255 ---; s. of N[; i; Sesphtha; name written as Paosiris; *P. Ryl.* II 199.22.

3256 ---; s. of Plution, s. of Syrus; Jan 100; farmer; land-holder?; Oxyrhynchite?; Oxy.?; land at Nemerae; writes for father and others; XLI 2960.47.

3257 ---; s. of Pausirion, s. of Eudaemon; m. Sinthonia; sp. Theodous; after 102; property owner; Oxy.; forfeits property (1/3 house in Temgenuthis qtr) to Demetrous as payt of loan; III 636.16.

3258 ---; ch. Pausirion; Sept 109; Psobthis, M. Top.; addr. for gs. Heras, lessee; *PSI* IX 1030.3.

3259 ---; ch. Thermuthion; 116; Oxy.; addr. for mat. gs. Harthonis (now dec.), hierotekton of Thoeris, Isis, Sarapis and assoc. gods and enrolled in Thoeris St qtr; XII 1550.14.

3260 ---; ch. Ammonous; 119; Oxyrhynchite?; Oxy.?; addr. for d.; XXXVI 2776.7.

3261 ---; ch. Theon; 131; Oxyrhynchite; Oxy.; addr. for s.; I 68.2.

3262 ---; s. of Petsiris; Jan 138; wheat seller?; Sesphtha, L. Top.; III 484.3.

3263 ---; s. of Theon, s. of Theon; m. Thaesis, d. of Didymus; gs. of Diogenous; 148/149; Oxyrhynchite, gymnasial class; Knights' Camp qtr; reg. in g. class in above qtr this yr; age 13 in 147/148; XLVI 3283.7.

3264 ---; ii; former owner of Theon, now freedman; *SB* VI 9372.2.

3265 ---; s. of Apollonius; ii; shipowner (corn transport); III 522.13.

3266 PAUSIS; 31; fisherman; Teis, Thmois. Top.; XIX 2234.9.

3267 PAUSI(S): s. of C̣ḥ[ ]; i; farmer; *P. Ryl.* 199.31.

3268 PAUSORAPIS; s. of Papontos; ii; landowner; *P. Erl.* 44 iii 35.

3269 PCAES(?); ch. Ammonius; 127/128; Oxyrhynchite; gymnasial class; Gymnasium St qtr?; addr. for gs. Ptolemaeus, in graphe of AD 4/5; XII 1452 ii 53.

3270 PE[ ]; ch. Petesnes; i BC - i; *OD Pisa* 510 + 568 Convesso ii 1.

3271 P̣Ẹ[-]; ch. Horion; 98-117; *PSI* VII 772.2.

3272 PE...[; ch. Pasis; early i; *OD Pisa* 450B Concavo ii X + 6.

3273 PEBAS (?)(P_3-bj); ch. Totoes; i BC - i; *OD Pisa* 541 Convesso i 2.

3274 ---; i BC - i; *OD Pisa* 779 + 242 Convesso X + 12.

3275 PEBOS; April 4; *OD Pisa* 511 + 512 i 5.

3276 ---; i BC - i; *OD Pisa* 1023 Convesso ii 1.

3277 ---; ch. Pamun; i; *OD Pisa* 129 X + 4.

3278 PEBRICHIS; s. of Horus; i BC - i; *OD Pisa* 360 Concavo X + 7.

3279 PECAS(?); ii; *P. Warren* 13.11.

3280 PECMIUS; s. of Onnophris; i BC - i; *OD Pisa* 280 X + 3.

3281 PECYSIS; s. of Petosiris; 73 or 44 BC; farmer; wheat seller; Oxy.?; bro. of Orsenouphis; Persian of Epigone; XIV 1639.1.

3282 ---; i BC - i; *OD Pisa* 117.2.

3283 ---; ch. Pecysis; 23; M. Top.?; doc. pr. Oxy.?; addr. for gd. Taseus; *P. Princ.* III 141.1.

3284 ---; s. of Pecysis; ch. Taseus; 23; M. Top.?; doc. pr. Oxy.?; guardian for d.; illiterate; *P. Princ.* III 141.1.

3285 ---; s. of Totoes, s. of Saras; 31/32?; *P. Mich. inv.* 69.2.

3286 ---; s. of Comon; 52/53; guardian to sister, Tausorapis; *PSI* IX 1029.2.

3287 ---; s. of Isierax; 97; Oxyrhynchite; II 371.3.

3288 ---; s. of Ammonius, s. of Ammonius; mid i; property owner; bro. of Theon; VII 1027.4.

3289 ---; s. of Diodorus; i; farmer; Sobthis; VIII 1145.2.

3290 ---; s. of Zoilus; sp. Lucia; ch. Sinthoonis; 100; Oxyrhynchite?; Oxy.?; addr. for d.; I 49.5.

3291 ---; s. of Diogenes; sp. Tausiris; ch. Thaesis; c. 107-112; property owner; property in North St qtr; *PSI* V 450 R i 10.

3292 PECYSIS; ch. Hermes; 117-137; Oxyrhynchite?; Cretan qtr; addr. for gs. Pecysis; I 105.[2], 8.

3293 ---; s. of Hermes, s. of Pecysis; m. Didyme, d. of Philotas; sp. Ptolema; ch. Ammonous; 117-137; property owner; Oxyrhynchite; Cretan qtr; age 44; signalement; I 105.[2], 8.

3294 ---; ch. Pecysis; 122/123; Senepta?, M. Top.; addr. for s.; XXXVIII 2866.8.

3295 ---; s. of Pecysis; 122/123; Senepta, M. Top.; XXXVIII 2866.8.

3296 ---; s. of Theon; m. Sinpetsiris; Feb 130?; Sesphtha, L. Top.; liturgist (appropriation of private donkeys); *P. Mich. inv.* 974.3.

3297 ---; sp. Teencegous; ch. Sinthonis, Pachnubis; ii; Tanais, M. Top.; addr. for d.; III 505.2.

3298 ---; s. of Asclas; ch. Pecysis; ii; *P. Erl.* 44 iii 28.

3299 ---; s. of Pecysis, s. of Asclas; ii; priest; landholder; *P. Erl.* 44 iii 28.

3300 ---; ch. Pecysis; ii; *P. Erl.* 44 ii 12.

3201 ---; s. of Pecysis; ii; landholder; *P. Erl.* 44 ii 12.

3202 ---; sp. Heraclous; ch. Syrus; ii; *P. Erl.* 44 iii 32.

3203 ---; sp. Tausiris; ch. Carousis; ii; *P. Erl.* 44 iii 33.

3304 ---; s. of Ammas; ii; landholder; *P. Erl.* 44 ii 9.

3305 ---; s. of Harbichis; m. Thaisous; ii; leases land at Antipera and Sento; *P. Erl.* 44 ii 6.

3206 ---; ch. Totoes; ii; doc. pr. Oxy.?; *PSI* VI 710.11.

3307 ---; s. of Totoes, s. of Pecysis; sp. Tapecysis?; ii; slave owner; hires slave Totoes to Dioscorus; doc. pr. Ocy.?; *PSI* VI 710.11.

3308 PEDON; s. of Callistratus, s. of Alexandrus; 117; Oxyrhynchite; Oxy.; age 36; witness; signalement; III 489.24.

3309 ---; s. of Callicornus; April 135; Oxyrhynchite?; Oxy.?; guardian of Ptolema, d. of Straton; I 106.23.

3310 PEISIS; (1) April 96; (2) May 96; strategus; (1) *P. Oslo* III 95.1; (2) *PSI Bartoletti Colombo* 1.1.

3311 PELLIS; 2 BC - 1; IV 811.1.

3312 PELUSIS; ch. Petechon; i; farmer; Koba; VIII 1145.2, 7.

3313 PELUX; ch. Horus; early ii; Oxyrhynchite?; Oxy.?; addr. for gs. Harmiysis alias Pelux and Amois; *P. Wisc.* I 13.4.

PELUX; see HARMIYSIS.

3314 PELYTIS; ch. Petechonsis; i BC - i; *OD Pisa* 68.1.

3315 PEMENCHES; i BC - i; Dd his dependant; *OD Pisa* 510 + 568 Convesso i 2.

3316 ---; i BC - i; *OD Pisa* 232.8.

3317 ---; i BC - i; *OD Pisa* 779 + 242 Convesso X + 9.

3318 ---; i BC - i; dependant of Harcales; *OD Pisa* 451 + 540 Convesso 5.

3319 ---; s. of Petesis; i BC - i; Dd his dependant (5); (1) *OD Pisa* 69 Convesso i 6; (2) 111 Convesso 6; (3) 502 X + 9; (4) 541 Concavo 1, 6; (5) 510 + 568 Concavo i X + 7.

3320 ---; i BC; *OD Pisa* 323 X + 2.

3321 ---; April 4; *OD Pisa* 511 + 512 i 10.

3322 PEMNAS; s. of Besas; 126; Oxyrhynchite; Oxy.; age 38; witnesses will; signalement; III 491.20.

3323 PEN; s. of Heraclei(des?); 135/136; landholder; Talao?, L. Top.; doc. pr. Oxy.?; *P. Iand.* VII 136.14.

3324 PENAUS; i BC - i; acts for Horus; *OD Pisa* 510 + 568 Convesso ii 3.

3325 P[E]NEUAES; s. of E.emothus?; m. Tasooue?; i - ii; age 17; *P. Harris* 72.2.

3326 PENNAMIS; s. of Amenneus; 80/81; presbyteros; Peeno, M. Top.; *Coll. Pap.* II 21.4.

3327 PENYRIS; sp. Psenosiris; ch. Tastraton; 124; Oxyrhynchite?; Oxy.?; addr. for d.; III 490.2.

3328 PERET; ch. Panouphis; 8; *OD Pisa* 1.10.

3329 ---; ch. Harchypsis; Aug 9; *OD Pisa* 429.1.

3330 PERNAEUS; i BC - i; *OD Pisa* 228 X + 11.

3331 PERNAEUS; i BC - i; *OD Pisa* 25 ii 20.

3332 ---; i BC - i; *OD Pisa* 25 i 17.

3333 PEROS; ch. Gaius; 89; mentions hamlet of Vestinus; name may be Aperos; *P. Fouad* 48.4.

3334 PEṚ[SIS]; ii; doc. pr. Oxy.?; *P. Mich. inv.* 3799.2.

3335 PERTAX; ch. Taarpaesis; 133; Oxyrhynchite; Oxy.; addr. for gs. Dionysius alias Papontos; I 100.6.

3336 PESCA; early i; called the elder; *OD Pisa* 456.4-5.

3337 PESOURIS; 49; Oxy.; called Syrus in I 38; I 37.4.

3338 ---; ch. Saras; 104/105; Oxyrhynchite; Oxy.; addr. for s.; XXXVIII 2852.3-4.

3339 PESOURIS; sp. Taarime; ii; Oxyrhynchite?; Oxy.; sp.'s will; III 647.5, 9.

3340 PETALUS; ch.]ṇtoṭhis; 71/72; Oxy.?; doc. pr. Oxy.?; addr. for s.; *P. Ryl.* II 95.4.

3341 PETAMENOPHIS; s. of Wḥj; late i BC - early i; *OD Pisa* 35 Concavo ii 9.

3342 ---; s. of T_3-ḳt(?); late i BC - i; *OD Pisa* 35 Convesso 21.

3343 PETARBEBECIS; s. of Harthotes; ch. Harthotes, Harthotes the younger; 100; Oxy.; addr. for s.; I 46.5-6.

3344 PETARPOCHRATION; s. of Panesneus; m. Tatnagous; 81-96; Temple of Ares greatest god; reg. in 3rd yr of Titus; died age 1; m. probably dec.; VI 984 R init.

3345 PETE-[ ]; Aug 3; *OD Pisa* 473 Concavo i 10.

3346 PETE-[ ]ns; ch. Plachisis; early i; *OD Pisa* 426.2.

3347 PETE-Wḥj; i BC - i; *OD Pisa* 460 Convesso ii X + 12.

3348 PETEACES; m. Taseus; ii; Tanais, M. Top.; XXXI 2572.2.

3349 PETEARPEBECIS; s. of Teos, s. of Teos; c. 81-96; landholder; Senocomis?; W. Top.; part share in Kleros of Zenodorus; I 47.6-7.

3350 PETEARPOCHRATES; ch. Imouthes; i BC - i; *OD Pisa* 281 + 94 X + 6.

3351 PETEARPSENESIS; s. of Petechonsis; i BC - i; *OD Pisa* 129 X + 2.

3352 ---; s. of Peteiomis; i BC - i; *OD Pisa* 99 i 6.

3353 PETEARSENTH( ); ch. Dioscous, Horus, Papontos; i; *P. Harris* 144.2, 3, 4.

3354 PETECHON; s. of Petosiris; s. of Petosiris; Mar/Apr 66; apprentice brass beater; Egzoeu qtr; app. to Heracleides; *PSI* VIII 871.9.

3355 ---; s. of Apollonius; i; farmer; presbyterus; Koba; descr. as the elder; VIII 1145.9.

3356 ---; s. of Pelusis; i; farmer; Koba; VIII 1145.2, 7.

3357 ---; ch. Horus (or Ammonius?); i; Koba?; addr. for s.; corres. from Horus, s. of Petechon, to Ammonius, s. of Petechon; VIII 1145.8.

3358 ---; s. of Salvius; ch. Cephalas; i; XIV 1756.5.

3359 ---; c. 100; herb seller?; *P. Yale* 77.25-26.

3360 ---; ii; Oxy.; XII 1584.15, 17.

3361 PETECHONSIS; April 5 BC; *OD Pisa* 936 Convesso 3.

3362 PETECHONSIS; April 5 BC; *OD Pisa* 936 Convesso 2.

3363 ---; s. of Petethotes; April 5 BC; *OD Pisa* 936 Convesso 9.

3364 ---; s. of Teos; April 5 BC; *OD Pisa* 936 Concavo 1.

3365 ---; ch. Ephonicus; April 5 BC; *OD Pisa* 936 Concavo 8.

3366 PETECHONSIS(?); April 5 BC; *OD Pisa* 936 Convesso 18.

3367 PETECHONSIS; ch. Horus; i BC; *OD Pisa* 55 i 2, ii 4.

3368 ---; s. of Horus; i BC; *OD Pisa* 289.1.

3369 ---; ch. Pates; (1) i BC; (2) i BC - i; (1) *OD Pisa* 55 ii 4; (2) 38 i X + 3.

3370 ---; s. of Petemunis; i BC; *OD Pisa* 34.1.

3371 ---; s. of Psentaes; i BC; *OD Pisa* 55 ii 6.

3372 ---; s. of Pamun; (1), (2) i BC - i; (2) i; (1) *OD Pisa* 510 + 568 Convesso i 6; (2) 755 Concavo X + 11; (3) 60 Concavo 4.

3373 ---; s. of Pa-itm; i BC - i; *OD Pisa* 276 X + 6.

3374 ---; ch. Petosiris; i BC - i; (1) *OD Pisa* 755 Convesso X + 18; (2) 510 + 568 Convesso i 12; (3) 22.6.

3375 ---; ch. Patous; i BC - i; (1) *OD Pisa* 276 X + 5; (2) 58.1.

3376 ---; s. of Haremphois; i BC - i; agent of Patous (5); *OD Pisa* 137 Convesso 4; (2) 460 Convesso i 46 X + 6; (3) 755 Convesso X + 11; (4) 755 Convesso X + 15; (5) 510 + 568 Concavo i X + 8; (6) 1264 Concavo 3.

3377 ---; s. of Harpaesis; i BC - i; (1) *OD Pisa* 243 + 473 i 7; (2) 137 Concavo 4.

3378 ---; s. of Pagonis; i BC - i; (1) *OD Pisa* 72 ii X + 6; (2) 470.6; (3) 8.10.

3379 ---; i BC - i; *OD Pisa* 99 i 5.

3380 ---; i BC - i; *OD Pisa* 25 ii 13.

3381 ---; ch. Gtws; i BC - i; *OD Pisa* 1163 bis Concavo B1.

3382 ---; ch. Haremphois; i BC - i; *OD Pisa* 1163 bis Convesso 4.

3383 ---; ch. Harpaesis; i BC - i; *OD Pisa* 25 i 4.

3384 ---; i BC - i; *OD Pisa* 5 i X + 10.

3385 ---; ch. Panechotes; i BC - i; *OD Pisa* 68.4.

3386 ---; ch. Patesis; i BC - i; *OD Pisa* 5 i X + 9.

3387 ---; s. of Ḏd; i BC - i; (1) *OD Pisa* 5 i X + 15; (2) 5 ii X + 11.

3388 PETECHONSIS; s. of Pelytis; i BC - i; *OD Pisa* 68.1.

3389 ---; ch. Pasis; i BC - i; (1) *OD Pisa* 69 Convesso i 12; (2) 111 Convesso 9.

3390 ---; s. of Senyphis; i BC - i; *OD Pisa* 243 + 472 i 8.

3391 ---; ch. Psenthotes; i BC - i; *OD Pisa* 470.4.

3392 ---; s. of Ḥr-gwr(?); i BC - i; *OD Pisa* 543 X + 6.

3393 ---; s. of Nechutes; i BC - i; *OD Pisa* 281 + 94 X + 11.

3394 ---; ch. Teos; i BC - i; *OD Pisa* 290 + 290A Concavo X + 3.

3395 ---; s. of Peteharpochrates; i BC - i; *OD Pisa* 510 + 568 Convesso i 7.

3396 ---; s. of Ḏd-Wn(?); i BC - i; *OD Pisa* 126 i 6.

3397 ---; i BC - i; *OD Pisa* 126 i 1.

3398 ---; i BC - i; *OD Pisa* 132 X + 2.

3399 ---; s. of Patous (P$_3$j-tw); i BC - i; *OD Pisa* 1163 bis Convesso 6.

3400 ---; s. of Petemestous; (1) i BC - i; (2) late i BC - early i; (1) *OD Pisa* 454.4; (2) 35 Convesso 9.

3401 ---; late i BC - early i; w. Harchypsis; *OD Pisa* 35 Convesso 13.

3402 ---; s. of Psen[...]; Aug 3; *OD Pisa* 473 Concavo i 6.

3403 ---; s. of Cephalon; Aug 3; *OD Pisa* 473 Convesso 1, 5.

3404 ---; s. of P$_3$-spj; April 4; dependant of Mn(?); *OD Pisa* 511 + 512 i 13.

3405 ---; Aug 7; *OD Pisa* 432.2.

3406 PETE]CHONSIS; s. of Patous; 8; *OD Pisa* 1.16.

3407 PETECHONSIS; 9; *DO Colon. inv.* 286.2.

3408 ---; s. of Ḫnsw-ḫb(?); 9; *DO Colon. inv.* 300.2.

3409 ---; early i; *OD Pisa* 320.1.

3410 ---; s. of P$_3$-rḫtj; early i; *OD Pisa* 164.4.

3411 ---; s. of P$_3$-sḥn; early i; *OD Pisa* 450B Concavo i X + 7.

3412 ---; ch. Petearpsenesis; i; *OD Pisa* 129 X + 2.

3413 PETEESIS; ch. Harthotes; i BC - i; *OD Pisa* 60 Convesso ii 6.

3414 ---; s. of Wḥj; late i BC - i; *OD Pisa* 35 Convesso 3.

3415 ---; s. of Kmj; late i BC - early i; *OD Pisa* 35 Convesso 4.

3416 PETEESIS; s. of Psen-t_3-wḥj; late i BC - early i; *OD Pisa* 35 Concavo ii 8.

3417 ---; s. of Patous; late i BC - early i; *OD Pisa* 35 Concavo ii 10.

3418 ---; s. of Philiscus, s. of Ammonius; m. Arasis, d. of Vettius; sp. Philotera; July 87; Senepta, M. Top.; guardian of wife; *PSI* III 203.2.

3419 ---; 91 or 107; Oxyrhynchite?; Oxy.?; addr. for gs., certifier of slave's emancipation; IV 722.32.

3420 PETẸẸUS; ch. Taseus; May 26; Tanais?, M. Top.; addr. for d.; *P. Ṙein.* II 103.2.

3421 PETEHARPOCHRATES; ch. Petechonsis; i BC - i; *OD Pisa* 510 + 568 Convesso i 7.

3422 PETEIOMIS; ch. Petearpsenesis; i BC - i; *OD Pisa* 99 i 6.

3423 PETEMESTOUS; ch. Petechonsis; (1) late i BC - early i; (2) i BC - i; (1) *OD Pisa* Convesso 9; (2) 454.4.

3424 ---; ch. Patesis; i BC - i; *OD Pisa* 99 i 3.

3425 ---; s. of Petosiris; early i; *OD Pisa* 249.1.

3426 PETEMESTUS; i BC - i; *OD Pisa* 779 + 242 Concavo 7.

3427 PETEMUNIS; s. of Wḥj; April 5 BC; *OD Pisa* 936 Concavo 7.

3428 ---; ch. Petechonsis; i BC; *OD Pisa* 34.1.

3429 ---; ch. [..].ls.t; i BC - i; *OD Pisa* 8.3.

3430 ---; s. of Abok; i BC - i; *OD Pisa* 510 + 568 Convesso ii 2.

3431 ---; i BC - i; *OD Pisa* 25 ii 23.

3432 ---; s. of T_3-ḳt(?); i BC - i; *OD Pisa* 217 Convesso X + 6.

3433 ---; i BC - i; *OD Pisa* 29 ii X + 13.

3434 ---; i BC - i; *OD Pisa* 504.3.

3435 ---; s. of P_3-šrj-ḳns; i BC - i; bro. of Haremphois; *OD Pisa* 29 ii X + 8.

3436 ---; ch. Harchypsis; i BC - i; (1) *OD Pisa* 127.6; (2) 541 Convesso i 1.

3437 ---; ch. Ghemapis; i BC - i; *OD Pisa* 69 Concavo 5.

3438 ---; s. of ^{c}Š$_3$; i BC - i; *OD Pisa* 111 Convesso 8.

3439 ---; s. of Sabinus; i BC - i; (1) *OD Pisa* 69 Concavo 4; (2) 137 Concavo 6.

3440 ---; i BC - i; *OD Pisa* 280 X + 6.

3441 ---; i BC - i; *OD Pisa* 1264 Convesso 3.

3442 PETEMUNIS; i BC - i; *OD Pisa* 290 + 290A Concavo X + 4.

3443 ---; s. of Psenpachiris; i BC - i; *OD Pisa* 25 i 5.

3444 ---; i BC - i; dependant of Pa-lg; *OD Pisa* 99 i 9.

3445 ---; s. of Petubastis; i BC - i; *OD Pisa* 99 i 4.

3446 ---; s. of Petesansneus; 8; *OD Pisa* 1.13.

3447 ---; 14-37; Oxy.; *P. Ryl.* IV 677.1.

3448 ---; ch. Panechotes; Jan 29; Kerkemunis?, U. Top.; addr. for s.; XXXVIII 2850.15-16.

3449 ---; early i; *OD Pisa* 320.1.

3450 ---; s. of Psenesis; i; *OD Pisa* 129 X + 7.

3451 P]ẸTEMUNIS; 117-138; Sinkepha; unnamed ch.; *PSI* V 475.17.

3452 PETEMUNIS; 132/133 or 153/154; Oxy.; XII 1518.22, 24.

3453 PETENUPHIS; ch. Hatres; i; Koba; addr. for s.; VIII 1145.17.

3454 PETES; i BC - i; *OD Pisa* 477 Convesso 7.

3455 PETESANSNEUS; ch. Petemunis; 8; *OD Pisa* 1. 13.

3456 PETESIRIS; ch. Pausiris; early i; Psobthis?, M. Top.; addr. for s.; *P. Wisc.* I 23.6.

3457 ---; Aug 107; *P. Wisc.* I 17 V 5.

3458 ---; Aug 107; *P. Wisc.* I 17 V 22.

3459 PETESIS; i BC - i; dependant of Ammonius; *OD Pisa* 29 ii X + 11.

3460 ---; s. of Petosiris; i BC - i; Libanus acts via him; (1) *OD Pisa* 510 + 568 Concavo i X + 9; (2) 510 + 568 Convesso i 19.

3461 ---; s. of Š̆w-tfn-t; i BC - i; *OD Pisa* 510 + 568 Convesso i 8.

3462 ---; s. of Herieus; i BC - i; *OD Pisa* 127.5.

3463 ---; ch. Pemenches; i BC - i; (1) *OD Pisa* 69 Convesso i 6; (2) 111 Convesso 6; (3) 502 X + 9; (4) 541 Concavo 1, 6; (5) 510 + 568 Concavo i X + 7.

3464 ---; i BC - i; works via Thoteus?; *OD Pisa* 111 Convesso 2.

3465 ---; ch. Apollonius; i BC - i; *OD Pisa* 5 i X + 8.

3466 ---; ch. Totoes; i BC - i; *OD Pisa* 126 i 5.

3467 ---; s. of Sn-Ḥp(?); i BC - i; *OD Pisa* 460 Convesso ii X + 14.

3468 PETESIS; s. of Kmj; late i BC - early i; *OD Pisa* 35 Convesso 10. 17.

3469 PETESNES; i BC - i; *OD Pisa* 543 X + 4.

3470 ---; ch. Harpochrates; i BC - i; *OD Pisa* 69 Convesso i 7.

3471 ---; s. of Pe[ ]; i BC - i; *OD Pisa* 510 + 568 Convesso ii 1.

3472 ---; ch. Petosiris; i BC - i; *OD Pisa* 25 ii 4.

3473 ---; ch. E-f-st_3-n.im-w; i BC - i; *OD Pisa* 8.18.

3474 PETE]SUCHUS; ch. Mnesitheus; (1) 29?; (2) July 42; (3) July 50; (4) Aug 50; (5) Aug 86; (6) 2nd half i; landholder?; Oxyrhynchite; Kerkeura, M. Top. (1); Tholthis?, Thmois. Top. (3); name restored (1); stemma in intro. (2); payment in Psychis, Heracleopolite (1); gs. Comon (6); death of s. (4); (1) XXXVIII 2842.5-6; (2) 2834.1-2; (3) 2836.2; (4) 2837.8-9; (5) 2843.9; (6) 2846.4.

3475 [P]ETESUCHUS; s. of Ballous; i; farmer; Sesphtha; *P. Ryl.* II 199.18.

3476 PETES(UCHUS); 2nd half i; VI 985 (descr.).

3477 ---; s. of Papo(ntos), s. of Harpae(sis); ii; landholder; Hippodrome qtr; *P. Princ.* II 46.1.

3478 PETESURIS; i BC - i; *OD Pisa* 35 Convesso 1.

3479 PETESYRIS; late i BC - early i; *OD Pisa* 35 Convesso 1.

3480 PETETHOTES; April 5 BC; *OD Pisa* 936 Convesso 9.

3481 PE]TETYMIS; ch. Harchypsis; i BC - i; *OD Pisa* 755 Convesso X + 5.

3482 PETETYMIS; ch. Onnophris; late i BC - i; *OD Pisa* 35 Concavo ii 16.

3483 ---; ch. Nectenibis; i; *OD Pisa* 60 Concavo 3.

3484 PETEURIS; s. of Petubastis; i BC - i; *OD Pisa* 477 Convesso 10.

3485 ---; i BC - i; *OD Pisa* 8.12, 13.

3486 ---; i BC - i; acts via Dd; *OD Pisa* 510 + 568 Concavo i X + 10.

3487 ---; s. of Horus-Dd; i BC - i; *OD Pisa* 460 Convesso ii X + 10.

3488 ---; s. of Patous; i BC - i; *OD Pisa* 460 Convesso i X + 7.

3489 ---; s. of Thoteus; 6; *OD Pisa* 1163.5.

3490 ---; 13; comogrammateus; Kerkeura, M. Top.; Oxy.; (1) IX 1188.2, 7; (2) XX 2277.5.

3491 PETEURIS; s. of Harthoonis; ch. Harthoonis; Oct 112; Oxyrhynchite; Oxy.; addr. for bro. Phatres; XXII 2351.12.

3492 ---; sp. Taaphynchis; ch. Paos; 116; Gymnasium St qtr; addr. for s., dec. tekton of Isis and other gods and pyraethes, and enr. in this qtr; XII 1550.17.

3493 ---; s. of Sarapion; ch. Herais; 122/123; Oxyrhynchite; III 592 (descr.) R 6.

3494 ---; s. of Eubion, s. of Ptollion; ch. Apollonius; 148/149; Oxyrhynchite, gymnasial class; Gymnasium St qtr; addr. for gs. Peteuris; father in list of 4/5; XLVI 3276.2.

3495 PET[EURI]S(?); s. of Apollonius; s. of Peteuris; sp. Heras; ch. Ammonius; 148/149; Oxyrhynchite, gymnasial class; Upper Camp qtr; enr. s. in g. class of 13 yr olds; XLVI 3276.2.

3496 PETEURIS; ii; friend of Plution; XLII 3080.1.

PETEUS; see PATOUS.

3497 PETOOUS; ch. Thoonis; 67 BC(?); doc. pr. Oxy.?; *P. Ryl.* II 65.2.

3498 PETOSARAPIS; s. of Thonis; 71/72; tax-farmer; Oxy.?; farms Bahria Oasis; *P. Ryl.* II 95.2.

---; see also PETOSORAPIS.

3499 ---; s. of [.]bi[....]; ch. Sinthonis; 96; Oxyrhynchite?; Oxy.?; addr. for d.; II 266.10.

3500 ---; s. of Thompecysis, s. of Sarapion; m. Sinthonis, d. of Petosarapis; sp. Thaesis (divorced); 96; Oxyrhynchite; Oxy.; II 266.6.

3501 ---; s. of Heracles, s. of Sarapas; early ii; father's will; bro. of Sarapas; III 649 (descr.).

3502 PETOSIRIS; ch. Orsenouphis, Pecysis; 73 or 44 BC; Oxy.?; addr. for s.; XIV 1639.1.

3503 ---; 67 BC?; grave digger; Oxy.?; *P. Ryl.* II 65.1.

3504 ---; s. of Thonis alias Patoiphis, s. of Thonis; 30/29 BC; temple lamplighter; Oxy.; l. of Temple of Thoeris; XII 1453.7.

3505 PETOSIRIS(?); ch. Onnophris; April 5 BC; *OD Pisa* 936 Convesso 7.

3506 ---; ch. Pausiris; i BC - i; *OD Pisa* 477 Concavo X + 7.

3507 PETOSIRIS; i BC - i; *OD Pisa* 23 ii 1.

3508 ---; s. of Pates; i BC - i; *OD Pisa* 28 X + 5.

3509 ---; s. of Petesnes; i BC - i; *OD Pisa* 25 ii 4.

3510 ---; ch. Harendotes; i BC - i; *OD Pisa* 25 i 20.

3511 PETOSIRIS; ch. Pausiris; i BC - i; (1) *OD Pisa* 25 ii 3; (2) 132 X + 8; (3) 470.3.

3512 ---; ch. P$_3$-tj-nb-...; i BC - i; *OD Pisa* 25 ii 16.

3513 ---; s. of Patous; dependant of Patous; i BC - i; (1) *OD Pisa* 25 i 21; (2) 779 + 242 Convesso X + 15; (3) 29 ii X + 14.

3514 ---; ch.]$^{c}{}_{3}$; i BC - i; *OD Pisa* 23 i X + 7.

3515 ---; ch.]-b$_3$; i BC - i; *OD Pisa* 23 i X + 9.

3516 ---; s. of Ḥr-Nḫt; i BC - i; *OD Pisa* 126 i 4.

3517 ---; s. of Haremphois; i BC - i; bro. Totoes; *OD Pisa* 69 Convesso i 3.

3518 ---; s. of Pa-$_3$ll; i BC - i; *OD Pisa* 126 i 9.

3519 ---; s. of Petubastis; i BC - i; *OD Pisa* 510 + 568 Convesso ii 8.

3520 ---; ch. Petesis; i BC - i; (1) *OD Pisa* 510 + 568 Concavo i X + 9; (2) Convesso i 19.

3521 ---; s. of Psen-w$_3$ḥ-t$_3$-ḳt(?); i BC - i; *OD Pisa* 87 X + 3.

3522 ---; s. of H̱rdw-Ḥp; i BC - i; *OD Pisa* 70.1.

3523 ---; i BC - i; *OD Pisa* 351 X + 3.

3524 ---; i BC - i; *OD Pisa* 1023 Convesso ii 5.

3525 PE]TOSIRIS; s. of Harpaesis; (1), (2) i BC - i; (3) July 7; (1) *OD Pisa* 561 + 562 + 795 i X + 4; (2) 779 + 242 Convesso X + 13; (3) 1131 Convesso 1.

3526 PETOSIRIS; s. of P$_3$-wrš; i BC - i; acts through P$_3$-nḥs; *OD Pisa* 451 + 540 Convesso 10.

3527 ---; ch. Harpaesis; i BC - i; *OD Pisa* 451 + 540 Convesso 9.

3528 ---; s. of Pausiris; i BC - i; (1) *OD Pisa* 451 + 540 Convesso 2; (2) 196 ii X + 2.

3529 ---; ch. Totoes; i BC - i; (1) *OD Pisa* 5 ii X + 8; (2) 196 ii X + 3.

3530 ---; s. of Mn; i BC - i; *OD Pisa* 5 i X + 14.

3531 ---; i BC - i; *OD Pisa* 5 i X + 5.

3532 ---; i BC - i; *OD Pisa* 69 Convesso ii 1.

3533 ---; s. of Gjbws; i BC - i; *OD Pisa* 111 Convesso 4.

3534 ---; s. of Horus; i BC - i; (1) *OD Pisa* 360 Concavo X + 5; (2) 276 X + 3; (3) 232.6.

3535 ---; i BC - i; *OD Pisa* 38 ii X + 2.

3536 PETOSIRIS; ch. Horus; i BC - i; (1) *OD Pisa* 290 + 290A Concavo X + 5; (2) 755 Concavo X + 9.

3537 ---; s. of Harendotes; i BC - i; (1) *OD Pisa* 377 Convesso 1 and passim; (2) 541 Convesso i 4.

3538 ---; s. of Petechonsis; i BC - i; P_3-stjws acts for him; (1) *OD Pisa* 22.6; (2) 755 Convesso X + 18; (3) 510 + 568 Convesso i 12.

3539 ---; s. of Harpchemis; (1) i BC - i; (2) i; (1) *OD Pisa* 129 X + 3; (2) 755 Concavo X + 4.

3540 ---; ch. Patous; (1) i BC - i; (2) i; (1) *OD Pisa* 111 Convesso 4; (2) 60 Convesso i 9.

3541 ---; s. of Teos; i BC - i; *OD Pisa* 532 X + 2.

3542 ---; i BC - i; *OD Pisa* 22.7.

3543 ---; s. of Pamun; i BC i; *OD Pisa* 126 ii 1.

3544 ---; end i BC; *OD Pisa* 293.1-2.

3545 ---; ch. Nectenibis; (1) April 4; (2) i; (1) *OD Pisa* 511 + 512 i 8; (2) 60 Convesso ii 5.

3546 ---; s. of Psen-Gdn; July 7; *OD Pisa* 1131 Concavo 6.

3547 ---; s. of Gll (Celol?); 8; *OD Pisa* 1.7.

3548 ---; s. of Dd(?); 8; *OD Pisa* 1.11.

3549 ---; June 9; *OD Pisa* 246.1.

3550 ---; ch. Horion; 19/20; Myrobalanus qtr; addr. for s.; II 254.2.

3551 ---; ch. Petosiris; July 66; Phthochis?, E. Top.; addr. for gs. Harmiysis; II 246.6.

3552 ---; s. of Petosiris; sp. Didyme; ch. Harmiysis; July 66; Phthochis?, E. Top.; addr. for s.; II 246.5-6.

3553 ---; ch. Petosiris; Mar/Apr 66; Egzoeu qtr?; addr. for s.; *PSI* VIII 871.4, 26.

3554 ---; s. of Petosiris; ch. Petechon; Mar/Apr 66; Egzoeu qtr?; reg. s. as apprentice brass beater w. Heracleides; illiterate; *PSI* VIII 871.4, 26.

3555 ---; s. of Artem [....; sp. ....]nis; ch. Pane[ ]; 71; Senekeleu?, W. Top.; addr. for s.; *P. Med. inv.* 71.70.4.

3556 ---; ch.]ẹsis; 71/72; Oxy.?; doc. pr. Oxy.?; s. a tax-farmer; *P. Ryl.* II 95.2.

3557 P]ETOSIRIS; s. of Harthonis; 71/72; tax-farmer; Oxy.?; doc. pr. Oxy.?; *P. Ryl.* II 95.3.

3558 PETOSIRIS; ch. Dionysia; 93; Athychis, U. Top.; addr. for d.; *P. Princ.* II 42 R 2.

3559 ---; d. of Harpaesis; sp. Harpaesis; ch. Thonis, Thomphyas; c. 98; Oxyrhynchite?; Oxy.?; addr. for s.; II 241.7.

3560 ---; ch. Petemestous; early i; *OD Pisa* 249.1.

3561 ---; s. of Šm^{c}; early i; *OD Pisa* 164.1.

3562 ---; April early i; dependant of Pamun; *OD Pisa* 423.2.

3563 ---; sp. Tapontos; ch. Tausiris; i; Pakerke, M. Top.; doc. pr. Oxy.?; addr. for d.; *P. Harris* 138 i 19.

3564 ---; s. of Pasis; i; *OD Pisa* 60 Convesso ii 1.

3565 ---; s. of Ḥr-p$_3$-ḳm(?); i; *OD Pisa* 60 Convesso i 11.

3566 ---; s. of Dionysius, s. of Epimachus; m. Thatres; 118; property owner; Oxyrhynchite; Oxy.; bro. of Epimachus; owns part house and court at Kerkethyris; III 503.3.

3567 ---; ch. Dionysius; 119; North St qtr; addr. for gs. Petosiris; XII 1547.2.

3568 ---; s. of Dionysius, s. of Petosiris; m. Mieus, d. of Horus; sp. Tetoeus; ch. Ti[ ]; 119; stone cutter; Oxyrhynchite; North St qtr; age 74; signalement; XII 1547.2.

3569 ---; s. of Thoonas, s. of Petosiris; m. Thaisous, d. of Papontos; 119; landholder; North St qtr; bro. of Tetoeus and Papontos; XII 1547.9.

3570 ---; s. of Thoonis; sp. Taps[ois?; ch. Apollonides; 119; Oxy.; addr. for s.; XII 1547.19.

3571 ---; 124; slave owner?; Oxy.; freedman is Panechotes; III 490.4, 9.

3572 ---; ch. Horus; 137/138; Sinageris, Hermopolite; addr. for gs.; *PSI* IV 315.3.

3573 ---; s. of Horus, s. of Petosiris; m. Chenpsois; 137/138; landholder; Sinageris, Hermopolite; leases land nr Po[ ]nis from Theon in Kleros of Hippalus; *PSI* IV 315.3.

3574 ---; 148/149; Oxyrhynchite, gymnasial class; Upper Camp qtr?; addr. for unnamed d., sp. of Di[-]; XLVI 3277.3.

3575 PEṬOṢIUS; ch. Charitous; March 79; Oxyrhynchite?; Oxy.; addr. for mat. gs. Didymus; II 243.5.

3576 PETOSORAPIS; s. of Haremphois; i BC - i; *OD Pisa* 25 i 18.

3577 ---; ch. Horus; i BC - i; *OD Pisa* 127.4.

3578 ---; i BC - i; *OD Pisa* 504.3.

3579 PE]TOSORAPIS; Aug 3; *OD Pisa* 473 Convesso 8.

3580 PETOSORAPIS; 8; *OD Pisa* 1.3.

3581 PETOSORAPIS; ch. Heracleides; Mar/Apr 66; Egzoeu qtr; addr. for s.; *PSI* VIII 871.14.

3582 ---; ch. Teseuris; 77; Oxy.; addr. for gd. Thermuthion; II 242.25.

3583 ---; sp. Heras; ch. Thnas, Tecosis; Nov 83; Oxyrhynchite?; Oxy.?; addr. for d.; X 1283.5, 8.

3584 ---; ch. Thonis; 83; Oxyrhynchite?; Oxy.?; addr. for gd. Tecosis; X 1282.11.

3585 ---; ch. Tausarapis; 94; Oxyrhynchite; Oxy.; addr. for mat. gs. Dionysius; I 73.18.

3586 ---; early i; *OD Pisa* 424.12.

3587 ---; ch. Petosorapis; Oxyrhynchite?; Thoeris St qtr; addr. for gs. Ptolemaeus; VII 1029.18.

3588 ---; s. of Petosorapis; ch. Ptolemaeus; 107; Oxyrhynchite?; Thoeris St qtr; addr. for s.; VII 1029.18.

3589 ---; ch. Sarapion; 117/118; property owner; Pammenes' Garden qtr; addr. for gs. Zoilus; XIV 1648.39.

3590 PETOUPHOIS; 81-96; VI 984 R fin.

3591 PETRAEUS; s. of Hermogenes; 31/32; Sinary, L. Top.; *P. Mich. inv.* 69.13.

3592 PETRONIUS; ch. Luci<u>s; i; Sobthis; addr. for s.; VIII 1145.21.

PETRONIUS; see also PETR[ONIUS] DIONYSIUS; P. PETRONIUS CELER.

3593 PETSEOUS; ch. Horus; i BC - i; *OD Pisa* 58.9, 11, 16.

3594 PETSEROTHONIS; ch. Harpaesis; c. 98; Oxyrhynchite?; Oxy.?; addr. for gs. Thonis; II 241.6.

3595 PETSIRIS; ch. Petsiris; 21; Sesphtha; L. Top.; addr. for s.; *P. Princ.* II 24.16.

3596 ---; s. of Petsiris; 21; shepherd; Sesphtha, L. Top.; sh. for Taarchorsia; *P. Princ.* II 24.16.

3597 ---; s. of Horus; sp. Taseus; May 26; Tanais, M. Top.; Persian of Epigone; illiterate; *P. Rein.* II 103.3.

3598 ---; s. of Cottes; 31/32?; *P. Mich. inv.* 69.3.

3599 ---; s. of Sarapion; m. Thaesis, d. of Heracleius; 48; guardian to aunt Thaesis; *P. Fouad* 35.2.

3600 ---; ch. Pausiris; Nov/Dec 64?; Palosis, Thmois. Top.; addr. for s.; IV 808 (descr.).

3601 ---; ch. Petsiris alias Antit( ); 83/84; Papsis?, Tychis Necotis; addr. for s.; II 290.22.

3602 PETSIRIS; alias ANTIT( ); s. of Petsiris; 83/84; landholder; Papsis?, Tychis Necotis; land there; II 290.22.

3603 ---; ch. Strouthes; 83/84 Papsis?, Tychis Necotis; addr. for gs. Strouthes; II 290.27.

---; see ANICETUS.

3604 ---; alias LIBO; s. of Panechotes; May 89; farmer; lessee; unnamed s. leases part of Seneca's estate; XLII 3051.3.

3605 PETSI(RIS); ch. Haryotes; i; Sesphtha?; addr. for s.; *P. Ryl.* II 199.17.

3606 PETSIRIS; sp. Athenarous; ch. Hermaeus; Sept 103; Oxyrhynchite?; Oxy.?; addr. for s.; sp. from Toka; XLI 2973.4-5.

3607 ---; s. of Horus; 127 or 128; Patne; *P. Lips.* 113.6.

3608 ---; ch. Pausiris; Jan 138; Sephtha?, L. Top.; addr. for s.; III 484.4.

3609 ---; ii; messenger of Demetrius to Heracleides; III 582 (descr.).

3610 PETSORONNOPHRIS; s. of Cheepheibis; 31/32; Sinary, L. Top.; *P. Mich. inv.* 69.14.

3611 PETUBASTIS; ch. Petemunis; i BC - i; *OD Pisa* 99 i 4.

3612 ---; ch. Patous; i BC - i; (1) *OD Pisa* 510 + 568 Concavo i X + 8; (2) ii 1.

3613 ---; s. of Patumis; i BC - i; *OD Pisa* 126 i 7.

3614 ---; ch. Peteuris; i BC - i; *OD Pisa* 477 Convesso 10.

3615 ---; ch. Petosiris; i BC - i; *OD Pisa* 510 + 568 Convesso ii 8.

3616 ---; i BC - i; dependant of Snn; *OD Pisa* 460 Convesso ii X + 13.

3617 ---; s. of Harpaesis; i BC - i; *OD Pisa* 755 Concavo X + 6.

3618 ---; i BC - i; *OD Pisa* 779 + 242 Convesso X + 8.

3619 ---; s. of Harpchemis; i BC - i; *OD Pisa* 1023 Convesso i 6.

3620 ---; ch. Totoes; i BC - i; (1) *OD Pisa* 5 ii X + 14; (2) 267.2.

3621 PETUBASTIS(?); ch. Pathotes; i BC - i; *OD Pisa* 502 X + 10.

3622 PETUBASTIS; Aug 3; agent for Platon; *OD Pisa* 473 Convesso 2.

3623 ---; Aug 7; *OD Pisa* 432.3.

3624 ---; s. of Horus; early i; called the ancient; *OD Pisa* 249.4.

3625 PETUSIUS; s. of Sarapion; June 52; bro. of Ammonius, Apollonia, Hermodotus; *SB* I 8034.10.

3626 PHẠ[....]TO( ); c. 1; IV 736.78.

3627 PHABANON; 122/123?; "brother" of Hephaestion and Didymus; II 73.4.

3628 PHALACRUS; 22; II 294.24.

PHALANX; see DIOGENES.

3629 ---; s. of Diogenes alias Phalanx, s. of Harpalus; 130; Oxyrhynchite; Oxy.; age 40; witness; signalement; III 492.19.

3630 PHANIAS; s. of Sarapion; Oct/Nov 21 BC; public farmer; cavalry colonist; slave owner?; Tacona, L. Top.; *P. Vindob. Worp.* 2.2.

3631 ---; 14-37; toparch; II 382 (descr.).

3632 ---; ch. Dionysius; 23/24 or 49/50; Oxy.; IV 789 (descr.).

3633 ---; ch. Amois; 55-68; Nemera; addr. for s.; *P. Ross. Georg.* II 13.6.

3634 ---; ch. Phanias alias Amois; March 79; Oxyrhynchite?; Oxy.?; addr. for gs. Dionysius alias Amois; II 243.7.

3635 ---; alias AMOIS; s. of Phanias; sp. Zenarion; ch. Dionysius alias Amois; March 79; Oxyrhynchite?; Hermaeum qtr; addr. for s.; II 243.7.

3636 ---; s. of Sarapion; 81-96; VIII 1105.1.

3637 ---; 81-96; nominee of Phanias, s. of Sarapion; VIII 1105.1.

3638 ---; (1) 95; (2) n.d.; (3) 99; (4), (5) c. 95-100 (n.d.?); (6) 100; superintendent of land distribution; w. Diogenes (2, 5) and w. Diogenes alias Hermias (4); (1) I 45.1; (2) I 175 (descr.); (3) II 343 (descr.)?; (4) 341 (descr.); (5) 342 (descr.); (6) I 46.1.

3639 ---; i; unnamed sp.; VIII 1148.3.

3640 ---; 132/133; unnamed child; *PSI* I 53 vi 89, 104.

3641 STATILIUS PHANIAS; ii; Roman; Oxy.; "father" of Andronicus; III 598 (descr.).

3642 PHAON; ch. Ptollis; Jan 132; Oxyrhynchite; Thoeris St qtr; addr. for gs. Phaon; III 478.21.

3643 ---; s. of Ptollis, s. of Phaon; m. Athena; sp. Dionysous (freedwoman); ch. Ptollis; Jan 132; Oxyrhynchite; Thoeris St qtr; dec.; in poll tax in 127/128; III 478.13, 20.

3644 PHARITON(?); ii; Oxy.; XII 1583.9.

3645 PHATRES; s. of Psentaes; i BC - i; *OD Pisa* 510 + 568 Convesso i 4.

3646 PHATRES; s. of Pamun; i BC - i; *OD Pisa* 106.7.

3647 ---; i BC - i; *OD Pisa* 454.1.

3648 ---; ch. Paor; Oct 5; *OD Pisa* 427.3.

3649 ---; s. of Apo(llonius?); ch. Ar...; July 44; Pela, W. Top.; addr. for d.; XII 1447.4.

3650 ---; ch. -us; 51/52 or 64/65; *P. Mil.* II 53.7.

3651 ---; 77; Oxy.; unnamed d.; gs. priest, perhaps Harthoonis, s. of Harthoonis, p. of Thoeris, Isis, Sarapis and assoc. gods; II 242.3.

3652 ---; ch. Anresis; 81-96; mat. gs. Onnophris of gymnasial class; VI 984 R (1).

3653 ---; ch. Teraus alias Thaubastis; 96; Oxyrhynchite?; Knights' Camp qtr; addr. for gs. Hatres; I 104.7.

3654 ---; s. of Harthoonis, s. of Harthoonis; Oct 112; priest of Thoeris, Isis, Sarapis and assoc. gods; landholder; lessor; Oxyrhynchite; Oxy.; owns part of Kleros of Nicaeus nr Tanais; XXII 2351.1.

---; see DIONYSIUS.

3655 ---; s. of Chaeras; ii; merchant?; doc. pr. Oxy.?; business w. Heracleides; *SB* VI 9025.16, 33.

3656 PHEREMPHIS; ch. Apia, Dionytas, Tapontos; Jan 121; Metroon qtr; addr. for ch.; *P. Fouad* 30.11.

3657 ---; ch. Sarapion; 130; Oxyrhynchite?; Oxy.?; addr. for s.; see XII 1539.13; III 492.23.

3658 PHILADELPHUS; gs. of Horus; m. Thaesis; 45-47; Little Oasis; addr. for m.; is elder s.; enslaved for insolvency?; XLII 3033.4.

3659 PHILAS; ch. Paapis; May 26; *P. Rein.* II 103.5.

3660 PHILEAS; s. of Saprion; ii; "brother" of Harpocration; XLIV 3199.1.

3661 PHILEROS; late i BC; Oxy.; married; XII 1479.12.

3662 TI. JULIUS PHILETUS; 90; Roman; Petne?, M. Top.; acts for Ti. Julius Basilides who had land there; I 72.17, 18.

3663 PHILETUS; ii; XXXI 2593.1.

3664 PHILINUS; Sept 6; *OD Pisa* 814 Convesso 3.

3665 ---; sp. -, d. of Eudaemon; ch. Philinus; i; *P. Med. inv.* 69.09.1.

3666 ---; s. of Philinus; gs. (mat.) of Eudaemon; i; *P. Med. inv.* 69.09.1.

3667 PHILINUS; c. 136; farmer; lessee; Oxyrhynchite?; Oxy.?; defendant; leased land in Seryphis; bro. of Anthestius; IV 707 ii 12.

3668 PHILION; ii; friend of Eirene; I 115.8.

3669 PHILISCUS; Feb 61; tax farmer (weavers' tax); Oxy.?; II 262.1.

3670 ---; ch. Sarapion; 66-72/73; s. has mortgaged property in Senepta, M. Top.; IX 1203 + *SB* IV 7339.12.

3671 ---; (1) Aug 79; (2) c. 79; agoranomus w. Taruthinus and Themistocles; (1) II 380 (descr.); (2) 375 (descr.).

3672 ---; s. of Philiscus; ch. Ptolema; (1) 86; (2) 94/95; ex-gymnasiarch; Oxyrhynchite; gymnasial class; Heracles Place qtr; (1) VII 1028.4; (2) II 257.28.

3673 ---; ch. Theogenes, Philiscus; 94/95; Oxyrhynchite, gymnasial class; Heracles Place qtr; ex-gymnasiarch; II 257.17, 28.

3674 ---; s. of Ammonius; sp. Arasis; ch. Peteesis; July 87; Senepta, M. Top.; addr. for s.; *PSI* III 203.2.

3675 ---; 89-91; Oxy.?; addr. for unnamed s., member of embassy to prefect; *PSI* XIV 1434.3, 8.

3676 ---; s. of Diogenes; 2nd half i; practor; Sesphtha, L. Top.; XXXVIII 2845.6.

3677 ---; ch. Diogenes; Oct 133; doc. pr. Oxy., W. Top.?; *P. Lips*. 114.4.

3678 ---; 134; bibliophylax, w. Herodes; Oxy.; III 515.1.

3679 PHILOLOGUS; late i; teacher in Alex.; XVIII 2190.7 and passim.

3680 PHILOMUSUS; late i BC; Alexandria; goes to Oxy.; XII 1479.8.

3681 PHILON; 93; landholder; Athychis, Enteiis, U. Top.; land at both; *P. Princ*. II 42 V ii 19, iii 34.

3682 ---; s. of Dionysius; Jan 121; property owner; Metroon qtr?; joint owner property there w. Aria, her bros., and others; *P. Fouad* 30.10.

3683 ---; sp. Taonnophris; ch. Eumoerus?; ii; Oxy.; (1) I 115.1; (2) 116.1.

3684 PHILONICUS; (1) Feb 122; (2) 122/123; (3) 122/123?; (4) Oct 123; strategus; Oxy.; (1) IV 714.1; (2) VI 957.1; (3) *P. Wisc*. II 73.24; (4) VI 898.26.

3685 PHILOSTEPH(ANOS); 81-96; VI 984 R fin.

3686 PHILOSTRATUS; s. of Zoilus; 66-72/73; Alexandria; property in Senepta wrongfully alienated to him; IX 1203 + *SB* IV 7339.5.

3687 PHILOTAS; ch. Didyme; 117-137; Oxyrhynchite?; Oxy.?; addr. for mat. gs. Pecysis; I 105.2.

3688 PHILOTERA; sp. Peteesis; July 87; wetnurse; Senepta, M. Top.; to suckle slave child Dionysius; sp. guardian; *PSI* III 203.[2] and passim.

3689 ---; d. of Origenes; sp. Chaeremon; ch. Adrastus; 133; Alex.; Alexandria; addr. for s.; I 100.5.

3690 PHILOTES; c.8 -]us; 30 BC - 14; s. farmer; *P. Rein.* II 99.1.

3691 PHILUMENE; sp. Ammonius; ch. [Ammoniu]s; 45; II 326 R 9.

3692 ---; d. of Heron; ch. Heron; (1) 82; (2) June 118; Oxy.; gss. are Themistocles and Heron; dec. in 2; (1) II 286.4; (2) *PSI* IV 281 R i 43.

3693 ---; sp. Mynius; ch. Tryphon; i - ii; *P. Harris* 72.32.

3694 ---; ch. Theon, Apollonius?; 117/138; res. in Apollonopolite nome; X 1293.1.

3695 PHILUMEN[US or E; 54-68; animal owner; Toka, M. Top.; *P. Inst. Fran.* I 21.3.

3696 PHILOUS; d. of Sarapion; sp. Sarapion; ch. Sarapion; i; property owner; Peeno, M. Top.; doc. pr. Oxy.?; addr. for s.; owned vacant lot in P.; *P. Harris* 138 iii 1, 2.

3697 PHILOXENUS; ch. Heracleides; March 79; Oxy.?; addr. for s.; II 243.19.

3698 ---; late i; XVIII 2190.12.

3699 PHILOX(ENUS); n.d.; *SB* I 1938 (c).

3700 PHILUS; ch. Procopianus; 137/138; *PSI* IV 315.3.

3701 PHILUTARION; c. 1; Oxy.; IV 739.20.

3702 PHNA; c. 1; unnamed d., dec.; IV 736.14.

3703 PHOEBA[MMON]; n.d.; *SB* I 1986 (a).

3704 PHOSPHORUS; July 23 BC; *P. Inst. Fran.* I 13.15.

3705 ---; i BC; IV 792 (descr.).

3706 PHRIBIS; s. of Heracleius; Sept 77; sitologus; Dermeithae, U. Top.; II 276.10.

3707 PHRONIMUS; ii; sent money by Cornelius; III 531.23.

3708 PICOS; s. of Horus; i BC - i; *OD Pisa* 117.1.

3709 PISAS; ii; brother to Ga[....]; XII 1584.14.

3710 PISICHIS; i BC - i; *OD Pisa* 25 i 19.

3711 PISYS; s. of Ammon, s. of Harpaesis; 87/88; farmer; Tanais, M. Top.; farm in Kleros of Theocritus; signalement; *Coll.*

Pap. I 22.2.

3712 PLACHISIS; s. of Pete-[ ]ns; early i; *OD Pisa* 426.2.

3713 PLANTA; ii; friend of Eirene; I 115.9.

3714 PLATON; Aug 3; works via Petubastis; *OD Pisa* 473 Concavo ii 2, Convesso 2.

3715 PLE[NIS; i BC - i; *OD Pisa* 137 Concavo 5.

3716 PLENIS; s. of Pates; i BC - i; *OD Pisa* 106.3.

3717 ---; s. of Kmj; April 4; *OD Pisa* 511 + 512 i 2.

3718 ---; early i; *OD Pisa* 450B Convesso ii X + 1.

3719 PLU[-; 132/133; *PSI* I 53 vi 103.

3720 PLULAN (?) (P_3lhwln_3); i BC - i; *OD Pisa* 28 X + 4.

3721 PLUSIA; 81-95; slave; Oxy.; s. of bride Sarapous; II 265.20, 25.

3722 PLUTARCHE; d. of Harpaesis; sp. Achilleus (1, dec.), Diogenes (2); ch. Thermuthion; (1) April 60; (2) March 61; Oxyrhynchite; Oxy.; (1) *P. Mich.* III 192.6; (2) 194.6.

3723 ---; d. of Sarapion; sp. Heracleides; ch. Heras; 94; Oxyrhynchite; Oxy.; addr. for s.; II 270.5.

3724 ---; d. of Theon; sp. Amois; ch. Ptollis; after 102; property owner; Oxyrhynchite; Oxy.; property in Temgenuthis qtr; addr. for s.; III 636.3.

3725 ---; m. Philumene; 117-138; see Plutarche, d. of Theon - writer here is a Theon; X 1293.31.

---; see EUDAEMONIS.

3726 PL[UTARCHUS]; s. of Sarapion; 37; banker; Oxy.; II 319.4-5.

3727 PLUTARCHUS; (1) 83/84; (2) 88; (3) c. 88 (n.d.?); agent for land distr. super. Tarutillius (1); "appt. epiteretes and cheiristes of the Katalochismoi of Oxy." (2); (1) XII 1462 i [3], ii 24; (2) I 174 (descr.); (3) II 345 (descr.).

3728 ---; ch. Plutarchus; 95; I 45.7.

3729 ---; s. of Plutarchus; ch. Plutarchus; 95; I 45.7.

3730 ---; s. of Plutarchus, s. of Plutarchus, gs. (mat.) of Tapotamon; 95; guardian of gm.; I 45.6.

3731 ---; ch. Plution; June 98; Oxyrhynchite, gymnasial class; South St qtr; addr. for s.; X 1266.21.

3732 ---; ch. Zoilus; i; hamlet of Nomus?; doc. pr. Oxy.?; addr. for gs. Plutarchus; *P. Harris* 138 i 2.

3733 PLUTARCHUS; s. of Zoilus, s. of Plutarchus; m. Thatres, d. of Theon; i; property owner; hamlet of Nomus; doc. pr. Oxy.?; property in Senepta; *P. Harris* 138 i 1.

3734 ---; s. of Pachnubis, s. of Totoes; Oct 108; Tanais, M. Top.; writes for illiterate father; XXXVIII 2874.54.

---; see TOTOES.

3735 ---; ch. Sarapion; 119/120; Oxyrhynchite; Oxy.; addr. for ggd. Julia, d. of Plutarchus; *PSI* XIII 1322.8.

3736 ---; s. of Sarapion, s. of Plutarchus; m. Isarous, d. of Ptolemaeus; sp. Flavia; ch. Julia; 119/120; property owner; Oxyrhynchite; bro. Ptolemaeus; *PSI* XIII 1322.2.

3737 ---; c. 136; farmer; lessee; Oxyrhynchite; Oxy.; leased land in Seryphis; IV 707 ii 14.

3738 PLUTAS; s. of Ptolemaeus; (1) 52/53; (2) ii; landholder; lessee; leases land nr Seryphis, W. Top., from Kleros of Sisines, Kleros of Nicanor and royal lands (1); land and bldgs at Psobthis (2); (1) *PSI* IX 1029.3; (2) *P. Inst. Fran.* III 15.19.

3739 PLUTION; ch. Plution; 55-68; *P. Ross. Georg.* II 13.13.

3740 ---; s. of Plution; 55-68; livestock owner; illiterate; *P. Ross. Georg.* II 13.13.

3741 ---; s. of Dionysius, s. of Heracleus; m. Ammonous, d. of Ammonius; 90; property owner; Teis, Thmois. Top.; *P. Ryl.* IV 597.2.

3742 ---; s. of Plutarchus; ch. Thermuthion; June 98; Oxyrhynchite, gymnasial class; South St qtr; sel. by str. in 72/73; X 1266.20-21.

3743 ---; s. of Psammis, s. of Dionysius alias Amois; m. Thermuthion, d. of Plutarchus; 98; Oxyrhynchite, gymnasial class; Oxy.; X 1266.33-34.

3744 ---; ch. Cephalas; Jan 100; Oxyrhynchite?; Oxy.?; addr. for s., farms at Nemerae; XLI 2960.7.

3745 ---; s. of Syrus; ch. Pausiris; Jan 100; farmer; landholder?; Oxyrhynchite; Oxy.?; land at Nemerae; other unnamed children; XLI 2960.7.

3746 ---; June 103-110; freedman; of Theon, writes for Horus and Panesneus; XLVI 3275.46.

3747 ---; s. of Besis(?), s. of Diogenes(?); 117; Oxyrhynchite; Oxy.; witness; age 45; signalement; readings uncertain; III 489.21.

3748 ---; s. of Ischyrion; sp. Sarapous; 117-138; property owner; Oxy.; 2 unnamed ch.; III 646 (descr.).

3749 ---; 119/120; 3 unnamed ch, 2 s., 1 d.; III 583 (descr.).

3750 PLUTION; s. of Diodorus, s. of Ptolemaeus; sp. Tatriphis, Dogymis; ch. Diodorus (by T.), Sarapion and Tnephersois (by D.); 127/128; Oxyrhynchite, gymnasial class; Gymnasium St qtr; epicrisis in 72/73; in census 89/90; now dec.; XII 1452 i 3.

---; see DIONYSIUS.

3751 ---; s. of Cratinus, s. of Demetrius; early ii; Oxyrhynchite; Oxy.; witness; III 493.13.

3752 ---; ch. Harmiysis; ii; Antipera; addr. for s.; *P. Erl.* 44 iii 24.

3753 ---; ii; XLII 3080.1-2.

3754 ---; ch. Plution; ii; Oxy.?; addr. for gs. Plution; *P. Mil.* II 51.1.

3755 ---; s. of Plution; sp. Thaesis; ch. Plution; ii; Oxy.?; addr. for s.; *P. Mil.* II 51.1.

3756 ---; s. of Plution, s. of Plution; m. Thaesis; sp. Ptolema; ii; Oxy.; *P. Mil.* II 51.1.

3757 ---; ii; visiting Oxy.?; I 113.15.

3758 ---; ch. Epimachus; ii; left s. share of camel stall; XLI 2981.22.

3759 ---; ch. Thermuthis; ii?; *PSI* XIV 1414.30.

3760 PLUTUS; ch. Aristas; 49/50; Oxyrhynchite; Knights' Camp qtr; addr. for s.; II 393 (descr.) 4.

3761 PLUT[US]?; 91/92; slave; Oxy.; age 32; sold to Didymus, formerly of Thermuthion; XXXVIII 2856.9.

3762 PLUTUS; s. of M( ); i; farmer; *P. Ryl.* II 199.29.

3763 ---; s. of Demetrius; ch. -]utus; i - ii; s. agent for Macer; *PSI* VI 687.6.

3764 PNEPHEROS; 35; II 323.1.

3765 ---; s. of Papontos; (1) 55; (2) 56; property owner; Oxyrhynchite; Temgenuthis qtr; age 65 (1); cousin of Thamunis; (1) I 99.3; (2) II 271.10.

3766 ---; sp. Tembius; ch. Papnoutis; i - ii; *P. Harris* 72.18.

3767 ---; sp. Techonsis; ch. Harmiysis; i - ii; *P. Harris* 72.5.

3768 ---; s. of Panetbes, s. of Harmaeis; m. Taorsenuphis; i - ii; age 19; *P. Harris* 72.26.

3769 ---; ch. Heras; 148/149; Oxyrhynchite, gymnasial class; Oxy.; addr. for gs.; XLVI 3280.2.

3770 ---; s. of Heras, s. of Pnepheros; m. Thatres; 148/149; Oxyrhynchite, gymnasial class; Oxy.; reg. unnamed s. in g. class this yr; XLVI 3280.2.

3771 PNEU...[or PNEB..[; ch.]..paeus; ii?; Senocomis, W. Top.; addr. for s.; *P. Fuad I Univ.* 32.6.

3772 PO......; 130; Oxyrhynchite?; Oxy.?; Sarapion adopted s.; III 492.23.

3773 POCCAOUS; s. of Pantauches; sp. Tausoreus; 132/133; Oxyrhynchite; Oxy.; guardian of sp.; *PSI* VIII 874 i 8.

3774 PO]C[O]OUS? or PE]C[O]OUS?; ch. Orsenouphis; Sept 103; Oxyrhynchite?; Oxy.?; addr. for gs. Horion; XLI 2973.6.

POLEṂ[ARCHUS](?); see NILUS.

3775 POLEMON; s. of Tryphon; 13/14; landholder?; applies to buy land in U. Top. (Thosbis and Tepouis) from idios logos; IV 721.2.

3776 PO]LEMON?; 41-54; banker; Oxy.; name may be Telemon; XXXIV 2720.2.

3777 CAECILIA POLLA; sp. Herodes; ch. Sarapion, Hexacon; 103/104; Roman?; leases olive garden, Psobthis, M. Top., to Horus; mentioned in III 506 of 143 (where s.'s addr. is Oxy.); III 639 (descr.).

3778 POLYDAS; ii; tax collector?; XXXVIII 2861.13.

3779 POLYDEUCES; ch. Epimachus; 55; II 261.10.

3780 ---; ch. Castor; after 81; Oxyrhynchite; Oxy.; addr. for gs. Sarapion; II 369.4.

3781 ---; s. of Heracleides, s. of Heracleides; sp. Didyme; 99; Oxyrhynchite; Oxy.; *P. Harris* 74.7.

3782 ---; s. of Dexi[theus?; 132/133 or 153/154; Oxy.; XII 1518.8.

3783 ---; s. of Ammonius; after 138/139; buys grain from Epimachus; *PSI* IV 281 R i 4.

3784 ---; ii; XXXIII 2679.10.

3785 POLYTIMUS; 63; slave; of C. Norbanus Ptolemaeus; XLV V 3250.4.

3786 POMPEIUS; i or ii; doc. pr.?; *P. Princ.* III 188.12, 19.

POMPEIUS; see POMPEIUS DIONYSODORUS, L. POMPEIUS NIGER.

3787 S. POMPEIUS; July 140; slave owner; Roman; *SB* XII 10894.3.

POMPONIUS; see SEPTIMIANUS.

PORCIUS; see M. PORCIUS EPITYNCHANON.

3788 POREPOMIS; ch. Horus; i; Pakerke, M. Top.; doc. pr. Oxy.?; addr. for gs. Horus; *P. Harris* 138 i 21.

3789 PORTIOUS; ch. P_3-ḥbs; early i; *OD Pisa* 234 Convesso 1.

3790 POSIDONIUS; late i; lecturer; res. in Alex.; XVIII 2190.35-36.

3791 ---; ch. Thaesis; 148/149; Oxyrhynchite, gymnasial class; Oxy.; ggs. Amois scrutinised this yr; XLVI 3278.3-4.

3792 POTAMMON; ch. Heraclas; mid ii; XLIV 3165.1-2.

3793 CLAUDIUS POTAMON; c. 47-54; m. Isidora, d. of Apollonius (Dionysius alias ...onius her adoptive father); Roman; ad. gf. is Alex., res. in Gamma distr.; XLVI 3271.2.

3794 POTAMON; early i; *OD Pisa* 435.1.

3795 ---; s. of Seuthes; ch. Potamon; end i; Oxyrhynchite; Oxy.; addr. for s.; *P. Sel.* 23.12.

3796 ---; s. of Potamon, s. of Seuthes; end i; slave owner; Oxyrhynchite; Oxy.; abroad buying slave; *P. Sel.* 23.12.

3797 ---; alias MAXIMUS; s. of Eudaemon, s. of Eudaemon; April 116; Oxyrhynchite; Oxy.; XXXVI 2759.5.

3798 ---; ch. Seuthes; 121; Senepta?, M. Top.; addr. for s.; III 499.14.

3799 ---; ii; *P. Oslo* II 49.1.

3800 ---; ii; landholder; *P. Erl.* 44 iii 30.

3801 POTHUS; 2 BC; reed gatherer/seller?; IV 742.2.

3802 POTHUS(?); s. of Sisois; ii; VI 1034 V.

3803 POUEBIS; 54-68; Peeno, M. Top.; addr. for gs. or s., shepherd; *P. Inst. Fran.* I 2.18.

3804 POUNSIS; 81-96; VI 984 R fin.

3805 PRACTICUS; Oct 111; slave; formerly of Ti. Julius Theon, now of his gs. Ti. Julius Theon, games victor; XLIV 3197.14.

3806 PREMOSIRIS; April 5 BC; *OD Pisa* 936 Convesso 10.

3807 ---; ch. Horus; April 4; *OD Pisa* 511 + 512 ii 3.

3808 PRIMA; c. 1; IV 736.17.

3809 ---; sp. Sarapion; ch. Demetria; Oct 80; Oxyrhynchite; Oxy.; II 248.4.

3810 ---; sp. Ptolemaeus; ch. Didymus; 123; *P. Lips.* 112.5.

3811 C. LONGIUS PRISCUS; 103; recruit, 3rd Ituraean Coh.; Roman; age 22; signalement; VII 1022.13.

3812 PRISCUS; 103; singularis, 3rd Ituraean Coh.; Roman; VII 1022.26.

3813 PRO[.]IUS; ch. Antonia; sp. Procope; ii; *P. Wurz.* 21 R A 1.

3814 PROCOPE; sp. Pro[.]ius; ch. Antonia; ii; Coptos?; addr. for d.; *P. Wurz.* 21 R B 10.

3815 PROCOPIANUS; s. of Philus; 137/138; agent for Theon alias Anthus; Alex.; *PSI* IV 315.2-3.

3816 PROETUS; ch. Achilleus; 21; Sinary, L. Top.; addr. for s.; X 1281.14.

3817 PROMACHUS; s. of Aristion; sp. Tauris; ch. Amyntas, Heniochus, Aristion; Aug 72?; Oxyrhynchite?; Oxy.; addr. for s.; XLI 2972.5.

3818 ---; s. of Aristion, s. of Promachus; m. Hagnes; gs. of Tauris; Aug 72?; property owner; Oxyrhynchite?; Nemerae, M. Top.; owns house and land there; XLI 2972.11.

3819 PROMETHEUS; ch. Dionys<ius>; Sept/Oct 110; III 575 (descr.) V.

3820 PROT[ ]; s. of Sarapas; 129; tax collector; Senao, Little Oasis; dec.; name Protarchus vel sim. *BL* III; *P. Harris* 147.4.

3821 PROTAS; ch. Apia; Oct 80; Oxyrhynchite; Oxy.; addr. for gss. Diogas and Publius; II 249.4.

3822 P]ROTUS; ii; landholder; farmer; Thosbis, U. Top.; *P. Inst. Fran.* III 15.2.

3823 PSAMIS; s. of Psamis; m. Thermuthis; i - ii; age 26; *P. Harris* 72.4.

3824 ---; sp. Thermuthis; ch. Psamis; i - ii; *P. Harris* 72.4.

3825 PSAMMIS; 91 or 107; agoranomus; Oxyrhynchite?; Oxy.; different from 3826 and 3827; IV 722.5.

3826 ---; 91 or 107; agoranomous; Oxyrhynchite?; Oxy.; different from 3825 and 3827; IV 722.5.

3827 ---; 91 or 107; agoranomus; Oxyrhynchite?; Oxy.; different from 3825 and 3826; IV 722.5.

3828 ---; s. of Ballarus; ch. Dionysius alias Amois; June 98; Oxyrhynchite, gymnasial class; Oxy.; reg. in 11; X 1266.7.

3829 ---; s. of Dionysius alias Amois, s. of Psammis; sp. Thermuthion; ch. Plution; June 98; Oxyrhynchite, gymnasial class; Oxy.; married 82; X 1266.40.

3830 PSATRES; 117-138; X 1293.40.

3831 PSAUTIS; 81-96; VI 984 R fin.

3832 PSELLA...; April 4; *OD Pisa* 511 + 512 i 6.

3833 PSEN-[...]; ch. Petechonsis; Aug 3; *OD Pisa* 473 Concavo i 6.

3834 ---; ch. Thoteus; i BC - i; *OD Pisa* 8.8.

3835 PSEN-[ ]; i BC - i; *OD Pisa* 8.22.

3836 ---; i BC - i; *OD Pisa* 72 ii X + 1.

3837 ---; i BC - i; *OD Pisa* 25 ii 11.

3838 PSEN-W_3ḥ-t_3-ḳt(?); ch. Petosiris; i BC - i; *OD Pisa* 87 X + 3.

3839 PSEN-Wḥj; i BC - i; *OD Pisa* 8.18-19.

3840 ---; early i; *OD Pisa* 42.4.

3841 PSEN-bt-w; i BC - i; *OD Pisa* 460 Convesso i X + 10.

3842 PSEN-p_3-jm; Aug 3; *OD Pisa* 473 Convesso 4.

3843 PSEN-p_3-^{c}l(?); i BC - i; *OD Pisa* 510 + 568 Concavo i X + 8.

3844 PSEN-lws; ch. Patesis; i BC - i; *OD Pisa* 25 i 14.

3845 PSEN-sl^{c}r; i BC - i; *OD Pisa* 69 Convesso i 5.

3846 PSEN-slm; i BC - i; *OD Pisa* 510 + 568 Concavo i X + 3.

3847 PSEN-ḳtḳw_3s; i BC - i; *OD Pisa* 25 i 12.

3848 PSEN-gbws; i BC - i; *OD Pisa* 44.4.

3849 PSEN-gḏn; ch. Petosiris; July 7; *OD Pisa* 1131 Concavo 6.

3850 PSEN-t_3-wḥj; ch. Peteesis; late i BC - early i; *OD Pisa* 35 Concavo ii 8.

3851 PSEN-t_3-wḥj(?); i BC - i; *OD Pisa* 460 Convesso ii X + 17.

3852 PSEN-[t_3-wḥ]j; i BC - i; *OD Pisa* 513 + 514 + 515 i X + 3-4.

3853 PSEN-t_3-wḥj; i BC - i; *OD Pisa* 541 Convesso ii 3.

3854 PSENAMUNIS; i BC - i; *OD Pisa* 513 + 514 + 515 i X + 10.

3855 ---; s. of Snn; i BC - i; *OD Pisa* 460 Convesso i X + 12.

3856 ---; s. of Thonis; ch. Psenamunis; Oct 62; Sesphtha?, L. Top.; addr. for s.; XXXVIII 2873.1.

3857 ---; s. of Psenamunis, s. of Thonis; Oct 62; farmer; lessee; Sesphtha, L. Top.; leased part of Seneca's estate (Diotimus' Kleros) from Ti. Claudius Theon; XXXVIII 2873.1.

3858 PSENA]ṂUNIS; m. Taụepha[ ]; gs. of Psenamunis; c. 92; Tacona, L. Top.; descr. as the elder; *P. Michael* 9.6.

3859 PSENAMUNIS; c. 92; Tacona, L. Top.; addr. for gs. Psenamunis; *P. Michael* 9.6.

3860 ---; ch. Taụepha[ ]; c. 92; Tacona?, L. Top.; addr. for mat. gs. Psenamunis; *P. Michael* 9.7.

3861 ---; ch. Serepodo(rus) (sic); i; Sesphtha; addr. for s. (or sp.); both names cancelled; *P. Ryl.* II 199.9.

3862 PSENATYMIS; ch. Totoes; July 7; *OD Pisa* 1131 Concavo 8.

3863 PSENBASTIS; i BC - i; dependant of Jm; *OD Pisa* 502 X + 8.

3864 PSENCALES; ch. Apollonius; i BC - i; *OD Pisa* 228 X + 6.

3865 PSENCHONSIS; s. of Tenis(?); i BC - i; *OD Pisa* 117.3.

3866 ---; i BC - i; *OD Pisa* 1023 Concavo 1.

3867 ---; s. of Psenetouotis; March 120; farmer; lessee on Nicanorian estate; XXIV 2410.29.

3868 PSENCUCEIUS; i BC - i; *OD Pisa* 502 X + 7.

3869 PSENDEMETRIUS; i BC - i; *OD Pisa* 25 i 6.

3870 PSENEBOS; ch. Pamunis; i; *OD Pisa* 129 X + 10.

3871 PSENERIEUS; ch. Patous; i BC - i; *OD Pisa* 29 ii X + 5.

3872 PSENESIS; ch. Harpaesis; i BC - i; Elephantine?; addr. for s.; *OD Pisa* 111 Concavo 8.

3873 ---; ch. Petemunis; i; *OD Pisa* 129 X + 7.

3874 ---; i; farmer; *P. Ryl.* II 199.30.

3875 ---; alias ISION; s. of Ptolemaeus; sp. Taarpaesis alias Isidora; ch. Ptolemaeus, Berenice, Isidora alias Apollonarion; Aug 133; Oxyrhynchite; in will of Taarpaesis; *P. Köln* II 100.14.

3876 PSENETOUOTIS; ch. Psenchonsis; March 120; XXIV 2410.29.

3877 PSENETYMIS; i BC - i; *OD Pisa* 117.2.

3878 PSENINARUS; i BC - i; *OD Pisa* 44.3.

3879 PSEN-KITON; early i; *OD Pisa* 153 X + 3, X + 5.

3880 PSENMAES; ch. Totoes; April 4; *OD Pisa* 511 + 512 i 7.

3881 PSENMEINIS; ch. Psosneus; 80/81; Peeno?, M. Top.; addr. for s.; *Coll. Pap.* II 21.4.

3882 PSEN-MELAS; 8; *OD Pisa* 1.8.

3883 PSENMENCHES; i; *OD Pisa* 129 X + 11.

3884 PSENMONTHES; i BC - i; Panechotes his dependant; *OD Pisa* 1023 Convesso i 4.

3885 PSENMUTHIS; i BC - i; *OD Pisa* 87 X + 11.

3886 ---; ch. Sisois; early i; *OD Pisa* 419.3.

3887 PSENOBASTIS; i BC - i; unnamed bro.; *OD Pisa* 513 + 514 + 515 i X + 16.

3888 PSENOSIRIS; ch. Panemgeus alias .eo...; 2nd half i; Sesphtha?, L. Top.; addr. for s.; XXXVIII 2845.9.

3889 PSEN[OSI]RIS; s. of Cephalas; 2nd half i; practor; Sesphtha, L. Top.; XXXVIII 2845.3.

3890 PSENOSIRIS; s. of Atreus; m. Specis; sp. Penyris; ch. Tastraton; 124; property owner; Oxyrhynchite?; Oxy.?; addr. for d.; prop. in Kriethyris; III 490.2.

3891 ---; sp. Sina[...; 126; Sesphtha?, L. Top.; doc. pr. Oxy.?; addr. for s., a stolistes; *P. Harris* 142.7.

3892 PSENPAAPIS; i BC - i; *OD Pisa* 460 Convesso ii X + 9.

3893 PSENPABIS; ch. Haremphois; Aug 9; *OD Pisa* 429.2.

3894 PSENPACHIRIS; ch. Petamunis; i BC - i; *OD Pisa* 25 i 5.

3895 PSENPALALIS; i BC - i; *OD Pisa* 44.2.

3896 ---; ch. Hermes; i BC - i; *OD Pisa* 561 + 562 + 795 X + 2.

3897 PSENPASENIS; i BC - i; *OD Pisa* 87 X + 1.

3898 PSENPASIS; i BC - i; *OD Pisa* 232.9.

3899 PSENPETECHONSIS; s. of Teous; i BC - i; *OD Pisa* 25 ii 2.

3900 PSENPETESNES; i BC - i; *OD Pisa* 29 ii X + 4.

3901 PSENPETESUCHUS; i; *OD Pisa* 129 X + 5.

3902 PSENPETIMUTHES; ch. Haremphois; i BC - i; *OD Pisa* 460 Convesso i X + 3.

3903 PSENPLENIS; early i; *OD Pisa* 164.3.

3904 PSENPOERIS; i BC; *OD Pisa* 323 X + 7.

3905 PSENPOLEMON; i BC - i; *OD Pisa* 111 Convesso 8.

3906 PSENPSENYRIS; s. of Tcales; i; *OD Pisa* 129 X + 6.

3907 PSENSARAS(?); i BC - i; Harpaesis his agent; *OD Pisa* 779 + 242 Concavo 2.

3908 PSENSNES; i BC - i; bro. Pamun; *OD Pisa* 25 i 2.

3909 PSENTAES; ch. Petechonsis; i BC; *OD Pisa* 55 ii 6.

3910 ---; i BC - i; *OD Pisa* 779 + 242 Convesso X + 6.

3911 ---; ch. Totoes; i BC - i; *OD Pisa* 816 X + 1.

3912 ---; i BC - i; *OD Pisa* 5 i X + 19.

3913 ---; ch. Phatres; I BC - i; *OD Pisa* 510 + 568 Convesso i 4.

3914 ---; i BC - i; *OD Pisa* 196 ii X + 6.

3915 ---; ch. Ir.t(?); i BC - i; *OD Pisa* 360 Convesso 1.

3916 PSENTHOTES; i BC - i; man of Ghwj; *OD Pisa* 8.1.

3917 PSENTHOTES; i BC - i; *OD Pisa* 106.7.

3918 ---; s. of Petechonsis; i BC - i; *OD Pisa* 470.4.

3919 ---; ch. Tenis?; i BC - i; *OD Pisa* 532 X + 7.

3920 ---; s. of Haremphois; i; *OD Pisa* 60 Convesso i 13.

3921 ---; ch. Paeris; i; *OD Pisa* 60 Convesso i 12.

3922 PSENTOTOES; early i; dependant of T_3-ḳt(?); *OD Pisa* 424.3.

3923 PSENTOUS; 81-96; VI 984 R fin.

3924 PSENTRES; s. of Gales; i BC - i; *OD Pisa* 1023 Convesso i 7.

3925 PSENYRIS; i BC - i; *OD Pisa* 510 + 568 Concavo ii 2.

3926 ---; s. of Patous; i BC - i; *OD Pisa* 69 Concavo 1.

3927 ---; s. of Somtous; i BC - i; *OD Pisa* 25 i 13.

3928 ---; s. of Tcales; i BC - i; *OD Pisa* 106.3.

3929 PSIRAITHES; 81-96; VI 984 R fin.

3930 PSOIS; s. of Allous; m. Tachois, d. of Dinchon; 31/32; Oxy.?; guardian for m.; signalement; *P. Ryl.* II 159.4.

3931 ---; 81-96; VI 984 R fin (list of names).

3932 ---; ii?; potter; in debt to Anthestianus; XLI 2996.1.

3933 PSOSNEUS; s. of Psenmeinis; 80/81; presbyteros; Peeno, M. Top.; *Coll. Pap.* II 21.3-4.

3934 PSUBIUS (PSOUBIOS); ch. Nicaea Sil[va]nus; c. 85; Oxyrhynchite; Jewish qtr; Jewish; II 335 (descr.).

3935 PTOL[-]; ch. Plutas; ii?; ch. has property in Psobthis; *P. Inst. Fran.* III 15.19.

3936 PTOLEM[; sp. Sinthonis; ch. Tereus; 81/82; Oxyrhynchite; *P. Mert.* III 118.11.

3937 PTOLEMA; d. of Hermippus; sp. Dionysius alias Didymus; ch. Dionysius; 66; II 272.23.

3938 ---; d. of Asinis; March 79; property owner; Oxy.?; owns land in Hermaeum qtr; II 243.19.

3939 ---; d. of Ischyrion; sp. Apollonius; ch. Zoilus; 90; Senepta, M. Top.; addr. for s.; I 72.4.

3940 ---; d. of Philiscus, s. of Philiscus; sp. Diogenes; 94/95; Oxyrhynchite; Heracles Place qtr; s. married to Isidora; in census 61/62; II 257.2.

3941 ---; i; II 298.34.

3942 PTOLEMA; sp. Pecysis; ch. Ammonous, Antas (s. of another man); 117-137; freedwoman; Oxyrhynchite?; Cretan qtr; freedwoman of Demetrius, s. of Hermippus; I 105.3.

3943 CLAUDIA PTOLEMA; 134/135; landowner; leases to Dioscorus royal land in Kleros of Xenon nr Sinary; IV 810 (descr.).

3944 PTOLEMA; c. 135; property owner; dec.; allegedly murdered by Sarapion; XVII 2111 i 23.

3945 ---; d. of Straton; m. Dionysia; April 135; Oxyrhynchite; Oxy.; illiterate; I 106.7.

3946 ---; d. of Apollonius, s. of Besas alias Ammonius; m. Taamois; sp. Plution; ii; Oxy.; C. Theon is guardian; *P. Mil.* II 51.2.

3947 ---; ii; doc. pr. Oxy.?; *SB* VI 9025.29-30.

3948 ---; d. of Diogenes; ii?; landholder; land at Terythis reg. in her name; *PSI* XIV 1414.31.

3949 PTOLEMAEUS; ch. Arsinoe; 63/62 BC; Cleopatra Aphrodite St?; addr. for d.; XIV 1644.13.

3950 ---; s. of Dionysius; m. Arsinoe, d. of Ptolemaeus; 63/62 BC; Macedonian of catoecic cavalry; Cleopatra Aphrodite St; XIV 1644.4.

3951 ---; ch. Spartacus; 44-37 BC; Cleopatra Aphrodite St?; addr. for s.; XIV 1635.3.

3952 ---; ch. Heliodorus; 30/29 BC; Oxy.; addr. for s.; XII 1453.12.

3953 ---; ch. Ptolemaeus, Ptolemaeus; 22 BC; VII 1061.5.

3954 ---; s. of Ptolemaeus; 22 BC; descr. as the younger; VII 1061.5.

3955 ---; s. of Ptolemaeus; 22 BC; elder bro. of P. the younger; VII 1061.14.

3956 ---; ch. Dionysius alias Amois, Apollonius; 22 BC; VII 1061 V.

3957 ---; 4/3 BC; tax farmer; Oxy.; farms 6 dr tax on asses w. Ariston at Oxy.; XII 1457.1.

3958 ---; late i BC; strategus; IV 803 (descr.).

3959 ---; i BC - i; descr. as major; *OD Pisa* 8.4.

3960 ---; i BC - i; *OD Pisa* 232.1, 8.

3961 ---; ch. Harchypsis; (1) i BC - i; (2) early i; (1) *OD Pisa* 510 + 568 Convesso i 11; (2) 424.16.

3962 ---; late i BC - early i; *OD Pisa* 35 Concavo i 5.

3963 ---; s. of Deph..sio(n); 17-19; slave owner; his freedman Thoonius a weaver; II 309.3.

3964 PTOLEMAEUS; 17-19; banker w. partner; II 309 iii 3, iv 2.

3965 ---; Sept/Oct 22; hyperetes; II 398 (descr.).

3966 ---; ch. Ammonius; 26; Isieum Tryphonos?, L. Top.; addr. for s.; VIII 1124.12.

3967 ---; ch. Theon; Jan 29; Pela?, W. Top.; addr. for s.; XXXVIII 2850.2-3.

3968 ---; ch. Didymus; 31/32; Oxy.; addr. for s.; *P. Ryl.* II 159.41.

3969 ---; 37; banker w. Dorion; II 312.2.

3970 ---; ch. Sarapion; 41; II 366 (descr.).

3971 ---; ch. Dionysius; 41/42; *PSI* XII 1235.13.

3972 ---; ch. Apollonius; 41-79; XLII 3061.19.

3973 ---; sp. Sarapias; ch. Ptollion; 48; *P. Fouad* 35.3.

3974 ---; ch. Plutas; 52/53; *PSI* IX 1029.3.

3975 ---; (1) July 60; (2) 62; (3) Mar/Apr 66; (4) July 66; basilicogrammateus, w. Ti. Claudius Asclepiades in 2; Oxy.; doc. 2 prov. Oxy.?; (1) XXXVIII 2851.2; (2) *SB* XII 10788.24; (3) *PSI* VIII 871.1; (4) II 246.3.

3976 ---; 62; tax registrar; doc. prov. Oxy.?; *SB* XII 10788.26.

3977 C. NORBANUS PTOLEMAEUS; 62; slave owner; slave Polytimus; XLV v 3250.4.

3978 P]TOLE[MAEUS; ch. Pausiris; Sept 66; Psobthis, L. Top.; addr. for gs. Epimachus; II 239.2.

3979 PTOLEMAEUS; ch. Pausirion; Sept 66; Oxyrhynchite; Oxy.; addr. for gs. Ptolemaeus; II 275.4.

3980 ---; s. of Pausirion, s. of Ptolemaeus; m. Ophelous, d. of Theon; Sept 66; weaver; Oxyrhynchite; Oxy.; illiterate; II 275.3.

3981 ---; ch. Leonides; 66-72/73; landholder; lessee?; Alex., Althaieus; dec.; land at Senepta in Kleros in Damon; IX 1203 + *SB* IV 7339.5.

3982 ---; s. of Sarapion; April 70; property owner; minor; *P. Oxy. inv.* 50.4B.24B(3-4)33.

3983 ---; ch. C. Julius Satornilus; 70; Alex., Phylaxithalassius, Althaieus; Oxy.?; addr. for s. (formerly Ptolemaeus) who owns land in Oxy.; XXII 2349.5.

3984 ---; alias C. JULIUS SATORNILUS; s. of Ptolemaeus; 70; Oxy.; owns land there; XXII 2349.5.

3985 ---; July 72; associate of sitologus; Seryphis, W. Top.; XLIV 3163.15.

3986 PTOLEMAEUS; s. of Ptolemaeus; sp. Senamunis; ch. Hagnes; Oct 72?; Nemerae, M. Top.; XLI 2972.7.

3987 ---; ch. Ptolemaeus; Oct 72?; Nemerae?, M. Top.; addr. for gd. Hagnes; XLI 2972.8.

3988 ---; Dec 75/Jan 76; Oxyrhynchite?; Oxy.?; addr. for gd. Thaesis; *P. Yale* 64.4.

3989 ---; ch. Thaisas; 78/79; Oxyrhynchite?; Oxy.?; addr. for gd. [..].[..]as; XXXVI 2756.5.

3990 ---; s. of Heracleus; m. Senphois the elder; ch. Heracles; 81-96; s. gymnasial class; VI 984 R init.

3991 ---; ch. Heracles, Ptollas; Nov 82; Oxyrhynchite?; Oxy.?; addr. for ss.; XXXVI 2773.2.

3992 M. ANTONIUS PTOLEMAEUS; s. of Sergius Ptolemaeus; 83; slave owner; Roman; Oxy.; I 94.3.

3993 SERGIUS PTOLEMAEUS; ch. M. Antonius Ptolemaeus; 83; Roman; Oxy.?; addr. for s.; I 94.3-4.

3994 PTOLEMAEUS; ch. Heracleides; 92; Oxyrhynchite?; Oxy.?; addr. for gs. Heracleides; XVIII 2185.7-8.

3995 ---; s. of Araeus; 92; farmer?; landholder?; lessee?; land at Peroth( )?; XVIII 2185.20.

3996 ---; ch. Ammonius; 94/95; Oxyrhynchite; Heracles Place qtr; II 257.36.

3997 ---; s. of Ammonius, s. of Ptolemaeus; ch. Isidora; 94/95; Oxyrhynchite; Heracles Place qtr; selected in 60/61; II 257.7-8.

3998 ---; ch. Diogenes; 95; land ceded to s. at Korobis in Kleros of Menoethius; I 45.3.

3999 ---; s. of Colylis; ch. Tapotamon; 95; d. has land at Korobis in Kleros of Menoethius; I 45.5.

4000 ---; May 96; unnamed s. hyperetes of Peisis; *PSI Bartoletti Colombo* 1.6.

4001 ---; 98-102; exegetes; priest; *P. Mert.* I 13.1.

4002 ---; s. of Onnophris; 98-117; Isieum Panga; lessee of land nr Nesla from Apollonous; *PSI* VIII 772.3.

4003 ---; s. of Asclepiades; 2nd half i; bro. Asclepiades; *P. Oslo* III 130.5.

4004 ---; ch. Sarapion; end i; Oxyrhynchite; Oxy.; addr. for gs. - alias Eusebes; *P. Sel.* 23.16.

4005 ---; alias GERMANUS; s. of Sarapion, s. of Ptolemaeus; m. Dionysia; end i; slave owner; Oxyrhynchite?; Oxy.?; addr. for bro. - alias Eusebes; *P. Sel.* 23.18.

4006 PTOL(EMAEUS); s. of Cepha(las); i Sesphtha; *P. Ryl.* II 199.12.

4007 PTOLEMAEUS; i; hyperetes; h. of Julius Asclepinus, str.; *PSI Bartoletti Colombo* 2.5.

4008 ---; i?; assoc. w. Diogenes; *P. Harris* 102.8.

4009 ---; i?; unnamed sp.; "brother" of Besius; *P. Harris* 102.1.

4010 ---; i - ii; *PSI* VII 814.18.

4011 ---; i - ii; Canopus; descr. as Canopite; III 599 (descr.).

4012 ---; ch. Zoilus; Jan 100; Nemerae?, M. Top.; addr. for s.; XLI 2960.10.

4013 ---; ch. Harendotes; 102; 10th qtr; addr. for s.; XII 1520.4.

4014 ---; Aug 106; *P. Wisc.* I 17 V 11.

4015 ---; Aug 106; *P. Wisc.* I 17 V 12.

4016 ---; s. of Petosorapis, s. of Petosorapis; 107; hieroglyph carver; Oxyrhynchite; Thoeris St qtr; only 5 h. carvers in Oxy.; VII 1029.18.

4017 ---; 107-116; *P. Stras.* 244.14.

4018 ---; s. of Ptolemaeus; ch. Ptolemaeus; 109; Oxyrhynchite?; Oxy.?; addr. for gs. Diogenes; III 482.23-24.

4019 ---; s. of Ptolemaeus; sp. Tecosis; ch. Diogenes; 109; Oxyrhynchite?; Oxy.?; addr. for s.; III 482.22-23.

4020 ---; ch. Areius, Sarapion; May 109; may not be Oxy.; XLII 3015.7.

4021 ---; ch. Diogenis; 117; Oxyrhynchite; Oxy.; III 489.5.

4022 ---; ch. Heracleides; 117; Oxyrhynchite?; Oxy.?; addr. for gs. Ammonis; III 489.25.

4023 ---; 119/120; bibliophylax w. Didymus; *PSI* XIII 1322.1.

4024 ---; ch. Isarous; 119/120; Oxyrhynchite; *PSI* XIII 1322.8.

4025 ---; s. of Sarapion, s. of Plutarchus; m. Isarous, d. of Ptolemaeus; 119/120; property owner; Oxyrhynchite; land from bro. Sarapion; *PSI* XIII 1322.21.

4026 ---; s. of Sarapion; c. 122/123; Phoboou distr., E. Top.; XXXVIII 2865.6.

4027 ---; ch. Ptolemaeus; 123; *P. Lips.* 112.4.

4028 ---; s. of Ptolemaeus; sp. Prima; ch. Didymus; 123; *P. Lips.* 112.4.

4029 ---; s. of Ammonius, s. of Pcaes?; ch. Diodorus; 127/128; Oxyrhynchite, gymnasial class; Gymnasium St qtr; in graphe of 4/5; addr. for gs. Plution; XII 1452 ii 53.

---; see THEON.

4030 PTOLEMAEUS; ch. Psenesis alias Ision; gs. Ptolemaeus; Aug 133; *P. Köln* II 100.13.

4031 ---; s. of Psenesis alias Ision, s. of Ptolemaeus; m. Taarpaesis alias Isidora; Aug 133; Oxy.; m. bequeathes property and land in South St qtr and Phoboou distr.; *P. Köln* II 100.[5], 6.

4032 ---; TI. CLAUDIUS PTOLEMAEUS; s. of Ti. Claudius Alexandrus; m. Claudia Theanous; May 134; Roman; Oxy.; parents freedmen; XXXVIII 2857.10.

4033 ---; ch. Apollonius; April 135; Oxy.; addr. for s.; I 106.3.

4034 ---; ch. Diophantus; c. 135; may not be an Oxy.; XVII 2111 i 20.

4035 ---; s. of Zoilus; Sept/Oct 137; writes for Ammoni(u)s, s. of Apollonides, and Ptollas, s. of Lucius; Ptolemais in text; IV 729.37.

4036 ---; 137; basilicogrammateus, w. Apolinarius, str.; *PSI* XII 1262 ii 9-10; iii 11.

4037 ---; July 140; unnamed s., banker; *SB* XII 10894.4.

4038 PT]OLEMAEUS; s. of P[-]; ch. Di[c. 10]; 148/149; Oxyrhynchite; gymnasial class; Upper Camp qtr?; addr. for s.; XLVI 3277.2.

4039 PTOLEMAEUS; ch. Thaesis; 148/149; Oxyrhynchite, gymnasial class; Upper Camp qtr; addr. for d.'s sp. Terentius; XLVI 3278.9.

4040 ---; early ii; exegetes; priest; Oxyrhynchite; Oxy.; succeeds Sarapion in both posts; X 1269.1.

4041 ---; early ii; "brother" of Horeis; XLII 3060.1.

4042 ---; ch. Antonius; ii; (1) III 523.1; (2) XVIII 2191 V.

4043 ---; sp. Cleopatra; ch. Glaucias, Sarapion; ii; Gymnasium St qtr; addr. for s.; *P. Princ.* II 46.4.

4044 ---; ch. Ammonius; ii; Oxy.; addr. for gd. Dionysia; *P. Mil.* II 39.1.

4045 ---; ii; archephodus; XLII 3058.10.

4046 ---; ii; Oxy.; messenger for Apia; XII 1581.9, 10.

4047 PTOLEMAIS; 103-117; pays via Taampemou, E. Top.; III 612 (descr.).

---; see DIONYSIA.

4048 PTOLLARION; early ii; property owner; Thoeris St qtr; *Coll. Pap.* I 50.9.

4049 PTOLLAROUS; d. of Chaeremon; sp. Sosibius; ch. Stephanus; Aug 102; Oxyrhynchite?; Oxy.?; addr. for s.; III 508.6.

4050 PTOLLAROUS; alias -; ii?; Pela, W. Top.; *P. Fuad I Univ.* 32.14.

4051 PT]OLLAS; late i BC; Alexandria; w. writer there; XII 1479.11.

4052 PTOLLAS; s. of Nicostratus; Sept 77; pilot of cargo boat; Oxy.; II 276.5, 6.

4053 ---; s. of Ptolemaeus; Nov 82; weaver?; Oxyrhynchite; Oxy.; Persian of Epigone; bro. of Heracles; XXXVI 2773.1.

4054 ---; 130; farmer; lessee; l. of Heracleides, s. of Antias; III 517.8-9.

4055 ---; s. of Lucius; Sept/Oct 137; farmer; sub-lessee of vineyard w. Ammoni(u)s; illiterate; IV 729.35.

4056 PTOLLEROS; ch. Dionytas; early ii; Oxyrhynchite?; Oxy.?; addr. for gs. Ptolleros; *P. Wisc.* I 13.19.

4057 ---; s. of Dionytas, s. of Ptolleros; early ii; Oxyrhynchite; Oxy.; signalement; *P. Wisc.* I 13.19.

4058 PTOLLION; ch. Theon; after 45-47; XLII 3033 V 3.

4059 ---; s. of Theon, s. of Ptollion; after 45-47; Shepherds' qtr?; under age; XLII 3033 V 4.

4060 ---; s. of Ptolemaeus; m. Sarapias; sp. Thaesis; ch. Sarapion (dec.); 48; *P. Fouad* 35.3.

4061 ---; s. of [Di]us(?); sp. Thermous; ch. Dius; 89-91; Oxy.; addr. for s.; II 274.9.

4062 ---; ch. Apollonius; 90; Senepta, M. Top.; Oxy.; addr. for gs. Zoilus; I 72.3.

4063 ---; s. of Diallus (form of name?); 99; VI 975.16.

4064 ---; c. 99-117; Oxy.; XLVI 3274 i 24.

4065 ---; ch. Theon; 130; Oxyrhynchite; Oxy.; addr. for gs. Ptollion; III 492.5.

4066 ---; s. of Theon, s. of Ptollion; m. Isareus, d. of Theon; 130; Oxyrhynchite; Oxy.; III 492.5.

4067 PTOLLI[ON]; ch. Eubion; 148/149; Oxyrhynchite, gymnasial class; Gymnasium St qtr; s. listed in 4/5; addr. for ggs. Apollonius; XLVI 3276.15-16.

4068 PTOLLION; ch. Nechthenicis; early ii; Phthochis, E. Top.; unnamed children; addr. for gd. Taptollion; *P. Wisc.* I 13.2.

4069 PTOLLIS; ch. Harmiysis; June 29; *SB* VIII 9827 (a) 2.

4070 ---; s. of Orthonoos; ch. Dionysius; (1) Oct 62; (2) 2nd half i; Sesphtha, L. Top.; addr. for s.; (1) XXXVIII 2873.2; (2) 2845.11.

4071 ---; ch. Horus; i; farmer; Koba; addr. for s.; VIII 1145.10.

4072 PTOLLIS; ch. Amois; after 102; Oxy.?; addr. for gs. Ptollis; III 636.2.

4073 ---; s. of Amois, s. of Ptollis; m. Plutarche; sp. Demetrous; 102; property owner; Oxy.; inherits prop. in Temgenuthis qtr from sp.; III 636.2.

4074 ---; s. of Phaon; sp. Athena; ch. Phaon; Jan 132; Oxyrhynchite; Thoeris St qtr; addr. for s.; III 478.14, 20.

4075 ---; s. of Phaon, s. of Ptollis; m. Dionysous (freedwoman); gs. of Athena; Jan 132; Oxyrhynchite?; Thoeris St qtr; 13, applies for selection; III 478.13.

4076 PTOLLOUS; d. of Amois, d. of Amois; m. Theudous; sp. Heliodorus; ch. Cleopatra; 132/133; age 60; 2nd unnamed ch. is 15; *PSI* I 53 i 5.

4077 PUBLIUS; s. of Teos, s. of Centaurus; m. Apia, d. of Protas; Oct 80; property owner; Oxyrhynchite; Pammenes' Garden qtr; house there; died 78; II 249.11.

4078 ---; s. of Publius; ii; xylometres?; XLI 2981.1, back.

4079 ---; ch. Publius; ii; XLI 2981.29.

---; see PUBLIUS PETRONIUS CELER.

4080 PUORIS; s. of Agron; m. Tamonnes; i - ii; age 20; *P. Harris* 72.15.

4081 ---; s. of Hermias; m. Tapontos; sp. Tnepheros; ch. Hermias; i - ii; age 51; *P. Harris* 72.16.

4082 ---; s. of Hermias; m. Tapontos; i - ii; age 35; descr. as the younger; *P. Harris* 72.16.

4083 PYLADES; s. of Heracleus; m. Tamochus; i - ii; age 28; *P. Harris* 72.21.

4084 PYRRHUS; c. 81; superintendent of land registers throughout Egypt; I 47.3.

4085 [PYRRH]US(?); sp. Apollonius; ch. Pet[euri]s?; 148/149; Oxyrhynchite, gymnasial class; Gymnasium St qtr; sp. scrutinised in 72/73; XLVI 3276.3.

4086 PYTHOCLIDES; i; advocate?; *P. Ryl.* II 270 (descr.).

QUINTUS; see Q. GAIUS PASSER; Q. FABIUS FABULLUS.

4087 ---; ch. Tiouda; 93/94; *PSI* X 1109.15.

4088 RHYNCHIS; s. of Magrus, s. of Hermolaus; m. Taonnophris; ii; hamlet of Sarapion, s. of Chaeremon; *P. Erl.* 59 R 2.

4089 RUFION; ch. Didyme; Aug 102; Oxy.?; addr. for gss. Rufus and Diocles; III 508.16-17.

4090 RUFUS; s. of Diocles, s. of Diocles; m. Didyme, d. of Rufion; Aug 102; property owner; Oxy.?; III 508.15.

4091 C. RUSTIUS; i; Roman; IV 745 V.

4092 Ṣ.[..].; s. of Heraclas; March 66; guardian of sister, Ṭaseus; XLI 2971.3.

4093 S[; sp. Saraeus; ch. Apollonous; 81/82; Oxyrhynchite?; Oxy.; addr. for d.; *P. Mert.* III 118.4.

4094 S- ; s. of S]ạrapion; may not be Oxy.; *P. Oslo* III 84.9.

4095 SA[ ]; late i - early ii; priest (?) of Thoeris, Isis, Sarapis and assoc. gods; *P. XV Congr.* 16.8.

4096 SA[..]EILLA; 22; II 294.7.

4097 SABINUS; late i BC; Alexandria; XII 1479.8.

4098 ---; ch. Petemunis; i BC - i; (1) *OD Pisa* 69 Concavo 4; (2) 137 Concavo 6.

4099 ---; 132/133; *PSI* I 53 ii 49.

4100 SAETAS; ii; III 532.4.

4101 SALVIUS; i; wool seller; XLII 3057.23.

4102 ---; ch. Petechon; i; XIV 1756.6.

4103 SAMBATHAEUS; ch. Sarapion; 8; *DO Colon. inv.* 78.2.

4104 ---; s. of Sambathaeus; 27/28; livestock owner; Pela, W. Top.; II 353.2.

4105 ---; ch. Sambathaeus, B....; 27/28; Pela?, W. Top.; addr. for s.; II 353.3.

4106 ---; ch. Harthotes; 31/32; Sinary?. L. Top.; addr. for s.; *P. Mich. inv.* 69.8.

4107 SAMBIUS; sp. Ammon; ch. Harphaesis; i - ii; *P. Harris* 72.14.

4108 SAMBOUS; d. of Dionysius; 83/84; landholder; Tychis Necotis; II 290.17.

4109 ---; d. of Amois, s. of Demetrius; m. Arsinoe; 104/105; property owner; Oxyrhynchite; Oxy.; XXXVIII 2852.2.

---; see DIONYSIA.

4110 SAMOUS; i BC - i; *OD Pisa* 25 ii 17.

4111 SAMPATYM[IS?]; d. of]onides; sp. Sarapion; ch. Sarapion; 68; XIV 1641.23.

4112 SAPRION; ch. Harpocration, Phileas; ii; XLIV 3199.16.

4113 SARAEUS; d. of Apion; sp. Tryphon; ch. Apion, Thoonis; (1) 36; (2) 36-50; (3) 37; (4) 49; (5) 49/50; (6) 59; (7) Sept 66; Oxyrhynchite; marries (1); Onnophris, s. of Antipater is guardian (1); has d. (2); s. apprentice weaver (7); (1) II 267.1; (2) 321.2; (3) 315.12; (4) I 37.4; (5) 38.4; (6) II 320.7; (7) 275.8.

4114 SARAEUS; d. of Nechthenibis; sp. S[ ]; ch. Apollonous; 81/82; Oxyrhynchite; Oxy.?; addr. for d.; *P. Mert.* III 118.5.

4115 ---; d. of Heracleides, s. of Diogenes alias Heracleides; gd. of Tausiris alias Thallous; ch. Dionysia, Herais; 89-97; Oxy.; addr. for d.; II 274.13.

4116 ---; d. of Leonides, s. of Alexandrus; m. Isidora, d. of Calas; sp. Diodorus; ch. Leonides, Diodorus, Thais; March 97; landholder; Oxyrhynchite; Oxy.; land at Nesla and Peeno; IV 713.8.

4117 SARAP( ); s. of ...erius; 2nd half i; practor; Sesphtha, L. Top.; XXXVIII 2845.4.

4118 SARAPAMMON; ii; III 611 (descr.).

4119 ---; ii; workshop owner?; Iseum; "brother" of Thaesis; XII 1488.1 V.

4120 ---; ii?; agent of Anthestianus; XLI 2996.4-5.

4121 SARAPAS; 31/32; Sinary, L. Top.; *P. Mich. inv.* 69.21.

4122 ---; m. Sarapous; gs. of Ammonius; 91 or 107; slave owner; Oxyrhynchite; Oxy.; bro. of Achilleus; signalement; IV 722.8.

4123 ---; Aug 106; *P. Wisc.* I 17 V 18.

4124 ---; Oct 111; slave; notary; s., formerly of Ti. Julius Theon, now of his gs., Ti. Julius Theon, games victor; XLIV 3197.13.

4125 ---; Oct 111; slave; of Ti. Julius Theon, games victor; XLIV 3197.16.

4126 ---; ch. Prot[ ]; 129; tax farmer (dyers' tax); Senao, Little Oasis; other unnamed children; *P. Harris* 147.4.

4127 ---; ch. Heracles; early ii; III 649 (descr.).

4128 ---; s. of Heracles, s. of Sarapas; early ii; bro. of Petosarapis; III 649 (descr.).

4129 ---; s. of Isas, s. of Isidorus; gs. of Soeris or Soerous; early ii; property owner; Oxyrhynchite?; Oxy.; bro. of Sarapous; minor; addr. for uncle Theonas alias Theon; X 1269.7.

4130 ---; early ii; XLII 3060.2.

4131 ---; s. of Pasion, s. of Sarapion; m. Berenice; early ii; Oxyrhynchite; Oxy.; bro. of Apollonius, Diogenes and another; III 493.6.

4132 ---; s. of Sarapion; ii; farmer; livestock owner?; XXXVI 2781.1.

4133 ---; ii; slave; of Apollonius, s. of Claudius Deme[trius; Thoeris St qtr; III 574 descr.) R.

4134 SARAPAS; s. of D[; ii; Tacona, L. Top.; *P. Inst. Fran.* I 4.2.

4135 ---; ii; XLII 3058.19.

4136 ---; s. of Athenaeus, s. of Sarapion; ii; fisherman; rents rights on canal of Themothis and doors of sluice at Phoboou; XLVI 3268.5.

4137 ---; sp. Apollonous; ch. Ophelas alias Besas; ii; Oxyrhynchite; Oxy.; addr. for s.; III 505.1.

4138 ---; ch. Horus; ii; Antipera; addr. for s.; *P. Erl.* 44 ii 5.

4139 ---; ii; XLVI 3313.12.

4140 ---; ii after 137; connected w. Horion and Horeis; XIV 1757.15.

4141 SARAPỊ( ); ch. Diogenis; 92; Oxyrhynchite?; Oxy.?; addr. for gṣ. Heracleides; XVIII 2185.8-9.

4142 SARAPIACUS; ii; overseer; XIV 1673.1.

4143 ---; ii; XXXI 2559.5.

4144 SARAPIADES; after 102; bibliophylax w. Sarapion; Oxy.; III 636.1.

4145 SARAPIANUS; i BC - i; dependant of Haremphois; *OD Pisa* 228 X + 8.

4146 SARAPIAS; sp. Ptolemaeus; ch. Ptollion; 48; *P. Fouad* 35.3.

---; see GAIA.

4147 ---; d. of Diogenes; sp. Theon; ch. Diogenes; end i; s. is Alex.; *P. Sel.* 23.14.

4148 ---; Aug 106; *P. Wisc.* I 17 V 15.

4149 ---; July 140; slave; Oxy.; born in Alex., sold by Cas[... to Sextus Pompeius [-; *SB* XII 10894.7.

4150 ---; ii; w. Apollonius writes to Dionysia; XLVI 3313.1.

4151 SARAPION; s. of Te( ); Nov 42 BC; Oxyrhynchite; witness; *P. Ryl.* IV 582.22.

4152 ---; Nov 42 BC; syngraphophylax; Oxy.; *P. Ryl.* IV 582.23.

4153 ---; ch. Phanias; Nov 21 BC; Tacona, L. Top.; addr. for s.; *P. Vindob. Worp.* 2.2.

4154 ---; 21/20 BC; made payments to priests of Thoeris, goldsmith Cephalas and stonecutters; IV 806 (descr.).

4155 ---; ch. Theon; 5/4 BC; W. Top.; *P. Oslo* II 26.22.

4156 ---; i BC; threshing floor guard; Isieum Pekysios; XII 1465.7.

4157 SARAPION; i BC; strategus; Oxy.; *P. Ryl.* IV 579.1.

4158 ---; i BC - i; *OD Pisa* 108 X + 4.

4159 ---; Aug 3; *OD Pisa* 473 Concavo ii 1.

4160 ---; 8; *OD Pisa* 1.12.

4161 ---; s. of Sambathaeus; ch. Thn^{c}r$_{3}$(?); 8; *DO Colon. inv.* 78.1.

4162 ---; 13; topogrammateus of M. Top.; (1) IX 1188.2, 7; (2) XX 2277.[5].

4163 ---; ch. Didymus; 18; *PSI* IV 320.4.

4164 ---; ch. M[ ](?); (1) 19; (2) 19/20; Oxy.?; addr. for s.; (1) II 253.5; (2) 252.[7].

4165 ---; ch. Dius; 20; II 305.27.

4166 ---; sp. Syra; 20-50; dated by association w. Heracleides, l. 1; II 281.6.

4167 ---; (1) 21; (2) Jan 26; (3) Jan 27; (4) Jan 29; toparch; W. Top.?; (1) *P. Princ.* II 24.23; (2) II 245.23; (3) 351.19; (4) XXXVIII 2850.24.

4168 ---; s. of Dorion; 22; property owner; "brother" of Dorion; in Alex. for court case; II 294.2.

4169 ---; ch. Sarapion; May 23; II 259.10.

4170 ---; s. of Sarapion; May 23; arrested, bailed by Theon; II 259.10.

---; see TEOS.

4171 ---; ch. Pamphilus; 35; see also S., father of Pl[utarchus]; II 323.11.

4172 ---; 36-50; s. or gs. guardian of Saraeus; II 321.3.

4173 ---; s. of Cleandrus; 36; banker; Sarapeum; II 267.4.

4174 [SARAPI]ON; ch. Pl[utarchus]; 37; Oxy.?; addr. for s.; II 319.5.

4175 SARAPION; s. of Ptolemaeus; 41; cedes catoecic land; II 366 (descr.).

4176 ---; 41-79; writes to "brother" of Archelaus, s. of Heraclas; XLII 3062.1.

4177 ---; s. of Dionysius, s. of Hippodamus; 41/42; *PSI* XII 1235.13.

4178 ---; alias DIDYMUS; s. of Heracleides; 43/44; property owner; leases land from royal farmlands nr Pela, W. Top., to -on; II 368.1.

4179 SARAPION; ch. Sarapion; Jan 44; Oxyrhynchite?; Oxy.?; addr. for s.; II 251.6.

4180 ---; s. of Sarapion; Jan 44; Oxyrhynchite?; Oxy.?; guardian of Thamunion, d. of Onnophris; II 251.6.

4181 ---; 45; Oxy.; goes to Alex.; II 283.2.

4182 ---; sp. Thaesis; ch. Petsiris; 48; *P. Fouad* 35.3.

4183 ---; s. of Ptollion, s. of Ptolemaeus; m. Thaesis, d. of Heracleius; gs. of Sarapias; ch. Tathoonas (under age); 48; dec.; m. trustee; *P. Fouad* 35.6.

4184 ---; April 48/Jan 49; Oxy.; X 1321 (descr.).

4185 ---; s. of Chaeremon; July 50; landholder; lessor; Tholthis, Thmois. Top.; Kleros of Pyrrhias; XXXVIII 2836.2.

4186 ---; s. of Theon; c. 50; weaver; Oxyrhynchite; Gymnasium St qtr; II 285.2.

4187 ---; ch. Ammonius, Petusius, Hermodotus, Apollonia; June 52; Oxy.?; addr. for s.; *SB* V 8034.4.

4188 ---; s. of Lochus; (1) 54; (2) early ii; banker; Oxyrhynchite; Sarapeum; addr. for gs. Lochus; (1) II 264.7; (2) III 493.13.

4189 ---; 55; banker w. partners; Oxy.; I 99.14.

4190 ---; ch. Diogenes; Aug 57; Oxy.; X 1316 (descr.).

4191 ---; s. of Dorcon; 59; *P. Fouad* 28.8, 18-19, 29.

4192 ---; ch. Ammonius; 60/61; Oxyrhynchite?; Oxy.?; addr. for gs.; II 250.12.

4193 ---; ch. Sarapion; Feb 61; Oxy.; addr. for s.; II 262.2.

4194 ---; s. of Sarapion; Feb 61; slave owner; weaver?; Oxy.; slave reg. in Temgenuthis qtr; II 262.2.

4195 ---; July 64; banker; Oxy.; acts via Ammonius; *P. Yale* 63.8.

4196 ---; July 64; banker; Oxy.; acts via Ammonius; descr. as the other Sarapion; *P. Yale* 63.8.

4197 ---; (1) July 64; (2) 64; bibliophylax, w. Theon; Oxy.; (1) *P. Mich.* III 179.2, 18; (2) *SB* XII 10788.46.

4198 ---; s. of Achilleus, s. of Achilleus; m. Thaisous, d. of Demetrius; Mar/Apr 66; writes for Petosiris; *PSI* VIII 871.29.

4199 ---; ch. Didymus; gs. Sarapion; 66; II 272.26.

4200 ---; s. of Didymus, s. of Sarapion; m. Dionysia, d. of Clarus; 66; II 272.26.

4201 ---; s. of Philiscus; 66-72/73; mortgaged property in Senepta, M. Top.; IX 1203 + *SB* IV 7339.12.

4202 SARAPION; ch. Sarapion; 68; Oxy.; XIV 1641.23.

4203 ---; s. of Sarapion; sp. Sampatym[is?]; ch. Sarapion; 68; Oxy.; XIV 1641.22.

4204 ---; s. of Sarapion, s. of Sarapion; m. Sampatym[is?], d. of]onides; 68; property owner; Oxy.; XIV 1641.22.

4205 ---; ch. Diogenes; April 70; Oxyrhynchite; Oxy.; addr. for gs.; *P. Oxy. inv.* 50.4B.24B.(3-4)2.

4206 ---; s. of Sarapion; April 70; property owner; *P. Oxy. inv.* 50.4B.24B.(3-4)33.

4207 ---; ch. Sarapion, Ptolemaeus; April 70; property owner; prob. dec.; bro. of Theon; *P. Oxy. inv.* 50.4B.24B.(3-4)33.

4208 ---; ch. Sinthoonis alias Ophelous; Aug 72?; Oxyrhynchite; Oxy.; addr. for gss. Dionysius and Mnesithes; XLI 2972.4-5.

4209 ---; Feb 75; farmer; Oasis; XII 1439.1.

4210 ---; 77-83; Claudius Antoninus his representative; II 330 (descr.).

4211 ---; s. of Didymus; sp. Charitous; ch. Didymus; March 79; Oxyrhynchite?; Oxy.?; addr. for s.; II 243.4.

4212 ---; s. of Alexandrus; Oct 80; Oxyrhynchite?; Oxy.?; guardian to Demetria; II 248.5.

4213 ---; s. of Theon; sp. Prima; ch. Demetria; Oct 80; land-holder; property owner; Oxyrhynchite; Broad St; land in Kleros of Ctesicles and of Epimachus in W. Top.; died 75/76; II 248.8.

4214 ---; s. of Sarapion; 80/81; XIV 1648.43.

4215 ---; ch. Heron, Sarapion; 80/81; XIV 1648.44.

4216 ---; s. of Sarapion; ch. Zoilus; 80/81; 117/118; property owner; bro. of Heron; XIV 1648.26, 43.

4217 ---; s. of Castor, s. of Polydeuces; m. Isarous; after 81; Oxyrhynchite; Oxy.; II 369.3.

4218 ---; ch. Isarous; after 81; Oxyrhynchite?; Oxy.?; addr. for d.; II 369.5.

4219 ---; ch. Phanias; 81-96; VIII 1105.1-2.

4220 ---; s. of Dionysius, s. of Sarapion; 83/84; Alex.?, Athenaeus?; Tychis Necotis; holds land there; bro. of Chaeremon and Dionysia; II 290.18.

4221 ---; ch. Dionysius; 83/84; Alex.?, Athenaeus?; Tychis Necotis; addr. for gch. Sarapion, Chaeremon, Dionysia; II 290.19.

4222 TI. CLAUDIUS SARAPION; ch. Ti. Claudius Theon; 83/84; Roman; Tychis Necotis; addr. for s.?; II 290.30.

4223 SARAPION; ch. Theon; (1), (2) c. 85; (3) 85/86; (1) II 328 (descr.); (2) 335 (descr.); (3) 336 (descr.).

4224 ---; ch. Harpochration; 88/89; Oxyrhynchite?; Oxy.?; addr. for gs. Dionysius; II 280.3.

4225 ---; ch. Thermous; 89-97; Oxy.?; addr. for gs. Dius; II 274.10.

4226 ---; ch. Pausiris; 89-97; Oxyrhynchite; addr. for gds. Dionysia and Herais; II 274.13.

4227 ---; ch. Demetrous; 89-97; property owner; Oxy.; dec.; property left to d. and unnamed s.; II 274.5.

4228 ---; alias DIOGENES; gs. of Sarapion; 89-97; property owner; Oxy.; owns prop. w. aunt Demetrous, d. of Sarapion; II 274.24.

4229 ---; s. of Diogenes; sp. Zenarion; Feb 91; property and slave owner; Oxyrhynchite; Temgenuthis qtr; owned house and slave weaver there; dec.; XLI 2957.9-10.

4230 ---; m. Heraclous; June 91; Oxy.; X 1317 (descr.).

4231 ---; 91/92; epiteretes; Oxy.; XXXVIII 2856.1.

4232 ---; s. of Sarapion, s. of Diophantus; m. Philous, d. of Sarapion; (1) 92; (2) i; property owner; Peeno, M. Top.; doc. 2 pr. Oxy.?; owns vacant lot in P., inherited from m.; (1) *PSI* VI 715.6; (2) *P. Harris* 138 iii 1.

4233 ---; s. of Diophantus; sp. Philous; ch. Sarapion; (1) 92; (2) i; Peeno?, M. Top.; doc. 2 pr. Oxy.?; addr. for s.; (1) *PSI* VI 715.6; (2) *P. Harris* 138 iii 1.

4234 ---; s. of Thracidas, s. of Hermogenes; Jan 93; Isieum Tryphonos, L. Top.; age 39; cedes catoecic land to Apollophanes - from holdings nr Sinary, L. Top., and from Kleros of Heracles, s. of Callicrates; signalement; *PSI* VIII 897.60, 93.

4235 ---; ch. Dionysius; Jan 93; s. has catoecic land nr Sinary, bordering that of Sarapion, s. of Thracidas; *PSI* VIII 897 ii 68.

4236 TI. CLAUDIUS SARAPION; (1) Jan 93; (2) Apr/May 94; ex-agoranomus of Alex. (2); Alex.; Theon his agent; age 38 (1); ceded land by Tsenuaris from Kleros of Cleandrides; signalement; (1) *PSI* VIII 897.6-7, 57; (2) II 364 (descr.).

4237 SARAPION; 94; agoranomus w. Dionysius, Theon, Sarapion (below) and Pasion; Oxy.; I 73.9.

4238 ---; 94; agoranomus w. Dionysius, Theon, Sarapion (above) and Pasion; Oxy.; I 73.8.

4239 ---; s. of Heracleides; sp. Clara; ch. Sarapion alias Clarus; 94; Oxyrhynchite; Oxy.; addr. for s.; II 270.6.

4240 ---; alias CLARUS; s. of Sarapion, s. of Heracleides; m. Clara, d. of Narcissus; 94; Oxyrhynchite; Oxy.; II 270.5.

4241 SARAPION; ch. Plutarche; 94; Oxyrhynchite; Oxy.; addr. for mat. gs. Heras; II 270.5.

4242 ---; ch. Thompecysis; 96; Oxyrhynchite?; Oxy.; addr. for gs. Petosarapis; II 266.6.

4243 ---; s. of Chaeremon; m. Tnepheros, d. of Annius; 96; slave owner; Oxyrhynchite; Oxy.; I 104.5.

4244 ---; s. of Theon; ch. [Heracleides?]; 97 (doc. date 197/198); landholder; Oxy.; doc. pr. Oxy.?; s. held palm grove nr Psinachis in Ars.; *P. Bour.* 16.10.

4245 ---; s. of T[-]; (1) 98-117; (2) end i; agent or notary of agoranomi; Oxy.; (1) *P. Sel.* 24.10; (2) 23.2.

4246 ---; ch. Apollonous 98-117; *PSI* VII 772.1.

4247 ---; sp. Didyme; 98-137; VI 968 (descr.).

4248 ---; early i; *OD Pisa* 425.5.

4249 ---; early i; *OD Pisa* 435.2.

4250 ---; 2nd half i; unnamed s. is bro. and guardian of unnamed widow of Asclepiades; *P. Oslo* 130.3.

4251 ---; s. of Belles; 2nd half i; vinedresser; VI 985 (descr.).

4252 ---; late i; "brother" of Dionysius; II 396 (descr.).

4253 ---; s. of Ptolemaeus; sp. Dionysia; ch. Ptolemaeus alias Germanus, Eusebes (an alias), and a d.; end i; Oxyrhynchite; Oxy.; addr. for s.; *P. Sel.* 23.16.

4254 ---; ch. Philous; i; Peeno?, M. Top.; doc. pr. Oxy.?; addr. for mat. gs. Sarapion; *P. Harris* 138 iii 2.

---; see DIOPHANTUS.

4255 ---; s. of Sarapion; sp. Ammonarion; ch. Areius, Anoup; i; Oxyrhynchite?; Oxy.; addr. for s.; *P. Harris* 138 iii 11.

4256 ---; ch. Sarapion; i; Oxyrhynchite?; Oxy.?; addr. for gss. Areius and Anoup; *P. Harris* 138 iii 11.

4257 ---; s. of Nechthosiris; sp. [....]nius; ch. Nechthosiris; i; Oxyrhynchite?; Oxy.?; addr. for s.; *P. Harris* 138 iii 13.

4258 ---; ch. Justus; i; other sons?; XXXVI 2786.1.

4259 ---; s. of Sar[apion; i; property owner; Oxyrhynchite; Sarapeum; part owner house there; *P. Ryl.* II 156.5.

4260 ---; i; Oxyrhynchite?; Oxy.?; age 48; guardian of Tames.[..., age 40; *P. Ryl.* II 156 V.

4261 ---; i; Oxy.; age 39; signalement; *P. Ryl.* II 156.32 V.

4262 ---; s. of Dionysius; i; XIV 1756.1, 13.

4263 SAR[APION; ch. Sarapion, Dionysius; i; Oxy.?; addr. for ss; *P. Ryl.* II 156.24.

4264 SARAPION; i; ch. or slave; II 298.21.

4265 ---; ch. Cephalas; i; Sesphtha, W. Top.; addr. for s.; *P. Ryl.* II 199.19.

4266 ---; i; II 298.36.

4267 ---; ch. Sarapion; i - early ii; Oxyrhynchite; addr. for gs. Aristandrus; *P. Oslo* III 114.14.

4268 ---; s. of Sarapion; sp. Arsinoe; ch. Aristandrus; i - early ii; Oxyrhynchite; *P. Oslo* III 114.14.

4269 TI. CLAUDIUS SARA[PION; i - ii; strategus?; Oxy.; *P. Princ.* II 25.1.

4270 SARAPION; s. of Pasion; ch. Sarapion, Pasion; (1) Mar 102; (2) early ii; Oxyrhynchite; Oxy.; addr. for s.; (1) XXXII 2342.4; (2) III 493.13, 15.

4271 ---; (1) after 102; (2) Feb/Mar? 108; bibliophylax w. Sarapiades (1), w. Theon (2); Oxy.; (1) III 636.1; (2) 483.32.

4272 ---; ch. Didymus; 103; Aphroditopolis; III 511.2.

4273 ---; s. of Herodes, s. of Exacon; m. Caecilia Polla; (1) 103/104; (2) Sept 109; (3) 116; (4) 121; (5) Nov 130; (6) 130; land, livestock and slave owner; lessor; Oxyrhynchite; Oxy.; leases olive gdn, Psobthis, M. Top., to Horus (1); w. bro. Exacon leases olive press to Heras (2); has livestock at Psobthis (3), land at Senepta, M. Top. (5); payt. made at Psobthis to him from a/c of Papontos, s. of Dorotheus, at Senepta (6); (1) III 639 (descr.); (2) *PSI* IX 1030.1; (3) I 74.5; (4) III 499.2; (5) IV 730.1; (6) III 517.9.

4274 ---; s. of Ammonius; ch. Ammonius, Pausanias; Nov 103; Oxyrhynchite?; Oxy.?; addr. for s.; *P. Mert.* I 14.4.

4275 ---; s. of Diogenes; sp. Didyme; ch. Diogenes alias Sarapion; Nov 103; Oxyrhynchite?; Oxy.?; addr. for s.; *P. Mert.* I 14.1.

---; see DIOGENES.

4276 ---; Aug 106; *P. Wisc.* I 17 V 14.

4277 ---; 107; lessor?; Episemon, U. Top.; XVIII 2188.9.

4278 ---; s. of Ptolemaeus; May 109; may not be Oxy.; bro. of Areius; XLII 3015.6.

4279 ---; Sept/Oct 110; lessor; III 575 (descr.) V.

4280 TI. JULIUS SARAPION; s. of Ti. Julius Theon; (1) Oct 111; (2) 122/123; hypomnematographus; landholder; slave owner; Roman; Alexandria; holds land at Senepta, M. Top.; bro. of Ti. Julius Theon; (1) XLIV 3197.2; (2) XXXVIII 2866.1-2.

4281 SARAPION; ch. Eudaemon; 113; South Quay qtr; addr. for s.; XII 1521.5.

4282 ---; s. of Syrus, s. of Apion; Aug 114 or 133; property owner; Hermaeum qtr; bro. of Apion, Nilus now called Polem[archus], Syrus and Thais; *SB* VIII 9824.3.

4283 ---; s. of Dionysius; ch. Sarapion; 117-137; Oxyrhynchite; Oxy.; addr. for s.; I 105.13.

4284 ---; s. of Sarapion, s. of Dionysius; 117-137; Oxyrhynchite; Oxy.; witness; I 105.13.

4285 ---; ch. Horion; 117-138; Oxy.; addr. for s.; I 178.3.

4286 ---; 117-138; Oxy.; III 648 (descr.).

4287 ---; s. of Hecaton (l. Hexagon); ch. Hecaton (l. Hexagon); 117-137; Oxyrhynchite?; Oxy.?; addr. for s.; I 105.14.

4288 ---; ch. Harpocration; 117; Oxyrhynchite?; North Quay qtr?; addr. for gs. Dionysius; III 489.4.

4289 ---; Dec 117/Jan 118; property owner; Pammenes' Garden qtr; sells part house there to Synistor and Zoilus; III 577 (descr.).

4290 ---; ch. Diogenes; 118; Oxyrhynchite; addr. for s.; *SB* VI 5678.3.

4291 SAR[AP]IO[N?; sp. Ammonous; 119; landholder; lessor; Oxyrhynchite; Oxy.; leases land nr Sko in holding of Theodorus and Aulaeus; XXXVI 2776.1.

4292 SARAPION; sp. Isarous; ch. Plutarchus, Ptolemaeus; 119/120; Oxyrhynchite; Oxy.; addr. for gd. Julia; *PSI* XIII 1322.2.

4293 ---; s. of Hierax; ch. Dionysius; 119/120; Oxyrhynchite; Oxy.; addr. for s.; *PSI* XIII 1322.5.

4294 ---; ch. Harsous or Arsous; Jan 121; Metroon qtr; addr. for s.; *P. Fouad* 30.13.

4295 ---; ch. Sarapion; Jan 121; Metroon qtr; addr. for s.; *P. Fouad* 30.14.

4296 ---; s. of Sarapion; Jan 121; property owner; Metroon qtr; owns property there; addr. jointly w. Apia and others; *P. Fouad* 30.14.

4297 ---; ch. Ptolemaeus; c. 122/123; Phoboou distr.?, E. Top.; addr. for s.; XXXVIII 2865.6.

4298 ---; ch. Dionysius; 122/123; *P. Lips.* 116.9.

4299 ---; 122/123; grammateus; of Julius Sarapion, hypomnematographus; XXXVIII 2866.1.

4300 ---; ch. Peteuris; 122/123; Oxyrhynchite; Oxy.; addr. for gd. Herais; (1) *SB* XII 10781.6; (2) III 592 (descr.) R 6.

4301 SARAPION; ch. Dionysius; 122/123; unnamed gs.; III 592 (descr.) V 5.

4302 ---; 122/123; unnamed ch.; III 592 (descr.) V 2.

4303 ---; ch. Heracleides; Aug 123; Pakerke, E. Top.; addr. for gs. Theon; XXXVIII 2864.1.

4304 [SAR]A[PI]ON; ch. Dionysius; 123; Oxyrhynchite?; Oxy.?; addr. for gs. ....aros; I 107.1-2.

4305 SARAPION; 124; Oxy.?; addr. for gs.; III 490.19.

4306 ---; ch. Heracleus; 126; Sesphtha?, L. Top.; doc. pr. Oxy.?; addr. for gs.; *P. Harris* 142.3.

4307 ---; s. of Dionysius; Aug 127; has a/c at Seryphis, Senocomis, Sen..( ); XXXVIII 2867.8.

4308 ---; ch. Sarapion; 127; Oxyrhynchite; Oxy.; addr. for ggs. Sarapion; III 496.2.

4309 ---; s. of Sarapion; ch. Sarapion; 127; Oxyrhynchite; Oxy.; addr. for gs. Sarapion; III 496.2.

4310 ---; s. of Sarapion, s. of Sarapion; sp. Thais; ch. Sarapion; 127; property owner; Oxyrhynchite; Oxy.; dec.?; another s.; III 496.2.

4311 ---; s. of Sarapion, s. of Sarapion; m. Thais, d. of Sarapion and Heraclous; ch. Thais; 127; property owner; Oxyrhynchite; Oxy.; III 496.2.

4312 ---; s. of Eudaemon, s. of Theon; m. Heras, d. of Didous; sp. Thais; 127; property and slave owner; Oxyrhynchite; Oxy.; bridegroom; III 496.2.

4313 ---; sp. Heraclous; ch. Thais; 127; Oxyrhynchite; Oxy.; addr. for gd. Thais; III 496.5.

4314 ---; 127 (doc. date 197/198); Oxyrhynchite; unnamed ch.; *P. Bour.* 16.16.

4315 ---; 127/128; misthotes, w. Ctesidemus, of usiac land; *P. Lips.* 113.1.

4316 ---; s. of Plution, s. of Diodorus; m. Dogymis; sp. Tnephersois; ch. Sarapion; 127/128; Oxyrhynchite, gymnasial class; Cretan qtr; died in Pammenes' Garden qtr; epicrisis in 99/100; reg. in poll tax 123/124; XII 1452.11, 37.

4317 ---; s. of Sarapion, s. of Plution; m. Tnephersois; gs. of Dogymis; 127/128; Oxyrhynchite, gymnasial class; Cretan qtr; born 113/114; epicrisis in 127/128; XII 1452 i 13, ii 39.

4318 ---; s. of Dio[.....; ch. Sarapion; 128/129; Oxy.; gs. Sarapion; X 1263.4.

4319 ---; s. of Sarapion, s. of Dio[.....; 128/129; slave owner; Oxy.; has freedman Dioscorus; X 1263.4.

4320 SARAPION; ch. Diogenis alias Tapontos; 129; Oxyrhynchite?; Oxy.?; addr. for mat. gs. Theon; I 75.8-9.

4321 ---; ch. Sarapion; 129; Oxyrhynchite; Oxy.?; addr. for gs. Pausanias; XXXVI 2774.2.

4322 ---; s. of Sarapion; sp. Apollonous; ch. Pausanias; 129; Oxyrhynchite; Oxy.; addr. for s.; XXXVI 2774.2.

4323 ---; ch. Sarapion; 130; Ibion Ammonii, L. Top.; addr. for ggs.; III 492.3.

4324 ---; s. of Apion (name not Apion in l. 3); sp. Heraclous; ch. Horion alias Theon; 130; Ibion Ammonii, L. Top.; addr. for s.; III 492.3, 16.

4325 ---; s. of Sarapion; sp. Tausiris alias Sarapous; ch. Heraclous; 130; Ibion Ammonii, L. Top.; addr. for gs. Horion alias Theon; III 492.3.

4326 ---; s. (1) of Pheremphis, (2) of Po[by adoption; 130; Oxyrhynchite; Oxy.; witness; age 37; III 492.23.

4327 ---; ch. Ammonius, Sarapion(?); 130; Isieum Tryphonos, L. Top.; addr. for gd. Thatres; III 492.2.

4328 ---; ch. Eubulia; 131; property owner; Oxyrhynchite; Oxy.; addr. for d.; dec.; bro. of Dionysius; I 68.8.

4329 ---; m. Eubulia, d. of Sarapion; 131; Oxyrhynchite; Oxy.; minor; I 68.8.

4330 ---; s. of Mnesitheus; 131; Oxyrhynchite; Oxy.; III 486.4.

4331 ---; s. of Sarapion; Nov 132; writes for Hermogenes; *PSI* I 53 iv 69.

4332 ---; ch. Sarapion; Nov 132; *PSI* I 53 iv 69.

4333 ---; ch. Theon; 132/133; gs. Onnophris; *PSI* VIII 874 i 2.

4334 ---; ch. Theon; 132/133; Alex., Propapposebasteius; Oxy.?; doc. pr. Oxy.?; details for gs. Ammonius; III 477.7.

4335 ---; s. of Gaius; sp. Ṭearous; 132/133; unnamed ch. in Pammenes' Garden qtr; *PSI* I 53 xi 184.

4336 ---; m. Didyme; April 133; weaver; *PSI* I 53 vii 109.

4337 ---; ch. Amois; April 133; *PSI* I 53 vii 130.

4338 ---; s. of Dionysius; 133-137; joint property owner; Oxyrhynchite; claims was displaced by neighbours from land at Seryphis owned w. bro.'s s. Dionysius; *P. Flor.* III 319.2.

4339 ---; ch. Thracidas?; c. 135; property owner; murdered Ptolema?; XVII 2111 i 22.

4340 CLA]UDIUS SARAPION; c. 135; advocate?; Roman?; Oxy.?; appears before Petronius Mamertinus; XVII 2111 i 7.

4341 SARAPION; c. 136; advocate for plaintiff Plutarchus; IV 707 ii 13.

4342 SARAPION; c. 136; heir, w. Andromachus; *P. Inst. Fran.* III 18.14.

4343 ---; Sept/Oct 137; farmer; lessee; lessor; sublets to Ptollas and Ammoni(u)s; IV 729.5 and passim.

4344 ---; s. of Asclepiades; 138-161; certifier of manumission; Oxy.; IV 723.4.

4345 S]ARAPION; ch. S- ; 138-161; may not be Oxy.; *P. Oslo* III 84.9.

4346 SARAPION; alias DIOSCORUS; after 138; agent?; Oxyrhynchite; Oxy.; *P. Yale* 65.7-8.

4347 ---; ch. Horion; 140/141; Lonemus distr.; Oxy.; addr. for s.; I 89.6.

4348 ---; ch. Arsinoe; 148/149; Oxyrhynchite, gymnasial class; Oxy.; addr. for d., sp. of Dionysius; XLVI 3281.3.

4349 ---; s. of Pausirion; m. -ris; 148/149; Oxyrhynchite, gymnasial class; Knights' Camp qtr; enr. in g. class of 13 yr olds here this yr; XLVI 3279.8.

4350 ---; s. of Harpocration; ch. Harpocration; 148/149; Oxyrhynchite, gymnasial class; 10th qtr?; addr. for gs. Sarapion; scr. in 72/73; XLVI 3282.4, 12.

4351 ---; s. of Harpocration, s. of Sarapion; m. Demetria alias Asclatarion; 148/149; Oxyrhynchite, gymnasial class; 10th qtr; enr. in g. class of 13 yr olds in 127/128; XLVI 3282.2.

4352 ---; ch. Pausiris; 168; gs. A[ ] still alive; XIV 1648.22.

---; see]RON.

---; see SERENUS.

4353 ---; ch. Amois; early ii; Oxyrhynchite?; Oxy.?; addr. for gs. Eudaemon alias Amois; witness to will; III 493.14.

4354 ---; s. of Sarapion, s. of Pasion; early ii; Oxyrhynchite; Oxy.; witness; bro. of Pasion who makes will?; III 493.13.

4355 ---; s. of Artemidorus; early ii; Alex., Auximetoreius; unnamed s.; III 497.22.

4356 ---; early ii; III 525.8.

4357 ---; early ii; exegetes; priest; Oxyrhynchite; Oxy.; predecessor of Ptolemaeus as ex.; X 1269.4, 12.

4358 SARAP(ION); s. of Horus; m. Sinthoonis; ii; landholder; Cretan qtr; *P. Princ.* II 46.7.

4359 SARAPION; ii; Oxy.; relative of Apia or Zoilus; XII 1581.5, 14.

4360 CLAUDIUS SARAPION; ii; III 523.3.

4361 SARAPION; ii; *P. Oslo* II 49.1.

4362 SARAPION; alias [G]AION; ii; slave; of Tasarapion; VIII 1149.7-8.

4363 ---; ch. Amois; ii; hamlet of Cosmos; doc. pr. Tebtynis; addr. for gs. Amois; *P. Mil. Vogl.* IV 211 a9, b5.

4364 ---; ch. Sarapas; ii; farmer; livestock owner; XXXVI 2781.1.

4365 ---; ch. Athenaeus; ii; gs. Sarapas; XLVI 3268.6.

4366 ---; ch. Justus; ii; Sinary, L. Top.; addr. for s.; XXXI 2574.3.

4367 ---; s. of Ptolemaeus; m. Cleopatra; ii; landholder; Gymnasium St qtr; bro. of Glaucias; *P. Princ.* II 46.5.

4368 ---; ii; has unnamed children; "brother" of Abascantus; XII 1582.15 V.

4369 ---; s. of Abascantus; ii; Oxy.; XII 1582.11.

4370 ---; ii; oxen seller?; Oxy.?; XLII 3063.17.

4371 ---; s. of Apei; ii; pawnbroker; III 530.13.

4372 ---; s. of Ammonius; sp. Diodora; ch. Sarapion alias Heraclas; ii; *P. Oslo* III 108.2.

4373 ---; alias HERACLAS; s. of Sarapion, s. of Ammonius; m. Diodora; ii; ref. to village of Taapemou; *P. Oslo* III 108.2.

4374 ---; m. Thaisous; ii; property owner; Pammenes' Garden qtr; III 505.7.

4375 ---; ii; strategus; Sebennyte, U. Top.; Oxy.; has "sister" and ?small child; VI 931.1.

---; see HEPHAESTION.

4376 ---; s. of Alexandrus; m. (or step-m.) Dionysia; ii; XLVI 3313.4, 23.

4377 ---; ch. Didymus; ii; III 610 (descr.).

4378 ---; s. of Apollonius; ii; III 609 (descr.).

4379 ---; s. of Gaius; ii; landholder; *P. Erl.* 44 iii 39.

4380 AURELIUS SARAPION; ii; Roman; bro. of Athenaeus; unnamed s.; XXXIII 2679.1-2.

4381 SARAPION; ii?; *PSI* XIV 1414.1.

4382 SARAPOUS; Feb 62; XXXVIII 2838.2.

4383 ---; ch. Demetrous; Oct 62; slave; Sesphtha?, L. Top.; XXXVIII 2873 V 35.

4384 ---; Jan/Feb 75; II 362 (descr.).

4385 ---; April 77; slave; age c. 8; sold by Bacche to Heliodora, d. of Heliodora; II 263.9.

4386 SARAPOUS; Aug 79; slave; age 30; II 380 (descr.).

4387 ---; sp. (?) Heracleides; 81-96; IV 795 (descr.).

4388 ---; d. of Zoilus; gd. (mat.) of Apollonius; sp. Dionysius; 81-96; Oxy.; dowry includes property nr Talao and slave Plusia; II 265.[6], 17.

4389 ---; ch. Achilleus, Sarapas; 91 or 107; Oxyrhynchite; Oxy.; addr. for sons; IV 722.11.

4390 ---; late i; Oxy.; sister or sp. of Theon, soldier; VIII 1154.1.

4391 ---; i; foster child; II 298.46.

4392 ---; sp. Plution; 117-138; Oxy.; two unnamed children; III 646 (descr.).

4393 ---; 127; Oxy.; slave of bridegroom Sarapion; III 496.7.

4394 ---; m. Nicarous; 127; Oxy.; slave of bridegroom Sarapion; sister of Epicharmus and Nicarous; III 496.7.

---; see TAUSIRIS.

4395 ---; d. of Isas, s. of Isidorus; gd. of Soeris or Soerous; early ii; property owner; Oxyrhynchite?; Oxy.?; addr. for uncle Theonas alias Theon; minor; sister of Sarapas; X 1269.8.

4396 ---; sp. Diogenes alias Cottus; ch. Is?]as; ii; Oxy.; addr. for s.; XII 1536.3.

4397 SARAS; c. 30; X 1292.8.

4398 ---; ch. Totoes; 31/32?; *P. Mich. inv.* 69.2.

4399 ---; s. of Pesouris; 104/105; Oxyrhynchite; Oxy.; guardian of Sambous, d. of Amois; XXXVIII 2852.3.

4400 ---; ch. Taaphynchis; 116; Oxy.; addr. for mat. gs. Paos, dec. tekton and pyraethes of Isis and other gods and enr. in Gymnasium St qtr; XII 1550.19.

4401 ---; s. of Marcus; 117-138; agent? for Theon, s. of Philumene; X 1293.5.

4402 ---; s. of Theogenes; Aug 123; Phoboou distr., E. Top.; XXXVIII 2863.5.

SARAS; see DIONYSIUS.

4403 SARMATES; s. of Wḥj; July 7; *OD Pisa* 1131 Concavo 3-4.

4404 SARON; s. of Belles; 8; *OD Pisa* 1.9.

4405 SARPOCRATIS; 81-96; VI 984 R fin.

4406 C. JULIUS SATORNILUS (formerly Ptolemaeus); s. of Ptolemaeus; 70; landholder; slave owner?; lessor; soldier of legio 22, century of Bius Serenus; Roman; formerly Alex.,

Phylaxithalassius, Althaieus; Oxy.; age 28; land in Senocomis, W. Top., and part of Kleros of Polemon; full signalement; XXII 2349.2.

4407 C. JULIUS SATURNINUS; 103; recruit in 3rd Ituraean cohort; Roman; age 23; signalement; VII 1022.19.

4408 SATYRUS; ch. -]us; 35; Alex., Althaieus; II 323.12.

4409 ---; sp. Harseis; ch. Acoris; ii; Cretan qtr; addr. for s.; *P. Princ.* II 46.6.

4410 SE[ ]; ii; doc. pr. Tebtynis; witness?; *P. Mil. Vogl.* IV 211 bl.

4411 SE...; ch. Apollos; i - ii; ch. slave of Ision?; *P. Harris* 72.34.

4412 SECUNDA; 22; property owner; II 294.9.

4413 SECUNDUS; Nov 45; practor; Oxy.; Hippodrome qtr; X 1258.2.

4414 ---; 59; agoranomus; "Apollonius formerly reg. as Secundus"; II 320.25.

---; see APOLLONIUS.

4415 ---; c. 1; also called Secundus; IV 736.50, 81.

4416 [.]L. SECUNDUS; 103; recruit in 3rd Ituraean cohort; Roman; age 20; VII 1022.17.

4417 ASINNIUS SECUNDUS; (1) 117-138?; (2) n.d.; decurion; Roman; doc. (1) prov.?; bros. Apollonius and Theon; (1) *P. Brem.* 56 (a)2 V; (2) *SB* I 4630.1.

4418 SECUNDUS; ii; III 531.24.

4419 SELENE; 79/80; II 373 (descr.).

4420 ---; d. of Apollonius; i; *P. Harris* 144.5.

4421 SELEUCUS; c. 35; slave?; II 295.3.

4422 SELEUE; early i; *OD Pisa* 456.3.

4423 SENAIAS; d. of Naarophibis; sp. Heraclas; ch. Ammonis; 2nd half i; Sinary?, L. Top.; addr. for s.; XXXVIII 2846.2.

4424 SENAMUNIS; d. of Dionysius; sp. Ptolemaeus; ch. Hagnes; Aug 72(?); Nemerae, M. Top.; addr. for d.; XLI 2972.8.

4425 SENBERENICE; early i; unnamed sp.; *OD Pisa* 424.6.

4426 SENCHEMENEUS; 81-96; VI 984 R fin.

4427 L. CALPURNIUS SENECA; ch. L. Calpurnius Serenus, L. Calpurnius Gaianus; 167; soldier, legio 2 Traiana Fortis; Roman; reg. 114-117; Oxy. (165/166); owns slaves Zosimus and Epagathus; *PSI* V 477.2.

4428 SENITHES; c. 1; IV 799 (descr.).

4429 SENONNOPHRIS; d. of Heracleus; 81-96; property owner; half house occupied by Eudaemon; sister of Ptolemaeus?; VI 984 R init.

4430 SENPANESNEUS; d. of Panesneus; m. Tanuris; 81-96; Temple of Ares greatest god; age 1; VI 984 R init.

4431 SENPARAITHIS; d. of Panesneus; m. Tatnagous; 81-96; Temple of Ares greatest god; m. possibly dec.; VI 984 R init.

4432 SENPHOIS; d. of Lycus, s. of Horus; sp. Ptolemaeus; ch. Heracles; 81-96; s. of gymnasial class; VI 984 R init.

4433 SENPTOLLIS; 81-96; VI 984 R fin.

4434 SENTHEUS; s. of Thoo(nis); i; pastophorus; member of Damarion's club; *P. Oslo* III 143.9.

4435 SENTH(EUS); ch. Pak[-; 98/99; Tholthis, L. Top.; addr. for gs. Diogenes; *P. Köln* II 86.5.

4436 SENTIANUS; ii; nomikos; Oxy.; III 578 (descr.).

4437 SENTOEUS; Jan 29; livestock owner; Pela, W. Top.; XXXVIII 2850.20.

4438 SENTRIS; 81-96; VI 984 R fin.

4439 SENYPHIS; ch. Petechonsis; i BC - i; *OD Pisa* 243 + 472 i 8.

4440 ---; 81-96; VI 984 R fin.

4441 SEPSARION; d. of Epimachus, s. of Dionysius; m. Thatres; 118; property owner; Oxyrhynchite; Oxy.; owns part house at Kerkethyris; guardian Hermas, s. of Theon; III 503.4.

4442 POMPONIUS SEPTIMIANUS; ii; III 589 (descr.).

4443 L. CALPURNIUS SERENUS; s. of L. Calpurnius Seneca; 167; slave owner; Roman; reg. 150-153; Oxy. (165/166); bro. L. Calpurnius Gaianus; slave Hermes Germanus; *PSI* V 447.7.

4444 SERENUS; sp. Isidora (also "sister"); ii; III 528.1.

4445 ---; ii; goldsmith; Oxy.; XII 1582.1, 8.

4446 SEREPODO(RUS) (sic); ch. Serepodo(rus) (sic); i; Sesphtha?; addr. for s.; *P. Ryl.* II 199.9.

4447 ---; s. of Serepodo(rus) (sic); i; farmer; Sesphtha; *P. Ryl.* II 199.9.

4448 ---; s. of Psenamunis; i; Sesphtha; *P. Ryl.* II 199.9.

SERGIUS; see SERGIUS PTOLEMAEUS.

4449 SEUTHAS; s. of On( ); Nov 42 BC; Oxyrhynchus; witness; *P. Ryl.* IV 582.22.

4450 SEUTHES; c. 45-47; Little Oasis?; unnamed sons take Thaesis and s. into slavery; XLII 3033.5.

4451 SEUTHES; s. of Diogenes, s. of Dionysius; March 66; weaver; XLI 2971.3.

4452 ---; ch. Potamon; (1) end i; (2) 121; landholder; Oxyrhynchite?; Senepta, M. Top.; addr. for gs. Potamon; (1) *P. Sel.* 23.12; (2) III 499.14.

4453 SEVERUS; 25/26; instructs Chaereas, str., re arrears of corn and money; II 291.6.

4454 BIUS SEVERUS; centurion of legio 22; Roman; XXII 2349.2.

4455 SEVERUS; n.d.; *SB* I 1985(a).

SEXTUS; see SEXTUS POMPEIUS.

4456 SIAG( ); ch. Apollo( ); 119/120; s. pays corn via Monimu, U. Top., and Sinary L. Top.; *P. Wisc.* II 39.4.

4457 NICAEA SIL[VA]NUS; s. of Psubius (Psoubios); c. 85; Oxyrhynchite, Jewish; Jewish qtr; buys 1/6 house Jewish qtr from Paulus; II 335 (descr.).

4458 [SIM]ON; s. of Tryphon; Sept 77; pilot of cargo boat; name restored in *CPJ* on analogy w. other Jewish names in 5-6; II 276.6.

4459 SINA . [...; sp. Psenosiris; 126; Sesphtha?, L. Top.; doc. pr. Oxy.?; addr. for s., stolistes; *P. Harris* 142.7.

4460 SINPETSIRIS; sp. Theon; ch. Pecysis; Feb 130(?); Sesphtha, L. Top.; addr. for s.; *P. Mich. inv.* 974.4.

4461 SINTH( ); s. of Achil(las) or Achil(leus); early Roman period; landholder?; *P. Mert.* III 104.6.

4462 SINTHEO(S); 19/20; Myrobalanus qtr; addr. for unnamed ch.; II 254.11.

4463 SINTHEUS; sp. Thonis (1), Onnophris (2); ch. Thaesis; 96; Oxyrhynchite?; Oxy.?; addr. for d.; II 266.3.

4464 ---; sp. Emechus; ch. Panetbes; i - ii; *P. Harris* 72.24.

4465 SINTHONIA; d. of Thonis; sp. Pausirion; ch. Pausiris; after 102; Oxyrhynchite; Oxy.; addr. for s.; III 636.16.

4466 SINTHONIS; ch. Harpochras; Sept 32; slave owner?; doc. pr. Oxy.?; unnamed s. in Coptos; unnamed d.; XXII 2353.1.

4467 ---; sp. Ptolem[; ch. Tereus; 81/82; Oxyrhynchite; Oxy.; addr. for d.; *P. Mert.* III 118.11.

4468 SINTHONIS(?); 85/86; buys land in Kleros of Euphron nr Th.thothis from Asclepiades; on name, cf. *P. Stras.* 266 (of c. 100); IV 794 (descr.).

4469 SINTHONIS; d. of Theon; sp. Lucius; ch. Lucia alias Thaisas; 94; Oxyrhynchite; Oxy.; addr. for d.; II 270.3.

4470 ---; d. of Petosarapis, s. of [.]bi[....]; sp. Thompecysis, Petosarapis; 96; Oxyrhynchite?; Oxy.?; addr. for s.; II 266.6-7, 10.

4471 SINTHONIS; d. of Hor[ ]; sp. Asclepiades; ch. Asclepiades; 100; landholder; age 47; signalement; s. guardian; cedes to Pausanias land from Kleros of Socrates; *P. Stras.* 266.14.

4472 ---; ch. Flavia; 119/120; Oxyrhynchite; Oxy.; addr. for gd. Julia; *PSI* XIII 1322.4.

4473 ---; d. of Pecysis; m. Teencegous; ch. Eudaemonis; ii; property owner; Tanais, M. Top.; buys courtyard in Oxy.; III 505.2.

4474 ---; sp. Ammonius; ch. Dionysia; ii; Oxy.?; addr. for d.; *P. Mil.* II 39.2.

4475 SINTHOONIS; alias OPHELOUS; d. of Sarapion; sp. Theon; ch. Dionysius, Mnesitheus; Aug 72(?); Oxyrhynchite; Oxy.; owned house in Nemerae; dec.; XLI 2972.4.

4476 ---; d. of Achilleus; sp. Theogenes; ch. Diogenes; 94/95; Oxyrhynchite; Heracles Place qtr; II 257.17.

4477 ---; d. of Thoonis, s. of Harthoonis; m. Tausarapis, d. of Tao( ); 98-117; priestess of Thoeris, Isis, Sarapis and assoc. gods; slave and property owner; Oxyrhynchite; Oxy.; age 40; signalement; bro. Harthoonis, priest of same gods; *P. Sel.* 24.3.

4478 ---; ch. ( )nis; 98-118; slave; Oxy.; d. slave of Sinthoonis, d. of Thoonis; *P. Sel.* 24.5.

4479 ---; sp. ..a..nus; ch. Paas; 99; Oxyrhynchite; *P. Princ.* II 32.4-5.

4480 ---; d. of Pecysis, s. of Zoilus; m. Lucia, d. of Longinus; 100; slave owner; Oxyrhynchite; Oxy.; I 49.5.

4481 SINTH(OONIS); sp. Horus; ch. Sarap(ion?); ii; Cretan qtr; addr. for s.; *P. Princ.* II 46.7.

4482 SINTOTOES (sic); d. of Apollonius; 137; Mermertha; *PSI* XII 1262 iii 3.

4483 ---; sp. Horus; ch. Thompecysis, Horus; Jan 139; Oxyrhynchite; North St qtr; *P. Oslo* III 105.11.

4484 SIPHMOUS; Nov 8; *OD Pisa* 421.2.

4485 SIR[ ]; s. of Harthoonis; ch. Horus; 135/136; Talao, L. Top.; doc. pr.?; addr. for s.; *P. Iand.* VII 136.10.

4486 SIRION; April 71; XXXIV 2725.6.

4487 SISOIS; d. of Stw_3s(?); i BC - i; *OD Pisa* 58.13.

4488 ---; (1) Oct 5; (2) Aug 7; (3) early i; (1) *OD Pisa* 427.1; (2) 432.1; (3) 425.1.

4489 ---; d. of Psenmuthis; early i; *OD Pisa* 419.2.

4490 ---; sp. Pothus?; ii; VII 1034 V.

4491 SISOUCHUS; July 72; assoc. of sitologus; Seryphis, W. Top.; XLIV 3163.13.

4492 SISYPHIS; s. of Ophieus; sp. Tereus; ch. Sisyphis; 81-96; unnamed gs.; VI 984 R (2).

4493 ---; s. of Sisyphis; s. of Ophieus; m. Tereus; 81-96; pastophorus of Apollo, the greatest god; age 60; lives in pastophorion of temple of Apollo; VI 984 R (2).

4494 SMARAGDUS; c. 130; slave; Oxy.; III 472 ii 14.

4495 SOCEUS; ch. Dieus; Sept 66; Oxy.; addr. for mat. gs. Zoilus; II 275.42.

4496 SOCRATES; ch. Papontos; 31/32; Sinary?, L. Top.; addr. for s.; *P. Mich. inv.* 69.9.

4497 SOCRATES; 112/113; III 586 (descr.).

4498 SOERIS (or SOEROUS); sp. Isidorus; ch. Theonas alias Theon, Isas; early ii; Oxyrhynchite?; Oxy.?; addr. for s.; name different in each line; X 1269.3, 14.

4499 SOERIS; d. of Harpochras; sp. Hatres; ch. Hareotes, Tnepheros; 96; property owner; Oxyrhynchite; Knights' Camp qtr; father freedman; I 104.4.

SOEROUS; see SOERIS.

4500 SOGENES; c. 1; IV 829 (descr.).

4501 SOIS; s. of Teos; Sept 73; priest (of Sarapis?); XLIV 3164.13.

4502 ---; ch. Onnophris; 86; Oxyrhynchite?; Hippodrome qtr; addr. for s.; VII 1208.16.

4503 SOMTOUS; ch. Psenyris; i BC - i; *OD Pisa* 25 i 13.

4504 ---; s. of Horus; i BC - i; *OD Pisa* 127.2.

4505 ---; ch. Horus; i BC - i; (1) *OD Pisa* 23 ii 5; (2) 532 X + 6.

4506 ---; ch. Pamun; i; *OD Pisa* 318.3.

4507 SUTORIUS SOSIBIUS; (1) 94/95; (2) 98; (3) 127/128; (4) - (8) 148/149; former strategus; Roman; str. in 72/73; (1) II 257.13; (2) X 1266.26; (3) XII 1452 ii 44-45; (4) XLVI 3276.11; (5) 3277.9; (6) 3279.14-15; (7) 3282.15; (8) 3283.10.

4508 SOSIBIUS; s. of Apollophanes; sp. Ptollarous; ch. Stephanus alias Amois; Aug 102; Oxyrhynchite?; Oxy.?; addr. for s.; III 508.5.

4509 S[O]SIPATRUS; ch. Ammonius; Oxy.; s. writes contract; XIV 1639.27.

4510 SOSTRATUS; ch. Nicanor; 78/79; Oxyrhynchite?; Thoeris St qtr; addr. for s.; XXXVI 2756.3.

4511 SOSUS; ii; XIV 1760.18.

4512 SOTADES; ch. Apollonius; (1) 20; (2) 48; slave owner; Thermutharion his freedwoman; (1) II 305.2; (2) 255.5.

4513 ---; 41-54; property owner; Oxyrhynchite?; owns house in Sarapeum, Ax...St; XXXIV 2720.19.

4514 ---; April 60; agoranomus; Oxyrhynchite?; Oxy.; assoc. w. Andromachus and Chaeremon; *P. Mich.* III 192.31.

4515 ---; ch. Ctesidem(us); 116; *P. Cair. Preis.* 32.2.

4516 ---; ch. Didymus; April 116; XXXVI 2759.2.

4517 SOTAS; 37; strategus; II 315.1.

4518 ---; Oct 65; writes for 2 unnamed women owning vineyard nr Ps[ ]as; *PSI* I 82.7.

4519 ---; ii; makes decision w. gymn. Demetrius and Adrastus re vines; XLII 3063.5.

4520 SOTER; alias DAMAS; ch. Soter; 98-102; Oxyrhynchite?; Oxy.?; addr. for s.; *P. Mert.* I 13.4-5.

4521 ---; s. of Soter alias Damas; 98-102; Oxyrhynchite; Oxy.; guardian of Thaesis, d. of Diogenes; *P. Mert.* I 13.4.

4522 SOTERICHUS; ch. Heracleius; (1) Jan 17; (2) 20; Oxy.; addr. for s.; (1) II 278.[2], 30; (2) 305.1.

4523 ---; s. of Lycas; May 91; beer seller; *PSI* III 181.3.

4524 ---; early ii; XVIII 2200.1.

4525 SOUẸ[RO]US(?); ii; doc. pr. Oxy.?; *SB* VI 9025.19.

4526 SPARTACUS; s. of Ptolemaeus; 44-37 BC; landholder; soldier; Cleopatra Aphrodite St?; catoecic land ceded to him; descr. as Ma[cedonian]; XIV 1635.3.

4527 ---; April 71; Oxy.?; "brother" of Adrastus; XXXIV 2725.14 and V.

4528 SPARTALAS; ch. Didymus, Callias; Jan 100; Oxyrhynchite; Oxy.; addr. for s.; XLI 2960.[2], 39, 41.

4529 SPARTAS; ch. Hermias; ii; III 591 (descr.).

4530 M. ANTONIUS SPENDON: i; phorologus; slave owner?; Roman; Eudaemon ?slave; nominates sitologi to epistrategus; XLVI 3273.2.

4531 SPHRAGIS; 81-96; VI 984 R bis.

4532 SPOCIS; sp. Atreus; ch. Psenosiris; 124; Oxy.?; addr. for gd. Tastraton; III 490.6.

STATILIUS; see PHANIAS.

4533 STEPHANUS; alias AMOIS; s. of Sosibius, s. of Apollophanes; m. Ptollarous, d. of Chaeremon; Aug 102; Oxyrhynchite; Oxy.; is security for two loans of Heraclas; III 508.5.

4534 STEPHANUS; Oct 120; Ibion Tan.e....reos?, Hermopolite nome; addr. for unnamed s. who exports from Sin..tape; XII 1440.4.

4535 ---; 130; grammateus of Horus; misthotes of Heracleides, s. of Antias; may live at Senepta or Sink( )pha; III 517.14.

4536 ---; s. of Canbarous; ch. Dosithes; 132/133 or 153/154; Oxy.; XII 1518.1, 6.

4537 NEMERIA STLACCIA; 6/5 BC; Roman; *PSI* X 1099.2.

4538 STOTOETES; i BC - i; *OD Pisa* 25 i 6.

4539 ---; s. of Horus; i BC - i; *OD Pisa* 228 X + 10.

4540 ---; ch. Horus; i BC - i; (1) *OD Pisa* 69 Concavo 6; (2) 72 ii X + 3; (3) 510 + 568 Convesso i 18; (4) 1264 Concavo 2.

4541 ---; Aug 3; *OD Pisa* 473 Convesso 3.

4542 STRATON; s. of Dionysius, s. of Hippalus; Feb 26; shepherd; Pela, W. Top.; descr. as the younger; II 245.18.

4543 ---; s. of Heliodorus; Oct 108; landholder; lessor; Oxyrhynchite; Oxy.; holds land nr Tanais in Kleros of Nicaeus; XXXVIII 2874.1.

4544 ---; sp. Dionysia; ch. Ptolema; 135; Oxyrhynchite?; Oxy.; addr. for d.; I 106.8.

4545 STRATONICUS; s. of Apion; 55; writes for Thoonis; II 304.30.

4546 STRATUS; c. 1; IV 736.97.

4547 STRUTHES; s. of Petsiris; ch. Struthes; 83/84; Papsis?, Tychis Necotis; addr. for s.; II 290.27.

4548 ---; s. of Struthes, s. of Petsiris; 83/84; landholder; Papsis?, Tychis Necotis; holds land there; II 290.27.

4549 SUCHUS; i BC - i; *OD Pisa* 69 Convesso ii 2.

4550 SUS; 81-96; part owner house in South Quay qtr; II 379 (descr.).

SUTORIUS; see SUTORIUS SOSIBIUS.

4551 SYNEROS; 30 BC - 14; XLIV 3208.1.

4552 SYNISTOR; sp. Athenarous; ch. Synistor; Sept 103; Toka?, M. Top.; addr. for s.; dec., wife remarried to Petsiris; XLI 2973.10.

4553 ---; s. of Synistor; m. Athenarous, d. of Eunomus; Sept 103; farmer; lessor; Toka?, M. Top.; land in Kleros of Callimachus and Bacchius; bro. on mother's side to Hermaeus; XLI 2973.10.

4554 ---; Dec 117/Jan 118; Pammenes' Garden qtr; buys part house w. Zoilus from Sarapion; III 577 (descr.).

4555 SYNTROPHUS; ii; I 113.26.

4556 SYRA; d. of Theon; sp. Sarapion; 20-50; dated by assoc. w. Heracleides in line 1; II 281.5.

4557 SYRAS; sp. Theonas; ch. Thaisous, Ammonas; c. 35; another unnamed d.; II 295.1.

4558 SYRUS; ch. Syrus; 49/50; Oxy.?; addr. for s., called Pesouris in I 37; I 38.3.

4559 ---; s. of Syrus; 49/50; Oxy.?; called Pesouris in I 37; I 38.3.

4560 ---; ch. Theon; 47; Oxy.?; addr. for s., II 269.22.

4561 ---; (= LUCIUS); s. of Apion; ch. L. Pompeius Niger; 61; property owner; Oxy.?; dec.; leaves property in Hermaeum qtr to s.; *SB* XII 10788.9.

4562 SYRUS; ch. Apollonius; Nov 83; Oxyrhynchite?; Oxy.?; addr. for gs. Amois; X 1282.9.

4563 ---; ch. Plution; Jan 100; Oxyrhynchite?; Oxy.?; addr. for s. who farms at Nemerae; XLI 2960.8.

4564 ---; s. of Syrus, s. of Apion; 114 or 133; property owner; Hermaeum qtr; bro. of Apion, Nilus now called Poleṃ[archus], Sarapion and Thais; *SB* VIII 9824.3.

4565 SYRUS; s. of Apion; ch. Apion, Nilus now called Poleṃ[archus], Syrus, Sarapion, Thais; Aug 114 or 133; property owner; Hermaeum qtr; *SB* VIII 9824.4.

4566 ---; s. of Pecysis; m. Heraclous; ii; landholder; *P. Erl.* 44 iii 32.

4567 ---; s. of Diodorus; m. Dionysia; ii; landholder; Shepherds' qtr; *P. Princ.* II 46.13.

4568 ---; ii; VII 1062.12.

4569 T[c. 9; d. of Chaeremon; ii; "sister" to Dionysius; Ariston sp.? or guardian?; may have children; XXXVI 2787.1.

4570 TA...; d. of Harpaesis alias Horus, s. of Thonis; sp. Eudaemon; ch. Thonis, Horus, Eudaemon; 126; Oxyrhynchite; Oxy.; sp. pastophorus at Mouchinor; III 491.4.

4571 T..AETE; sp. Panetbes; ch. Harmaeis; i - ii; *P. Harris* 72.27.

4572 T[.....]ESIUS; 98-117; joint agoranomus; Oxy.; *P. Sel.* 24.10.

4573 TẠ ...ṚṬ[..; ch. Apollonius?; i; property owner; Sarapeum qtr; owns part house; age 45; guardian is Apollonius, age 24; *P. Ryl.* II 156.[28], V.

4574 TAAGRELLSA; d. of Apellas; 60/61; Oxyrhynchite; Oxy.; property in Lycians' Camp qtr; unnamed sp.; II 250.15.

TAAMOIS; see DIONYSIA.

4575 ---; sp. Heraclas; c. 110-112; Oxyrhynchite; Oxy.; XXXVI 2758.9-10.

4576 TAAMOIS; d. of Zoilus; 124; Oxyrhynchite?; Oxy.?; addr. for s., cousin and guardian of Tastraton; III 490.3.

4577 ---; d. of Panemgeus, s. of Dioscorus; m. Tauris, d. of Horus; 132/133; property owner; Oxyrhynchite; minor; has share w. bro. Anteis and sister Tausoreus of unoccupied house in Hermaeum qtr; tutors Onnophris and Heras; *PSI* VIII 874 i 5.

4578 ---; sp. Horus; ch. Heras; 132/133; *PSI* VIII 874 i 4.

4579 ---; ii; III 530.28.

4580 ---; sp. Apollonius; ch. Ptolema; ii; Oxy.?; addr. for d.; *P. Mil.* II 51.3.

4581 TAANUPHIS; 81-96; VI 984 R fin.

4582 TAAPHYNCHIS; d. of Thonion; 94; landholder?; land mortgaged to her in Kleros of Demetrius in Seryphis; II 270.20.

4583 ---; d. of Saras; sp. Peteuris; ch. Paos; 116; Gymnasium St qtr; addr. for s., dec. tekton and pyraethes of Isis and other gods and enr. in this qtr; XII 1550.18.

4584 TAARCHORSIA; 21; livestock owner; reg. animals which pasture nr Pela, W. Top.; shepherd Petsiris; *P. Princ.* II 24.4.

4585 TAAREOTIS; sp. Apollonius; ch. Heracles; i - ii; *P. Harris* 72.28.

4586 TAARPAESIS; c. 1; IV 736.70.

4587 ---; Oct 98; property owner; house in South Quay qtr; *P. Genov.* II 62.13.

4588 ---; alias ISIDORA; d. of Apollonius, s. of Apollonius; m. Tsenamunis; sp. Psenesis alias Ision; ch. Ptolemaeus, Berenice, Isidora alias Apollonarion; Aug 133; land and property owner; Oxy.; guardian bro. Apollonius; house in South Quay qtr; land in Phoboou; age 59; gss. Ision and Psenis; signalement; illiterate; signs will in Pimpasi (or Pimpaui); *P. Köln* II 100.3 and passim.

4589 ---; d. of Pertax; sp. Horus; ch. Dionysius alias Papontos; 133; Oxyrhynchite; Oxy.; I 100.6.

4590 TAARIME; d. of M[- ; m. Thatres; sp. Pesouris; ii; Oxyrhynchite; III 647.[2], 18.

4591 TAARTHONIS; sp. Onnophris; ch. Onnophris; 96; Oxyrhynchite?; Oxy.?; addr. for s.; II 266.5.

4592 TABYNIS; ch. Hermogenes; 31/32; Sinary?, L. Top.; addr. for s.; *P. Mich. inv.* 69.7.

4593 TACHECYSIS; sp. Becis; ch. Horus; ii; Sento; addr. for s.; *P. Erl.* 44 iii 27.

4594 TACHNUMIS; sp. Papiris; ch. Totoes, Thoonis alias Alk.[..]?; Oct 112; Tanais, M. Top.; addr. for s.; XXII 2357.7.

4595 TACHOIS; d. of Dinchon; sp. Allous; ch. Psois; 31/32; landholder; Oxy.?; land at Pela; signalement; *P. Ryl.* II 159.3.

4596 TACOIS(?); 81-96; part owner, house in South Quay qtr; II 379 (descr.).

4597 [TA?]HERMAS; late i BC; Oxy.; XII 1479.12.

4598 TAIER[-]; ch. Papontos; July 87; addr. for s.; *PSI* III 203.3.

4599 TAL[...]APTAS; 14-37; Thmois. Top.?; doc. pr. Oxy.?; *P. Cornell* 54.6.

4600 TAMENNEUS; sp. Thoonis?; 6-35; property owner; Gooseherders' Lane qtr; property at above; II 256.[2], 5.

4601 TAMES.[...; i. Oxy.?; doc. pr. Oxy.?; age 40; guardian is Sarapion, age 48; *P. Ryl.* II 156, V.

4602 TAMMOTUS; sp. Horus; ch. Heracles; i - ii; *P. Harris* 72.22.

4603 TAMOCHUS; sp. Heraclammon; ch. Papontos; i - ii; *P. Harris* 72.1.

4604 ---; sp. Heracleius; ch. Pylades; i - ii; *P. Harris* 72.21.

4605 TAMONNES; sp. Agron; ch. Puoris; i - ii; *P. Harris* 72.15.

4606 TAMONOUS; d. of Harpaesis; sp. Horus; ch. Horus; Pakerke, M. Top.; doc. pr. Oxy.?; addr. for s.; *P. Harris* 138 i 21.

4607 TAMYSTHA; sp. Apollos; ch. Heracles; i - ii; *P. Harris* 72.7.

4608 TAN....IS; 2nd half i; *P. Oslo* III 130.7.

4609 TANAROOUS; sp. Adrastus; ch. Thamunion; 94; Oxyrhynchite; Oxy.; addr. for d., aged c. 50; I 73.11.

4610 TANECHOTARION alias EUTERPE; d. of Diogenes; sp. Apollonius; ch. Apollonius; Dec 134/Jan 135; Oxyrhynchite?; Oxy.?; addr. for s.; IV 726.6-7.

4611 TANECHOTES; s. of Horion; 83/84; landholder; Papsis?, Tychis Necotis; holds land there; II 290.15.

4612 TANEMEUS; sp. Tryphon; ch. Melas; i - ii; *P. Harris* 72.31.

4613 TANEN(TERIS); sp. Dioscorus; ch. Dioscorus; ii; Upper Parembole qtr; addr. for s.; *P. Princ.* II 46.8.

4614 TANURIS; sp. Panesneus; ch. Thaesis, Senpanesneus; 81-96; temple of Ares greatest god; age 30; VI 984 R init.

4615 TAO-; ch. Tausorapis; 98-117; Oxy.; *P. Sel.* 24.3.

4616 TAONNOPHRIS; 74/75; II 372 (descr.).

4617 ---; d. of Panesies; sp. Tryphon; ch. Heraclas; 91 or 107; Oxyrhynchite?; Oxy.?; addr. for s.; IV 722.22.

4618 ---; sp. Philon; ch. Eumoerus; ii; Oxy.; (1) I 115.1; (2) 116.1.

4619 TAONNOPHRIS; sp. Magrus; ch. Rhynchis; ii; hamlet of Sarapion, s. of Chaeremon; addr. for s.; *P. Erl.* 59 R 3.

4620 TAORSENUPHIS; sp. Panetbes; ch. Pnepheros; i - ii; *P. Harris* 72.26.

4621 TAORSE[US; Dec 75/Jan 76; Oxyrhynchite?; Oxy.?; addr. for unnamed s.; *P. Yale* 64.5.

4622 TAORSEUS; d. of Thompsemis, s. of Thoonis; sp. Onnophris; ch. Chaeremon; 86; Oxyrhynchite; Oxy.; husband (dec.) and s. reg. here; VII 1028.6.

4623 TAOS; 6-35; property owner; Oxy.; house in Gooseherders' Lane qtr; has guardian; II 256.4.

4624 TAOTOUS; (TAOS?); sp. Apollonius; ch. -]n; ii; Oxyrhynchite; addr. for s.; *SB* VI 9372.1.

4625 TAËOUCON(?); ii; "sister" of Horion; III 608 (descr.).

4626 TAPECYSIS; sp. Pecysis?; ii; doc. pr. Oxy.?; *PSI* VI 710.11.

4627 TAPETOURIS; sp. Papnoutis; ch. Paopetes; i - ii; *P. Harris* 72.19.

4628 TAPHIBIS; 81-96; VI 984 R fin.

4629 TAPONTOS; d. of Colluthus; sp. Petosiris; ch. Tausiris; i; Pakerke, M. Top.; doc. pr. Oxy.?; addr. for d.; *P. Harris* 138 i 20.

4630 ---; d. of Dionysius; sp. Papontos; ch. Papontos; i; Senepta, M. Top.; addr. for s.; *P. Harris* 138 i 12.

4631 ---; sp. Hermias; ch. Puoris, Puoris the younger; i - ii; *P. Harris* 72.16, 20.

4632 ---; d. of Pheremphis; Jan 121; property owner; Metroon qtr; joint owner w. sibs Apia and Dionytas; *P. Fouad* 30.12.

---; see DIOGENIS.

4633 TAPOTAMON; s. of Ptolemaeus, s. of Colylis; 95; landholder; farmer; land at Korobis in Menoetius' Kleros ceded to Diogenes, s. of Ptolemaeus; I 45.4-5.

4634 ---; sp. Comon; ch. Apollo; ii; Cretan qtr; addr. for s.; *P. Princ.* II 46.9.

4435 TAPSOBAIS; 81-96; VI 984 R fin.

4436 TAPSOIS; d. of Comon; sp. Diogenes; ch. Dionysius; Jan 90; Oxy.; *PSI* VIII 942.7.

4437 [TAPS?]OIS; d. of Paos, s. of Peteuris; sp. Harthonis; ch. Theon; gd. of Taaphynchis; 116; Thoeris St qtr; addr. for sp., dec., hierotekton of Thoeris, Isis, Sarapis and assoc. gods; XII 1550.5.

4638 TAPS[OIS?; d. of Paulus; sp. Petosiris; ch. Apollonides; 119; Oxy.; addr. for s.; XII 1547.19.

4639 TAPSOIS; ch. Horus; 133; Oxyrhynchite; Oxy.; addr. for s.; I 100.7.

4640 ---; ii; XXXVI 2787.6.

4641 TAPTICHI(S); 81-96; VI 984 R fin.

4642 TAPTOLLION; gd. of Ptollion; early ii; landholder; property owner; Phthocis, E. Top.; land there and at Posombus Aristomachu; age 35; *P. Wisc.* I 13.2 and passim.

4643 TAPTOLLOUS; d. of Caecili(us); c. 1; IV 736.55.

4644 TAREINUS; ch. Apollonis, Epimachus; ii; *P. Erl.* 44 iii 36.

4645 TAROU(THINAS?); ch. Thais; i BC; *PSI* I 64.1.

4646 TARUTHINUS; (1) Aug 79; (2) c. 79; agoranomus w. Themistocles and Philiscus; (1) II 380 (descr.); (2) 375 (descr.).

4647 TARUTILLIUS; 83/84; land distribution superintendent; see also I 165 (descr.) of 81; XII 1462 i [1], ii 22.

4648 ---; ch. Hermas; 119/120; Monimu, U. Top.; addr. for s.; *P. Wisc.* II 39.3.

4649 TASARAPION; ii; slave owner; s. is Sarapion alias Gaion; VIII 1149.6.

4650 TASENTHEUS; d. of Onnophris; 83/84; landholder; Tychis Necotis; land there; II 290.25.

4651 TASEUS; d. of Pausiris; m. Tecosis; 42/41 BC; slave owner; Oxyrhynchite; Oxy.; *PSI* V 549.5.

4652 ---; 6-35; Oxyrhynchite?; Gooseherders' Lane qtr; addr. for ch., sp. of Cronius; II 256.12.

4653 ---; d. of Pecysis, s. of Pecysis; 23; M. Top?; doc. pr. Oxy.?; illiterate; father guardian; *P. Princ.* III 141.1.

4654 ---; d. of Peteeus; sp. Petsiris; May 26; slave owner; Tanais, M. Top.; receives slave Thermutharion from Paapis; illiterate; signalement; *P. Rein.* II 103.2.

4655 ---; m. Tausorapis; sp. Amois; ch. Zois; Oct 62; Sesphtha?, L. Top.; XXVIII 2873 V 31.

4656 ---; d. of Heraclas; sp. Apollo..[..]; ch. Heraclas; March 66; bro. S .... is guardian; XLI 2971.1.

4657 ---; d. of Aphynchis; i; *P. Harris* 144.1.

4658 ---; sp. Onnophris; ch. Onnophris, Teos; 107; 10th qtr; addr. for sons; VII 1029.3.

4659 ---; ch. Peteaces; ii; Tanais, M. Top.; addr. for s.; XXXI 2572.2.

4660 TASIONYS; alias DIONYSIA; d. of Dionysius; Jan 121; property owner; Oxyrhynchite; Metroon qtr; owns property there w. Ammonius; guardian Demetrius; neighbour of Aria; *P. Fouad* 30.2.

4661 TASIS; sp. Horion; 19/20; property owner; Myrobalanus qtr; house in temple of Duo Adelphi; II 254.7.

4662 TASOOUE; sp. E.emothus; ch. Peneuaes; i - ii; *P. Harris* 72. 2.

4663 TASSEUOUS; ii; XLI 2981.23.

4664 TASTRATON; d. of Psenosiris, s. of Atreus; m. Penyris; gd. of Spocis; 124; property owner; Oxyrhynchite; Oxy.; prop. in Krietyris; married to cousin; illiterate; signalement; III 490.2.

4665 TATHOONAS; d. of Sarapion, s. of Ptollion; gd. of Thaesis; 48; Oasite nome; father dec.; Thaesis, aunt, trustee; *P. Fouad* 35.6.

4666 TATHOTIS; d. of Harpaesis; i; *P. Harris* 144.8.

4667 TATNAGOUS; sp. Panesneus (dec.?); ch. Senparaithis, Petarpochration (dec.); 81-96; temple of Ares greatest god?; VI 984 R init.

4668 TATREIPHIS; d. of Theon; sp. Harpaesis; ch. Theon; Oct 98; Oxyrhynchite; *P. Genov.* II 62.3.

4669 TATRIPHIS; d. of Amois; sp. Plution; ch. Diodorus; 127/128; Oxyrhynchite; Gymnasium St qtr; addr. for sp.; XII 1452 i 5.

4670 TAUEPHA[; d. of Psenamunis; ch. Psenamunis; c. 92; Tacona, L. Top.; addr. for s.; *P. Michael* 9.7.

4671 TAUPHOIS; 81-96; VI 984 R fin.

4672 TAURINUS; c. 1; IV 799 (descr.).

4673 ---; late i; camel driver; II 300.4.

4674 TAURIS; d. of Apollonius, s. of Menches; July 64; property owner; Oxyrhynchite; Knights' Camp qtr; *P. Mich.* III 179.3.

4675 ---; d. of Heniochus; sp. Promachus; ch. Ariston, Amyntas, Heniochus; Aug 72(?); Oxyrhynchite?; Oxy.?; addr. for s.; XLI 2972.6.

4676 ---; sp. Cephalon; ch. Faustus; 129; Oxyrhynchite?; Oxy.?; addr. for s.; *P. Cornell* 46.3.

4677 ---; d. of Horus; sp. Panemgeus; ch. Anteis, Taamois, Tausoreus; 132/133; Oxyrhynchite; Oxy.; sp. owned property in Hermaeum qtr; *PSI* VIII 874 i 7.

4678 ---; sp. Amois; ch. Apollonius; ii; Oxyrhynchite?; Oxy.?; addr. for s.; III 498.5.

4679 TAURIS (TAURUS?); s. of Harbichis; 19/20; property owner; Myrobalanus qtr; part house in temple of Duo Adelphi; II 254.7.

4680 TAUSARAPIS; d. of Petosorapis; sp. Harpocration; ch. Dionysius; 94; Oxyrhynchite; Oxy.; addr. for s.; I 73.18.

4681 TAUSIRIS; d. of Papontos; 55; property owner; Oxyrhynchite; Oxy.; house west of Temgenuthis qtr; I 99.9.

4682 ---; d. of Petosiris; m. Tapontos, d. of Colluthus; i; landholder; Pakerke, M. Top.; doc. pr. Oxy.?; cedes land to Horus, s. of Horus; *P. Harris* 138 i 19.

4683 ---; alias THALLOUS; sp. Diogenes alias Heracleides; ch. Heracleides; 89-97; Oxy.; addr. for ggd. Dionysia and Herais; II 274.50-51.

4684 ---; 101; Psobthis, E. Top.; addr. for unnamed d.; III 510.2.

4685 ---; sp. Pecysis; ch. Thaesis; c. 107-112; North St qtr; *PSI* V 450 R i 9.

4686 ---; alias SARAPOUS; sp. Sarapion; ch. Heraclous; 130; Ibion Ammonii; addr. for gs. Horion alias Theon; III 492.3.

4687 ---; sp. Pecysis; ch. Carousis; ii; *P. Erl.* 44 iii 33.

4688 TAUSORAPIS; d. of Comon; 52/53; landowner; lessor; leases to Plutas land nr Seryphis, W. Top., from Kleros of Sisines and from that of Nicanor; bro. and guardian Pecysis; *PSI* IX 1029.1.

4689 ---; ch. Taseus; Oct 62; Sesphtha?, L. Top.; addr. for gd. Zois; XXXVIII 2873 V 32.

4690 ---; d. of Areionis; sp. Narcissus; ch. Theon; 71; Oxyrhynchite; Oxy.; addr. for s.; *P. Med. inv.* 71.70.9.

4691 ---; d. of Harthoonis; sp. Harpaesis; ch. Apis; 77; Oxy.; addr. for s., priest of Thoeris, Isis, Sarapis and assoc. gods; II 242.4.

4692 ---; d. of Tao( ); sp. Thoonis; ch. Sinthoonis, Harthoonis; 98-117; Oxyrhynchite?; Oxy.?; addr. for children, priest and priestess; *P. Sel.* 24.3.

4693 TAUSOREUS; d. of Panemgeus, s. of Dioscorus; m. Tauris, d. of Horus; sp. Poccaous; 132/133; property owner; Oxyrhynchite; owns w. bro. Anteis and sister Taamois property in Hermaeum qtr; *PSI* VIII 574 i 6.

4694 TAUTOSIRIS; d. of Thoonis, s. of Ammonius; Aug 106; Oxyrhynchite; Oxy.; s. aged 13 reg. in 10th qtr; Tautoris in text; *P. Wisc.* I 17.6-7.

4695 TBECIS; d. of Hierax, s. of Thoonis; 81-96; property owner; Oxyrhynchite; Sarapis St qtr; mortgaged house to Thoonis, s. of Thoonis; VIII 1105.14.

4696 ---; sp. Heracleides; ii; *P. Inst. Fran.* III 5.10.

4697 TBES...; i BC - i; *OD Pisa* 22.5.

4698 TCALES; ch. Monthis; i BC - i; *OD Pisa* 779 + 242 Concavo 4.

4699 ---; ch. * Psenpsenyris; (1) i BC - i; (2) i; ch.'s name Psenyris in 1; (1) *OD Pisa* 106.3; (2) 129 X + 6.

4700 TE( ); ch. Sarapion; Nov 42 BC; Oxy.; addr. for s.; *P. Ryl.* IV 582.22.

4701 TE..ICOS.CUS?; 68; XIV 1641.24.

4702 TEAIPSIS; 81-96; VI 984 R fin.

4703 TEAROUS; ch. Sarapion; 132/133; unnamed ch. reg. in Pammenes' Garden qtr; *PSI* I 53 xi 184.

4704 TECHONSIS; sp. Pnepheros; ch. Harmiysis; i - ii; *P. Harris* 72.5.

4705 TECHOSOUS; 98-117; slave; IV 809 (descr.).

4706 TECOSIS; sp. Pausiris; ch. Taseus; 42/41 BC; Oxyrhynchite; Oxy.; addr. for d.; *PSI* V 549.5.

4707 ---; sp. Apollonius; ch. Amois; Nov 83; Oxyrhynchite?; Oxy.?; addr. for s.; X 1282.10.

4708 ---; d. of Petosorapis; m. Heras, d. of Heracleides; sp. Paapis; ch. Thompachrates; Nov 83; Oxyrhynchite?; Oxy.; addr. for s.; X 1282.8.

4709 ---; d. of Thonis, s. of Petosorapis; m. Eseneus; sp. Amois; Nov 83; Oxyrhynchite; Oxy.; sp. guardian; X 1282.11.

4710 ---; d. of Harthoonis, s. of Ptolemaeus; ch. Diogenes; 109; Oxyrhynchite?; Oxy.?; addr. for s.; III 482.24-25.

4711 ---; sp. Dropides; ch. Heras; 137; Oxyrhynchite; Oxy.; addr. for s.; *PSI* XII 1262 iii 2.

4712 TEENCEGOUS; ii; sp. Pecysis; ch. Sinthonis, Pachnubis; ii; Tanais, M. Top.; addr. for d.; III 505.3.

4713 TEIRON; (1) 42/43; (2) 61; bibliophylax w. Bacchius; (1) *PSI* XII 1235.6; (2) *SB* XII 10788.1.

4714 TELESPHORUS; Oct 111; slave; formerly of Ti. Julius Theon, now of his gs., Ti. Julius Theon, games victor; XLIV 3197.14.

4715 ---; Oct 111; slave; repairer; formerly of Ti. Julius Theon, now of his s., Ti. Julius Sarapion; XLIV 3197.10.

4716 TEMBIUS; sp. Pnepheros; ch. Papnoutis; i - ii; *P. Harris* 72.18.

4717 TENIS; d. of Pausiris; i BC - i; agent for Cathytes; *OD Pisa* 477 Convesso 2.

4718 TENIS(?); ch. Psenchonsis; i BC - i; *OD Pisa* 117.3.

4719 ---; d. of Psenthotes; i BC - i; *OD Pisa* 532 X + 7.

4720 TENIS; d. of Horus; i BC - i; *OD Pisa* 243 + 472 i 4, 12.

4721 TEON; s. of Nechthenibis; 107; farmer; lessee; Episemon, U. Top.; illiterate; XVIII 2188.17.

4722 TEOS; 16/15 BC; taxpayer; IV 832 (descr.) ii.

4723 ---; ch. Petechonsis; (1) April 5 BC; (2) i BC - i; ch.'s name Psenpetechonsis in 2; (1) *OD Pisa* 936 Concavo 1; (2) 25 ii 2.

4724 ---; April 5 BC; *OD Pisa* 936 Convesso 11, 13.

4725 ---; 5/4 BC; joint landholder; W. Top.; land there; *P. Oslo* II 26.29.

4726 ---; i BC; *OD Pisa* 323 X + 8.

4727 ---; ch. Petosiris; i BC - i; *OD Pisa* 532 X + 2.

4728 ---; s. of Haryotes; i BC - i; *OD Pisa* 668.3.

4729 ---; i BC - i; called the elder; *OD Pisa* 137 Concavo 3.

4730 ---; s. of Harimuthes; i BC - i; *OD Pisa* 228 X + 3, X + 12.

4731 ---; i BC - i; *OD Pisa* 232.1, 6.

4732 ---; i BC - i; *OD Pisa* 106.6.

4733 ---; s. of Harpaesis; i BC - i; *OD Pisa* 477 Convesso 7.

4734 ---; s. of Petechonsis; i BC - i; *OD Pisa* 290 + 290A Concavo X + 3.

4735 ---; alias SARAPION; 31/32; tax collector?; Sinary, L. Top.; *P. Mich. inv.* 69.17.

4736 ---; ch. Sois; Sept 73; XLIV 3164.13.

4737 ---; s. of Centaurus; sp. Apia; ch. Diogas, Publius; Oct 80; Oxyrhynchite?; Oxy.?; addr. for sons who own property in Pammenes' Garden qtr; III 249.2.

4738 ---; ch. Petearpebecis; c. 81-86; Senocomis?, W. Top.; addr. for gs. Teos; I 47.7.

4739 ---; s. of Petearpebecis, s. of Teos; c. 81-86; priest of Thoeris, Isis, Sarapis and assoc. gods; landholder; Senocomis, W. Top.; land there in Kleros of Zenodorus ceded to him from Didymus alias Amoitas; I 47.6.

4740 ---; i; *OD Pisa* 129 X + 8.

4741 ---; ch. Thonis; i; s. is pastophorus; *P. Oslo* III 143.2.

4742 ---; s. of Onnophris, s. of Teos; m. Taseus; 107; hieroglyph carver; Oxyrhynchite; 10th qtr; only 5 h. carvers in Oxy.; called neoteros; VII 1029.2, 12.

4743 ---; ch. Onnophris; 107; Oxyrhynchite; 10th qtr; addr. for gs. Teos and Onnophris; VII 1029.2.

4744 ---; ch. Herais; Aug 133; Oxyrhynchite; ch. formerly owned part house in South St qtr; *P. Köln* II 100.12.

4745 TEOS; c. 138 (n.d.); hierotekton of Athena Thoeris, w. Thonis; Oxyrhynchite; Oxy.; III 579 (descr.).

4746 TEOS?; ii?; Senocomis, W. Top.; unnamed ch.; *P. Fuad I Univ.* 32.5.

4747 TERAUS; alias THAUBASTIS; d. of Phatres; ch. Hatres; 96; Oxyrhynchite; Knights' Camp qtr; addr. for s.; I 104.6-7.

4748 TERECHA( ); 81-96; VI 984 R fin.

4749 TERENTIUS; s. of Diogenes, s. of Miccalus; m. Thaesis; sp. Thaesis; ch. Amois; 148/149; Oxyrhynchite, gymnasial class; Upper Camp qtr; reg s. in g. class of 13 yr olds in above distr. this yr; XLVI 3278.1.

4750 TEREUS; sp. Sisyphis; 81-96; s. is pastophorus of Apollo; VI 984 R (2).

4751 ---; d. of Ptolem[ ]; m. Sinthonis; 81/82; Oxyrhynchite; cares for foundling Theanous; sp. in gs. of Chareis; *P. Mert.* III 118.10.

4752 TERO[.]O[ ]; ch. -chus; 83/84; Alex.; s. cedes catoecic land in Sinary, L. Top.; XII 1462.20.

4753 TEROS; d. of Gaius; 132/133; unnamed ch.; age 40; *PSI* I 53 i 12.

4754 TERPNUS; Oct 111; slave; formerly of Ti. Julius Theon, now of his s., Ti. Julius Theon, ex-strategus and archidikast; XLIV 3197.7.

4755 TESAURIS; sp. Onnophris; ch. Asclas, Osmolchis; 107; Oxyrhynchite?; 10th qtr?; addr. for ss.; VII 1029.4.

4756 TESEURIS; d. of Apion; 64; property owner; doc. pr. Oxy.?; owns w. nephew L. Pompeius Niger, quarter house in Hermaeum qtr inherited from bro. Syrus; *SB* XII 10788.60.

4757 ---; d. of Petosorapis; sp. Dionysius; ch. Thermuthion; 77; Oxyrhynchite; Oxy.; II 242.24.

4758 TETEO(US) or TETOEO(US); d. of Eudaemon; sp. Thoonis; ch. Thoonis, Eudaemon, Didymus?; 93; II 289 i 3 and passim.

4759 TETEORIS; d. of P ...; Dec 81; property owner; Oxyrhynchite; Oxy.; descr. as Persian; s. guardian; XII 1471.6-7.

4760 TETEURIS; sp. Pausirion; ch. Heras; Sept 109; Psobthis, M. Top.; addr. for s.; *PSI* IX 1030.3.

4761 TETHEUS; sp. Dieuches; ch. Panouphis; 131; Talao, L. Top.; addr. for s.; *SB* VI 9190.6.

4762 ---; ch. Dionytas and Theonas (1), Dionysius (2); (1) early ii; (2) ii; accom. by Dionytas and Theon (2); (1) XII 1481.1 and V; (2) III 530.1.

4763 TETOEUS; d. of Thoonas, d. of Petosiris; m. Thaisous, d. of Papontos; sp. Petosiris; ch. Ti[ ]; 119; landowner; Oxyrhynchite; North St qtr; sister of Petosiris and Papontos; XII 1547.7.

4764 THACORIS; d. of Amenneus; sp. Amenneus; ch. Artemidorus; ii; Oxyrhynchite; Oxy.; addr. for s.; III 505.1.

TETOEO(US); see TETEO(US).

4765 TEUPHOUS; 81-96; Oxy.; VI 984 R fin.

4766 TH[ ]; 54-68; livestock owner; Toka, M. Top.; livestock now owned by Philumen[us/e]; *P. Inst. Fran.* I 21.7.

4767 TH[ ]; sp. Arsinoe; ch. Apollophanes; Jan 93; Alex.? Neocosmius, Genearcheius?; tribe and deme for s., to whom ceded catoecic land nr Sinary; *PSI* VIII 897.61.

4768 THAECHMERE(?); 19/20; property owner; Myrobalanus qtr; part house in temple of Duo Adelphi; II 254.8-9.

4769 THAES(?); 135/136; landholder; Talao, L. Top.; *P. Iand.* VII 136.13.

4770 THAESION; ii; doc. pr. Oxy.?; unnamed children; greeted by Heracleides; *SB* VI 9025.29.

4771 THAESIS; c. 1; IV 736.68.

4772 ---; d. of Horus; ch. Philadelphus; c. 45-47; Little Oasis; enslaved for insolvency?; another unnamed s.; XLII 3033.2.

4773 ---; d. of Heracleius; sp. Ptollion; ch. Sarapion dec.; 48; gd. Tathoonas; money owing in Oxy., Oasite and Ars. nomes; *P. Fouad* 35.[2] and passim.

4774 ---; d. of Heracleius; sp. Sarapion; ch. Petsiris; 48; *P. Fouad* 35.2.

4775 ---; d. of Besas; sp. Aperos; Dec 75/Jan 76; Oxyrhynchite; Oxy.; *P. Yale* 64.3.

4776 ---; sp. Harthoonis; ch. Cephalon; 77; Oxyrhynchite; Oxy.; II 242.27.

4777 ---; 82; unnamed ch.; Oxy.?; II 286.10.

4778 ---; d. of Panesneus; m. Tanouris; 81-96; temple of greatest god Ares; age 6; VI 984 R init.

4779 ---; d. of Thonis, s. of Amithonis; m. Sintheus; sp. Petosarapis (divorced); 96; Oxyrhynchite; Oxy.; II 266.3.

4780 ---; d. of Diogenes, s. of Thonis; m. Zois, d. of Antipater; sp. Heron; 98-102; Oxyrhynchite; Oxy.; Soter, s. of Soter is guardian; *P. Mert.* I 13.2.

4781 THA[ESIS?]; d. of Horus; sp. Heras; ch. Heras; 99; Oxyrhynchite; *P. Princ.* II 32.2.

4782 THAESIS; alias ISIS; end i; slave; age c. 18; *P. Sel.* 23.15.

4783 ---; sp. Monius; ch. Haryotes; i - ii; *P. Harris* 72.30.

4784 ---; sp. Erion; ch. Harpaesis; i - ii; *P. Harris* 72.3.

4785 THAESIS; d. of Pecysis; m. Tausiris, d. of Diogenes; c. 107-112; North St qtr; *PSI* V 450 R i 21-22.

4786 ---; sp. Pachnubis; ch. Totoes alias Plutarchus, Pachnubis; Oct 112; Tanais, M. Top.; addr. for sons; XXII 2351.6.

---; see THAISOUS.

4787 ---; m. (or owner) Tho..( ); 119; slave; North St qtr; age c. 30; XII 1547.27.

4788 ---; sp. Thonasychis; ch. Eudaemon; 126; Oxyrhynchite?; Oxy.; addr. for s.; III 491.2.

4789 ---; sp. Dionysius; ch. Dionysius; Aug 127; Lenon, nr Pela; addr. for s.; *P. Oxy. inv.?* 3.

4790 ---; sp. Thompecysis; ch. Horus; Jan 139; property owner; Oxyrhynchite; South St qtr; unnamed g. sons; *P. Oslo* III 105.4.

4791 ---; d. of Posidonius; sp. Diogenes; ch. Terentius; 148/149; Oxyrhynchite, gymnasial class; Upper Camp qtr; addr. for s.; XLVI 3278.3.

4792 ---; d. of Ptolemaeus; sp. Terentius; ch. Amois; 148/149; Oxyrhynchite, gymnasial class; Upper Camp qtr; s. reg. in g. class in above distr. this yr; XLVI 3278.9.

4793 ---; d. of Didymus; sp. Theon; ch. Pausiris; 148/149; Oxyrhynchite, gymnasial class; Knights' Camp qtr; s. reg. in g. class in above distr. this yr; XLVI 3283.7.

---; see THAISOUS.

4794 ---; sp. Heracleus; ch. Cephalion; ii; Talao, L. Top.; addr. for s.; XXXI 2573.2.

4795 ---; ii; XXXI 2594.16.

4796 ---; sp. Plution; ch. Plution; ii; Oxy.?; addr. for s.; *P. Mil.* II 51.1.

4797 ---; ii; Isieum; sister of Sarapammon; XII 1488.1-2 V.

4798 ---; d. of Tarou(thinas?); i BC; sp. is a s. of Hermogenes; *PSI* I 64.1.

4799 THAIS; 24/25; livestock owner; Talao; II 350 (descr.).

4800 ---; d. of Amenneus; sp. Thoonis; 41-54; property owner; Oxyrhynchite?; Oxy.; house in Sarapeum, st. of Ax...; age c. 32; XXXIV 2720.2.

4801 ---; d. of Diodorus, s. of Diodorus; m. Saraeus, d. of Leonides; gd. of Isidora; March 97; landholder; Oxyrhynchite; Oxy.; inherited m.'s land in Nesla and Peeno; sister to Leonides and Diodorus; IV 713.22.

4802 THAIṢ[ ]; i; *P. Med. inv.* 69.09.3.

4803 THAIS; d. of Syrus, s. of Apion; Aug 114 or 133; property owner; Hermaeum qtr; sister of Apion, Nilus now called Polemạ[archus], Syrus and Sarapion; *SB* VIII 9824.10.

4804 ---; sp. Theon (?); ch. -on; 124; Oxyrhynchite?; Oxy.?; addr. for s.; III 490.21.

4805 ---; d. of Sarapion; sp. Sarapion; m. Heraclous; ch. Sarapion; 127; slave owner; Oxyrhynchite; Oxy.; unnamed s. guardian; III 496.2, 5.

4806 ---; d. of Sarapion, s. of Sarapion; sp. Sarapion (married 127); gd. of Thais; 127; Oxyrhynchite; Oxy.; III 496.2.

4807 ---; d. of Chaeremon; sp. Heliodorus; ch. Apollonius; Nov 129; Oxyrhynchite?; Oxy.?; addr. for s.; VII 1024.15.

4808 ---; ii; Coptos resident?; unnamed d.; *P. Wurz.* 21 Rb 15.

4809 THAISAS; d. of Ptolemaeus; ch. [..].[..]as; 78/79; Oxyrhynchite?; Oxy?; addr. for d.; XXXVI 2756.4.

---; see LUCIA.

4810 THAISOUS; d. of Theonas; m. Syras; c. 35; II 295.1.

4811 ---; d. of Demetrius; sp. Achilleus; ch. Sarapion, Thermuthion; (1) Mar/Apr 66; (2) 91/92; Oxyrhynchite; Oxy.; addr. for d.; (1) *PSI* VIII 871.30; (2) XXXVIII 2856.13.

4812 ---; m. Zois, d. of -ius; sp. Heracleides; 89; hamlet of Vestinus?; w. unnamed guardian and sp. borrows from Gaius; *P. Fouad* 48.7.

4813 ---; i; II 298.12.

4814 ---; sp. Theon; late i; II 300.1.

4815 ---; d. of Epimachus; ch. Alexandrus; end i; addr. for s.; *P. Sel.* 23.9.

4816 ---; alias THAESIS; d. of Heracleides, s. of Olympus; m. Heracleia; sp. Epicrates alias Apion; ch. Aphroditous alias Demarous; 100 or 119; landholder?; Heracleopolis; land at Psobthis?; d. in Oxy.; age 45; signalement; III 504.[4], 33.

4817 ---; alias THAESIS; 115/116; slave; of Nicanor and Diogenes; I 97.11.

4818 ---; d. of Papo(ntos); sp. Thoonas; ch. Papontos, Tetoeus, Petosiris; 119; North St qtr; addr. for children; XII 1547.22.

4819 ---; ch. Sarapion; ii; Pammenes' Garden qtr; addr. for s.; III 505.8.

4820 ---; ii; descr. as "the little" one; III 530.26.

4821 ---; sp. Harbichis; ch. Pecysis; ii; Antipera; addr. for s.; *P. Erl.* 44 ii 6.

4822 ---; ch. -ius; ii; *P. Erl.* 44 ii 15.

4823 THAI(SOUS); ii; Antipera; addr. for unnamed s.; *P. Erl.* 44 ii 19.

THALLOUS; see TAUSIRIS.

4824 THALLOUSA; 81-96; V 984 R fin.

4825 THALLUS; ch. Theodous; after 102; Oxyrhynchite; Oxy.; addr. for d.; III 636.18.

4826 THAMOU[....; after 79; may not be Oxy.; rep. for Thauetion; XXXVI 2757 ii 3.

4827 THAMUNION (= THAMUNIS); d. of Onnophris; sp. Dionysius; ch. Thoonis, Tryphon, Onnophris; (1) 25; (2) 36; (3) 37; (4) Jan 44; (5) 55; (6) Sept 66; property owner; Oxyrhynchite; Hippodrome qtr (1), Temgenuthis qtr (4); Tryphon aged 3 in 41 Augustus, Thoonis aged 1 in 42 Aug. (1); guardian is unnamed s. of -eros (3); illiterate; age 58 (4); Thoonis reg. in T. qtr (4); owns house north of T. qtr; (1) II 288.39; (2) 322.[1], 5; (3) 319.[1]; (4) 251.3; (5) I 99.3; (6) II 275.2.

4828 ---; i; Oxy.; age 20; signalement; *P. Ryl.* II 156.[31], 37.

4829 ---; d. of Adrastus; sp. Dionysius; m. Tanaroous; 94; slave owner; Oxyrhynchite; Oxy.; age c. 50; signalement; I 73.10.

4830 THARION; 81-96; VI 984 R fin.

4831 THASARION; ii?; *P. Harris* 104.13.

4832 THATRES; d. of Theon; sp. Zoilus; ch. Plutarchus; i; hamlet of Nomus; addr. for s.; *P. Harris* 138 i 2.

4833 ---; sp. Epimachus; ch. Sepsarion, Dionysius, Harsiesis; 118; Oxyrhynchite; Oxy.; addr. for d. Sepsarion; III 503.4.

4834 ---; sp. Dionysius; ch. Epimachus, Petosiris; 118; Oxyrhynchite; Oxy.; addr. for sons; III 503.3.

4835 ---; d. of Ammonius, s. of Sarapion; m. Tsenthotumis; 130; property and slave owner; Knights' Camp qtr, formerly of Isieum Tryphonos, L. Top.; age 73; signalement; III 492.2 and passim.

4836 ---; sp. Pnepheros; 148/149; Oxyrhynchite, gymnasial class; unnamed s. enr. in g. class this yr; XLVI 3280.3.

4837 ---; sp. M[ ]; ch. Taarime; ii; Oxyrhynchite; Oxy.; III 647.3.

4838 ---; ch. Totoes; ii; slave; doc. pr. Oxy.?; slave of Pecysis, s. of Totoes; *PSI* VI 710.13.

4839 THAUBARION; d. of Theon?, s. of Sarapion; sp. (also bro.) Ammonius; ch. Nilammon; 132/133; Alex., Proapposebasteius?, Althaieus?; Oxy.; dec.; addr. for s.; III 477.14.

THAUBASTIS; see TERAUS.

4840 THAUETION; after 79; plaintiff, w. Thamoụ[. as rep.; Oxyrhynchite?; XXXVI 2757 ii 3.

4841 THEADETUS; ch. -]on; ii; Oxy.; XII 1536.4.

4842 THEAGENES; 122/123; sitologus of Sinkepha distr. and ? of Phoboou; *P. Lips.* 116.1, 10.

4843 THEANOUS; 81/82; slave; Oxy.; *P. Mert.* III 118.16.

4844 CLAUDIA THEANOUS; sp. Ti. Claudius Alexandrus; ch. Ti. Claudius Ptolemaeus; May 134; freedwoman of Ti.?; Roman; Oxy.; XXXVIII 2857.2.

4845 THED(ETUS); s. of Jacobus; 93; landholder; land at Enteiis, Athychis, Po[ ] (U. Top.); (1) *P. Princ.* II 42 V ii 19, 21, iii 32.

4846 TH]EGENIUS?; ii?; Alexandria?; doc. pr. Oxy.?; family arrives in Oxy. from Alex., name restored in *BL* III; *P. Harris* 103.1.

4847 THEMISTOCLES; July/Aug 67; Alex., ?tribe, Eileithyius; may be same as in II 373 (descr.); II 377 (descr.).

4848 ---; 74; farmer?; lessee?; XIV 1661.5.

4849 ---; (1) Aug 79; (2) c. 79; agoranomus w. Taruthinus and Philiscus; (1) II 380 (descr.); 375 (descr.).

4850 ---; 79/80; Alex., Caesareius; guardian of Apollonia; II 373 (descr.).

4851 ---; gs. of Philumene; June 118; he and Heron deny claims of Diogenes that gm. owed money; *PSI* IV 281 R i 44.

4852 THE]NAMUNIS; ch. Demetrous; 37; Oxy.; accused of assault on Saraeus; name may be Psenamunis; II 315.8.

4853 THEO..( ); early i; II 389 (descr.).

4854 THEODORUS; c. 1; IV 736.33.

4855 ---; n.d.; *SB* I 1938(g).

4856 THEODOTUS; n.d.; *SB* I 1986(b).

4857 THE[OD]OUS; d. of Thallus; sp. Pausiris; after 102; property owner; Oxy.; owns part house in Temgenuthis qtr w. sp.; III 636.18.

4858 THEOG[ENES; ch. Theogenes; 44/45; Nesla, U. Top.; addr. for s.; II 279.2.

4859 THEOGENES; s. of Theog[enes; 44/45; farmer; lessee; Nesla, U. Top.; leases domain land there; II 279.2.

4860 ---; ch. Theogenes; April 70; *P. Osy. inv.* 50.4B.24B(3-4)5.

4861 ---; s. of Theogenes; April 70; dike overseer; M. Top.; replaced by Diogenes; *P. Oxy. inv.* 50.4B.24B(3-4)5.

4862 THEOGENES; gs. of Diogenes; m. Isidora, d. of Ptolemaeus and Ptolema; 94/95; Oxyrhynchite, gymnasial class; Heracles Place qtr; age 13; II 257.7.

4863 ---; s. of Philiscus; m. Sinthoonis, d. of Achilleus; ch. Diogenes; 94/95; Oxyrhynchite, gymnasial class; Heracles Place qtr; in graphe of 4/5; II 257.1-2 and passim.

4864 ---; ch. Diogenes; 2nd half i; Sesphtha (or Psenosiris), L. Top.; addr. for s.; XXXVIII 2845.15.

4865 ---; ch. Saras, Theogenes; Aug 123; Phoboou distr.?, E. Top.; addr. for ss.?; XXXVIII 2863.6.

4866 ---; s. of Theogenes; Aug 123; Phoboou distr.?, E. Top.; XXXVIII 2863.5.

4867 THEOLYMPION; d. of Neoptolemus; sp. Dionysius; ch. Hermaeus alias Hermaeon; 117; Oxyrhynchite?; Oxy.?; addr. for s.; *P. Harris* 85.5.

4868 THEON; ch. Theon alias Thoonis; 73 or 44 BC; Oxy.?; addr. for s.; XIV 1639.2.

4869 ---; alias THOONIS; s. of Theon; 73 or 44 BC; soldier?; Oxy.?; descr. as of the catoecic cavalry; XIV 1639.2.

4870 ---; ch. Theon; July 44 BC; Oxyrhynchite; Cleopatra Aphrodite St; addr. for s.; XIV 1629.5.

4871 ---; s. of Theon; July 44 BC; landholder; lessor; soldier (catoecic cavalry); Oxyrhynchite; Cleopatra Aphrodite St; land at Paimis; XIV 1629.4.

4872 -; alias THEON; Sept 31 BC; syngenes and strategus; *P. Wurz.* 5.1.

4873 THEON; 30 BC - 14; XLIV 3208.1.

4874 ---; s. of Ischyrion; 22 BC; house owner; VII 1061 V.

4875 ---; s. of Sarapion; 5/4 BC; landholder; W. Top.; land there; *P. Oslo* II 26.22.

4876 ---; ch. Demetrius; Oct 4 BC; s. lessor; *SB* XII i 10942.38.

4877 ---; i BC; Oxy.; *PSI* IX 1079.3.

4878 ---; c. 1; IV 799 (descr.).

4879 ---; 16; "brother" of Heracleides, basilicogrammateus; IV 746.1.

4880 ---; 18; in charge of reg. of land grants; bro. Eudaemon appointee; *PSI* IV 320.8.

4881 ---; s. of Ammonius; (1) 19; (2) May 23; Oxyrhynchite; Temgenuthis qtr; part owner house there; descr. as the younger (1), as Persian of Epigone (2); (1) II 253.21; (2) 259.2.

4882 THEON; 19/20; topogrammateus, comogrammateus w. Eutychides; Oxy.; (1) II 252.1; (2) 254.1.

4883 ---; ch. Syra; 20-50; property owner; dated by association w. Heracleides archidikast in l. 1; II 281.5.

4884 ---; c. 25; "brother" of Heracleides; II 292.1.

4885 ---; ch. Heracleides; May 26; *P. Rein.* II 103.36.

4886 ---; ch. Dionysius; Oct 26; s. owns land at Isieum Tryphonos; VIII 1124.22.

4887 ---; s. of Ptolemaeus; Jan 29; livestock owner; Pela, W. Top.; XXXVIII 2850.2.

4888 ---; ch. Apollos; 30; X 1291.11.

4889 ---; (1) 33/34; (2) 40/41; toparch; II 354 (descr.); (2) 355 (descr.).

4890 ---; s. of Paaesis; 36; writes for Onnophris, s. of Antipater; II 267.29.

4891 ---; 41-79; eisagogeus; XLII 3062.15.

4892 ---; 41-79; strategus; Panopolis; XLII 3062.17.

4893 ---; July 44; sitologus; Pela, W. Top.; XII 1447.2.

4894 ---; s. of Panechotes; 44/45; unnamed sons farmed crown land at Nesla, U. Top.; II 279.8.

4895 ---; s. of Ptollion; ch. Ptollion; after 45-47; XLII 3033 V 2.

4896 ---; 48; appointee of agoranomi (in assoc. w. -atus); *P. Fouad* 35.16.

4897 ---; 49; advocate?; Oxy.; I 37.27.

4898 ---; s. of Eudaemon; July 50; landholder; Tholthis, Thmois. Top.; former part owner of Kleros of Pyrrhias; XXXVIII 2836.10.

4899 ---; ch. Sarapion; 50; Oxyrhynchite; Gymnasium St qtr; addr. for s.; II 285.2.

4900 ---; c. 50; IV 709 V.

4901 ---; s. of Antiochus; sp. Demetria; 55; Alex., Auximetoreius, Leneius; Oxy.; guardian of Demetria, sp.'s gm.; II 261.5.

4902 ---; June 56; Oxy.; II 310.3.

4903 ---; ch. Theon, Zoilus; Aug 57; Oxy.; X 1316 (descr.).

4904 ---; s. of Theon; Aug 57; Oxy.; bro. of Zoilus; X 1316 (descr.).

4905 ---; s. of Syrus; 57; agent for banker Archibius; Oxy.?; II 269.22.

4906 THEON; ch. Epinicius; (1) Sept 58; (2) Oct 62; Oxyrhynchite?; Hermaeum qtr; addr. for s., a master carver; (1) *P. Mich.* III 171.5; (2) 172.13.

4907 ---; s. of Onnophris; (1) July 59; (2) 66-72-73; hyperetes of strategus (Ammonius, 1; Ti. Claudius Herodes, 2); Oxy.; (1) II 260.19; (2) IX 1203 + *SB* IV 7339.31.

4908 ---; Oct 62; tax farmer (weavers' tax); Oxy.; *P. Mich.* 172.1.

4909 TI. CLAUDIUS THEON; s. of Ti. Claudius Sarapion; (1) Oct 62; (2) 83/84; (3) May 89; (4) 101; ex-gymnasiarch and ex-agoranomus of Alex. (3); landholder; lessee; Roman; land at Sesphtha, L. Top. (1), at Tychis Necotis (2), and formerly at Psobthis, E. Top. (4); leases estate of Seneca (1, 3); on possible identification of these 4, see XLII 3051, intro. and n. 1; (1) XXXVIII 2873.5; (2) II 290.29; (3) XLII 3051.1; (4) III 510.16.

4910 ---; (1) July 64; (2) 64; bibliophylax w. Sarapion; Oxy.; (1) *P. Mich* III 179.2; (2) *SB* XII 10788.46.

4911 ---; ch. Theon; Sept 66; Temenuthis distr.; addr. for gs. Theon; called the younger; *CPR* V ii 1.5.

4912 ---; s. of Theon; sp. Isis; ch. Theon; Sept 66; Temenuthis distr.; addr. for s.; *CPR* V ii 1.4.

4913 ---; s. of Theon, s. of Theon; m. Isis, d. of Diogenes; Sept 66; Temenuthis distr.; *CPR* V ii 1.4.

4914 ---; ch. Ophelous; Sept 66; Oxyrhynchite; Oxy.; addr. for mat. gs. Ptolemaeus; II 275.5.

4915 ---; s. of Aristandrus; 66-72/73; Oxyrhynchite; Oxy.; father had property in Senepta; IX 1203 + *SB* IV 7339.2.

4916 ---; April 70; property owner; Oxy.; bro. of Sarapion; *P. Oxy. inv.* 50.4B.24B(3-4)34.

4917 ---; s. of Narcissus, s. of Narcissus; m. Tausorapis, d. of Areionis; 71; Oxyrhynchite; Oxy.; *P. Med. inv.* 71.70.8, 14.

4918 ---; s. of Theon; sp. Sinthoonis alias Ophelous; ch. Dionysius, Mnesitheus; (1) July 72; (2) Aug 72?; Oxyrhynchite?; Oxy.?; addr. for ss.; (1) XLIV 3163.7; (2) XLI 2972.3.

4919 ---; ch. Theon; Aug 72?; Oxyrhynchite?; Oxy.?; addr. for gss. Dionysius and Mnesitheus; XLI 2972.4.

4920 ---; sp. Apollonia; ch. Demetria; 77-83; I 170.5.

4921 ---; March 79; banker w. associates; Oxy.; II 243.45.

4922 ---; ch. Sarapion; Oct 80; Oxyrhynchite; Oxy.; addr. for s.; II 248.8.

4923 ---; (1), (2) Oct 80; (3) 80 or 90; (4) 86-88; (5) Jan 90; (6) March 90; (7) April 90; (8) 90; (9) March 108; bibliophylax w. Epimachus (1, 2, 4-6, 8), w. Theon (3), w.

Sarapion (9); Oxy.; (1) II 248.1; (2) 249.1; (3) 359 (descr.); (4) *PSI* XII 1235.2; (5) VIII 942.2; (6) II 247.2; (7) I 72.1; (8) *P. Ryl.* IV 597.1; (9) III 483.32.

4924 THEON; ch. Dionysia; 81-95; Oxyrhynchite; gs. Dionysius being married; II 265.2.

4925 ---; ch. Amois; Nov 83; Oxyrhynchite?; Oxy.?; addr. for gs. Papontos, dec.; X 1282.20.

4926 ---; s. of Dionysius, s. of Dionysius; 83; Oxyrhynchite; Oxy.; addr. for s.; I 94.5

4927 ---; s. of Didymus; 83/84; landholder; Papsis?, Tychis Necotis; has land there; bro. of Demetrius; II 290.12.

4928 ---; s. of Sarapion; (1), (2) c. 85; (3) 85/86; (1) II 328 (descr.); (2) 335 (descr.); (3) 336 (descr.).

4929 ---; s. of Dionysius, s. of Leon; m. Isione; (1) Aug 86; (2) 93/94; Oxyrhynchite; Oxy.; age c. 43; guardian of slave Euphrosyne; tutor of Dionysius; signalement; (1) XXXVIII 2843.16; (2) *PSI* X 1109.2.

4930 ---; (1) Aug 86; (2) 94; (3) 98-117; agoranomus w. Dionysius and Dius (1), w. Dionysius, 2 Sarapions and Pasion (2); Oxyrhynchite?; Oxy.; (1) XXXVIII 2843.4; (2) I 73.7; (3) *P. Sel.* 24.2.

4931 ---; 86; city secretary w. Apollonius; Oxy.; VII 1028.5.

4932 ---; s. of Harpaesis; ch. Harpalus; after 89; Oxy.?; doc. pr. Oxy.?; addr. for s.; *P. Lips.* 120.5.

4933 ---; ch. Amois; 90; Senepta?, M. Top.; addr. for s. aged c. 61; I 72.23.

4934 ---; April/May 94; agent of Ti. Claudius Sarapion; II 364 (descr.).

4935 ---; ch. Sinthonis; 94; Oxyrhynchite; Oxy.; addr. for gd. Lucia alias Thaisas; II 270.3.

4936 ---; s. of Nicippus, s. of Nicippus; sp. Gaia alias Sarapias; Alex., Phylaxithalassius or Althaieus; Oxy.?; II 273.8.

4937 ---; s. of Harpaesis, s. of Harpaesis; m. Tatreiphis, d. of Theon; (1) April 96; (2) May 96; (3) Oct 98; (4) i; physician; Oxyrhynchite; Oxy.; reports on condition of Alexandra, slave of Claudia Dionysia (1); asked by Paesis to treat -is (2); sent patient by hyperetes Ptolemaeus (of str.; 4); father's name incorrectly Harpalus in 4; (1) *P. Oslo* III 95.2; (2) *PSI Bartoletti Colombo* 1.2; (3) *P. Genov.* II 62.3; (4) *PSI Bartoletti Colombo* 2.2.

4938 ---; ch. Sarapion; 97; Oxy.; gs. [Heracleides?] holds land in Oxy. and Ars. nomes; *P. Bour.* 16.10.

4939 ---; ch. Tatreiphis; Oct 98; Oxyrhynchite; Oxy.; addr. for mat. gs. Theon; *P. Genov.* II 62.4.

4940 THEON; ch. Dionysius; 99; Oxyrhynchite?; Oxy.?; addr. for gs. Dionysius; descr. as the elder; *P. Harris* 74.15.

4941 ---; ch. [Demetr]ia, Dionytas, Didymus; 99-117; Oxy.?; addr. for d.; XLVI 3274 i 3, ii 32.

4942 ---; s. of Ammonius, s. of Ammonius; c. mid i; property owner; bro. of Pecysis; VII 1027.2, 3.

4943 ---; 2nd half i; property owner; Oxy.; *P. Yale* 66.6.

4944 ---; s. of Ampheion; 2nd half i; practor; Sesphtha (or Psenosiris), L. Top.; XXXVIII 2845.14.

4945 ---; ch. Thatres; i; hamlet of Nomus; doc. pr. Oxy.?; addr. for mat. gs. Plutarchus; *P. Harris* 138 i 2.

4946 ---; i; hamlet of Nomus; doc. pr. Oxy.?; unnamed s. and gs.; addr. for gs.; *P. Harris* 138 i 1.

4947 ---; i; banker?; *P. Med. inv.* 71.47.8.

4948 THEON(?); i?; livestock owner; IV 807 i 3.

4949 THEON; s. of Nicobulus; sp. Thaisous; late i; elaiochristes at gymnasium; Oxy.; II 300.6.

4950 ---; late i; rep. of Dionysius and partners; II 329 (descr.).

4951 ---; late i; II 300.8.

4952 ---; late i; soldier?; bro. (sp.?) of Sarapous; VIII 1154.1.

4953 ---; late i; unnamed s. and gs. Alexandrus; *P. Sel.* 23.9.

4954 ---; s. of Heracleides; sp. Sarapias; ch. Diogenes; late i; Alex., Propapposebasteius, Althaieus; tribe and deme for s.; *P. Sel.* 23.13.

4955 ---; ch.? Nilus, Diogas; late i; Oxy.?; XVIII 2190.1.

4956 ---; late i; teacher; Alexandria?; XVIII 2190.14.

4957 ---; ch. Arsinoe; i - early ii; Oxyrhynchite; Oxy.; addr. for mat. gs. Aristandrus; *P. Oslo* III 114.14.

4958 ---; s. of Heracleus; m. Demetria; i - ii; age 20; *P. Harris* 72.33.

4959 ---; ch. Horion; i - ii; Isieum Tryphonos?; s. owned property nr Talao; addr. for gd. Melanous; *PSI* VI 687.1.

4960 ---; 100; banker, partner of Theon (1); has partners (2); Oxy.; (1) I 49.1; (2) 50.1.

4961 ---; 100; banker, partner of Theon; Oxy.; I 49.1.

4962 ---; s. of Mnesitheus; sp.]Heme.[....; ch. Mnesitheus; after 102; Oxy.?; addr. for gd.; III 636.6, 22.

4963 ---; ch. Plutarche; after 102; Oxy.?; addr. for mat. gs. Ptollis; III 636.3.

4964 THEON; June c. 103-110; slave owner; previously owned Plution, now freedman; XLVI 3275.47.

4965 ---; Aug 106; *P. Wisc.* I 17 V 8.

4966 ---; s. of T(?); Aug 106; *P. Wisc.* I 17 V 13.

4967 ---; Aug 106; *P. Wisc.* I 17 V 16.

4968 ---; Aug 106; *P. Wisc.* I 17 V 25.

4969 ---; s. of Diogenes; c. 107-112; bro.? of Pecysis; *PSI* V 450 R 1, 15.

4970 C. JULIUS THEON; ch. C. Julius; 107/108; landholder; ex high priest and hypomnematographus; Roman; Alexandria; XII 1434.9.

4971 TI. JULIUS THEON; gs. of Ti. Julius Theon; nephew of Ti. Julius Theon and of Ti. Julius Sarapion; Oct 111; landholder; slave owner; Roman; Alexandria; has land in other nomes; games victor; XLIV 3197.2.

4972 ---; s. of Ti. Julius Theon; (1) Oct 111; (2) 122/123; (3) Aug 127; ex-strategus of the city, archidikastes (1); gymnasiarch (3); landholder; slave owner; Roman; Alexandria; land in other nomes (1), in Phoboou distr., E. Top and Seryphis distr., W. Top. (3); (1) XLIV 3197.1; (2) XXXVIII 2865.1; (3) 2867.1-2.

4973 ---; ch. Ti. Julius Theon, Ti. Julius Sarapion; Oct 111; ex-hypomnematographus; ex-gymnasiarch; slave owner; Roman; Alexandria; XLIV 3197.3.

4974 THEON; ch. Diogenes; Oct 111; XLIV 3197.7.

4975 ---; s. of Harthonis; sp. Thermuthion; ch. Harthonis; 116; Oxy.; addr. for s., dec. hierotekton of Thoeris, Isis, Sarapis and assoc. gods and enr. in Thoeris St qtr; XII 1550.4.

4976 ---; s. of Harthonis, s. of Theon; m. [Taps?]ois, d. of Paos; 116; hierotekton of Thoeris, Thoeris, Isis, Sarapis and assoc. gods; father enr. in Thoeris St qtr; XII 1550.3.

4977 ---; Feb 117; Oxyrhynchite, gymnasial class; Oxy.; *P. Med. inv.* 72.16.7.

4978 ---; ch. Hermas; 118; Oxyrhynchite?; Oxy.; addr. for s.; III 503.5.

4979 ---; m. Philumene; (1) 117-138; (2) n.d.; bro. of Asinnius Secundus and Apollonius; on identification of Theon, see *P. Brem.* 56 intro.; (1) X 1293.1; (2) *SB* I 4630.8.

4980 ---; m. Thermuthion, d. of Ne]chthenibis; 119; North St qtr; XII 1547.32.

4981 ---; ch. Theon; Jan 121; Oxyrhynchite; Oxy.; addr. for gs. Demetrius; *P. Fouad* 30.6.

4982 ---; s. of Theon; ch. Demetrius; Jan 121; Oxyrhynchite; Oxy.; addr. for s.; *P. Fouad* 30.6.

4983 THEON; s. of Hephaestion; 122/123; III 592 (descr.) V 3.

4984 ---; s. of Achilles; 122/123; grain transfer to a/c of Arsinoe; *P. Lips.* 116.10.

4985 ---; ch. Arsinoe; (1) 122/123; (2) Aug 123; Pakerke distr.?, E. Top.; (1) *P. Lips.* 116.5; (2) XXXVIII 2864.4.

4986 ---; 122/123?; *P. Wisc.* II 73.14-15, 22.

4987 ---; s. of Heracleides, s. of Sarapion; m. Aline; Aug 123; landholder; Pakerke distr., E. Top.; XXXVIII 2864.1.

4988 ---; sp. Thais?; ch. -on; 124; Oxyrhynchite?; Oxy.?; addr. for s.; III 490.21.

4989 ---; ch. Zoilus; 126; Oxyrhynchite?; Oxy.?; addr. for gs. Theon; III 491.19.

4990 ---; s. of Zoilus, s. of Theon; 126; Oxyrhynchite; Oxy.; age 39; signalement; witness; III 491.19.

4991 ---; ch. Eudaemon; 127; Oxyrhynchite; Oxy.; addr. for gs. Sarapion, being married; III 496.2.

4992 ---; ch. Diogenes; 129; Alex., Sosicosmius, Althaieus?; Alexandria?; details for gs. Agathodaemon; XXXVI 2774.1.

4993 ---; alias PTOLEMAEUS; (1) 129; (2) 131 or 132; bibliophylax, w. Diogenes (1), w. Tryphon (2); Oxy.; (1) I 75.1; (2) III 584 (descr.) R and V.

4994 ---; ch. Theon; 129; Oxyrhynchite?; Shepherds' qtr; addr. for ggs. Theon; I 75.7.

4995 ---; s. of Theon; sp. Diogenis alias Tapontos; ch. Theon; 129; Oxyrhynchite?; Shepherds' qtr; addr. for gs. Theon; I 75.2.

4996 ---; s. of Theon, s. of Theon; m. Thermuthis, d. of Apion; gs. of Diogenis alias Tapontos; 129; landholder; property owner; Oxyrhynchite; Shepherds' qtr; I 75.2.

4997 ---; s. of Theon, s. of Theon; m. Diogenis alias Tapontos, d. of Sarapion; sp. Thermuthis; ch. Theon, Diogenis; 129; landholder; property owner; Oxyrhynchite; Shepherds' qtr; I 75.2.

---; see HERACLEIDES.

4998 ---; sp. Sinpetsiris; ch. Pecysis; Feb 130?; Sesphtha, L. Top.; addr. for s.; *P. Mich. inv.* 974.3.

4999 ---; ch. Theon alias Apollonius; 130; Oxyrhynchite; Oxy.; addr. for ggs. Theon; III 492.6, 8.

5000 ---; alias APOLLONIUS; s. of Theon; sp. Helene; ch. Theon; 130; Oxyrhynchite; Oxy.; addr. for gs. Theon; III 492.6, 8.

5001 ---; s. of Theon alias Apollonius, s. of Theon; m. Helene; sp. Isareus; ch. Theon; 130; Oxyrhynchite; Oxy.; addr. for s.; denied access to house in l. 8; III 492.6, 8.

5002 THEON; s. of Theon, s. of Theon alias Apollonius; m. Isareus, d. of Theon; gs. of Helene; 130; Oxyrhynchite; Oxy.; III 492.[5], 8.

5003 ---; ch. Agatheinus; 130; Oxyrhynchite; Oxy.; addr. for gs. Theon, witness to will; III 492.23.

5004 ---; s. of Agatheinus, s. of Theon; 130; Oxyrhynchite; Oxy.; age 61; signalement; witness to will; III 492.22.

5005 ---; ch. Isareus; 130; Oxyrhynchite; Oxy.; addr. for mat. gs. Ptollion; III 492.5.

5006 ---; s. of Ptollion; sp. Isareus; ch. Ptollion; 130; Oxyrhynchite; Oxy.; addr. for s.; III 492.5.

---; see HORION.

5007 ---; 130; sitologus; Sinkepha; III 517.6.

5008 ---; s. of Pausiris; 131; Oxyrhynchite; Oxy.; I 68.2.

5009 ---; s. of Sarapion; sp. Thermuthion; ch. Onnophris; 132/133; *PSI* VIII 874 i 2.

5010 ---; s. of Sarapion; ch. Ammonius, Thaubarion?; 132/133; Alex., Propapposebasteius, Althaieus; Oxy.; details for s.; III 477.6.

5011 ---; s. of Onnophris, s. of Thonis; Aug 133; scribe; Oxy.; age 53; writes for Taarpaesis and Apollonius; signalement; *P. Köln* II 100.[28], 37.

5012 ---; 134; grammateus of bibliophylakes; Oxy.; III 515.8.

5013 ---; ch. Theon; 136; Alex., Sosicosmius, Althaieus; details for gs.; *P. Inst. Fran.* III 18.10.

5014 ---; s. of Theon; 136; Alex., Sosicosmius, Althaieus; details for unnamed s.; *P. Inst. Fran.* III 18.10.

5015 ---; 137; Alex., Eirenophylakios, Althaieus; III 625 (descr.).

5016 ---; alias ANTHUS; s. of Ammonianus; 137/138; landowner; Alex.; leases land from Hippalus' holding nr Po[]nis to Petosiris of Hermopolite; *PSI* IV 315.1.

5017 ---; s. of Diogenes, s. of Dieuches; ch. Dieuches; after 138/139; Oxy.; guardian to Epimachus; *PSI* IV 281 R i 2, 29 and passim.

5018 ---; s. of Heracleides; ch. Tseei; 138-161; Oxyrhynchite?; Oxy.?; addr. for d. and gs. Diodorus; IV 723.2.

5019 ---; ch. Ammonius; Aug 148; Oxy.; addr. for gs. Theon; *P. Iand.* VII 139.6.

5020 ---; s. of Ammonius, s. of Theon; Aug 148; ex-dyke inspector w. Theon; Oxy.; inspector in 140; *P. Iand.* VII 139.5.

5021 THEON; s. of Ammonius; m. Is]ido[te?, d. of D]eius; Aug 148; ex-dyke inspector; Oxy.; inspector in 140, now dec.; *P. Iand.* VII 139.7.

5022 ---; s. of Ammonius; ch. Ammonius; 148/149; Oxyrhynchite, gymnasial class; Pammenes' Garden qtr; reg. in g. class this distr. 4/5; XLVI 3283.14.

5023 ---; s. of Ammonius, s. of Theon; ch. Theon; 148/149; Oxyrhynchite, gymnasial class; Pammenes' Garden qtr; reg. in g. class this distr. 72/73; XLVI 3283.2, 12.

5024 ---; s. of Theon, s. of Ammonius; sp. Diogenous; ch. Theon; 148/149; Oxyrhynchite, gymnasial class; Pammenes' Garden qtr; reg. in g. class this distr. 91/92; XLVI 3283.1.

5025 ---; s. of Theon, s. of Theon; m. Diogenous; sp. Thaesis; ch. Pausiris; 148/149; Oxyrhynchite, gymnasial class; Knights' Camp qtr; reg. s. in g. class of 13 yr olds in this distr.; was himself reg. in Pammenes' Garden qtr; XLVI 3283.2.

---; see THEONAS.

5026 ---; ch. Diogenes; early ii; Oxyrhynchite?; Oxy.?; addr. for gs. Apollon, witness to will; III 493.14.

5027 ---; gs. of Achilleus; m. Demetria; sp. Ammonous; early ii; Alex., Propapposebasteius, Althaieus; bridegroom; III 497.5 and passim.

5028 ---; ch. Theon; ii, before 161; Oxy.; *P. Stras.* 534.1.

5029 ---; s. of Theon; ii, before 161; landowner; Oxy.; leases out land in Kleros of Call[is?]tus; *P. Stras.* 534.1.

5030 ---; s. of Demetrius, s. of Lacon; mid ii; farmer; Syron Kome?, W. Top.; XLIV 3165.5.

5031 ---; s. of Eudaemon; ii; athlete; XIV 1759.1.

5032 ---; ii; freedman; Oxy.; fr. of Pausiris; foster d. Dionysia; *SB* VI 9372.2.

5033 ---; ii; III 530.7.

5034 ---; ii; "brother" of Diogenis and Eteocleia; bro.? of Pannus; absent in Senao, W. Top.; XII 1584.1.

5035 ---; s. of Alexandrus; m. (or step-m.) Dionysia; ii; bro. of Sarapion and Aristocleia; XLVI 3313.24.

5036 C. THEON; s. of Harthoonis; ii; Oxy.; guardian to Ptolema; *P. Mil.* II 51.4.

5037 THEON; s. of Athenaeus; ii; friend of Apollonius, bro. of Theonas; XLII 3059.8.

5038 ---; s. of Apollo( ); ii; banker; XLI 2980 back.

5039 ---; ii; unnamed s. or self gymnasiarch designate; *P. Oslo* III 108.1.

5040 THEON; ii; friend of Ammonius whom he calls bro.; XLI 2980.1.

5041 ---; ii, after 138; XIV 1757.22.

5042 ---; ii?; rec. by Aurelius Archelaus, beneficiarius; I 32.5.

5043 ---; n.d.; *SB* I 1938(b).

5044 THEONAS; 27; may be Theon; II 293.10.

5045 ---; sp. Syras; ch. Thaisous, Ammonas; c. 35; unnamed d.; II 295 margin.

5046 ---; 104; in Alex., on business?; VIII 1155.1.

5047 TI. CLAUDIUS THEONAS; May 134; freedman; Roman; XXXVIII 2857.17.

5048 THEONAS; alias THEON; s. of Isidorus; m. Soeris or Soerous; early ii; Oxyrhynchite; Oxy.; guardian of niece and nephew; called Theon in l. 34; X 1269.2, 13, 34.

5049 ---; s. of Tetheus; (1) early ii; (2) ii; soldier; bro. of Dionytas; (1) XII 1481.1 V; (2) III 530.24.

5050 ---; ii; bro. of Apollonius; XLII 3059.6.

5051 THEOPHILUS; c. 1; politarch; IV 745.4.

5052 THEOPOMPION; d. of Heracleides; m. Ammonarion alias Theopompion, d. of Diogenes; end i; slave owner; Oxyrhynchite; Oxy.; *P. Sel.* 23.5.

---; see AMMONARION.

THEOPOMPUS; see DIONYSIUS.

5053 ---; ii. writes to Sarapion, str. U. Top., Sebennyte nome; VI 931.1.

5054 ---; s. of Athenạ[ ]; ii?; Senocomis?, W. Top.; *P. Fuad I Univ.* 32.8.

5055 THEOXENUS; 66/65 or 15/14 BC; IV 836 (descr.).

5056 ---; 140/141; sitologus; Lọnẹmus distr.; I 89.8.

5057 THẸPṢEIS; d. of Didymus; ch. .....us; 86/87?; Oxyrhynchite; Shepherds' qtr; s. aged 13; name may be Thysois, vel sim.; II 258.11.

5058 THERḄ[ ]; 26? (from *P. Rein.* II 103); slave owner; Oxy.; sp. is s. of Demetrius; *P. Rein.* II 104.2.

5059 THERMOUS; d. of Sarapion; sp. Ptollion; ch. Dius; 89-97; Oxy.?; addr. for s.; II 274.9.

5060 THERMUTHARION; d. of Thoonis; sp. Heracleius; (1) 20; (2) 48; property owner; freedwoman of Sotades; age 65 (2); signalement; (1) II 305.2; (2) 255.3.

5061 THERMUTHARION; May 26; slave; raised by Paapis; slave of Taseus at Tanais, M. Top.; *P. Rein.* II 103.7.

5062 ---; ii; III 530.29.

5063 THERMUTHION; d. of Achilleus, s. of Pastous; m. Plutarche, d. of Harpaesis; sp. Dioscous (div. in 2); (1) April 60; (2) March 61; property owner; Oxyrhynchite; Oxy.; part house in Hippodrome qtr (1); step-f. is Diogenes, s. of Pasion (2); *P. Mich.* III 192.4-5; (2) 194.4.

5064 ---; d. of Dionysius, s. of Thoonis; m. Teseuris, d. of Petosarapis; sp. Cephalon; 77; property owner; Oxyrhynchite; Oxy.; II 242.2, 3.

5065 ---; d. of Heracleides; sp. Gaius; ch. Gaius, Heracleides; (1) 77-83; (2) 89; Oxy.; addr. for s.; (1) I 170.11; (2) *P. Fouad* 48.4.

5066 ---; d. of Achilles, s. of Achilles; m. Thaisous, d. of Demetrius; 91/92; slave owner; Oxyrhynchite; Oxy.; bro. Sarapion; XXXVIII 2856.11.

5067 ---; d. of Plution, s. of Plutarchus; sp. Psammis; ch. Plution; 98; Oxyrhynchite; Oxy.; married in 82; X 1266.16.

5068 ---; d. of Pausiris; sp. Theon; ch. Harthonis; 116; Thoeris St qtr; addr. for s. dec. hierotekton of Thoeris, Isis, Sarapis and assoc. gods and enr. in above qtr; XII 1550.13.

5069 ---; d. of Ne]chthenibis; ch. Theon; 119; North St qtr?; addr. for s.; XII 1547.32.

5070 ---; sp. Panemgeus; ch. Papontos alias Leontas; Feb 130?; Sesphtha?, L. Top.; addr. for s.; *P. Mich. inv.* 974.6.

5071 ---; d. of Onnophris; sp. Theon; ch. Onnophris; 132/133; *PSI* VIII 874 i 3.

5072 ---; ii; friend of Eirene; I 115.7-8.

5073 ---; ii; Oxyrhynchite; unnamed child; III 647.11.

5074 THERMUTHI(O)N; n.d.; Oxy.; *SB* I 1987(a).

5075 THERMUTHIS; sp. Psamis; ch. Psamis; i - ii; *P. Harris* 72.4.

5076 ---; sp. Antigonus; ch. Antas; i - ii; *P. Harris* 72.12.

5077 ---; sp. Horion; ch. Chaeremon; i - ii; *P. Harris* 72.13.

5078 ---; sp. Harmaeis; ch. Panetbes; i - ii; *P. Harris* 72.25.

5079 ---; 122/123?; *P. Wisc.* II 73.19.

5080 ---; d. of Apion; sp. Theon; ch. Theon, Diogenis; 129; Oxyrhynchite; Shepherds' qtr; I 75.3.

5081 ---; d. of Plution; sp. Dionysius?; ch. Dionysammon?; ii?; *PSI* XIV 1414.30.

5082 THEUDOUS; sp. Amois; ch. Ptollous; 132/133; *PSI* I 53 i 6.

5083 THNAS; d. of Petosorapis; m. Heras, d. of Heracleides; sp. Papontos (dec.); Nov 83; property owner; Oxyrhynchite; Oxy.; guardian is Thompachrates; X 1282.5.

5084 THOMPACHRATES; s. of Paapis; m. Tecosis, d. of Petosorapis and Heras; Nov 83; Oxyrhynchite; Oxy.; guardian of aunt Thnas; X 1282.7.

5085 ---; i; pastophorus; *P. Oslo* III 143.3.

5086 THOMPECYSIS; i BC(?); *P. Inst. Fran.* I 36.5.

5087 ---; s. of Sarapion; sp. Sinthonis; ch. Petosarapis; 96; Oxyrhynchite?; Oxy.?; addr. for s.; II 266.6.

5088 ---; mid i; unnamed s.; *P. Inst. Fran.* III 30.1.

5089 ---; s. of Horus; sp. Thaesis; ch. Horus; Jan 139; Oxyrhynchite; Oxy.; addr. for s.; *P. Oslo* III 105.3.

5090 ---; s. of Horus, s. of Thompecysis; m. Sintotoes; gs. of Thaesis; Jan 139; Oxyrhynchite; South St qtr; previously reg. at gm.'s property, transferred by father to own half house; *P. Oslo* III 105.9.

5091 THOMPEIDISIS; s. of Comoapis; 126; Oxyrhynchite; Oxy.; addr. for unnamed s., witness to will; III 491.22.

5092 THOMPHYAS; d. of Harpaesis, s. of Petserothonis; m. Petosiris, d. of Harpaesis; c. 98; property owner; Oxyrhynchite; Gymnasium St qtr; owns part house there, mortgaged to bro. Thonis; II 241.29.

5093 THOMPSEMIS; s. of Thoonis; ch. Taorseus; 86; Oxyrhynchite; Thoeris St qtr; guardian of d.; died in 80; VII 1028.6.

5094 THONASYCHIS; s. of Thonis; sp. Thaesis; ch. Eudaemon; 126; Oxyrhynchite?; Oxy.; addr. for s., pastophorus; III 491.2.

5095 THONION; ch. Taaphynchis; 94; land at Seryphis mortgaged to d.; II 270.20.

5096 THONIS; s. of Harpaesis; 30/29 BC; Oxy.; writes for Paapis, temple lamplighter; XII 1453.32.

5097 ---; ch. Paapis; 30/29 BC; Oxy.; addr. for s.; XII 1453.6.

5098 ---; ch. Thonia alias Patoiphis; 30/29 BC; Oxy.; addr. for s.; XII 1453.2.

5099 ---; alias PATOIPHIS; s. of Thonis; ch. Petosiris; 30/29 BC; temple lamplighter; Oxy.; lampl. of temple of Sarapis and Isieum; XII 1453.1-2.

5100 ---; July 23 BC; Oxy.; *P. Inst. Fran.* I 13.28.

5101 ---; ch. Thoonis; 4/3 BC; Oxyrhynchite?; Sarapis St qtr; addr. for s.; XII 1457.4.

5102 THONIS; ch. Lastas; 41-79; Teis?, Thmois. Top.; addr. for s.; XLII 3061.10.

5103 ---; ch. Psenamunis; Oct 62; Sesphtha?, L. Top.; addr. for gs.; XXXVIII 2873.2.

5104 ---; ch. Thonis; 71/72; Oxy.?; doc. pr. Oxy.?; addr. for s.; *P. Ryl.* II 95.3.

5105 ---; s. of Thonis; 71/72; tax farmer; Oxy.?; doc. pr. Oxy.?; *P. Ryl.* II 95.3.

5106 ---; ch. Petosarapis; 71/72; OXY.?; doc. pr. Oxy.?; addr. for s.; *P. Ryl.* II 95.2.

5107 ---; s. of Petosorapis; sp. Eseneus; ch. Tecosis; Nov 83; Oxyrhynchite?; Oxy.; addr. for d.; X 1282.11.

5108 ---; s. of Amithonis; sp. Sintheus; ch. Thaesis; 96; Oxyrhynchite?; Oxy.; addr. for d.; II 266.3.

5109 ---; s. of Harpaesis, s. of Petserothonis; m. Petosiris, d. of Harpaesis; c. 98; archipastophorus of Thoeris, Isis, Sarapis, Osiris and assoc. gods; Oxyrhynchite; Oxy.; II 241.4.

5110 ---; ch. Diogenes; 98-102; Oxyrhynchite?; Oxy.; addr. for gd. Thaesis; *P. Mert.* I 13.2.

5111 ---; s. of Horus; early i; Psobthis, M. Top.; *P. Wisc.* I 23.3.

5112 ---; s. of Teos; i; pastophorus; *P. Oslo* III 143.2.

5113 ---; ch. Pasion; Jan 100; Nemerae, M. Top.; addr. for s., farming there; XLI 2960.11.

5114 ---; ch. Sinthonia; after 102; Oxyrhynchite; Oxy.; addr. for mat. gs. Pausiris; III 636.16.

5115 ---; ch. Harpaesis alias Horus; 126; Oxyrhynchite?; Oxy.; addr. for gd. Ta...; III 491.10.

5116 ---; ch. Thonasychis; 126; Oxyrhynchite?; Oxy.; addr. for gs. Eudaemon; III 491.2.

5117 ---; s. of Eudaemon, s. of Thonasychis; m. Ta..., d. of Harpaesis alias Horus; gs. of Thaesis; 126; Oxyrhynchite; Oxy.; minor?; III 491.4.

5118 ---; s. of Pamm( ); 126; Oxyrhynchite?; Oxy.?; signalement; witness of will; III 491.23.

5119 ---; ch. Onnophris; Aug 133; Oxy.; addr. for gs. Theon; *P. Köln* II 100.29.

5120 ---; c. 138 (n.d.); hierotekton of Athena Thoeris, w. Teos; Oxyrhynchite; Oxy.; III 579 (descr.).

5121 THOONAS; s. of Petosiris; sp. Thaisous; ch. Tetoeus, Petosiris, Papontos; 119; landowner; North St qtr; dec.; XII 1547.8, 17, 22, 25.

THOONIS; see THEON

5122 ---; s. of Petoous; 67 BC; gravedigger; Oxy.?; doc. pr. Oxy.?; *P. Ryl.* II 65.2.

5123 ---; Aug 35 BC; connect w. Oxy. via name; *P. Ryl.* IV 593.1.

5124 ---; Oct 4 BC; landholder; leases land from Demetrius; cultivates land formerly of Neoptolemaeus; Thoonius in text; *SB* XII i 10942.6, 12.

5125 ---; s. of Thonis; 4/3 BC; property and livestock owner; Oxyrhynchite; Sarapeum; pays 6 dr. tax on asses; XII 1457.4.

5126 ---; 6-35; Oxy.; addr. for 2 unnamed s.; married to sister; II 256.1.

5127 ---; s. of Tryphon, s. of Didymus; m. Timos; (1) 12/13; (2) 25; weaver; Hippodrome qtr; age 22 (1); (1) II 314.7; (2) 288.40.

5128 ---; s. of Dionysius, s. of Tryphon; m. Thamunion, d. of Onnophris; gs. of Timos; (1) 12/13; (2) 25; (3) 37; (4) Jan 44; Oxyrhynchite; Hippodrome qtr (2), Temgenuthis qtr (4); age 1 (1); (1) II 314.6; (2) 288.[42]; (3) 319.12; (4) 251. 7.

5129 ---; s. of Ammonius; (1) 19; (2) 19/20; Oxyrhynchite?; Oxy.?; bro. reg. in Oxy.; (1) II 253.[15]; (2) 252.2.

5130 ---; s. of Patbeus; 20; priest of Thoeris, Isis, Sarapis and assoc. gods; II 305.3.

5131 ---; 31/32; landholder; Pela, W. Top.; land there; *P. Ryl.* II 159.13.

5132 ---; 41; II 366 (descr.).

5133 ---; sp. Thais; 41-54; Oxyrhynchite?; Oxy.; age c. 42; signalement; guardian of wife; XXXIV 2720.3.

5134 ---; ch. Thoonis; 48; *P. Fouad* 35.12.

5135 ---; s. of Thoonis; 48; in debt to Thaesis; *P. Fouad* 35.12.

5136 ---; ch. Thermutharion; 48; II 255.4.

---; see HERACLES.

5137 ---; s. of Thoonis, s. of Onnophris; m. Teteo(us) or Tetoeo(us), d. of Eudaemon; (1) 55; (2) 83; livestock owner; Oxy.; bro. of Eudaemon; illiterate; (1) II 304.1, 29; (2) 289 i 2 and passim.

5138 ---; s. of Onnophris; sp. Teteo(us) or Tetoeo(us); ch. Thoonis, Eudaemon, Didymus?; (1) 55; (2) 83; Oxy.; addr. for s. Thoonis; (1) II 304.2; (2) 289 i 2 and passim.

5139 ---; July 64; Oxy.; *P. Yale* 63.19.

5140 ---; s. of Tryphon, s. of Dionysius; m. Saraeus, d. of Apion; gs. of Thamunis; 66; weaver (apprentice); Oxyrhynchite; Oxy.; II 275.7-8.

5141 THOONIS; ch. Dionysius; 77; Oxyrhynchite; Oxy.; addr. for gd. Thermuthion; II 242.24.

5142 ---; ch. Hierax; 81-96; Oxyrhynchite; Oxy.; addr. for gd. Tbecis; VIII 1105.15.

5143 ---; ch. Thoonis; 81-96; Oxyrhynchite; Oxy.; addr. for gs. Thoonis; VIII 1105.4.

5144 ---; s. of Thoonis; ch. Thoonis; 81-96; Oxyrhynchite; Oxy.; addr. for s.; VIII 1105.3.

5145 ---; s. of Thoonis, s. of Thoonis; 81-96; Oxyrhynchite; Oxy.; house in Sarapis St qtr mortgaged to him; VIII 1105.1.

5146 ---; s. of Harthoonis; 83/84; Papsis, Tychis Necotis; addr. for s.; II 290.15.

5147 ---; ch. Thompsemis; 86; Oxyrhynchite; Thoeris St qtr; addr. for s.; VII 1028.7.

5148 ---; s. of Harpaesis; 93; landholder; Athychis, U. Top.; land there; (1) *P. Princ.* II 42 R 7; (2) V ii 26.

5149 ---; s. of Harthoonis; sp. Tausorapis; ch. Sinthoonis, Harthoonis; 98-117; Oxyrhynchite; Oxy.; addr. for d.; ch. priest and priestess of Thoeris, Isis, Sarapis and assoc. gods; *P. Sel.* 24.3.

5150 ---; Sentheus; i; s. pastophorus; *P. Oslo* III 143.9.

5151 ---; late i - early ii; *P. XV Congr.* 16.10.

5152 ---; s. of Ammonius, s. of Noeris; ch. Tautosiris; Aug 106; Oxyrhynchite; 10th qtr; died 84; *P. Wisc.* I 17 R 7.

5153 ---; alias Alk.[..]; s. of Papiris; Oct 112; Tanais?, M. Top.; XXII 2351.82.

5154 ---; ch. Petosiris; 119; Oxy.; addr. for gs. Apollonides; may be Thoonas, father of Petosiris; XII 1547.19.

5155 ---; ch. Zoilus; ii; s. has land in Taampemou and Oxy.; *P. Inst. Fran.* III 15.14.

5156 THOONIUS; 17-19; freedman; weaver; landholder; fr. of Ptolemaeus; II 309 i 2 and passim.

5157 THOTES (Ḏḥwtj); i BC - i; dependant of Whj; agent for Petesis; *OD Pisa* 111 Convesso 2.

5158 ---; ch. Nechutes; i BC - i; *OD Pisa* 25 i 16.

5159 THOTEUS (Ḏḥwtj-iw); April 5 BC; *OD Pisa* 936 Convesso 8.

5160 ---; i BC - i; *OD Pisa* 510 + 568 Concavo ii 5.

5161 ---; ch. Harpaesis; i BC - i; (1) *OD Pisa* 243 + 472 i 6; (2) 667.2.

5162 ---; s. of Pabis; i BC - i; *OD Pisa* 755 Convesso X + 10.

5163 THOTEUS; ch. Pamun; i BC - i; *OD Pisa* 1023 Convesso i 5.

5164 ---; s. of Harpaesis; i BC - i; *OD Pisa* 22.1.

5165 ---; s. of Kmj; i BC - i; *OD Pisa* 667.4.

5166 ---; s. of Psen-[...]; i BC - i; *OD Pisa* 8.8.

5167 ---; i BC - i; *OD Pisa* 243 + 472 i 14.

5168 ---; ch. Peteuris; 6; *OD Pisa* 1163.5.

5169 THRACIDAS; late i BC; XII 1479 V.

5170 ---; s. of Hermogenes; ch. Sarapion; Jan 93; Isieum Tryphonos, L. Top.; addr. for s. who cedes catoecic land nr Sinary; *PSI* VIII 897.60.

5171 THRACIDAS? (THRAKITA); s. of Com(on); i; farmer; Koba; VIII 1145.12, 16.

5172 THRACIDAS; s. of Sarapion?; c. 135; property owner; may not be Oxy.; XVII 2111 i 21.

5173 THRASYBOULUS; late i BC; XII 1479.2.

5174 THRASYMACHUS; 97; conceded land at Peeno; IV 713.26.

5175 TI[ ]; s. of Petosiris, s. of Dionysius; m. Tetoeus, d. of Thoonas; 119; stone cutter; North St qtr; age 45; signalement; XII 1547.17.

5176 TIBERIUS; see CLAUDIUS; IULIUS; TI. CLAUDIUS ASCLEPIADES, DI[ ], HERODES, SARAPION, THEON; TI. IULIUS BASILIDES, PHILETAS.

5177 TIBERIUS; May 134; slave owner; Roman; Oxy.; has freedmen Ti. Claudius Alexandrus, Ti. Claudius Demetrius, Ti. Theanous; XXXVIII 2857.1.

5178 TIMOS; sp. Tryphon; ch. Didymus, Dionysius, Thoonis; 25; Hippodrome qtr; II 288.37.

5179 TIOUDA; d. of Quintus; sp. Dionysius; ch. Comon; 93/94; Roman?; Hippodrome qtr; addr. for s.; *PSI* X 1109.15.

5180 TITIUS; 31; soldier; Teis, Thmois. Top.; XIX 2234.13.

TITUS; see CLEMENS; HERACLEIDES.

5181 TLEP[OLEMUS?]; ch. Heracleides; 30 BC - 14; *P. Rein.* II 99.11.

5182 ---; alias TM[A]RUS?; after 79; may not be Oxy.; XXXVI 2757 i 3.

5183 TNE - ; Nov 132; female; age 14; sister of Didyme; *PSI* I 53 iv 52.

5184 TNEPHEROS; d. of Annius; sp. Chaeremon; ch. Sarapion; 96; Oxyrhynchite; Oxy.; addr. for s.; I 104.5.

5185 TNEPHEROS; d. of Hatres; m. Soeris; gd. of Teraus alias Thaubastis; 96; Oxyrhynchite; Oxy.; is married; I 104.23.

5186 ---; sp. Heras; ch. Heras; 99; Oxyrhynchite?; Sarapis St qtr; addr. for s.; III 481.13-14.

5187 ---; sp. Puoris; ch. Hermias; i - ii; *P. Harris* 72.17.

5188 TNEPHERSOIS; ch. [Th]aseeus or [P]aseeus; end i; slave; Oxy.; *P. Sel.* 23.7.

5189 ---; d. of Plution, s. of Diodorus; m. Dogymis; sp. Sarapion; ch. Sarapion; 127/128; Oxyrhynchite, gymnasial class; Gymnasium St qtr; full sister of sp.; XII 1452 i 11, ii 38.

5190 ---; early ii; X 1269.31.

5191 TOONSIS; 81-96; VI 984 R fin.

5192 TOTHES; Oct 120; nomophylax; Hermopolite nome?; XII 1440.7.

5193 TOTOES; ch. Heracleides; 30/29 BC; Oxy.; addr. for s.; XII 1453.3.

5194 TOTOES(?); April 5 BC; *OD Pisa* 936 Convesso 1.

5195 TOTOES; ch. Pates; i BC; *OD Pisa* 227.1.

5196 ---; i BC - i; *OD Pisa* 460 Convesso ii X + 2.

5197 ---; s. of P_3-rmt-m_3j(?); i BC - i; *OD Pisa* 735 Concavo X + 10.

5198 ---; s. of Osir[; i BC - i; *OD Pisa* 561 + 562 + 795 ii 20.

5199 ---; i BC - i; *OD Pisa* 58.15.

5200 ---; ch. Horus; i BC - i; (1) *OD Pisa* 58.10; (2) 510 + 568 Convesso i 10.

5201 ---; s. of Haremphois; i BC - i; bro. Petosiris; (1) *OD Pisa* 69 Convesso i 2; (2) 1264 Concavo 4.

5202 ---; s. of Petubastis; i BC - i; (1) *OD Pisa* 5 ii X + 14; (2) 267.2.

5203 ---; s. of Petosiris; i BC - i; (1) *OD Pisa* 196 ii X + 3; (2) 5 ii X + 8.

5204 ---; s. of Onnophris; i BC - i; (1) *OD Pisa* 5 i X + 7; (2) 5 ii X + 8.

5205 ---; ch. Chonsous; i BC - i; *OD Pisa* 127.1.

5206 ---; s. of Pabais(?); i BC - i; *OD Pisa* 541 Convesso i 2.

5207 ---; s. of Petesis; i BC - i; *OD Pisa* 126 i 5.

5208 ---; s. of Psentaes; i BC - i; *OD Pisa* 816 X + 1, X + 2.

5209 ---; i BC - i; workman; *OD Pisa* 25 ii 14.

5210 TOTOES; i BC - i; *OD Pisa* 477 Concavo X + 8.

5211 ---; i BC - i; *OD Pisa* 541 Convesso i 5, 7.

5212 ---; i BC - i; *OD Pisa* 5 i X + 6.

5213 ---; i BC - i; *OD Pisa* 196 ii X + 4.

5214 ---; i BC - i; *OD Pisa* 196 i X + 2.

5215 ---; ch. Patous; late i BC - early i; *OD Pisa* 35 Concavo ii 13.

5216 ---; Aug 3; *OD Pisa* 473 Convesso 7.

5217 ---; s. of Psenmaes; April 4; *OD Pisa* 511 + 512 i 7, ii 1.

5218 ---; Sept 6; *OD Pisa* 814 Concavo 2.

5219 ---; s. of Psenatumis; July 7; *OD Pisa* 1131 Concavo 8.

5220 ---; s. of Horus; (1) July 7; (2) i; (1) *OD Pisa* 1131 Convesso 5; (2) 318.6.

5221 ---; s. of Saras; ch. Pecysis; 31/32; *P. Mich. inv.* 69.2.

5222 ---; s. of Lycus; 31/32; Sinary, L. Top.; *P. Mich. inv.* 69.16.

5223 ---; early i; *OD Pisa* 419.5.

5224 ---; s. of Pasis; i; *OD Pisa* 60 Convesso i 14.

5225 ---; late i - early ii; unnamed gs. a priest of Thoeris, Isis, Sarapis and assoc. gods; *P XV Congr.* 16.4.

5226 ---; s. of Tryphon; ch. Pachnubis; (1) Oct 108; (2) Oct 112; Tanais, M. Top.; gss. Totoes alias Plutarchus and Pachnubis; (1) XXXVIII 2874.2-3; (2) XXII 2351.6.

5227 ---; alias PLUTARCHUS; s. of Pachnubis, s. of Totoes; m. Thaesis; Oct 112; farmer; lessee; Tanais, M. Top.; Persian of Epigone; rents part of Kleros of Nicaeus; XXII 2351.4.

5228 ---; ch. Papiris; Oct 112; Tanais, M. Top.; addr. for gs. Totoes; XXII 2351.7.

5229 ---; s. of Papiris, s. of Totoes; m. Tachnumis; Oct 112; farmer; lessee; Tanais, M. Top.; Persian of Epigone; rents part of Kleros of Nicaeus; XXII 2351.6.

5230 ---; s. of Aperos; 132/133; unnamed s. aged 3; *PSI* I 53 i 2.

5231 ---; s. of Heleis; sp. -ia; ch. -is; 132/133; *PSI* I 53 i 14.

5232 ---; s. of Pecysis; ch. Pecysis; ii; doc. pr. Oxy.?; *PSI* VI 710.11.

5233 ---; m. Thatres; ii; slave; doc. pr. Oxy.?; house born slave of Pecysis hired by Dioscorus; *PSI* VI 710.13.

5234 TOTOEUS; ch. Horus; 30/29 BC; Oxy.; s. writes for temple lamplighter Heracleides; XII 1453.38.

5235 ---; s. of Onnophris; 83/84; Tychis Necotis; Petsiris alias Antit( ) pays tax via him; II 290.23.

5236 TOUTHEUS; sp. Zopyrus; ch. Pausirion; i; Oxyrhynchite?; Oxy.?; doc. pr. Oxy.?; addr. for s.; *P. Harris* 138 i 14.

5237 TRIADELPHIS; d. of Asclepiades; sp. Diophantus; ch. Diophantus alias Sarapion; i; Oxyrhynchite?; Oxy.; addr. for s.; *P. Harris* 138 iii margin and 4.

5238 TRIADELPHUS; ii; shipowner; III 522.1.

5239 TRIG( ); ch. Apollo( ); ii; *PSI* IV 281 V 62.

5240 TROILUS(?); ch. Amoitas; 99; Oxy.?; addr. for s.; III 481.24.

5241 TROPHON (or TREPHON); Oct 111; slave; formerly of Ti. Julius Theon, now of his s. Ti. Julius Sarapion; XLIV 3197.10.

5242 TRYPHAENA; d. of [H]orion?; 59; Oxyrhynchite; Oxy.; unnamed sister; II 320.3.

5243 ---; sp. Ariston; ch. Heliodorus; end i; Oxyrhynchite; Oxy.; addr. for s.; *P. Sel.* 23.11.

5244 ---; 137; unnamed child; *PSI* XII 1262 i 1.

5245 TRYPHAS; c. 11 IV 736.56.

5246 ---; ii; VII 1062 V.

5247 TRYPHON; Aug 7 BC; overseer?, assoc. w. Heracleides; Oxy.; *P. Ryl.* IV 603.2.

5248 ---; s. of Didymus; sp. Timos; ch. Didymus, Dionysius, Thoonis; (1) 12/13; (2) 25; (3) Sept 66; master weaver; Oxyrhynchite; Hippodrome qtr (2); age 65 (1); gs. Tryphon; (1) II 314.2; (2) 288.36; (3) 275.2.

5249 ---; s. of Dionysius, s. of Tryphon; m. Thamunis (dec. in 18), d. of Onnophris; sp. Demetrous (4), Saraeus (6, 8, 9 etc); ch. unnamed d. (8), Thoonis, Apion; gs. of Timos; (1) 12/13; (2) 15-22; (3) 22/23; (4) 25; (5) Dec 35; (6) June 36; (7) Sept 36; (8) 36-50; (9) June/July 37; (10) Dec 37; (11) 49/50; (12) Nov 50; (13) 50; (14) 50/51; (15) April 52; (16) Aug 54; (17), (18), Nov 55; (19) June 56; (20) May 57; (21), (22) June 59; (23) July 59; (24) Sept 66; landholder; property and livestock owner; weaver; Hippodrome qtr (3, 4), Temgenuthis, qtr (13, 18, 19); age 4 (1); owns house in Shepherds' qtr (14,21); buys house in T. qtr (18); released from military service, bad eyesight (15); illiterate; Persian of Epigone; full signalement (18); (1) II 314.5; (2) 235.2; (3) 311.3; (4) 288.39; (5) 282.2; (6) 267.1; (7) 322.3; (8) 321.1; (9) 315.2; (10) 319.[3]; (11) I 38.2; (12) II 324.9; (13) 308.2; (14) 316.2; (15) I 39.8; (16) II 264.1; (17) 304.1; (18) I 99.2; (19) II 310.3; (20) 269.1; (21) 318.[4], 14; (22) 320.5; (23) 306.6; (24) 275.1.

5250 TRYPHON; ch. Polemon; 13/14; IV 721.2.

5251 ---; ch. [Sim]on(?); Sept 77; Oxy.; addr. for s.; pilot of cargo boat; II 276.6.

5252 ---; sp. Taonnophris; ch. Heraclas; 91 or 107; Oxyrhynchite?; Oxy.?; addr. for s.; IV 722.21.

5253 ---; ch. Astyanax; 95; Alex., Phylaxithalassius; Oxy.; addr. for gs. Pausanias alias Dionysius, Heracleius; II 273.12.

5254 ---; 98-117; may not be Oxy.; XLII 3015.13.

5255 ---; sp. Tanemeus; ch. Melas; i - ii; *P. Harris* 72.31.

5256 ---; s. of Mynius; m. Philumene; i - ii; age 46; *P. Harris* 72.32.

5257 ---; ch. Toto[eus]; Oct 108; Tanais, M. Top.; addr. for gs.; XXXVIII 2874.3.

5258 ---; s. of Aristandrus. s. of [....]minis; (1) 121; (2) 137; landholder; lessor; Oxyrhynchite; Oxy.; land at Senepta, Kleros of Dion; (1) III 499.1; (2) *PSI* XII 1262 ii 1.

5259 ---; 131 or 132; bibliophylax w. Theon alias Ptolemaeus; III 584 (descr.) R and V.

5260 TR]YPHON; 132/133; unnamed s., aged 17, weaver; *PSI* I 53 xi 176.

5261 TRYPHON; early ii; XLII 3060.12, 16.

5262 ---; ch. Heras; ii; Ibiotapheum qtr; addr. for s.; *P. Princ.* II 46.14.

5263 ---; ii?; assoc. w. Eudaemon; *P. Harris* 103.11.

5264 TSEEI; d. of Theon, s. of Heracleides; sp. Agatheinus; ch. Diodorus; 138-161; Oxyrhynchite?; Oxy.?; addr. for s.; IV 723.2.

5265 TSENAMMONAS; d. of Panechotes; sp. Pausiris; ch. Panechotes; March 90; property owner; Oxyrhynchite; Knights' Camp qtr; dec.; house in above; unnamed child; II 247.6.

5266 TSENAMUNIS; sp. Apollonius; ch. Taarpaesis alias Isidora; Aug 133; Oxyrhynchite; Oxy.; addr. for d.; *P. Köln* II 100.3.

5267 TSENPALEMIS; 40/41; livestock owner; II 355 (descr.).

5268 TSENTHOTUMIS; sp. Ammonius; ch. Thatres; 130; Isieum Tryphonos; addr. for d.; III 492.2.

5269 TSENUARIS; d. of Onnophris, s. of Harpsois; sp. Diogenes; ch. Onnophris; Jan 93; Oxyrhynchite; illiterate; cedes land from Kleros of Cleandrides to Ti. Claudius Sarapion; age over 70; *PSI* VIII 897.3, 40. 55.

5270 TSENYRIS; d. of Ergeo(tes?); 83/84; landholder; Papsis, Tychis Necotis; land there; II 290.26.

5271 TSINTOTOES; d. of Apollonius; 137; Mermertha; *PSI* XII 1262 iii 4.

5272 TURIUS; i BC - i; *OD Pisa* 510 + 568 Convesso ii 4.

5273 TYCHAROUS; 126; slave of Diogenes; Oxy.; III 634 (descr.).

5274 TYCHE; c. 1; IV 736.18.

5275 TYRANNUS; (1) c. 25; (2) 25/26; dioecetes; bro. of Hermias; (1) II 292.1; (2) 291.1.

5276 ---; i; advocate?; *P. Ryl.* II 270 (descr.).

5277 TYRUS; ch. Zois; i - ii; gd. Melanous res. in Isieum Tryphonos; *PSI* VI 687.1.

ULPIUS; see DIOSCURIDES.

5278 M. ANTONIUS VALENS; 103; recruit, 3rd Ituraean Cohort; Roman; age 22; signalement; VII 1022.21.

5279 M. IULIUS VALERIANUS; ii; veteran of fleet; Roman; purchases unproductive state land at Senepta, M. Top.; XII 1508.1, 5.

VALERIUS; see HERACLEIDES.

5280 ---; s. of Apollonius; Nov 130; farmer; lessee; Senepta, M. Top.; Persian of Epigone; leases domain land from Sarapion, s. of Herodes; IV 730.2.

5281 VERETHONIS; i; pastophorus; *P. Oslo* III 143.10.

5282 VESTINUS; ii; donkey driver?; III 531.6-7.

5283 VETTIUS; ch. Arasis; July 87; Senepta?, M. Top.; addr. for gd. Philotera; *PSI* III 203.2.

VETURIUS; see. C. VETURIUS GEMELLUS.

5284 VIBIUS; 5/4 BC; centurion; landholder; Roman; W. Top.; land there; *P. Oslo* II 26.23.

5285 T. MALIUS VILLUS; ii; Roman; nr village of Ker-; guardian to sister Malia Iusta; *P. Flor.* III 381.4-5.

5286 XAN( ); Nov 42 BC; Oxy.; witness; *P. Ryl.* IV 582.22.

5287 XENON; ch. Heracles; c. 1; IV 785 (descr.).

5288 ---; 25-37; officer in charge of land distr.; land ceded in Thmois. Top.; *PSI* X 1118.4.

5289 ---; ch. Hecaton; c. 52/53 (date of R); Oxy.; *PSI* IX 1029 V 9.

5290 ---; July 66; agent; Oxy.; II 246.35.

5291 ---; 89; Dionysius his rep. (1); (1) II 332 (descr.); (2) 333 (descr.).

5292 XENO(N); early i; II 389 (descr.).

5293 XENUS; ii; Oxy.; XII 1584.24.

5294 ZENARION; d. of Dionysius; sp. Phanias alias Amois; ch. Dionysius alias Amois; March 79; property owner; Oxyrhynchite; Oxy.; dec.; part house in Hermaeum qtr; II 243.8.

5295 ---; sp. Heron(?); 82; landholder; Oxy.; II 286.2.

5296 ---; d. of Heracleides, s. of Hephaestion; sp. Sarapion; Feb 91; Oxyrhynchite; Temgenuthis qtr; addr. for dec. sp.; unnamed d.; reports death of slave weaver Diogas; XLI 2957.3.

5297 ZENAS; s. of Zenas, s. of Heras; m. Areia, d. of ..ticus; (1) i - ii; (2) ii; landholder; Oxyrhynchite; Heracles Place qtr; aged 13 in 88/89; leases land at Antipera and Sento; *PSI* VII 731.6; (2) *P. Erl.* 44 iii 22.

5298 ---; s. of Heras; sp. Areia; ch. Heras alias Gaius, Zenas; (1) i - ii; (2) c. 107-112; (3) 117-137; (4) ii; Oxyrhynchite; Heracles Place qtr?; addr. for s.; (1) *PSI* VII 731.6; (2) IV 450 R 1, 23; (3) I 105.18; (4) *P. Erl.* 44 iii 22.

5299 ZENODORUS; ch. Dioscorus; 57; Oxy.; II 269.1.

5300 ZM[.]..; c. 1; IV 736.4.

5301 ZOILAS; c. 100; *P. Yale* 77.31.

5302 ZOILUS; 6/5 BC; banker w. Dionysius; Sarapeum; (1) *P. Yale* 60.4; (2) *PSI* X 1099.4.

5303 ---; ch. Zoilus; (1) 50; (2) 55; Oxy.?; addr. for s.; (1) II 324.11; (2) 304.22.

5304 ---; s. of Zoilus; (1) 50; (2) 55; Oxy.; writes for Tryphon; (1) II 324.10; (2) 304.22.

---; see APHYNCHIS.

5305 ---; s. of Theon; Aug 57; Oxy.; X 1316 (descr.).

5306 ---; s. of Horus, s. of Zoilus; m. Dieus, d. of Soceus; (1) 57; (2) Sept 66; Oxy.; writes for Dioscorus, s. of Zenodorus (1), and for Ptolemaeus, weaver (2); (1) II 269.17; (2) 275.41.

5307 ---; ch. Horus; Sept 66; Oxy.; addr. for gs. Zoilus; II 275.41.

5308 ---; ch. Philostratus; 66-72/73; Alexandria; addr. for s.; IX 1203 + *SB* IV 7339.5.

5309 ---; ch. Sarapous; 81-96; Oxy.; ch. being married; II 265.41.

5310 ---; s. of Apollonius, s. of Ptollion; m. Ptolema, d. of Ischyrion; 90; agent for M. Porcius; Senepta, M. Top.; age c. 48; signalement; illiterate; I 72.2.

5311 ZOILUS; s. of Plutarchus; sp. Thatres; ch. Plutarchus; i?; hamlet of Nomus; doc. pr. Oxy.?; addr. for s.; *P. Harris* 138 i 2.

5312 ---; i?; wine merchant; *P. Erl.* 93.6.

5313 ---; s. of Ptolemaeus; Jan 100; farmer; landholder?; Nemerae, M. Top.; XLI 2960.9-10.

5314 ---; ch. Pecysis; 100; Oxyrhynchite; Oxy.; addr. for gd. Sinthoonis; I 49.6.

5315 ---; s. of Sarapion, s. of Petosorapis; ch. Terathonis, Saras, Theon; 117/118; property and land owner; Pammenes' Garden qtr; land also held in U. Top. and Thmois. Top.; XIV 1648.26.

5316 ---; Dec 117/Jan 118; Pammenes' Garden qtr; buys part house w. Synistor from Sarapion; III 577 (descr.).

5317 ---; s. of Panechotes; ch. Zoilus; 117-137; Oxyrhynchite?; Oxy.; addr. for s.; I 105.16.

5318 ---; s. of Zoilus, s. of Panechotes; 117-137; Oxyrhynchite?; Oxy.; age 48; witness of will; signalement; I 105.16.

5319 ---; ch. Taamois; 124; Oxyrhynchite?; Oxy.; addr. for gs., cousin of Tastraton; III 490.3.

5320 ---; s. of Theon, s. of Theon; 126; Oxyrhynchite; Oxy.; addr. for s., witness to will; III 491.19.

5321 ---; s. of Apion; sp. Neilarous; ch. Apion; 130; Oxyrhynchite?; Oxy.; addr. for s.; III 492.18.

5322 ---; Jan 132; bibliophylax w. Hadrion; Oxy.; III 478.1.

5323 ---; ch. Ptolemaeus alias Ptolemais; 137; Oxy.; IV 729.37.

5324 ---; early ii; III 649 (descr.).

5325 ---; ii; VII 1062.16.

5326 ---; ch. Apollonius; ii; I 164 (descr.).

5327 ---; ii; *P. Inst. Fran.* I 4.4.

5328 ---; ii VII 1034 V 1.

5329 ---; s. of Thoonis; ii; landholder; land nr (Ta)ampemou and property in Oxy.; *P. Inst. Fran.* III 15.14.

5330 ---; ii; "brother" of Apia; Oxy.; XII 1581.[1]V.

5331 ZOIS; 30; "sister" of Ischyrion and Hermogenes?; X 1291.1.

5332 ---; d. of Amois, s. of Dionysius; m. Taseus; Oct 62; Sesphtha?, L. Top.; age c. 45; XXXVIII 2873 V 30.

5333 ---; d. of -ius; ch. Thaisous; 89; *P. Fouad* 48.6.

5334 ZOIS; d. of Antipater; sp. Diogenes; ch. Thaesis; 98-102; Oxyrhynchite?; Oxy.; addr. for d.; *P. Mert.* I 13.3.

5335 ---; d. of Tyrus; sp. Horion; ch. Malanous; i - ii; Isieum Tryphones?; addr. for d.; sp. owns catoecic land nr Talao; *PSI* VI 687.1.

5336 ZOPYRUS; sp. Toutheus; ch. Pausirion; Oxyrhynchite; Oxy.?; addr. for s.; *P. Harris* 138 i 13.

5337 CLAUDIA ZOSIME; alias HERMIONE; c. 135; Roman; may not be an Oxy.; unnamed ch; claims tax relief in Mendesian nome under lex laetoria; XVII 2111 i 13.

5338 ..A..NUS; s. of Horus; sp. Sinthoonis; ch. Paatis; 99; Oxy.?; addr. for s.; *P. Princ.* II 32.4.

5339 ...]ALLIAS; ii; Oxyrhynchite; doc. pr. Tebtynis; restored by editor as Ser]allias; *P. Mil. Vogl.* IV 211 a3.

5340 ....AROS; s. of Dionysius, s. of [Sar]a[pi]on; 123; Oxyrhynchite; Oxy.; I 107.1.

5341]AS; gd. of Ammonius; 132/133; unnamed ch.; lives at same house as unnamed bro., s. of Tryphon; *PSI* I 53 xi 178.

5342 [..].[..]AS; m. Thaisas, d. of Ptolemaeus; sp. Nicanor; ch. Isidorus; 78/79; Oxyrhynchite; Thoeris St qtr; XXXVI 2765.4.

5343]ASEEUS; m. Tnephersois; end i; slave; Oxy.; age c. 28; slave of Theopompion; here emancipated; name may be Th]aseeus or P]aseeus; *P. Sel.* 23.7.

5344 [..].ẠṢṬẠS(?); 27; Oxy.; XVIII 2148.9.

5345]ATUS; 48; appointee of agoranomi; appt. w. Theon; reg. appointment by Thaesis of Ptollion; *P. Fouad* 35.16.

5346 .]BỊ[....]; ch. Petosarapis; 96; Oxyrhynchite?; Oxy.?; addṛ. for gd. Sinthonis; II 266.11.

5347]CE; s. of Atreus (Hatres?); ch. Diogenes; Dec 78/Jan 76; Oxyrhynchite?; Oxy.?; addr. for s.; *P. Yale* 64.7.

5348 ...CHAS; s. of [...]mis; sp. Helene; ch. N[...]lus; i; Senepta, M. Top.; doc. pr. Oxy.?; addr. for s.; *P. Harris* 138 i 4.

5349 ...]CHONSIS; April 5 BC; *OD Pisa* 936 Convesso 6.

5350 ....]CHUS; s. of Tero[.]o[; 83/84; Alex., Zeneius?; cedes land in Sinary, L. Top.; "brother" is [ ]us, s. of Dioscorus, but father's name different; XII 1462.20.

5351 .....DIUS; 98-117; agoranomus; Oxy.; *P. Sel.* 24.10.

5352]ḌORUS; ii; cosmetes; Oxy.?; *P. Warren* 13.24.

-E; see DIONYSIA.

-E; see ISIDORA.

5353 [..]EIA; d.of Apollonius; sp. Mnesitheus; ch. Demetrous; after 102; Oxy.; addr. for d. who owned part house in Temgenuthis qtr; III 636.7.

5354].EIBIUS; s. of Ch...[; i - ii; *PSI* VII 814.29.

5355 ..ERIUS; Sept 16; friend or relative of Hermophilus; IV 746.5.

5356 ...ERIUS; ch. Sarap( ); 2nd half i; Sesphtha, L. Top.; addr. for s.; XXXVIII 2845.4.

5357 .[..]EROS; ch. Leon; 36; II 267.26.

5358]ESIS; Nov 45; Oxyrhynchite; Hippodrome qtr; unnamed s.; X 1258.1.

5359]ESIS; s. of Petosiris; 71/72; tax farmer?; *P. Ryl.* II 92.2.

5360]ESIUS; 98-117; agoranomus; *P. Sel.* 24.10.

5361 ...EURIS; s. of Nicostratus; Jan 28; livestock owner; Pela, W. Top.; II 351.2

5362]IA; sp. Totoes; ch. -is; 132/133; *PSI* I 53 i 15.

5363]ION; ch. Aperos; 148/149; Oxy.?; addr. for gs.; XLVI 3279.18.

5364]IS; d. of Totoes, s. of Heleis; m. -ia; sp. Heliodorus; 132/133; age 25; no trade; unnamed d. aged 5; *PSI* I 53 i 14.

5365 ...IS; d. of Harsiesis; May 96; treated by Theon at request of Peisis; *PSI Bartoletti Colombo* 1.11.

5366]ISIS; s. of Pasis; i; *OD Pisa* 60 Convesso i 3.

5367]IUS; ch. Heracleides; 54/53 BC; s. leases land from Asclepiades in Kleros of Alexandrus nr Seryphis; *PSI* X 1097.2.

5368 ---; ch. Zois; 89; *P. Fouad* 48.7.

5369 ---; m. Thaisous; ii; landholder; *P. Erl.* 44 ii 15.

5370]LAS; ii; unnamed s. leases land at Antipera; *P. Erl.* 44 ii 20.

5371 .[.]LBANON; 31/32; Sinary?, L. Top.; *P. Mich. inv.* 60.23.

-LUFENNIUS; see MACER.

5372 [..]MIDES; i; Oxy.; age 55; *P. Ryl.* II 156 V.

5373 ....]MINIS; ch. Aristandrus; 137; Oxy.?; addr. for gs. Tryphon; *PSI* XII 1262 ii 1.

5374 [...]MIS; ch. [...]chas; i; Senepta?, M. Top.; doc. pr. Oxy.?; addr. for gs. N[...]lus; *P. Harris* 138 i 4.

5375 ..MUS; ch. Eunomus; Sept 103; Toka, M. Top.; addr. for gd. Athenarous; XLI 2973.3.

5376 [...]N; s. of Leon; sp. Pausirion; ch. Hellenis; i; Oxyrhynchite; Oxy.; *P. Harris* 138 i 16.

5377 ....]NIS; d. of Didymus; sp. Petosiris; ch. Pane[ ]; 71; Senekeleu?, W. Top.; addr. for s.; *P. Med. inv.* 71.70.5.

5378]NIS; m. Sinthoonis; 98-117; slave; age c. 17; signalement; slave of Sinthoonis, d. of Thoonis; *P. Sel.* 24.5.

5379 [....]NIUS; sp. Sarapion; ch. Nechthosiris; i; Oxyrhynchite?; Oxy.?; addr. for s.; *P. Harris* 138 iii 13.

5380]NIUS; ii; Oxy.?; addr. for gs. Didymus; *P. Palau Rib. inv.* 150.2.

5381]ṆTOṬḤIS; s. of Petalus; 71/72; tax farmer; Oxy.?; connection w. Oxy. through other names in doc.; *P. Ryl.* II 95.4.

5382]NUS; s. of Appian; ii; doc. pr. Oxy.?; summoned by Heracleides; *SB* VI 9025.30.

5383 ....OḌ.IMOṆ[..; Oct 111; slave; of Ti. Julius Theon, games victor; XLIV 3197.16.

5384]ON; s. of Apollonius; 43/44; leases land from royal farmlands nr Pela from Sarapion; II 368.2.

5385 ---; s. of Latinus; ii; Oxy.; *P. Stras.* 299 R 17.

5386 ---; s. of Isidorus; 1st half i; Oxy.?; addr. for unnamed s., banker in Sarapeum; *P. Inst. Fran.* III 30.4.

5387 [...]ON; ch. Papontos; i; Senepta?, M. Top.; doc. pr. Oxy.?; addr. for gs. Papontos; *P. Harris* 138 i 12.

5388]ONIDES; ch. Sampatym[is?; 68; Oxy.; XIV 1614.23.

...ONIUS; see DIONYSIUS.

5389]..PAEUS; s. of Pneu..[or Pneb..[; ii; Senocomis, W. Top.; *P. Fuad I Univ.* 32.6.

5390 [...]PSAMOUS; s. of Haryotes; i; farmer; Sesphtha; *P. Ryl.* II 199.16.

5391]PSERSOIS; sp. Heliodorus; ch. Dionysius; 132/133; *PSI* I 53 i 4.

5392]ṚENUS; ii?; Pela, W. Top.; *P. Fuad I Univ.* 32.15.

5393 [....]..RIO( ); s. of Lagous; i; farmer; Sesphtha; *P. Ryl.* II 199.15.

5394 c. 5]RIS; d. of Panechotes; sp. Pausirion; ch. Sarapion; 148/149; Oxyrhynchite; gymnasial class; Knights' Camp qtr; s. enr. this yr in 13 yr olds; XLVI 3279.9.

5395].[.]RON; alias SARAPION; ii; Pela, W. Top.; *P. Fuad I Univ.* 32.13.

5396]Ṛ OS; s. of Apollophanes; 6-35; Oxy.; II 256.4.

5397 ..RSIS; s. of Epag[athus; ii; Oxyrhynchite; witness to will; III 647.16.

5398 ..]TENORUS?; s. of Diogenes; ii; Oxy.; witness to will; III 647.14.

5399 ...TES; ii; Oxy.; witness to will; III 647.13.

5400]TETHEUS; d. of Artemidorus; ii; Oxy.; *P. Flor.* III 381.3.

5401 ..TICUS; ch. Areia; i - ii; Roman (s.v. Areia); *PSI* VII 731.7.

5402 ....]TOEIUS; s. of Cames; Sept 31 BC; river fisherman; Tholthis, Thmois. Top.; *P. Wurz.* 5.2.

5403 c. 8]US; s. of Philotes; 30 BC - 14; farmer of public land; *P. Rein.* II 99.1.

5404 ...US; ch. Helene; i; Senepta?, M. Top.; addr. for mat. gs. N[...]lus; *P. Harris* 138 i 5.

5405]US; s. of Phatres; 51/52; or 64/65; *P. Mil.* II 53.7.

5406 ---; s. of Apollonius; May/June 101; landholder; doc. pr. Oxy.?; held catoecic land in A[ ], returns it; *P. Bour.* 16.15.

5407 ---; s. of Diogenes; ii; Posbthis; *P. Erl.* 59 R 7.

5408 ---; s. of Diodotus, s. of Demainetus; ii; *P. Flor.* III 381.14.

5409 .]US LUCRETIU[S -; c. 92; soldier?; *P. Michael* 9.133.

5410]UTUS; s. of Plutus, s. of Demetrius; i - ii; phronistes; agent for Macer; *PSI* VI 687.6.

5411]YRIS; d. of Papontos; i; hamlet of Nomus; *P. Harris* 138 i 1.

5412 3psns[(?); Aug 3; read 3psms (Apsemis?),n. ad. loc.; *OD Pisa* 473 Concavo ii 4.

5413 3llj; i BC - i; *OD Pisa* 243 + 472 i 10.

5414 In-w-p_3-mw; i BC - i; *OD Pisa* 132 X + 5.

5415 Ir.t(?); i BC - i; *OD Pisa* 360 Convesso 1.

5416 Jb; s. of Wḥj; i BC - i; *OD Pisa* 22.4.

5417 Jm; i BC - i; Psenbastis his dependant; *OD Pisa* 502 X + 8.

5418 E-ir-^{c}w; early i; *OD Pisa* 293.5.

5419 E-ir-tj; ch. ^{c}nh-Ij-m-ḥtp; i BC - i; *OD Pisa* 460 Convesso i X + 8.

5420 E-n-in.iw; s. of Kmj; early i; *OD Pisa* 450A Concavo i 12.

5421 E-n-st$_3$-n.im-n; early i; *OD Pisa* 450A Concavo i 11.

5422 E-n-st$_3$-n.im.n.m.s$_3$-n$_3$e-n-šj; early i; *OD Pisa* 450A Concavo i 5-6.

5423 E-f-st$_3$-n.im-w; s of Petesnes; i BC - i; *OD Pisa* 8.18.

5424 ^{c}$_3$; s. of Pabis; i BC - i; *OD Pisa* 281 + 94 X + 5.

5425 ^{c}$_3$; i BC - i; *OD Pisa* 38 X + 10, 13.

5426 ^{c}š$_3$; ch. Petemunis; i BC - i; *OD Pisa* 111 Convesso 8.

5427 ^{c}nḫ-Ij-m-ḥtp; s. of E-ir-tj; i BC - i; *OD Pisa* 460 Convesso i X + 8.

5428 ---; i BC - i; *OD Pisa* 460 Convesso i X + 7.

5429 ---; i BC - i; *OD Pisa* 755 Concavo X + 5.

5430 W$_3$ḥ-p$_3$-^{c}$_3$; ch. Celol; i BC - i; *OD Pisa* 543 X + 4.

5431 W$_3$ḥ-p$_3$-pr-^{c}$_3$(?); i BC - i; *OD Pisa* 541 Convesso ii 1.

5432 W$_3$ḥ-p$_3$-ḫr-j; early i; *OD Pisa* 293.7.

5433 W$_3$ḥ-n$_3$-ḳl$_3$; s. of W^{c}nb; early i; *OD Pisa* 234 Convesso 8.

5434 W$_3$ḥ-t$_3$-ḳt(?); early i; *OD Pisa* 450B Convesso ii X + 3.

5435 ---; ch. Kmj; (1), (2), (3), (4), i BC - i; (5) late i BC - early i; (1) *OD Pisa* 29 ii X + 2; (2) 8.16, 24; (3) 360 Concavo X + 3, X + 4; (4) 667.2; (5) 35 Convesso 6.

5436 W^c-nb; ch. W$_3$ḥ-n$_3$-ḳl$_3$; early i; *OD Pisa* 234 Convesso 8.

5437 Wn; s. of Sgj; i BC - i; *OD Pisa* 460 Convesso ii X + 6.

5438 Wn-Inn; i BC - i; *OD Pisa* 106.6.

5439 Wn-nfr-iw(?); i; *OD Pisa* 60 Convesso i 4.

5440 Wrš; ch. Pamunis (Pamun); i BC - i; *OD Pisa* 460 Convesso ii X + 3.

5441 Wḥj; ch. Petemunis; April 5 BC; *OD Pisa* 936 Concavo 7.

5442 Wḥ[j(?); i BC - i; *OD Pisa* 256.2.

5443 Wḥj; i BC - i; *OD Pisa* 8.12, 24.

5444 ---; i BC - i; *OD Pisa* 58.11.

5445 ---; ch. Harendotes; i BC - i; *OD Pisa* 513 + 514 + 515 i X + 6.

5446 ---; ch. Jb, Haremphois; i BC - i; *OD Pisa* 22.4.

5447 ---; s. of Haremphois; i BC - i; *OD Pisa* 22.5.

5448 Wḥj; i BC - i; *OD Pisa* 513 + 514 + 515 ii X + 3.

5449 ---; i BC - i; Petesis his dependant; *OD Pisa* 111 Convesso 2.

5450 ---; i BC - i; *OD Pisa* 360 Convesso 5.

5451 ---; i BC - i; *OD Pisa* 667.7.

5452 ---; i BC - i; *OD Pisa* 281 + 94 X + 1, X + 7, X + 9, X + 12.

5453 ---; ch. Peteesis; late i BC - early i; *OD Pisa* 35 Convesso 3.

5454 ---; ch. Patous(?); late i BC - early i; *OD Pisa* 35 Convesso 11.

5455 ---; ch. Petamenophis; late i BC - early i; *OD Pisa* 35 Concavo ii 9.

5456 ---; late i BC - early i; *OD Pisa* 35 Convesso 7.

5457 ---; Aug 3; *OD Pisa* 473 Convesso 5.

5458 ---; ch. Sarmates; July 7; *OD Pisa* 1131 Concavo 4.

5459 ---; early i; *OD Pisa* 234 Convesso 2.

5460 ---; early i; *OD Pisa* 450A Concavo i 13.

5461 ---; i; *OD Pisa* 39 i X + 3, 6.

5462 Wsr; i BC - i; *OD Pisa* 779 + 242 Concavo 8.

5463 Bw-j-pḥ; s. of T$_3$-ḳt(?); early i; *OD Pisa* 450A Concavo i 2.

5464 Bw-j-pḥ-mw; s. of Kmj; early i; *OD Pisa* 450A Concavo i 7.

5465 ---; early i; *OD Pisa* 450A Concavo i 3.

Bw-nfr; see HARPAESIS.

5466 P$_3$-[ ]; i BC - i; *OD Pisa* 87 X + 5.

5467 P$_3$-...[; ch. Haremphois; i BC - i; *OD Pisa* 25 ii 21.

5468 P$_3$-....; i BC - i; *OD Pisa* 5 ii X + 7.

5469 P$_3$-...; i BC - i; *OD Pisa* 276 X + 9.

5470 P$_3$-irj; ch. N$_3$-ḥtrw; i BC - i; *OD Pisa* 22.6.

5471 P$_3$-irj; early i; *OD Pisa* 419.11.

5472 P$_3$-$^{c}{}_3$[; i BC - i; *OD Pisa* 755 Convesso X + 17.

5473 P$_3$-wjnn; i BC - i; *OD Pisa* 280 X + 5.

5474 P$_3$-wrš; ch. Petosiris; i BC - i; *OD Pisa* 451 + 540 Convesso 10.

5475 ---; s. of Nfr-iw; i BC - i; *OD Pisa* 5 i X + 11.

5476 P$_3$-wš; i BC - i; *OD Pisa* 72 ii X + 3.

5477 ---; i BC - i; *OD Pisa* 276 X + 8.

5478 P$_3$-[m]bwr; s. of Kmj; April 5 BC; *OD Pisa* 936 Concavo 10.

5479 P$_3$-mlhw; i BC - i; *OD Pisa* 1264 Convesso 1.

5480 P$_3$-nš(?); i BC - i; *OD Pisa* 543 X + 5.

5481 P$_3$j-n$_3$-ḫt.w...; i BC - i; *OD Pisa* 532 X + 8.

5482 P$_3$-nḥs; i BC - i; agent for Petosiris; *OD Pisa* 451 + 540 Convesso 10.

5483 P$_3$-rj.t; ch. Nectenibis; i BC - i; *OD Pisa* 504.7.

5484 P$_3$-rmt-Ib; i BC - i; *OD Pisa* 1023 Convesso ii 3.

5485 P$_3$-rmt-m$_3$j(?); ch. Totoes; i BC - i; *OD Pisa* 755 Concavo X + 10.

5486 P$_3$-rmt-nbj(?); n.d.; *DO Colon. inv.* 53.

5487 P$_3$-rmt-.....hnjn; April 4; *OD Pisa* 511 + 512 i 9.

5488 P$_3$-rḫtj; ch. Petechonsis; early i; *OD Pisa* 164.4.

5489 P$_3$-lljs; i BC - i; *OD Pisa* 69 Concavo 5.

5490 P$_3$-lḫ; i BC - i; *OD Pisa* 137 Convesso 9.

5491 P$_3$-ḥbs; early i; *OD Pisa* 450A Concavo ii 1.

5492 ---; s. of Portious; early i; Harpaesis his dependant; *OD Pisa* 234 Convesso 1.

5493 P$_3$-ḥr-s$_3$-ls.t (Paorsaisis?); i BC - i; *OD Pisa* 126 i 3.

5494 P$_3$-ḫ$_3^{(c)}$; i BC - i; *OD Pisa* 470.8.

5495 P$_3$-ḫf; i BC - i; *OD Pisa* 137 Convesso 5.

5496 P$_3$-ḫnsw(?); 9; dyke man; *DO Colon. inv.* 300.1.

5497 P$_3$-sp; ch. Harpaesis; i BC - i; *OD Pisa* 502 X + 6.

5498 P$_3$-spj; ch. Harpaesis; (1), (2) i BC - i; (3) Sept 6; (4) i; (1) *OD Pisa* 23 ii 6; (2) 25 ii 8; (3) 814 Convesso 8; (4) 318.2.

5499 ---; s. of Menon; i BC - i; *OD Pisa* 111 Convesso 7.

5500 ---; ch. Petechonsis; April 4; *OD Pisa* 511 + 512 i 13.

5501 P$_3$-sn-mbwr; i BC - i; *OD Pisa* 460 Convesso i X + 11.

5502 P$_3$-sḥn; ch. Petechonsis; early i; *OD Pisa* 450B Concavo i X + 7.

5503 P$_3$-sẖ-ḥt-ntr; i BC - i; *OD Pisa* 38 i X + 11.

5504 P$_3$-swg(?); i BC - i; *OD Pisa* 779 + 242 Convesso X + 11.

5505 P$_3$j-st$_3$(?); ch. Harpaesis; i BC - i; *OD Pisa* 779 + 242 Convesso X + 14.

5506 P$_3$-stjws; i BC - i; acts for Petosiris; *OD Pisa* 510 + 568 Convesso i 12.

5507 P$_3$-šwtj; ch. Horus; i BC - i; *OD Pisa* 451 + 540 Convesso 4.

5508 P$_3$-šr-p$_3$-mw(?); n.d.; *DO Colon. inv.* 280.

5509 P$_3$-šrj-p$_3$-$_3$b$_3$ (*Psenpebos); ch. Pamun; (1) i BC - i; (2) i; (1) *OD Pisa* 25 i 7; (2) 129 X + 10.

5510 P$_3$-šrj-p$_3$-lj-snj(?); April 5 BC; *OD Pisa* 936 Concavo 11.

5511 P$_3$-šrj-ḳns; ch. Haremphois, Petamunis; i BC - i; *OD Pisa* 29 ii X + 7, X + 8.

5512 P$_3$-šrj-ḳtn($_3$); i BC - i; *OD Pisa* 23 ii 3.

5513 P$_3$-tj-jm (*Peteiomis?); ch. Apollonius; i; *OD Pisa* 318.5.

5514 P$_3$-tj-nb-...; s. of Petosiris; i BC - i; *OD Pisa* 25 ii 16.

5515 P$_3$-tš; i BC - i; Arieus his dependant; *OD Pisa* 69 Convesso i 11.

5516 P$_3$-ḏjḥ...; i BC - i; *OD Pisa* 561 + 562 + 795 i X + 11.

5517 P$_3$-dj-ḫnsw; n.d. *DO Colon. inv.* 280.

5518 Pa-itm; ch. Petechonsis; i BC - i; *OD Pisa* 276 X + 6.

5519 Pa-ptḥ; ch. Ḥwn; i; *OD Pisa* 60 Convesso i 8.

5520 Pa-mwt; ch. Harpaesis; i BC - i; *OD Pisa* 276 X + 2.

5521 Pa-lg; i BC - i; Petemunis his dependant; *OD Pisa* 99 i 9.

5522 Pa-ḥj; i BC - i; *OD Pisa* 454.2.

5523 Pa-ḫ$_3$^{c}; April 5 BC; *OD Pisa* 936 Concavo 3.

5524 Pa-sp; s. of Snn; i BC - i; *OD Pisa* 460 Convesso i X + 9.

5525 Pa-spjn; i BC - i; *OD Pisa* 137 Convesso 3.

5526 Pa-ḳj; i BC - i; *OD Pisa* 132 X + 11.

5527 Pa-ggi; i BC - i; *OD Pisa* 204.1.

5528 Pa-t$_3$-ḳllj; i BC - i; *OD Pisa* 243 + 472 i 5.

5529 Pa-tbḫtj(?); i; *OD Pisa* 60 Convesso i 15.

5530 Pr-imnt.t; ch. Menches; i BC - i; *OD Pisa* 22.9.

5531 Prprs; i BC - i; *OD Pisa* 106.5.

5532 Prgs; s. of Harpaesis; i BC - i; *OD Pisa* 5 ii X + 12.

5533 ---; i BC - i; *OD Pisa* 5 ii X + 10.

5534 Psl$_3$(?); i BC - i; *OD Pisa* 779 + 242 Convesso X + 2.

5535 M$_3$^{c}(?)-[...]; i BC - i; *OD Pisa* 25 i 9.

5536 Mn; ch. Petosiris; i BC - i; *OD Pisa* 5 i X + 14.

5537 Mn(?); April 4; Petechonsis his dependant; *OD Pisa* 511 + 512 i 13.

5538 Mltj; 8; *OD Pisa* 1.5.

5539 N$_3$-ḥtrw; s. of P -irj; i BC - i; *OD Pisa* 22.6.

5540 N$_3$-klm$_3$; early i; *OD Pisa* 450A Concavo i 9.

5541 Njlws(?); i BC - i; *OD Pisa* 137 Concavo 4.

5542 Nfr-iw; ch. P$_3$-ws; i BC - i; *OD Pisa* 5 i X + 11.

5543 R-in.w; s. of Kmj; i BC - i; *OD Pisa* 132 X + 7.

5544 Rmtn; i BC - i; *OD Pisa* 360 Concavo X + 5.

5545 R-t$_3$-ḳl$_3$-mn; early i; *OD Pisa* 450A Concavo i 4.

5546 L^c$_3$ (Lu); i BC - i; *OD Pisa* 280 X + 4.

5547 Lpws(?); i BC - i; *OD Pisa* 779 + 242 Convesso X + 10.

5548 H$_3$-nfr; i BC - i; *OD Pisa* 22.3.

5549 Hmj; i BC - i; *OD Pisa* 667.8.

5550 Hrjw-B$_3$st.t; ch. Pateus; Sept 6; (1) *OD Pisa* 431.10; (2) 432.2, 4, 7.

5551 Hrjn; Sept 6; *OD Pisa* 431.7.

5552 Hrjn$_3$.....; Sept 6; *OD Pisa* 814 Concavo 1.

5553 Hrḳs; i BC - i; *OD Pisa* 816 X + 2.

5554 Ḥwn; s. of Pa-Ptḥ; i; *OD Pisa* 60 Convesso i 8.

5555 ---; s. of Celol; i; *OD Pisa* 60 Convesso i 7.

5556 Ḥbs; i; *OD Pisa* 60 Concavo 2.

5557 Ḥr-p$_3$-ḳm(?); ch. Petosiris; i; *OD Pisa* 60 Convesso i 11.

5558 Ḥr-p$_3$-ḳtr(?); late i BC - early i; (1) *OD Pisa* 35 Convesso 8; (2) Concavo ii 5.

5559 Ḥr-mn; s. of Harpaesis; i BC - i; *OD Pisa* 5 ii X + 13.

5560 ---; i BC - i; *OD Pisa* 5 ii X + 5.

5561 Ḥr-mn; ch. Harthotes; i BC - i; *OD Pisa* 5 i X + 13.

5562 Ḥrmjs(Hermes?); i BC - i; *OD Pisa* 543 X + 7.

5563 Ḥr-nḫt; ch. Petosiris; i BC - i; *OD Pisa* 126 i 4.

5564 Ḥr-ḥbj; ch. Onnophris; i BC - i; *OD Pisa* 196 ii X + 5.

5565 Ḥr-smn(?); i; *OD Pisa* 60 Convesso ii 2, 4.

5566 Ḥḳws; s. of Patous; i BC - i; *OD Pisa* 1163 bis Convesso 3.

5567 Ḥr-gwr(?); ch. Petechonsis; i BC - i; *OD Pisa* 543 X + 6.

5568 Ḥlgj; i BC - i; agent for Harpaesis; *OD Pisa* 111 Concavo 1, 3.

5569 ---; i BC - i; *OD Pisa* 510 + 568 Convesso ii 7.

5570 Ḥtws; s. of Harpaesis; (1) i BC; (2) i BC - i; (1) *OD Pisa* 55 ii 10; (2) 38 i X + 5.

5571 ---; i BC - i; *OD Pisa* 132 X + 6.

5572 Ḥtb; ch. Horus; i BC - i; *OD Pisa* 68.3.

5573 Ḫnj(?); ch. T_3-ḳt(?); early i; *OD Pisa* 424.4.

5574 Ḫnsw-ḫb(?); ch. Petechonsis; 9; *DO Colon. inv.* 300.2.

5575 H̱rdw-ḥp; ch. Petosiris; i BC - i; *OD Pisa* 70.1.

5576 Sj-p_3-mwt; i BC - i; name as Sifmu in Italian; *OD Pisa* 117.1.

5577 S^cw(?); ch. Patous; i BC - i; *OD Pisa* 228 X + 7.

5578 Spj; ch. Pasis; i BC - i; *OD Pisa* 451 + 540 Convesso 8.

5579 ---; i BC - i; *OD Pisa* 137 Convesso 6.

5580 Smj; s. of Arieus; Sept 6; *OD Pisa* 431.4.

5581 $Smtrw_3$; i BC - i; slave owner; slave Patesis; *OD Pisa* 108 X + 2.

5582 Sn-ḥp(?); ch. Petesis; i BC - i; *OD Pisa* 460 Convesso ii X + 4.

5583 Snmns; i BC - i; Pamias his dependant; *OD Pisa* 502 X + 5.

5584 Snn; ch. Nechutes; i BC - i; *OD Pisa* 755 Concavo X + 7.

5585 ---; ch. Psenamunis; i BC - i; *OD Pisa* 460 Convesso i X + 12.

5586 ---; ch. Pa-sp; i BC - i; *OD Pisa* 460 Convesso i X + 9.

5587 ---; i BC - i; Petubastis his dependant; *OD Pisa* 460 Convesso ii X + 13.

5588 Srj; i BC - i; *OD Pisa* 360 Concavo X + 2.

5589 Srj; i BC - i; *OD Pisa* 69 Convesso i 13.

5590 Srtn$_3$; i BC - i; *OD Pisa* 25 i 23.

5591 Slj; s. of Harsiesis; i BC - i; *OD Pisa* 1163 bis Convesso 2.

5592 Sẖl$_3$; i BC - i; *OD Pisa* 25 i 9.

5593 Sḳrw[; i BC - i; *OD Pisa* 108 X + 5.

5594 Sgj; ch. Wn; i BC - i; *OD Pisa* 460 Convesso ii X + 6.

5595 Sgn(j)s; ch. Haremphois; i BC - i; *OD Pisa* 23 i X + 11.

5596 Stjgjn; i BC - i; *OD Pisa* 217 Convesso X + 4.

5597 Stw$_3$s(?); i BC - i; *OD Pisa* 58.13.

5598 Šw-tf̣n.t; ch. Petesis; i BC - i; *OD Pisa* 510 + 568 Convesso i 8.

5599 Šp; ch. Harpocrates; i; *OD Pisa* 60 Convesso i 10.

5600 Šm^{c}; i BC - i; *OD Pisa* 351 X + 1.

5601 ---; i B C - i; *OD Pisa* 69 Convesso i 4.

5602 ---; i BC - i; *OD Pisa* 111 Concavo 8.

5603 ---; ch. Petosiris; early i; *OD Pisa* 164.1.

5604 Šmr; i BC - i; *OD Pisa* 779 + 242 Convesso X + 7.

5605 ---; ch. Pasis i; *OD Pisa* 60 Concavo 1.

5606 Šmrw; ch. Pasis; i BC - i; *OD Pisa* 502 X + 10.

5607 ---; ch. Ḏd; i BC - i; *OD Pisa* 87 X + 6.

5608 Ḳrḳt; i BC - i; *OD Pisa* 1163 bis Concavo B 2, 3.

5609 Ḳl[ ]; i BC - i; *OD Pisa* 755 Convesso X + 16.

5610 Ḳlp; i BC - i; *OD Pisa* 99 i 7.

5611 Kpbs; Aug 3; bro. Cathytes; *OD Pisa* 473 Concavo i 4.

5612 Kmj; ch. P$_3$-[m]bwr; April 5 BC; *OD Pisa* 936 Concavo 10.

5613 ---; i BC; *OD Pisa* 55.1.

5614 ---; s. of Hatres; i BC - i; *OD Pisa* 58.9.

5615 ---; s. of W$_3$ḥ-t$_3$-ḳt(?); (1), (2), (3) i BC - i; (4) late i BC - early i; (1) *OD Pisa* 8.16, 23-24; (2) 29 ii X + 2; (3) 360 Concavo X + 3; (4) 35 Convesso 6.

5616 ---; s. of T$_3$-ḳt; i BC - i; *OD Pisa* 377 Convesso 4, 6; Concavo 3.

5617 ---; s. of Ḏjḥ; i BC - i; *OD Pisa* 513 + 514 + 515 i X + 7.

5618 Kmj; ch. Haremphois(?); i BC - i; *OD Pisa* 29 ii X + 9.

5619 ---; ch. Harpaesis; i BC - i; *OD Pisa* 232.9.

5620 ---; ch. Patous; i BC - i; *OD Pisa* 137 Convesso 2.

5621 ---; ch. Pausiris; i BC - i; *OD Pisa* 38 i X + 12.

5622 Kmj; ch. Thoteus; i BC - i; *OD Pisa* 667.4.

5623 ---; s. of W_3ḥ-t_3-ḳt; i BC - i; *OD Pisa* 667.2.

5624 ---; ch. R-in-w; i BC - i; *OD Pisa* 132 X + 7.

5625 ---; i BC - i; *OD Pisa* 8.2, 5, 6, 8, 13, 15, 17, 20.

5626 ---; i BC - i; *OD Pisa* 22.3, 6, 8, 11.

5627 ---; i BC - i; *OD Pisa* 58.8, 10, 12.

5628 ---; i BC - i; *OD Pisa* 217 Convesso X + 7, Concavo ii X + 6.

5629 ---; i BC - i; *OD Pisa* 256.4.

5630 ---; i BC - i; *OD Pisa* 218 + 94 X + 4, X + 8, X + 10.

5631 ---; i BC - i; *OD Pisa* 360 Convesso 2, 3.

5632 ---; i BC - i; *OD Pisa* 377 Convesso 9, Concavo 7, 15.

5633 Kmj(?); i BC - i; *OD Pisa* 460 Concavo X + 2.

5634 Kmj; i BC - i; *OD Pisa* 541 Convesso i 3, 5, Concavo 4.

5635 ---; i BC - i; *OD Pisa* 561 + 562 + 795 i X + 10.

5636 ---; late i BC - early i; *OD Pisa* 35 Concavo ii 14, Convesso 23.

5637 ---; ch. Peteesis; late i BC - early i; *OD Pisa* 35 Convesso 4, 10.

5638 ---; ch. Harchypsis; late i BC - early i; *OD Pisa* 35 Convesso 13.

5639 ---; ch. Pasis; (1) late i BC - early i; (2) i; (1) *OD Pisa* 35 Convesso 2; (2) 39 i X + 4, 5, 7, 8.

5640 ---; Aug 3; *OD Pisa* 473 Concavo ii 3.

5641 ---; ch. Plenis; April 4; *OD Pisa* 511 + 512 i 2.

5642 ---; early i; *OD Pisa* 450A Concavo i 1.

5643 ---; ch. Bw-j-pḥ-mw; early i; *OD Pisa* 450A Concavo i 7.

5644 ---; ch. E-n-in.iw; early i; *OD Pisa* 450A Concavo i 12.

5645 Gjbws; ch. Petosiris; i BC - i; *OD Pisa* 111 Convesso 4.

5646 Gwms; i BC - i; *OD Pisa* 460 Convesso ii X + 12.

5647 Gwr; i BC - i; *OD Pisa* 755 Concavo X + 12.

5648 Gm-w-r.ḥr-n; early i; *OD Pisa* 293.6.

5649 Gm-n$_3$-gwr-r.ḥr-n; early i; *OD Pisa* 293.2-3.

5650 Gm-n-p$_3$-ẖrj; early i; *OD Pisa* 293.4.

5651 Gntjs; i BC - i; *OD Pisa* 510 + 568 Convesso i 15.

5652 Gll (Celol?); ch. Petosiris; 8; *OD Pisa* 1.7.

5653 Gllj; i BC - i; *OD Pisa* 510 + 568 Concavo ii 6.

5654 Ghwj; i BC - i; Psenthotes his dependant; *OD Pisa* 8.1.

5655 Gtws; s. of Petechonsis; i BC - i; *OD Pisa* 1163 bis Concavo B 1.

5656 Gtpns; i BC - i; *OD Pisa* 29 ii X + 5.

5657 T$_3$-rj.t-ḥrj-t; early i; *OD Pisa* 456.6.

5658 T$_3$-ḳt(?); i BC - i; *OD Pisa* 256.3.

5659 ---; i BC - i; *OD Pisa* 473 Convesso 3, 5, 13, Concavo 5, 8.

5660 ---; i BC - i; *OD Pisa* 513 + 514 + 515 i X + 15.

5661 ---; i BC - i; *OD Pisa* 541 Convesso i 6.

5662 ---; i BC - i; *OD Pisa* 516 + 562 + 795 i X + 12.

5663 ---; ch. Petemunis; i BC - i; *OD Pisa* 217 Convesso X + 6.

5664 ---; ch. Kmj; i BC - i; *OD Pisa* 377 Convesso 4, 6, Concavo 3.

5665 T$_3$-ḳt(?)l ch. Pausiris; i BC - i; *OD Pisa* 243 + 472 i 1.

5666 T$_3$-ḳt; ch. Pausiris; i BC - i; *OD Pisa* 38 i X + 13.

5667 T$_3$-ḳt(?); ch. Petamenophis; late i BC - early i; *OD Pisa* 35 Convesso 21.

5668 ---; late i BC - early i; agent for Pasis; *OD Pisa* 35 Convesso 2, 9.

5669 ---; ch. Pasis; late i BC - early i; *OD Pisa* 35 Convesso 5.

5670 ---; ch. Bw-j-pḥ; early i; *OD Pisa* 450A Concavo i 2.

5671 ---; early i; *OD Pisa* 450B Concavo ii X + 2.

5672 ---; s. of Hnj(?); early i; Psentotoes his servant-dependant; *OD Pisa* 424.4.

5673 Tbt; ch. Onnophris(?); i BC - i; *OD Pisa* 243 + 472 i 9.

5674 Tm$_3$; early i; *OD Pisa* 450A Concavo i 8.

5675 Tri$_3$s(?); s. of Nechutes; i BC - i; *OD Pisa* 25 ii 1.

5676 Trm; i BC - i; *OD Pisa* 1163 bis Concavo B 2, 3, 5.

5677 Thn^{c}r$_{3}$(?); s. of Sarapion, s. of Sambathaeus; 8; *DO Colon. inv.* 78.2.

5678 Tt...; i BC - i; *OD Pisa* 5 ii X + 6.

5679 I̱j-^{c}ḳ-hḅs; i BC - i; *OD Pisa* 243 + 472 i 11.

5680 Ḏjḥ; ch. Kmj; i BC - i; *OD Pisa* 513 + 514 + 515 i X + 7.

5681 Ḏḥwtj-ir-rḫ-f; i BC - i; *OD Pisa* 87 X + 4.

5682 Ḏd; April 5 BC; *OD Pisa* 936 Convesso 14.

5683 ---; s. of Harpaesis; i BC - i; *OD Pisa* 217 Convesso X + 1.

5684 ---; s. of Harmelles; i BC - i; *OD Pisa* 87 X + 7.

5685 ---; s. of Horus; i BC - i; (1) *OD Pisa* 5 i X + 16; (2) 779 + 242 Concavo 5.

5686 ---; s. of Inarus; i BC - i; agent for Peteuris; (1) *OD Pisa* 69 Convesso i 8; (2) 510 + 568 Convesso i 5, Concavo i X + 10.

5687 ---; s. of Pabis; i BC - i; *OD Pisa* 127.3.

5688 ---; ch. Petechonsis; i BC - i; *OD Pisa* 5 i X + 15, ii X + 11.

5689 ---; s. of Šmrw; i BC - i; *OD Pisa* 87 X + 6.

5690 ---; i BC - i; descr. as major; *OD Pisa* 816 X + 5.

5691 ---; i BC - i; dependant of Pemenches; (1) *OD Pisa* 510 + 568 Convesso i 2; (2) Concavo i X + 7.

5692 ---; i BC - i; *OD Pisa* 755 Convesso X + 13.

5693 ---; i BC - i; *OD Pisa* 816 X + 4.

5694 ---; s. of Herieus; Sept 6; *OD Pisa* 814 Convesso 6.

5695 Ḏd(?); ch. Petechonsis; ch. Horus; Aug 7; *OD Pisa* 432.2.

5696 ---; ch. Petosiris; 8; *OD Pisa* 1.11.

5697 Ḏd-wn(?); i BC - i; *OD Pisa* 126 i 6.

5698 ---; ch.]nfr; i BC - i; *OD Pisa* 22.11.

5699 Ḏd-wn; 9; *DO Colon. inv.* 95.1.

5700 -]iw; i BC - i; *OD Pisa* 5 i X + 18.

5701 [...]-ls.t; s. of Petamunis; i BC - i; *OD Pisa* 8.3.

5702]^{c}$_{3}$; s. of Petosiris; i BC - i; *OD Pisa* 23 i X + 7.

5703]-b$_{3}$; s. of Petosiris; i BC - i; *OD Pisa* 23 i X + 9.

5704]nfr; s. of Dd-wn(?); i BC - i; *OD Pisa* 22.11.

5705]-nfr; i BC - i; *OD Pisa* 561 + 562 + 793 i X + 13.

5706]-glmn; i BC - i; *OD Pisa* 755 Convesso X + 12.

INDEX OF TEXTS CITED

I PAPYRI

P. Mich. inv. 69 [H.C. Youtie, *ZPE* 28 (1978) 255-258], 974 [H.C. Youtie, *ZPE* 28 (1978) 245-248], 3799 [H.C. Youtie, *ZPE* 24 (1977) 127-128].

P. Michael 9.

P. Mil. 39 [= *SB* VI 9517], 51 [= *SB* VI 9000], 53 [= *SB* X 10441].

P. Mil. Vogl. IV 211, 235.

P. Oslo II 15, 26, 49; III 95, 105, 108, 114, 130, 143.

I 32 [= *Ch. L.* IV 267, *Sel. Pap.* I 122], 34 [= *Chrest. Mitt.* 188], 37 [= *Chrest. Mitt.* 79, *FIRA* III 170], 38 [= *Chrest. Mitt.* 58], 39 [= *Chrest. Wilck.* 456], 44 [= *Chrest. Wilck.* 275], 45 [= *Chrest. Mitt.* 222], 46, 47, 48, 49 [= *Chrest Mitt.* 359], 50, 68 [= *Chrest. Mitt.* 228], 72, 73, 74, 75, 89, 94 [= *Chrest. Mitt.* 344], 95 [= *Chrest. Mitt* 267, *Sel. Pap.* I 32], 97, 98, 99, 100 [= *C.P. Jud.* III 454], 104, 105 [= *Chrest. Mitt.* 303], 106 [= *Chrest. Mitt.* 308], 107, 110 [= *Chrest. Wilck.* 99], 113, 115 [= *Chrest. Wilck.* 479], 116, 164 (descr.), 165 (descr.), 167 (descr.), 170 [M.G. Raschke, *BASP* 13 (1976) 17-29], 174 (descr.), 175 (descr.), 178 [= *SB* VIII 9766], 187 (descr.), 188 (descr.).

II 235, 239, 241, 242, 243 [= *Chrest. Mitt.* 182], 244, 245, 246 [= *Chrest. Wilck.* 242], 247, 248, 249, 250, 251, 252 [= *Chrest. Wilck.* 215], 253, 254, 255 [= *Chrest. Wilck.* 201], 256, 257 [= *Chrest. Wilck.* 147], 258 [= *Chrest. Wilck.* 216], 259 [= *Chrest. Mitt.* 101], 260 [= *Chrest. Mitt.* 74], 261 [= *Chrest. Mitt.* 346, *Sel. Pap.* I 60], 262, 263, 264 [= *Chrest. Mitt.* 266], 265, 266 [= *Chrest. Mitt.* 292, *Sel. Pap.* I 7], 267 [= *Chrest. Mitt.* 281], 268 [= *Chrest. Mitt.* 299], 269 [= *Sel. Pap.* I 69], 270 [= *Chrest. Mitt.* 236, *Sel. Pap.* I 57], 271, 272, 273 [= *Chrest. Mitt.* 221], 274 [= *Chrest. Mitt.* 193, *FIRA* III 104], 275 [= *Chrest. Wilck.* 324, *Sel. Pap.* I 13], 276 [= *C.P. Jud.* II 422, *Doc. Eser. Rom.* 68], 277, 278 [= *Chrest. Mitt.* 165], 279 [= *Chrest. Wilck.* 348], 280, 281 [= *Chrest. Mitt.* 66], 282 [= *Chrest. Mitt.* 117], 283, 284, 285, 286 [= *Chrest. Mitt.* 232], 287, 288, 289, 290, 291, 292 [= *Sel. Pap.* I 106], 293, 294, 295, 296, 297, 298, 299 [= *Sel. Pap.* I 108], 300, 304 [= *SB* X 10246], 305 [= *SB* X 10222], 306 [= *P. Cair. Preis.* 43], 308 [= *SB* X 10243], 309 [= *SB* X 10221], 310 [= *SB* X 10247], 311 [= *SB* X 10223], 312 [= *SB* X 10237], 313 [= *SB* X 10242], 314 [= *SB* X 10220], 315 [= *SB* X 10239], 316 [= *SB* X 10245], 317 [= I 39], 318 [= *SB* X 10249], 319 [= *SB* X 10238], 320 [= *SB* X 10248 and J.D. Thomas, *ZPE* 16 (1975) 309-314], 321 [= *SB* X 10235], 322 [= *SB* X 10236], 323 [= *SB* X 10234], 324 [= *SB* X 10244], 325 [= *SB* X 10240], 326 [= *SB* X 10241], 327 (descr.), 328 (descr.), 329 (descr.), 330 (descr.), 331 (descr.), 332 (descr.), 333 (descr.), 334 (descr.), 335 [= *C.P. Jud* II 423], 336 (descr.), 337 (descr.), 338 (descr.), 339 [= VIII 1105], 340 (descr.), 341 (descr.), 342 (descr.), 343 (descr.), 344 (descr.), 345 (descr.), 346 (descr.), 347 (descr.), 348 (descr.), 349 [= *SB* I 5616], 350 (descr.), 351 [= *SB* XII 10795], 352 (descr.), 353 [= *C.P. Jud* III 482], 354 (descr.), 355 (descr.), 356 (descr.), 359 (descr.), 362 (descr.), 364 (descr.), 366 (descr.), 368 [= *SPP* IV p.116], 369 [= *SB* VIII 9765], 371 [J. Bingen, *Au Temps où On Lisait le Grec en Égypte* (Brussels 1977) 28], 372 (descr.), 373 (descr.), 374

XVII 2111, 2148.

XVIII 2185, 2188, 2190, 2191, 2199, 2200.

XIX 2234.

XX 2277, 2281.

XXII 2342, 2349, 2353.

XXIV 2410.

XXVII 2471.

XXXI 2559, 2572, 2573, 2574, 2582, 2583, 2592, 2593, 2594, 2613.

XXXIII 2669, 2670, 2679.

XXXIV 2720, 2725, 2726.

XXXVI 2756, 2757, 2758, 2759, 2772, 2773, 2774, 2776, 2781, 2786, 2787, 2791.

XXXVIII 2834 - 2846, 2850, 2851, 2852, 2856, 2857, 2860, 2861, 2863 - 2867, 2873, 2874.

XLI 2957, 2958, 2959, 2960, 2970, 2971, 2972, 2973, 2979, 2980, 2981, 2987, 2996.

XLII 3015, 3025, 3033, 3051, 3057, 3058, 3059, 3060, 3061, 3062, 3063, 3070, 3080.

XLIV 3163, 3164, 3165, 3197, 3199, 3208.

XLV 3240, 3250, 3264 [= *Coll. Pap.* I 21].

XLVI 3268, 3271, 3273, 3274, 3275, 3276 - 3284, 3312, 3313.

P. Oxy. inv. 20.3B.34/B [R. Hübner, *ZPE* 30 (1978) 198-200], 50.4B.24B(3-4) [R. Hübner, *ZPE* 24 (1977) 43-53], *inv.*? [M. Hombert, *Hommages Cl. Préaux* (Brussels 1975) 601-604].

P. Palau Rib. inv. 150 [S. Daris, *Stud. Pap.* 15 (1976) 126-29].

P. Princ. II 24, 25, 32, 42 [= *C.P. Jud.* II 425], 46; III 141, 147 [= *SB* X 10532], 188.

P. Rein. II 98, 99, 103 + *P. Ryl.* II 178, 104.

P. Ross Georg. II 13.

P. Ryl. II 65, 95, 156, 159, 199, 270 (descr.); IV 579, 582, 593, 597, 603, 675, 677.

P. Select. 22, 23, 24.

PSI I 40, 53, 64, 82; III 181, 203; IV 281, 315, 320; V 447, 450, 457, 475, 549; VI 687, 692, 710, 715; VII 731, 772, 814; VIII 871, 874, 897, 942, 952; IX 1029, 1030, 1079; X 1097, 1099, 1109, 1118; XII 1235, 1262; XIII 1322, 1356; XIV 1414, 1433, 1434.

II OSTRACA

OD Pisa 513 + 514 + 515, 1163 bis, 1163, 126, 29, 22, 668, 532, 504, 1264, 473, 377 [in E. Bresciani et al., *SCO* 24 (1975) 70-92].

III INSCRIPTIONS

SB I 1403, 1539, 1933, 1938, 1961, 1985, 1986, 1987.

INDEX OF TEXTS CITED BY DATE

For reff. to republications, see index of Texts Cited.

19 BC
II 277.

16/15 BC
IV 832 (descr.).

15/14 BC or 66/65 BC
IV 836 (descr.).

10/9 BC
IV 817 (descr.).

8/7 BC
P. Inst. Fran. I 5.

7 BC
P. Ryl. IV 603.

6/5 BC
IV 816 (descr.); *PSI* X 1099; *P. Yale* 60.

5 BC
IV 812 (descr.); *OD Pisa* 936 [*SCO* 22 (1973)].

5/4 BC
P. Oslo. II 26.

4 BC
SB XII 10942.

4/3 BC
XII 1457.

3 BC
XLI 2979.

2 BC
IV 742, 743.

1 BC
IV 744.

i BC
P. Inst. Fran. I 36 (?); IV 717, 784 (descr.), 792 (descr.), 803 (descr.); XII 1465, 1479; *P. Ryl.* IV 579; *PSI* I 64 (?), IX 1079; *OD Pisa* 118, 149, 323, 227, 289, 55, 34 [*SCO* 17 (1968)], 293 [*SCO* 22 (1973)].

i BC - i
OD Pisa 228, 84, 23, 80, 99, 28, 25 [*SCO* 19/20 (1970/1)]; 35, 454, 816, 72, 196, 5, 68, 44, 69, 111, 477, 360, 502, 127, 243 + 472, 132, 38, 470, 543, 667, 267, 117, 106, 281 + 94, 290 + 290A, 541 [*SCO* 21 (1972)]; 137, 276, 232, 460, 256, 108, 351, 70, 204, 280, 755, 87, 217, 308, 561 + 562 + 795, 779 + 242, 1023, 451 + 540, 58, 510 + 568, 8 [*SCO* 22 (1973)]; 513 + 514 + 515, 1163 bis, 126, 29, 22, 668, 532, 504, 1264, 377 [*SCO* 24 (1975)].

Early Roman or c.1
P. Mert. III 104; IV 736, 739, 745, 785 (descr.), 791 (descr.), 799 (descr.), 807, 811, 815 (descr.), 822 (descr.), 829 (descr.).

19/20
II 252, 254.

20
II 305.

20/21
P. Inst. Fran. III 43.

c.20 - 50
II 235, 281.

21
II 386 (descr.); X 1281; *P. Princ.* II 24; *SB* XII 10794.

22
II 294.

22/23
II 311.

23
II 244, 259, 287; *P. Princ.* III 141.

23/24 or 49/50
IV 789 (descr.).

24/25
II 350 (descr.), 398 (descr.).

25
II 288, 292 (circa).

25/26
II 291.

25 - 37
PSI X 1118.

26
II 245; VIII 1124; *P. Rein.* II 103, 104 (?).

27
II 293, 356 (descr.); XVII 2148.

27/28
II 353.

28
II 351, 352 (descr.).

29
XXXVIII 2842 (?), 2850; *SB* VIII 9827 (a) and (b).

30
X 1291, 1292 (circa).

c.30 - 35
II 282.

31
XIX 2234.

49
P. Mich. III 170; I 37; XXXI 2582.

49/50
I 38; II 393; IV 789 (descr.) (or 23/24).

50
II 284 (circa), 285 (circa), 308, 324; IV 709 (circa); XXVII 2471; XXXVIII 2836, 2837.

50/51
II 316.

52
I 39; *SB* V 8034.

52/53
PSI VI 692 (?); IX 1029.

53
P. Wisc. I 4.

54
II 264, 297.

54 - 68
P. Inst. Fran. I 21; *P. Ross Georg.* II 13; *SB* X 10256.

55
I 99; II 261, 304.

56
II 271, 310.

57
II 269; X 1316 (descr.).

58
P. Mich. III 171; II 268.

59
P. Fouad 28; II 260, 306, 318, 320.

60
P. Mich. III 191, 192; XXXVIII 2851.

60/61
II 250.

61
P. Mich. III 194; II 262.

61 - 64
SB XII 10788.

62
P. Mich. III 172; XXXVIII 2838, 2873; XLI 2970.

c.63
XLV 3250.

79
II 243, 375 (descr.) (circa), 380 (descr.).

79/80
II 373 (descr.); *P. Oxy. inv.* 20.3B.34/B.

After 79
XXXVI 2757.

80
II 248, 249, 359 (descr.) (or 90).

80/81
Coll. Pap. I 21.

81
I 165 (descr.); XII 1471.

81/82
P. Mert. III 118.

81 - 83
II 334 (descr.).

81 - 96
I 44, 47; II 265, 379 (descr.); IV 795 (descr.); VI 984 (descr.); VIII 1105.

After 81
II 369.

82
II 286; XXXVI 2773.

83
P. Fam. Teb. 15.98-105; I 94; II 289, 331 (descr.); X 1282.

83/84
II 290; XII 1462.

85
II 328 (descr.) (circa), 335 (descr.); XXXVIII 2841.

85/86
II 336 (descr.); IV 794 (descr.).

86
I 48; VII 1028; XXXVIII 2843.

86/87 (?)
II 258.

86 - 88
PSI XII 1235.

87
PSI III 203.

87/88
Coll. Pap. I 22; *P. Princ.* III 147.

98 - 102
P. Mert. I 13.

98 - 117
IV 809 (descr.); XLVI 3274; *P. Select.* 24; *PSI* VII 772; *SB* XII 10946.

98 - 137
VI 968 (descr.).

99
P. Harris 74; II 343 (descr.); II 481, 581 (descr.); VI 975; XLI 2958, 2959; *P. Princ.* II 32.

99/100
II 338 (descr.).

i
P. Bon. 43; *P. Erl.* 93; *P. Harris* 102, 138, 144; *P. Inst. Fran.* III 30; *P. Med. inv.* 69.09 + 69.08, 71.47; *P. Mil.* 53; *P. Mil. Vogl.* IV 235; *P. Oslo* III 130, 143; I 47; II 296, 298, 299, 300, 327 (descr.), 329 (descr.), 344 (descr.), 348 (descr.), 349, 389 (descr.), 396 (descr.), 397 (descr.), 399 (descr.), 400 (descr.); IV 839 (descr.); VI 985 (descr.), VII 1027; VIII 1145, 1148, 1153, 1154; XIV 1756; XVIII 2190; XXXVI 2786; XXXVIII 2835, 2844, 2845, 2846; XLII 3061, 3062, 3070; XLVI 3273; *P. Ryl.* II 156, 199, 270 (descr.); *P. Select* 23; *PSI* XII 1356; *PSI Bartoletti Colombo* 2; *P. Wisc.* I 23; *P. Yale* 66; *SB* III 7258; XII 10765; *OD Pisa* 425, 423, 435, 426, 249, 39, 318, 129 [*SCO* 19/20 (1970/1)]; 60 [*SCO* 21 (1972)]; 419, 42, 164, 320, 424, 234, 153, 456 [*SCO* 22 (1973)].

i - ii
P. Bour. 16; *P. Harris* 72, 96; *P. Oslo* III 114.14-15; III 599 (descr.); VI 791 (descr.); XXXI 2592; XLII 3057; *P. Princ.* II 25; III 188; *PSI* VI 687; VII 731, 814; *P. XV. Congr.* 16.

100
I 46, 49, 50; II 346 (descr.); III 641 (descr.); XLI 2960; *P. Stras.* 266 (circa); *P. Yale* 77 (circa).

101
III 510.

102
III 508; XII 1520; XXII 2342; *PSI* VIII 952.

After 102
III 636.

103
P. Mert. I 14; III 511; VII 1022; XLI 2973.

103/104
III 639 (descr.).

c.103 - 110
XLVI 3275.

115/116
I 97.

116
P. Harris 89; I 74; III 601; XII 1550; XXXVI 2759.

117
P. Harris 85; *P. Med. inv.* 72.16; III 489; VII 1023.

117/118
P. Fam. Teb. 18 (circa); IV 837 (descr.); IX 1189.

117 - 138
P. Brem. 56 (?); I 105, 178, 188 (descr.); III 646 (descr.), 648 (descr.); X 1293; XVIII 2199; *PSI* V 457.11-12, 475.

118
III 503, 577 (descr.); XLII 3025; *SB* I 5678.

119
IV 786 (descr.); XII 1547; XXXVI 2776.

119/120
III 583 (descr.); *PSI* XIII 1322; *P. Wisc.* II 39.

120
XII 1440; XXIV 2410.

121
P. Fouad 30; III 499.

122
IV 714.

122/123
P. Lips. 116; III 592; VI 957 (descr.); XXXVIII 2866; *P. Wisc.* II 73 (?).

123
P. Lips. 112; I 107; VI 898; XXXVIII 2863, 2864.

124
III 490.

126
P. Harris 142; III 491.

126/127
III 634 (descr.), 651 (descr.).

127
I 34; III 496; XXXIII 2670; XXXVIII 2867; *P. Oxy. inv.?*.

127/128
XII 1452.

127 or 128
P. Lips. 113.

c.128
XII 1422.

141/142
I 98.

148
P. Iand. VII 139.

148/149
XLVI 3276 - 3284.

ii
Coll. Pap. 50; *P. Erl.* 44, 96; *P. Fuad I Univ.* 32; *P. Hamb.* I 79; *P. Harris* 95, 103, 104, 106; *P. Iand.* VI 107; *P. Inst. Fran.* I 4; III 5, 15(?); *P. Med. inv.* 12; *P. Mert.* III 109; *P. Mich. inv.* 3799; *P. Mil.* 39, 51; *P. Mil. Vogl.* IV 211; *P. Oslo* II 15, 49; III 108; I 32, 110, 113, 115, 116, 164 (descr.), 167 (descr.), 170, 187 (descr.); III 493, 497, 498 504, 505, 522-526, 528-532, 574, 576 (descr.), 578 (descr.), 582 (descr.), 587 (descr.), 589 (descr.), 591 (descr.), 598 (descr.), 602, 608 (descr.)-611 (descr.), 633 (descr.), 642 (descr.), 644 (descr.), 647, 649; IV 741; VI 931, 967 (descr.), 969 (descr.); VII 1034, 1062; VIII 1125, 1149; IX 1212, 1213; X 1269; XII 1481, 1482, 1484, 1488, 1508, 1518, 1536, 1581-1584; XIV 1648, 1673, 1757-1760; XVIII 2191, 2200; XX 2281; XXXI 2559, 2572-2574, 2583, 2593, 2594, 2613; XXXIII 2679; XXXIV 2726; XXXVI 2781, 2787, 2791; XXXVIII 2860, 2861; XLI 2980, 2981, 2996; XLII 3015, 3058-3060, 3063, 3080; XLIV 3199; XLVI 3268, 3312, 3313; *P. Palau Rib. inv.* 150; *P. Princ.* II 46; *P. Select* 22; *PSI* IV 281; VI 710; XIV 1414; *P. Stras.* 184, 299, 534; *P. Warren* 13; *P. Wisc.* I 13; *P. Wurz.* 21; *SB* V 9025; VI 9372.

n.d.
DO Colon. inv. 39, 49, 50, 53, 89, 280; *SB* I 1403, 1539, 1933, 1938, 1961, 1985-1987.